SOCIETY

MANNERS & POLITICS

IN THE UNITED STATES

BY

MICHAEL CHEVALIER

[1839]

REPRINTS OF ECONOMIC CLASSICS

AUGUSTUS M. KELLEY · PUBLISHERS
NEW YORK · 1966

LIBRARY OF CONGRESS CATALOGUE CARD NUMBER

66 - 21661

PRINTED IN THE UNITED STATES OF AMERICA

by SENTRY PRESS, NEW YORK, N. Y. 10019

SOCIETY, MANNERS AND POLITICS

IN THE

UNITED STATES:

BEING A

SERIES OF LETTERS ON NORTH AMERICA.

BY MICHAEL CHEVALIER.

TRANSLATED FROM THE THIRD PARIS EDITION.

BOSTON:
WEEKS, JORDAN AND COMPANY.
1839.

NOTICE.

M. CHEVALIER was sent to this country in 1834, under the patronage of Thiers, then Minister of the Interior, in France, to inspect our public works. But attracted by the novel spectacle presented by society in the United States, he extended the time of his stay and the sphere of his observations amongst us, and spent two years in visiting nearly all parts of the Union, and studying the workings of our social and political machinery. His letters give the results of his observations, the impressions made on his mind, his speculations in regard to the future destiny of our institutions, rather than a detailed narrative of facts and events, which, however, is introduced when necessary for illustration or proof. The translator is not, of course, to be considered responsible for all the opinions and statements of the original ; but it will be found, in his judgment, that M. Chevalier has studied with diligence and sagacity, drawn his conclusions with caution and discrimination, and stated his views in a clear, forcible, and interesting manner. He seems to be perfectly free from any narrowness or prejudice, ready to recognise whatever is good or of good tendency, whether in character, manners, modes of life, political and social institutions, habits, or opinions, without regard to mere personal likes and dislikes; and to be equally frank in condemning, whenever he perceives, in our practices, a violation of our own principles, or of those of an enlightened philosophy. He tells many home truths to all parties and classes. Some passages of the letters and many of the notes, which have no particular interest in this country, have been omitted. M. Chevalier's work has been very favourably received in his own country, where it has passed through several editions.   T. G. BRADFORD.

Boston, October, 1839.

CONTENTS.

4   CONTENTS.

NOTES AT THE END OF THE VOLUME.

LETTERS ON NORTH AMERICA.

INTRODUCTION.

1. THAT form of civilization which has prevailed among the European nations, has moved, in its march over the globe, from east to west. From its cradles in the depths of old Asia and Upper Egypt, it advanced, by successive stages, to the shores of the Atlantic, along which it spread itself from the southern point of Spain to the northern extremity of the British Isles and the Scandinavian peninsula. It seemed to have here reached its goal when Christopher Columbus showed it the way to the New World. At each stage it has taken up a new faith, new manners, new laws, new customs, a different language, dress, and food, different modes of life, public and private. The great questions touching the relation of man to God, to his fellows, and to the universe, and domestic, social, and political order, which had all been solved at the beginning of the halt, were, after a while, brought again into discussion, and then civilization, starting again on her march, has moved onward toward the west, to give them a new solution.

This stream, setting from the east toward the west, is formed by the junction of two others flowing from the two great Bible races of Japhet and Shem; which, coming from the north and the south, meet and mingle together, and are replenished from their respective sources, during each period of our civilization, through all the episodes, which obstruct and chequer this majestic pilgrimage. By turns, each of these forces, whose combined action constitutes the motive power that carries mankind forward in its course, has been overborne by the other. Thence it is, that our civilization, instead of advancing in a straight line from east to west, has swerved in its march, either from the north toward the south, or from the south toward the north, taking a winding and devious course, and gathering up, by turns, purer drops from the blood of Shem or of Japhet. There has been, however, this difference between the North and the South; that the South has most often acted upon the North by sending to it the germs of civilization, without overrunning it with a new race; while the North has awakened the slumbering civilization of the South by pouring over it swarms of hardy barbarians, *audax Japeti genus.* Thus is fulfilled the great prophecy concerning Japhet, that *" he shall dwell in the tents of Shem."*

2. Independent of our civilization and distinct from it, there is another in the furthest East, whose centre is China, and whose outposts are Japan, and which embraces its hundreds of millions of men. It moves in a direction contrary to our own, from west to east, and its locomotive powers are slight; we might compare the respective speed of these two civilizations to the two great revolutions of the globe, the annual revolution in its orbit, and that which gives rise to the precession of the equinoxes. This oriental civilization, like that of the west, has repeatedly regenerated itself by a new mixture of the man of the North with the man of the South. The race of Japhet, which gave us our Barbarians, and, before the Barbarians, had given us the Pelasgians, Scythians, Celts, and Thracians, and has since given us the Turks and Sclavonians, has also furnished the East with its

Mongols and Manchoos. The family of Gengis Khan, which conquered the East, also pushed its victorious hordes, at the same time, to the Rhine.

The Eastern civilization, less active and less easily set in motion than the Western, probably because it has not enough of the blood of Shem, and has too much of that of the inferior races, has not risen to the same degree of improvement with its sister. But we must do it the justice to confess, that to it belongs the honor of several capital inventions and discoveries, such as the mariners' compass, printing, and gun-powder, on which we pride ourselves; and we must moreover acknowledge that it has solved the problem, to keep under one law, for an indefinite number of ages, a population greater than that of all Europe. The Roman empire, whose population was less than that of China, stood whole only three hundred years. The spiritual authority of the Pope extended over less territory than that of the Roman empire, and was absolutely acknowledged only from Charlemagne to Luther.

3. The two civilizations, thus gathered together at the two extremities of the old continent, and turning their backs upon each other, were separated by an immense space before the western had fixed itself in America; now, more than half the intervening distance is passed; Mexico and South America are covered with offsets from the latter, on the side which looks toward Asia, as well as on that which fronts us: the United States cannot long delay to extend themselves from sea to sea; the Islands of the South Sea are beginning to be peopled by Europeans. From this point of view, it is clear that America, placed between the two civilizations, is reserved for high destinies, and that the progress of population in the New World is a matter of the deepest interest to the whole human race.

The connecting of the two civilizations is certainly the broadest subject that can occupy the human mind ; it is, in the eyes of the friend of man, an event of all others most big with hope. It embraces, politically, the association of all peoples, the balance of the world, of which the balance of Europe is only a part ; in religion, the whole law of the human family, the true *catholicism :* morally, the most harmonious reciprocal action of the two opposite natures, which divide each race, each sex, each people, and each family, and which are typified in the Bible by Cain and Abel; intellectually, the complete encyclopædia and the universal language ; industrially, a definite plan for developing the resources of the globe. In our time this question is no longer merely speculative ; it is now something more than merely food for the dreams of philosophers ; it should be the subject of the meditations of statesmen.

Since the age of Louis XIV., the merchants, who are the pioneers of state policy, have striven with a constantly increasing ardor, to open relations with China, because they have felt the importance of a regular system of exchanges between Europe and a mass of two hundred million of producers and consumers. The emancipation of North America, and quite lately the abolition of the English East India Company's monopoly, have given to the efforts of commerce an irresistible force ; before this power, the laws which close up the celestial empire are nothing. China is encircled, on the south, by the English and their tributaries ; on the north, by the Cossacks, the van-guard of Russia ; British and American fleets prowl along her coasts ; the sleepy Spaniards of Mexico and the Philippines think of the days of the galleons, and keep their half-opened eyes fixed upon her. The human race has just come into possession of new means of communication, which shorten distance in an unexpected degree. The two civilizations will soon reach each other and mingle together; it will be the greatest event in the history of man.

4. Before the art of navigation was brought to perfection, before Christopher Columbus and Vasco da Gama, Europe had had communications with China through the medium of the Arabs, independently of the cavarans which traversed Central Asia. The Arabs, conquerors and missionaries placed between the two civilizations, had spread themselves by turns toward the East and the West. That people, so active by starts, has been to the East the messenger of the West, and to the West, the courier and factor of the East. Unhappily since the Western civilization has shone with the greatest brilliancy in Europe, Arabia has flung out but feeble gleams of light; since Providence has filled us with a devouring activity, the Arabians are fallen into a deep lethargy; on that side, therefore, the intercourse, which was never complete nor speedy, has almost ceased. But if, as some suppose, the Arab race is about to rouse itself from its long stupor, at the voice and by the aid of Europe, the latter will then have a powerful ally in its efforts to seize and hold Asia, or to transmit to her the means of working out her own restoration, and this illustrious race will thus contribute essentially to the marriage of the two civilizations.

5. Our civilization, in its march westward, has sometimes turned back towards the East; thus it has had its Argonauts, its Agamemnons, and its Alexanders, and more lately its heroes of the crusades and its Portuguese captains. These partial movements were but temporary interruptions of its solemn march toward the West; they were merely countercurrents, resembling the eddies which always exist in the currents of rivers. Until our own time, Europe has founded no durable and important

establishment in Asia; in proportion as our civilization advanced westwards, the countries which it left behind escaped from its influence, and the distance between it and the oriental civilization, became greater. Alexander is the only person of whom China could feel any fear, and he passed away like the lightning flash. The Parthians, the Saracens, or the Turks, were the impregnable bulwarks of eastern Asia. The mission of Europe was, above all things, to reach and settle a new hemisphere.

At present, the incontestible superiority of the western nations in wealth, in mechanical skill, in means of transportation, in government, in the art of war, enables them to make their way across the Old World toward the remotest recesses of Asia. The nations whom we are accustomed to call oriental, but who are only inhabitants of the *Lesser East*, have ceased to be formidable adversaries to Europe; they delivered up their swords, at Heliopolis, Navarino, and Adrianople. The colonization of America is now at length completed from Hudson's Bay to Cape Horn, but Europe can and ought to move towards the East as well as towards the West; the isthmus of Suez has as good a chance as the isthmus of Panama, to become the route of western civilization to the *Greater East*.

6.   Our European civilization has a twofold source, the Romans and the Teutonic nations. Setting aside for the present Russia, who is a new comer, and who already, however, equals the most powerful of the elder states, it is subdivided into two families, each of which is marked by its strong likeness to one of the mother nations, which have contributed to give birth to both. Thus there is the Latin Europe, and the Teutonic Europe; the former comprises the south, the latter the people of the north; the former is Roman Catholic, the latter Protestant; the one speaks Teutonic languages, and the other, idioms,

in which Latin is predominant. These two branches, Latin and German, re-appear in the New World ; South America, like southern Europe, is Roman Catholic and Latin ; North America belongs to the Protestant Anglo-Saxon population.

In the great enterprise of bringing together European and Asiatic civilization, the Teutonic and Latin nations may both find a field of action ; both occupy in Europe and America, by land and sea, admirable outposts and excellent positions round that imperturbable Asia, into which it is their object to force their way. But, during the last age, the superiority which formerly belonged to the Latin family, has passed into the hands of the Teutonic race, owing partly to the energy of England in the Old World, and that of her sons in the New, and partly to the loosening of the old religious and moral ties among the Latin nations. The Sclavonic race, which has lately shown itself, and which now forms a third group of nations in Europe, seems ready to contest with the Latin race even the possession of the second rank ; it is only the Russians and Anglo-Saxons that interest themselves about Further Asia, and press upon its frontiers by land and by sea. The people of the Latin stock must not, however, stand idle in the coming struggle, or the case will go against them by default ; an excellent opportunity is now offered to regain their lost rank.

7. In our three-headed Europe, Teutonic, Latin, and Sclavonic, two nations, France and Austria, present themselves under less distinct features, and with less exclusive characters than the others. France shares in the Teutonic and Latin natures ; in religion, she is Catholic in feeling, but Protestant out of caprice ; she unites the nervous understanding of the Germans with the elegant taste of the southern nations. Austria, by the education and origin of the people of her different states, is half Sclavonic, half

Teutonic, and she is connected with the Latin family by her religion. France and Austria are, then, the natural mediums of communication, the one between the Germans and Latins, and the other between the Germans and Sclavonians; Austria is chiefly Teutonic, as France is essentially Latin. From this mixed character of France and Austria, we may conclude, that whenever the balance of Europe, or the harmonious combination of all European nations in one common object, shall become subjects of discussion, both will exercise a decisive influence, and their hearty co-operation in a common cause will make them irresistible. Austria has a more central position than France; she has a greater number of points of contact with the different types of western civilization; but France combines the invaluable advantages of a more homogeneous constitution, and a more flexible temperament; she has a physiognomy more strongly marked, a mission more clearly defined, and above all, she has more of the social spirit. She is at the head of the Latin group; she is its protectress.

8. In the events which seem about to dawn upon us, France may, then, take a most important share; she is the depositary of the destinies of all the Latin nations of both continents. She alone can save the whole family from being swallowed up by a double flood of Sclavonians and Germans. To her it belongs to rouse them from the lethargy into which they are plunged in both hemispheres, to raise them to the level of other nations, and to enable them again to take a stand in the world; she also is called upon, perhaps more than any other power, to encourage the new spirit, which seems to be re-animating the Arabians, and through them to shake the East. Thus the political theatre, seen from a French point of view, shows, in a distant back-ground, the meeting of the Oriental and the Western civilizations, in which we are called upon to act as medi-

ators, and in the fore-ground, the education, by France, of all the Latin nations, and of many of the Arab tribes living around the Mediterranean.

There may be a difference of opinion as to the time when these revolutions, which are to agitate the depths of Asia, will take place; I am one of those who think it not far off. I can easily conceive, also, that some persons should wish to lessen the circle of French influence, and confine it to the southern countries of Europe; although to me France seems called upon to exercise a benevolent and wholesome care over the people of South America, who are not yet fit to take care of themselves, and although the old traditions of the crusades, the conquest of Algiers, and the recollection of the expedition into Egypt, seem to promise us one of the first parts in the drama which will be acted on the eastern shores of the Mediterranean.

As for the European nations of the Latin family, no one, I suppose, can have any doubts concerning our supremacy over them, or concerning our duties, both to them and to ourselves, in relation to them. We have been notoriously the head of the family since the time of Louis XIV., and we can neither shrink from the burdens, nor from the privileges of our situation. Our superiority is acknowledged by all its members, our protection has been accepted by all, whenever it has been offered without selfish views. Happy would it have been for France, if, content with this high prerogative, her princes, and above all he who has added new lustre to the name of Emperor, had not been obstinately bent on the unnatural purpose of extending their authority over the members of the Teutonic family!

9. Since the weight has been thrown into the Saxon scale, since the English race has overborne France and Spain in Asia, in America, and in Europe, new institutions, new rules of government, new ideas, new modes of action,

in social, political, and individual life, have sprung up among the English, and more especially among their successors in the New World; everything connected with labor and the condition of the greater number of working men, has been carried to a degree of perfection before unheard of. It seems as if, by the aid of these improvements, the superiority of the Anglo-Saxons over the Latin family, must go on constantly increasing. The French, of all the Latin nations, are most favorably placed, and the only one well placed, to avail themselves of these improvements by adapting them to their own exigencies. We are full of energy; never has our mind been more fairly thrown open; never were our hearts more ready to throb for noble enterprises.

But we must set ourselves at work without delay; we must do this, setting aside all considerations of general policy, and of the contact, whether more or less remote, of the two civilizations. It is a matter of the last necessity in regard to ourselves, even supposing that we have not to transmit to the southern nations of Europe, of whom we are the eldest, and to the inhabitants of the Levant, those improvements which their situation demands, and which they are ready to receive at our hands; our own welfare, our own existence is at stake. How, and under what form shall we be able to make the innovations of the English race our own? This difficult and complicated question has been the chief object of my attention during my residence in the New World; I do not claim the honor of having even partially solved it. But I shall feel satisfied, if the thoughts suggested to me by the sight of an order of things so unlike our own, falling under the eyes of one more far-sighted than myself, shall put him in the way of its solution.

LETTER I.

RAILROAD FROM LONDON TO PARIS.

LONDON, Nov. 1, 1833.

W HILE railroads are talked of at Paris, they are made
here.   That from London to Birmingham is already begun ; it will be 112 miles in length, and all the stock, to
the amount of 12,000,000 dollars, has been taken up by
subscription ; this road will be continued by another of
nearly the same length, from Birmingham to Liverpool,
and in five years Liverpool and London will be only eight
hours apart.   Whilst the English capitalists are executing
these great undertakings, the Parisian capitalists look on,
but do not stir ; they do not even form projects.   Not one
of them seems to have seriously considered, that even in
the present state of things, there is more than twice the
number of travellers between Paris and Versailles, than
between Liverpool and Manchester, although the railroad
between the last named places has been opened three years.
In London, therefore, they count little upon the aid of
French capitalists in the construction of a railroad from
that city to Paris ; they desire it, they would be glad to be
able to go from one capital to the other in fifteen hours,
and at trifling expense ; all classes are delighted with the
idea of such a thing.   But they feel that such a work is
neither expedient nor feasible, without the joint action of
both nations ; and as they dare not hope for the co-operation of France, little is said about it as a serious affair.

Among all the acquisitions, which, since the end of the
last century, have enriched the domain of science, none
has opened a wider field than Volta's discoveries relative
to the motion of electricity, and its development by con-

tact.   The phenomena resulting from the two poles of the
Voltaic battery offer an inexhaustible mine to the physical
philosopher; there is no fact in science more general in its
nature, for if any two bodies whatsoever touch each other,
they form at once, by their mutual action and reaction, a
Voltaic pile of greater or less energy.   This physical fact
has its counterpart in the moral order of things; if you
bring together two men who have hitherto been separated
from each other, in however slight a degree they may
have any striking quality, their friction will certainly produce a spark.   If instead of two men, the two poles of
your battery are two nations, the result is greater in the
proportion of a nation to an individual.   If these two nations are England and France, that is to say, the two most
enlightened and most powerful people in the world, this
sort of Voltaic phenomenon then acquires a prodigious intensity; it involves nothing less than the safety of an old
or the creation of a new civilization.

    The predominant qualities, good or bad, of France and
England, may be arranged in a series of parallels, the corresponding terms in each of which will be complements
of each other.   England is pre-eminent in affairs, and the
qualities which belong to them, coolness, economy, precision, method, perseverance; taste and genius for the fine
arts, with the enthusiasm, the recklessness, the caprice,
the irregular habits, the wastefulness, at least in time and
words, which characterise the artist, have fallen to the lot
of France.   On one side, is reason, cautious and sober, but
sure-footed, good sense, creeping along the ground; on
the other, imagination with her brilliant audacity, but also
with her ignorance of things and method, her starts and
trips.   Here, an admirable energy in struggling against
nature and metamorphosing the physical features of the
globe; there, an unequalled intellectual activity, and the
gift of warming the heart of mankind with its fires.   In

England, treasures of industry and heaps of gold; in France, treasures of thought, wells of science, torrents of inspiration. In proud Albion, staid, but cheerless manners, reserve pushed to a chilling excess; in our fair France, easiness of manners carried to licentiousness, the old Gaulish gaiety, often savoring somewhat of the camp, a something of the free and easy bordering on the promiscuous (*un sans-façon expansif qui frise la promiscuité*). On both sides a large dose of pride; among our neighbors, a calculating, ambitious pride; the pride of the statesman and the merchant, which feeds only on power and wealth; which for the country desires conquests, vast colonies, all the Gibraltars and St Helenas, eagle's nests by which all seas and all shores are commanded; and which for oneself pants for riches, an aristocratic park, a seat in the House of Lords, a tomb in Westminster Abbey. Amongst us, a vain-glorious pride, which longs for the unreal, for ideal pleasures; a thirst after applause for self, after glory for our country; a pride, which, for France, would be satisfied with the admiration of the world, for self, with castles in the air, a ribband, an epaulet, a line of Béranger as a funeral oration; the pride of the actor on the stage, of the knight in the lists. On the north of the Channel, prevail religion and positive faith; on the south, scepticism, mingled with enthusiasm. There a deep sentiment of order and respect for rank, combined with a haughty feeling of the dignity of man; here, a people eager for equality, excitable, restless, turbulent, yet docile, often even to weakness, confiding, even to credulity, easily cajoled by its flatterers, submitting to be trampled under foot like a carcase, during the period of its lethargy, and at times given over to the most courtier-like obsequiousness. Among the English the reverence for tradition, among the French the passion for novelty, predominates; among the former respect for the law, and obedience to man, on condition that his supreme rule shall be the law ; among the latter, the worship of great men, and submission to the laws if they are defended by the sword of Cæsar. On one side the ruler of the seas, on the other the arbiter of the continent, rousing the world at their pleasure, the one by its lever of gold, the other by the sound of its voice alone. Surely from the reciprocal influences of two nations thus constituted and thus situated on the globe, the most important effects should result, not only on the general cause of civilization, but on their own mutual improvement.

The industrial development is not, indeed, the development of the whole man, but since the beginning of the nineteenth century, no people can be allowed to reckon itself in the first rank of nations, if it is not advanced in the industrial career, if it cannot labor and produce. No people will be powerful that is not rich, and there is now no other way of growing rich but by work. In regard to production and labor, we have much to learn from England, and it is a lesson which is to be learned by the eyes rather than by the ears, by observation better than by reading. If, then, there were a railroad between London and Paris, the French, who have now little knowledge of business, would go to London, where the instinct of method is in the blood, to learn. Our speculators would go to see how simply, promptly, and plainly great enterprises are carried on ; our shop-keepers and buyers have to learn from England that to overcharge and to haggle have no connexion with buying and selling advantageously ; our capitalists and merchants, that there can be no durable commercial prosperity nor security for capital, where there is no system of credit ; they would see the operations of the Bank of England with its branches and the private banks, and perhaps they might be incited to bring home, with the needful modification, institutions and practices so

profitable at once to the share holders and to the public.
They would here imbibe the spirit of association, which
in London sweats at every pore.*   All of us might here
see in what consists and how is realised, that comfort, that
care of the person, so essential to the peace and quiet of
one's life, and Paris might perhaps be led to free itself from
the filth of centuries, which formerly gave it its name,
and against which eighteen hundred years later, Voltaire,
whom the ancient monarchy and the faith of our fathers
could not withstand, warred in vain.   As we are full of
self-love, we should return from England ashamed of the
wretched state of our agriculture, our roads, and our elementary schools, humbled at the insignificance of our foreign commerce, and solicitous to vie with our neighbors.
I need not stop to point out what the English might come
to seek among us, they are already converts in this matter,
they swarm in Paris, while it would be easy to count up
the Frenchmen who have been in London.   Without saying what the English would get in Paris, I may affirm
that they would leave plenty of sovereigns there.   To
Paris, the city of pleasures, the terrestrial paradise of strangers, the railroad would be a gold mine, and the English,
getting familiar with France, would find profitable invest-
ments for their capital among us, which would give life
and energy to useful enterprises.

The railroad from London to Paris would be a commercial enterprise of the first importance ; it would also be a
political instrument, a strong bond of union between England and France.   But it is more' especially as a means of

---

* Thus the London merchants dispense with the care, trouble, and expense of a money-chest on their own premises, and all money operations are
transacted by a small number of bankers at the *Clearing House.* The
amount of these transactions often rises to fifteen millions sterling [a day],
independently of those which are not strictly commercial, and of those of
the retailers, which do not pass through the hands of bankers. See *Bab-
bage's Economy of Machinery.*

education, that it should be most highly recommended, for
there is no fear that the other points of view will be over-
looked. The industrial arts, I said before, are learned
chiefly through the eyes; this is particularly true in regard
to the operatives, for in them, owing to their manner of
life, the world of sensation prevails over the world of ideas.
Now the progress of the mechanical arts depends not less
on the workmen than on the foremen and superintendents
of the works; it would be expedient, therefore, to send a
certain number of picked operatives to pass a suitable time
in England, just as the Board of Public Works (*Ponts et
Chaussées*) is now in the habit of sending a few engineers
thither. The railroad, by reducing the expense and trouble
of the journey, would probably furnish an opportunity of
despatching companies of artisans selected from among
those most worthy of the privilege. According to the
plan of a merchant of Lyons, a very sensible man, this
might be done on a large scale and at little expense; and
he further proposed a system of reciprocity, by which
English workmen should be employed in France and
French operatives in England. It is not impossible that
this project may one day be made the basis of a new law,
designed to further the views of our excellent law of primary education; but the railroad between London and
Paris must first be constructed.

Of the small number of Frenchmen who have visited
England,* very few have been led by motives of business.
Most have undertaken the voyage from vague feelings of
curiosity, or merely for pleasure; and the objects of their
notice have been the picturesque, the poetical. They

---

* The whole number of passengers to and from Calais, through which
most of the travellers between England and France pass, is only about forty
thousand yearly. This is not more than the number passing between Havre
and New York.

have visited the Gothic ruins of the monasteries and castles, the cave of Fingal, and the lakes of Scotland, admired the costume of the Highlanders, the horses and jockeys of the great lords, and the blooming complexion of the women.   They have walked through one or two parks, visited the hot-houses where all the plants of the world are collected, braving, behind the glass, the cloudy sky of Great Britain.   They have been through the dock-yards and military arsenals, when they could get leave, under the escort of a sergeant, seen the young beauties of Almacks and the old curiosities of the Tower, and travelled over England, just as they would make the tour of Italy or Switzerland.   If the subject of industry has occupied their attention a moment, it is only in reference to the fashion of some opera decoration.   They have, to be sure, stood amazed at the thousands of vessels whose masts stretch out of sight along the Thames or in the docks;* they have been delighted with the extent of the great manufacturing towns, the magnitude of the manufactories, and the height of their chimneys, with the magical brilliancy of the gas-lights, with the daring bridges of stone or iron, and with the fantastical appearance of the forge-fires in the night.   But they have never asked, how came England to have such a vast number of ships, how has she multiplied and extended her manufactures to such an amazing degree, and how created these towns, so simple in their architecture, but so fastidiously neat in their spacious streets ; they have not thought to ask the causes of all this wealth and prosperity.

Yet he who expects to return satisfied from England should visit her as the Queen of industry ; he should see the city rather than Regent's Park, the East India House

---

* It is estimated that 25,000 vessels enter the port of London yearly.

rather than Windsor Castle, seek out the Bank before St. Paul's, the Clearing House before Somerset House, take more interest in the docks and Commercial House, than in the armor preserved in the Tower. He should go to the warehouses, the counting-houses, the workshops, in pursuit of the genius of Great Britain. He must tear himself from the magnificent hospitality of the English country seats, and give up his time to the mines and the forges, which furnish industry with its daily bread, its coal and iron. (Notes 1 and 2 at the end of the volume.) He must mingle with the stout and active workmen, quite as much as with the more refined society in the saloons of the nobility. For myself, I have found nothing in London which has struck me as more original, and given me greater pleasure, than a shop in Old Change, whose ware-rooms contain twenty times as many goods as the largest warehouse in Paris, and whose business transactions amount to two millions sterling a year, and the great brewery of Barclay, Perkins & Co. near London Bridge, the order and arrangement of which are still more striking than its vast extent.

As I stood in this brewery, on a floor on which, distributed in different rooms, there were ninetynine vats, some of them holding 500,000 or 600,000 bottles, I thought of the famous Heidelberg tun which I had seen some years ago. It is the only object in a tolerable state of preservation in the delicious chateau of the Palatine counts, and it is faithfully visited by all travellers who go to see that fine ruin, perhaps the finest relic of the feudal times. What a difference now between the old chateau of Heidelberg with its tun, and the colossal establishment of the English brewer with its regiment of tuns! The old castle crumbles to pieces; the rich Gothic sculptures are wearing away. In vain has a French artist (and, strange coincidence ! that artist himself another relic of the feudal age, an *émigré,* who with a praiseworthy zeal has been for a long time the self-constituted guardian of this fine old monument,) in vain has he urged the government of Baden, to whom the castle belongs, to take some measures for its preservation. Each year some new dilapidation is caused by the frosts of winter and the storms of autumn ; the old chateau will soon become a shapeless mass, the very stones will probably be sold, and nothing will remain, but the drawings of M. de Graimbert, to show what it has been. The Knights' Hall is stripped of its roof—the arches, which support the superb terrace whence the eye wanders over the lovely vale of the Neckar and its beautiful heights,—those arches, rent by the powder of Louvois, —will some day sink. Meanwhile, the brewery is enriched one day with a new building, and the next with a new steam-engine ; and in case of any damage by fire, as recently happened, the loss is immediately repaired ; in the place of the building destroyed by the flames, rises one more splendid, in which the free use of iron will be a protection against new ravages.

The statues of the Palatine electors are overthrown in their niches ; no son of their vassals will set them up again ; but at the brewery everything is in perfect order ; each tool hangs on its nail, each kettle is kept well-rubbed and bright. The stables of the noble prince are a heap of ruins ; in the stables of the brewer, rivalling those of Chantilly, where the great Condé entertained kings, one hundred and fifty horses, fit steeds for Goliah, are objects of as careful attention, as those, perhaps, which surrounded the persons of the first Electors and their gallant knights. The old tun has been empty for a century and a half ; the curious may enter it, and take its measure ; once only has M. de Graimbert seen it spout wine ; it was in 1813, in

honour of the emperor Alexander and his allies, the sovereigns of Austria and Prussia.   Even then it was only a
pious fraud, the old tun was not full, the wine flowed from
a base barrel which had been stuck in it the night before.
The ninetynine vats of Barclay, Perkins & Co. are always
full of beer ; that which is daily drawn off, and sent all
over the United Kingdom and North America, and finds
its way even to the East Indies, would fill the classical
tun of the Palatine Casimir.*   The secret of this contrast may easily be explained ; the great feudal tun could
only be filled by the produce of the feudal impositions,
whilst the vats of the brewery are filled by the voluntary
co-operation of three hundred men, sure of gathering daily
the fruits of their industry ; the Heidelberg tun was emp-
tied only to administer to the pleasures of the prince or
his favorites, while the vats of the brewer quench the
thirst of a numerous population, which works hard, receives good pay, and pays its providers well.

The silence and desolation of the old castle, contrasted
with the bustle and prosperity of the English brewery,
are a striking emblem of the feudal system compared with
the modern power of peace and creative industry.   All
nations, in proportion as they have the power to change
the warlike qualities of the feudal age into the useful
qualities of the labourer, or as they want the capacity thus
to re-cast themselves, may read their own destiny, either
in the state of the flourishing manufactory, or in that of
the deserted and crumbling castle.   Happy the people,
who, like France and England, have had strength to shake
off the past, and who, in the quiet enjoyment of their
liberties, have only to concern themselves about the future !
Woe to that people, which will not, or cannot, tear itself
away from the past !   That people is worn out ; it will

---

* 50,000 gallons.

die of consumption, and will leave behind nothing but ruins, poetical, perhaps, but still none the less ruins, that is, death and desolation : unless indeed a new blood be infused into its veins, or in other words, unless it be conquered like unhappy Poland.

LETTER II.

LIVERPOOL AND THE RAILROAD.

LIVERPOOL, Nov. 7, 1833.

I HAVE just come back from Manchester by the railroad, which is a fine piece of work ; I know of nothing that gives a higher idea of the power of man. There are impressions which one cannot describe ; such is that of being hurried along at the rate of half a mile a minute, or thirty miles an hour (the speed of the train as we started from Manchester,) without being the least incommoded, and with the most complete feeling of security, for only one accident has happened since the opening of the road, and that was owing to the imprudence of the individual who perished. You pass over and under roads, rivers, and canals ; you cross other railroads, and a great number of other roads, without any trouble or confusion. The great forethought and spirit of order which in England they suck in with their mothers' milk, preside in every part, and make it impossible that the trains should fall foul of each other, or that the cars should run down unlucky travellers, or the farmers' wagons ; all along the route are gates, which open and shut at the precise moment of time, and watchmen on the look out. How many persons in France would be benefitted by this short trip, did it serve only as a lesson of order and forecast! And then the Mount Olive cut is as well worth seeing as Roland's Breach; the Wapping tunnel will bear a comparison with the caves of Campan; the dike across Chat Moss seems to me as full of interest as the remains of the most famous Roman ways, not excepting even the Appian itself; and there is a column, which, though only a chimney for a steam-engine, is not, perhaps, less perfect in its proportions than Pompey's Pillar. Many tourists, even persons who have not been made weary of sight-seeing in Switzerland and Italy, would find Chester Bridge, which is not, indeed, on the road, but is nevertheless very near it, quite as worthy of a visit as the Devil's Bridge; not to mention that the burning cinders which the engine strews along the route, might suggest to the traveller, without any great stretch of fancy, the idea of being transported in a fiery car, certainly the most poetical of all vehicles.

Those who doubt the policy of introducing railroads into France, and think it prudent to wait for more light, cite, among other arguments, the experiments continually making in England to apply locomotive engines to common roads, the success of which, they think, would save the expense of rails. There is no doubt that railroads, like every other new invention, are susceptible of improvement; but they will always be expensive, and while other nations keep up such *schools* as the Manchester and Liverpool railroad, and we stand looking on with folded arms, we shall soon find ourselves, by excess of caution, fallen behind all Europe in manufactures and commerce. As for the steam-engines of Gurney, Dance, or anybody else, there is no hope that they will enable us to save the expense of rails. I think it, indeed, very probable that engines may be made to take the place of horses on roads kept in such a state as the English highways; but upon any road whatsoever, and whatever motive power is employed, engines or horses, in order to reach a great speed, from twentyfive to thirty miles an hour, for instance, it is absolutely necessary to cut through hills, and to fill up or bridge over the valleys, just as is done for railroads. Besides this great speed forbids the free circulation of vehicles, and makes it necessary to avoid the level of the frequented routes, and to pass over or under them by means of tunnels or bridges. None of the inconveniences, or liabilities of railroads would be avoided by this system; the expense would be almost the same, for the most costly portion of the work in railroads is the cuts and embankments, the bridges and viaducts; the iron required for the rails forms less than one-third of the expenditure. The expenses of superintending the routes would be the same. Besides, the road once graded, there would be a great gain in laying rails, that is, in making a complete railroad, however little might be the amount of transportation; for on a Macadamised road the force of friction is ten times that on iron rails, so that the use of these new locomotive carriages can never supply the place of railways.

The correctness of these views is proved by what is now doing in England; while the new steam carriages are getting ready for regular service, railroad companies are already at work or are organizing in all quarters. Two works are now in progress which will connect Liverpool with London, by way of Birmingham; the whole length will be one hundred and ninetyfive miles. Although a trial of the new carriages is making on the Birmingham road, shares in the railroad between that town and London are at a high premium. Another company is preparing to construct a railroad from London to Bath and Bristol, a distance of one hundred and fifteen miles; companies are also formed for connecting London with Southampton, on

the Havre route to Paris, and with Brighton, on the Dieppe
route ; other shorter works are projected. It is not that
the experiments of Gurney and Dance are unknown or
slighted ; on the contrary, their importance is fully felt ;
the newspapers are full of them, and they even excite
some enthusiasm. In this country, where it is a settled
maxim that the labourer is worthy of his hire, I saw vessels
all along the road which had been gratuitously brought
and filled by the inhabitants for the use of one of these
steam-carriages ; unluckily the carriage did not arrive
when it was expected ; it had got out of order, as it too
often does.

The Liverpool and Manchester railroad owes its brilliant
success to the substantial and permanent nature of the
interest which binds together the two towns. It would
be impossible to realize a more complete division of labor ;
Manchester, with the country twenty miles round it, is
nothing but a workshop ; Liverpool manufactures nothing,
but merely sells what her neighbours produce. Liverpool
is not, whatever the guide book may say, another Venice,
rising from the waves ; it is a counting-house, and nothing but a counting-house, though on a vast scale,
and under the most perfect regulations, of any in the
world. The business is all done in a space smaller
than the *Place du Carrousel,* where are the handsome
Exchange, the Town House, and all the banking houses,
&c. At four or five o'clock each one shuts up his cell (for
the offices deserve this name), and retires to his house or
his country seat, for many of the residences are on the
other side of the Mersey. Liverpool and Manchester are
surrounded by a double and three fold series of canals ; the
Duke of Bridgewater's canal, the Leeds and Liverpool,
the Sankey, Leigh, Bolton and Bury, Mersey and Irwell
canals, without taking into account the rivers Irwell, Mersey, and Weaver, which though small, form fine bays at

their mouths, and are more easily and regularly navigable than our great rivers, while the navigation is carried on with a promptitude and despatch wholly unknown in France. Since the peace these two towns have enjoyed such a high degree of prosperity, that ten years ago these means of communication, with the addition of a fine road, were found to be insufficient. The counting-house and the manufactory wished to be nearer to each other; accordingly, on the 10th of May, 1824, a memorial, signed by one hundred and fifty merchants, declared the necessity of new routes; and a railroad was decided on. The work was begun in June, 1826, and the road was opened in due form, on the 15th of September, 1830. A tunnel is now constructing, one mile and a quarter in length, which will carry the railroad into the heart of the town, and will cost about 800,000 dollars.

The chief article of English commerce, that in which it has no rival, and which opens all the ports of the world to English vessels, is cottons of all descriptions. The value of the produce and manufactures annually exported from the United Kingdom, during the last ten years, has averaged 190 millions of dollars.* That of cottons alone has ranged from 80 to 90 millions, and the greater part is made in Manchester and the vicinity.† This single fact would sufficiently explain the commercial importance of Liverpool; add to this that Liverpool is in the neighbourhood of the founderies and forges of Staffordshire and Shropshire, and the manufactories of Birmingham and

---

* The annual exports of France are little more than half this sum. (See Note 3, at the end of the volume.)

† The population of Lancashire, in which are situated Liverpool and Manchester, increased, between 1801 and 1831, from 672,731 to 1,336,854, that is, it doubled. The increase of population in the rest of the United Kingdom was only fifty per cent.

Sheffield; that the diminished width of the island, in the 53d degree of latitude, enables her to reach out her hands at once to the eastern and western coasts ; that she is the centre of the business between England and Ireland ; that she approaches, at the same time, Scotland and Wales; that she is the head quarters of steam navigation in England, and it will be seen at a glance that Liverpool is the seat of a prodigious commerce, inferior only to that of London.   Eleven thousand vessels measuring 1,400,000 tons, enter her nine docks every year; two-fifths of the whole exports of England are shipped hence, and more than one-fifth of the British customs duty, or nearly 20,000,000 dollars (equal to the total sum of the French customs), are collected here.   Since the modification of the East India Company's charter, the Liverpool merchants flatter themselves with the hope of securing a great part of the India trade, which has hitherto been monopolized by London ; they aspire to rival the commerce of the capital, and it must be confessed that they are taking the right road to success.

In tracing the history of Liverpool, Manchester, or any other English town, we are struck with a fact which is full of good omen for France ; it is this, that a people never engages heartily and successfully in commerce and manufactures, until it feels itself safe from civil or religious despotism ; but once assured on that point, it moves rapidly and right forward in its industrial career.   So long as England was restrained in her franchises or her faith, she was possessed with one idea, how to throw off the yoke ; once freed from this care, she has achieved in the different branches of industry what no nation has ever done before.   In the beginning of the last century, not long after the expulsion of the Stuarts, when Liverpool had only 5,000 inhabitants, with no commerce but a feeble coasting trade, some of her merchants conceived the idea of competing with Bristol, which then monopolized the West Indian trade. Bristol exported to America the products of the fisheries in the German Ocean, and some fustians and checks manufactured in Germany, and the Liverpool adventurers took cargoes of Scotch stuffs; but the attempt was unsuccessful, the Scotch goods were of inferior quality. Manchester then relieved them from this difficulty; there were already some manufacturers in that place, who imitated and surpassed the German articles, and thus provided, the merchants of Liverpool were able to sustain a competition with those of Bristol. The smuggling trade with the Spanish colonies, and the slave trade, undertaken in competition with Bristol, continued to enrich Liverpool and consequently Manchester. In 1764, when Bristol fitted out 32 ships for Africa and 74 for America, Liverpool ran 105 to the former and 141 to the latter; in the same year 1589 vessels entered the port of Liverpool, while only 675 arrived at Bristol. At present Bristol is a second-rate mart compared with Liverpool; not that the former has declined; on the contrary, it is a wealthy city, with a trade tenfold what it was a hundred years ago. But in the midst of the general progress, Liverpool has advanced at high speed. It now contains 180,000 inhabitants, or, including the suburbs, 225,000, without reckoning the floating population of strangers and sailors. During the siege of Calais, when Edward III. collected all the strength of England, this town found it difficult to furnish one vessel, carrying six men; in 1829, it owned 806 vessels of 161,780 tons burthen, manned by 9,091 sailors. (See Note 4, at the end of the volume.) During the wars of the French Revolution, Liverpool was able to bear her share of the burdens of the country, and to spend 170,000 dollars annually in works of public utility and in embellishing the town. In 1797 she volunteered to raise a troop of horse and eight companies of foot at her own charge ; in 1798 she raised a regiment of volunteers and the sum of 80,000 dollars, and in 1803, when Napoleon threatened England with invasion, two regiments of infantry and 600 artillerists. In the same period a host of useful and charitable institutions were founded by subscription, and the Exchange was built at the cost of 600,000 dollars. All this is the work of one century ; hardly had James II. reached Saint Germain, when the first dock in Liverpool was opened ; within thirty years the Mersey and Irwęll were canalled. It was the same throughout England. We must not exaggerate and abuse historical parallels, but, unless we shut our eyes, it is impossible not to perceive a striking analogy between the state of England after the fall of the Stuarts, and that of France since 1830. With both people there is a feeling of profound security in regard to their liberties, a deep conviction that they have gained a decisive victory, and that they have nothing to fear from the encroachments of the civil power or of a religious corporation ; the same wish to see political reforms gives rise to substantial and palpable improvement in the condition of the people, and the same disposition on the part of the government to enlighten and realize the popular will.

The old dynasties of England and France fell in consequence of their efforts to give political power to the clergy, rather than from any attempt to restore the feudal system with its brutality and its rapacity ; for the deposed princes themselves were neither rapacious nor violent. The English revolution, however, was far from giving birth to irreligion ; Liverpool,—which is, so to speak, of to-day, which bears the stamp, not of England as she was in the sixteenth or the fourteenth century, but of England as she was in the eighteenth century, as she is in our own time,—Liverpool is a proof of this. There is no town in France which numbers as many churches as Liverpool, where there are thirtyseven of the establishment, in addition to fortythree dissenters' chapels and meeting houses, Presbyterian, Baptist, Methodist, Unitarian, Quaker, Jewish, and Roman Catholic ; the last have here five chapels. Most of these have been built since 1750, and nearly one half since 1800 ; I have a list under my eye, and the dates are 1803, 1810, 1813, 1814, 1815, 1815, 1815, 1816, 1821, 1826, 1826, 1827, 1827, 1830, 1831. Are we to believe that this analogy will hold good on our own soil, and that as she grows rich by industry, France will return to the religious sentiment ? I wish it, I hope it ; we are already past the time when atheism was fashionable in France ; it will not, however, be under the flag of the Anglican church, or of any other protestant sect that France will rally ; she must have a more imposing and pompous worship.

LETTER III.

WAR OF THE PRESIDENT OF THE UNITED STATES UPON THE BANK.

NEW YORK, JANUARY 1, 1834.

THIS country is now in the crisis of a high industrial fever, which has assumed a political character, and is of a very serious nature ; for the industrial interest, in this country, is the most important. Last year, when the dispute between the Northern and Southern States, relative to the tariff was settled, (see Note 5, at the end of

the volume,) the wise and prudent thanked God, that
the danger, which had threatened their country, had
been averted ; there seemed to them nothing further to
obstruct its triumphant career of conquests over nature,
with an ever accelerated rapidity and increased success.
A series of causes, to appearance of slight moment, has
changed these hopes into fears. Some trifling circumstances revived the old quarrel between the democratic
party, to which the President belongs, and the Bank
of the United States, and both sides grew warm.
(See Note 6, at the end of the volume.) President
Jackson, a man of good intentions and ardent patriotism,
but too hasty towards those who venture to contradict
him, declared a deadly war against the Bank, and pushed
it with all the energy and fury, in the same cut-and-thrust
style, that he had the war against the Indians and English
twenty years before. He set his veto to the bill that had
passed both houses of Congress, renewing the Bank charter, which was about to expire in three years. Not satisfied with this blow, he withdrew from the hands of the
Bank the public money, which, by the provisions of its
charter, had been deposited in them, and which gave it
the means of very materially extending its operations ;
for the excess of the deposits over the exigencies of the
government amount to not less than ten millions. The
Bank, which had paid to the government a bonus of
1,500,000 dollars for the privilege of being the depository of the public funds, cried out loudly against this
measure, and with good reason, for no one denies, that no
institution in the union is better able to meet all its liabilities. It has reduced its discounts, first, because the
removal of the public deposits has diminished the amount
of specie in its vaults, and also, as it declares, whether
right or wrong, because its very existence being threatened
by the President's veto, it is prudent to restrain the sphere of

its operations, and to prepare in time for the final settlement of its concerns. As this institution takes the lead in the financial world, the other banks, even those to which the public deposits have been transferred, have been obliged, in their turn, to restrict their operations. Not only are they afraid to extend their discounts in proportion to the amount of these deposits, but they are obliged to contract them, because they find themselves, as objects of the favour of government in this respect, in a state of hostility with the Bank of the United States, and it is necessary to be on their guard in the presence of so formidable an adversary. Thus are the sources of credit suddenly dried up. Now credit is the life-blood of the prosperity of the United States; without credit, the populous towns which are springing up on all sides, as if by magic, the opulent States, which, far away from the Atlantic and beyond the Alleghanies, stretch along the Ohio and the Mississippi, would become a solitary wilderness, savage forests or pathless swamps. The city of New York alone has twenty banks, the annual average discounts of which, during the last eight years, have amounted to one hundred millions. At Paris, where the transactions are certainly more extensive than in New York, the discounts of the Bank of France, in 1831, amounted to 223 million francs, and in 1832 to 151 millions.* The amount of the discounts of the Philadelphia banks, in 1831, was 150 millions. A general shock to credit, however transient, is here more terrible than the most frightful earthquake.

If I did not fear to lengthen out this letter beyond measure, I would give some details concerning the struggle

---

* The maximum of the discounts of the Bank of France was in 1810, when it amounted to 710 million francs. In 1813, they were 640 millions, in 1826, 689 millions; at these two periods the Bank made a great effort to sustain commerce. It had less courage in the crisis of 1831—32.

between the two parties, concerning their tactics and their
measures in Congress and out of it, concerning Mr Clay's
speeches and General Jackson's home thrusts. But I think
it more important at present, to call your attention to the
part which the Bank of the United States has played since
its establishment, and to the causes which stirred up
against it that mass of hatred and distrust, from which
General Jackson derives confidence in his measures. For
it is not merely his own dislike that he gratifies; from the
last elections, which in almost all the States are based on
universal suffrage, it is plain that the numerical majority
of the population is, at this moment, opposed to the
Bank.

The Americans had already used and abused systems of
credit while under the English rule. As soon as they had
achieved their independence, they became bolder in their
enterprises, more sanguine, or, if you please, more rash in
their speculations. They stood in great need of credit;
the number of banks was multiplied, and many abuses
crept in. The State legislatures made no difficulty in
granting bank-charters to whoever asked for them, and in
this respect they have not changed their practice. If they
imposed some restraints, they had no means of ascertain-
ing or securing their strict observance. The banks, therefore, often issued an amount of bills wholly disproportion-
ate to their real capital, not merely twice or thrice, but ten
times the value of their specie and other means. The
originators of the bank often chose themselves directors,
and discounted no paper but their own, or rather they lent
to themselves the whole circulation of the bank, on the
bare deposit of the bank shares. This was an ingenious
process to enable whoever pleased to coin current money,
without ingots of gold or silver. The mismanagement of
these banking companies has sometimes been such, that
instances have occurred where the officers of the bank

have, on their own authority, opened a credit for them-selves, and generally admitted their friends to share in the privilege. Thus it was discovered, that the cashier of the City Bank in Baltimore had lent himself 166,548 dollars, and had made loans to one of his friends to the amount of 185,382 dollars; all the other officers had taken the same liberty, with the exception of one clerk and the porter.

The banks abusing the privilege of issuing bills, that is to say of making loans, individuals abused the privilege of borrowing; hence mad speculations, and consequently losses by the lender and borrower. The banks cloaked theirs by new issues of paper, individuals theirs by new loans; but there were many failures of speculators, and some of banks. The latter excited the public indignation without reforming any one. The honest and moderate working classes, the farmers* and mechanics, who found that in the end they were the dupes of the speculators, since by the depreciation of the paper money, which they had taken as so much specie, they came in for a share of the loss, but had no part in the gain, that is, in the divi-dends, conceived a violent hatred against the banking sys-tem. To this particular cause of dislike, was added that aversion which may be found in Europe and everywhere else, felt by persons of methodical habits, gaining little by hard labour, but gaining regularly, against those who are im-patient to make their fortune, and to make it at all events, and who waste what they make in the most unbounded luxury and by the most foolish enterprises, in less time than they have been in acquiring it. Then there was the natural jeal-ousy of simplicity against cunning, of slow and heavy minds against the shrewd penetration of others. There

---

* The Americans have retained the English word *farmer*, which proper-ly signifies one who cultivates a hired soil, *fermier*, although among them the cultivators are proprietors.

was also that suspicious distrust of all new influences, and all power that aims to strike its roots deep, a distrust, which is essential to the American, and which is the source, explanation, and safe-guard of his republican institutions. In short, in 1811, when the old Bank of the United States, which was on a much smaller scale than the present Bank, petitioned Congress for a renewal of its charter, an appeal was made to the farmers and mechanics, and, as at the present day, the hobgoblin of a *new aristocracy, and the worst of all, an aristocracy of money*, was summoned up ; the petition was not granted.

Soon after, in 1812, war broke out between England and the United States. The natural effect of war is to diminish confidence, to make the merchants timid, speculators cautious. Most of the banks, having been managed with little prudence in better times, were soon unable to meet the call for specie by the public ; they solicited and obtained from their respective legislatures leave to suspend specie payments. Their bills had a forced circulation. At the peace of 1815 the banks were not able to resume specie payments, and the system of inconvertible paper money was persevered in. Imagine then two hundred and fortysix classes of paper money,* circulating side by side, having all degrees of value, according to the good or bad credit of the bank which issued them, at 20 per cent., 30 per cent., or 50 per cent. discount. Gold and silver had entirely disappeared ; there was no longer any standard of price and value ; the amount of bills in circulation had become prodigious.† To the bills of the banks was added a great amount of individual obligations of still less value, issued by private persons as suited their wants, and which circulated more or less freely in the

---

* The number of banks at that time.

† There was more paper in circulation in 1816 than in 1834, when the extent and value of business were very much greater.

neighbourhood. It was a frightful scene of confusion, a Babel, where all business became impracticable from the utter impossibility of the parties understanding each other.

It was now felt that, to restore order in the bosom of this chaos, there was needed a regulating power, capable of commanding confidence, with ample funds to enable it to pay out specie freely, and whose presence and, in case of necessity, whose authority, should serve to recall the local banks to their duty. In 1816, the present Bank of the United States was, therefore, chartered by Congress for a term of 20 years, with a capital of 35 millions, and it went into operation on the 1st of January, 1817. The seat of the mother-bank is Philadelphia, and it has 25 branches scattered over the Union. By its interference and assistance specie payments were resumed by the New York, Philadelphia, Baltimore, Richmond, Norfolk Banks on the 20th February, 1817, and in course of time all the other Banks followed the example. This resumption of specie payments was, first for the banks and then for individuals, the signal, the occasion, the rule of a general settling up of old accounts. As there had been much prodigality, unsuccessful speculations, and dead loss, accumulated through a period of 20 years, there was now a complete breaking up; many banks failed or suspended their operations, and from 1811 to 1830, 165 banks were reduced to one or the other of these alternatives. This state of things lasted three years; they were three years of crisis, three years of suffering for industry, that is, for the people of the United States; for this people is identified with its commerce. The trials of this period have left a deep and lasting impression. Hatred of speculators and of the Banking system has taken root in the hearts of the mass of the people, and now springs up in hostility to the Bank of the United States, which, in the eyes of the multitude, is the representative of the system, although it is itself innocent of the mischief, and can alone prevent its recurrence.

The antipathy of the greatest number against the banks has then a reasonable cause, but it is not, therefore, any the less blind and unjust. They see nothing but abuses, and shut their eyes against the advantages. The great extension of credit, which resulted from the great number of banks, and from the absence of all restraint on their proceedings, has been beneficial to all classes, to the farmers and mechanics not less than to the merchants. The banks have served the Americans as a lever to transfer to their soil, to the general profit, the agriculture and manufactures of Europe, and to cover their country with roads, canals, factories, schools, churches, and, in a word, with every thing that goes to make up civilization. Without the banks, the cultivator could not have had the first advances, nor the implements necessary for the cultivation of his farm, and if the credit system has given facilities for stock-jobbing to speculators, it has also enabled him, although indirectly, to buy at the rate of one, two, or three dollars an acre, and to cultivate lands, which are now, in his hands, worth tenfold or a hundred fold their first cost. The mechanics who attack the banking system, forget that they owe to it that growth of manufacturing industry, which has raised their wages from one dollar to two dollars a day. They forget that it furnishes the means by which many of their number raise themselves to competence or wealth; for in this country every enterprising man, of a respectable character, is sure of obtaining credit, and thenceforth his fortune depends upon his own exertions.*

---

* The mechanics and farmers have no credit open at the banks, but the traders from whom they buy their tools, implements, raw material, and provisions, having that advantage, are able to deal with them on favourable terms; the farmer and mechanic are thus benefitted indirectly, if not immediately, by the banks.

At the end of 1819, commerce revived, the financial system of the United States seemed settled on a sure basis. Since that time, some shocks have been felt, as in 1822, and in 1825, the latter the reaction of the great English crisis, but in both cases the storm soon passed away. The root of the evil was struck on the day that the Bank of the United States went into operation. This great establishment, which committed some errors at first and paid the penalty, has for a long time been conducted with the most consummate prudence. Most of the leading commercial men, that is to say, most of the talents, of the country are attached to it as directors, and its foreign correspondents or associates are the houses whose credit is most firmly established, such as the Barings of London, and the Hottinguers of Paris. It exercises the necessary control over all the local banks, obliges them to restrain their emissions by calling upon them for specie, or by refusing to receive their bills when the issues are excessive. It was by its agency that the currency of the United States was established on so large a basis, that, in 1831, the banks were able, without any effort, to discount the amount of 800,000,000 dollars, in the principal cities of the Union, or 1,100,000,000 for the whole country.

Now, this state of prosperity seems to be coming to an end. Here, in New York, the banks have ceased to discount, and on good paper, for two or three months, 15, 18, and 24 per cent. per annum have been paid, the usual rate of the Bank of the United States, and of most of the local banks, being 6 per cent. At Philadelphia, 18 per cent. per annum has been given on excellent paper at short dates. At Baltimore, merchants of great wealth have been obliged to stop payment. Nobody buys; nobody can sell. Orders for foreign goods are held back; and as every body here is engaged in business, this state of things threatens all interests, is the subject of all conver-

sations, of all writing, and of all thoughts. God grant
that the sight of the impending danger may calm the passions, and that the good sense of the community may
banish empty prejudices and false fears! God grant that
both parties may forget their mutual animosities in their
anxiety for the common welfare! This should be our
prayer, not only for the sake of the destinies of this great
nation, but also because our silk manufacturers and the
owners of our vineyards, will pay a part of the expenses
of the campaign against the banks in general, which the
radical party is about to open, by a mortal contest, with
the Bank of the United States.

LETTER IV.

DEMOCRACY — THE BANK.

NEW YORK, JANUARY 11, 1834.

THE financial crisis brought on by the quarrel between
the President and the Bank, has not become more serious;
there is a great scarcity of money, that is, a great diminution of credit, but the failures are not yet numerous or
considerable. The last arrivals from Europe have brought
us the news that several of the trades in Paris and at
Lyons have refused to work. What is taking place here
in regard to the Bank, is analogous to what is passing in
France among the tailors, bakers, and carpenters, and
what occurs daily in England among the manufacturing
operatives. In Europe, and particularly in France, it is
the rising of a democracy or rather a radicalism, which is

yet in embryo, and which, if it please God, will never come to maturity. In America, it is the despotic humour of a full grown democracy, passing more and more into radicalism, the longer it rules without a rival and without a counterpoise.

It seems to me improbable that the journeymen carpenters, tailors, and bakers of Paris, should ever give the law to their masters. Among us, the middling class (*bourgeoisie*) is beginning to feel that it is its duty to improve the condition of the working class. It has the authority, but it is conscious that the people has the physical force. The people has counted its own ranks and those of the *bourgeoisie*, but it feels that it is not enough to have the number; it sees that it has nothing to expect from violence, and that it can back its friends only by improved habits of order and morality. On both sides their reciprocal rights are mutually acknowledged ; each fears and respects the other. Here, on the contrary, it is perfectly natural that the democracy should rule the capitalists, merchants, and manufacturers ; it possesses at once the physical force and the political power ; the middling and upper classes inspire it neither with fear nor with respect. The equilibrium is gone ; there is no guarantee against the popular caprice in the United States, but the good sense of the people ; it must be allowed that this good sense is quite extraordinary, but it is not infallible. A popular despotism is as easily deluded by flatterers, as any other despotism.

The Bank of the United States is at this time experiencing the truth of this observation. I have already alluded to some of the crying abuses which have excited a violent hatred against the banks in general, although without the aid of the banks it would have been impossible for the United States to have increased in population, wealth, and territory as they have done. These abuses were and are the acts of the local banks, and not of the Mammoth Bank. On the contrary, the latter, by the control which it exercises over the local banks for its own security, checks and limits these abuses, if it does not completely prevent them. The legislatures of the different States have been repeatedly called to deliberate on the question of abolishing all banks and breaking up the banking system ; but they have generally thought, and justly, that the remedy would be worse than the disease. They have attempted to cure the disorder by restrictive provisions in the charter of new banks. The State of of New York, in 1829, embraced the whole subject in the Safety-Fund Act, which established a mutual supervision of the banks over each other, under the direction of the Bank Commissioners, and creates at their common expense a safety fund, designed to indemnify the public in case of the failure of any one of the banks. But these measures of repression or prevention have generally proved inefficacious, either from a defect in the means of coercion possessed by the government, or from a reluctance to use the powers conferred by the laws.

In their report of the 31st of January, 1833, the New York Bank Commissioners urgently call the attention of the legislature to the serious dangers which may result from these institutions as they are now organized, particularly in the country, and to their excessive issues in proportion to the small quantity of specie in their vaults. With two millions in specie, the banks of the State had, at that time, a circulation of above twelve millions. But this report itself proves, that the commissioners did not dare to fulfil the duties imposed on them by the Safety-Fund act ; they had the authority to shut up the offending banks. Their warnings have not prevented the legislature from chartering new banks by the dozen. This year it will have to act on 105 petitions for charters, that is, eighteen more than the actual number of banks in the State. To be sure in the present instance, the *let alone* principle will probably be violated, for the Governor's Message of January 7, 1834, urges the two houses to arrest the flood. This Bank mania, as Jefferson called it, is created by the profits of banking, which is, and more especially was, before the institution of the Bank of the United States, the best kind of speculation, exactly in the ratio of the abuses attending it.*

In the local banks, especially in the country banks, the chief aim of the president and directors is, at all events, come what may, to make the semi-annual dividend as large as possible. By extending their operations excessively, they may, if they lose the public confidence, be driven to a failure; but in the United States the prospect of such a disaster is much less terrible to the greater number of merchants, and even to the smaller companies, than it is in Europe. (See *Note* 7, at the end of the volume.) When a bank fails, there is, indeed, a great outcry, because the number of victims is large, and the loss extends to all classes; for most of the bills being of the denomination of five dollars and under, they are very generally distributed in the hands of the labourers, as well as of the wealthier classes. But just in proportion to the distribution of

---

* The dividends of the Bank of North America were, in 1792, 15 per cent.; in 1793, 13 1-2; from 1794 to 1799 inclusive, 12 per cent.; from 1804 to 1810, 9 per cent. Those of the old Bank of the United States varied from 7 5-8 to 10 per cent. Those of the Pennsylvania Bank, from 1792 to 1810, from 8 to 10. The Bank of the United States regularly divides 7 per cent. to the share-holders. In the city of New York the average dividends of the banks in 1832, was 6.14 per cent.; of the country banks 9 per cent. It must not be forgotten that the legal rate of interest is higher in the United States than in Europe; it is 6 per cent. in Pennsylvania, 7 in New York, from 8 to 9 in the Southern States, and 10 in Louisiana. In the Western States there is no regulation of interest by law, but the ordinary rate is very high.

the loss over the greater number of persons, is the quickness with which the clamor ceases. The president, the cashier, the directors, and others principally interested, readily find means to recover from the blow, by obtaining credit elsewhere, and the whole affair is at an end.

The Bank of the United States, on the contrary, directed by men of large fortune and established reputation, connected in business with the principal houses in Europe, charged with a vast responsibility, subject to the supervision of the Federal government, which names five of the directors out of twentyfive, and officiously watched by an army of journalists, is interested and obliged to follow another course. Not that it has not committed some errors ; but it paid dear for them, and has never repeated them. Neither are its rules and regulations perfect ; the experience of twenty years will doubtless suggest some modifications. But even its adversaries admit that it has been admirably managed. They pretended, at first, that the public money was not safe in its vaults, but they are at present ashamed to insist upon this point, as the investigation made by the House of Representatives proved the absurdity of the charge. The accusations now brought against it are of a political character.

Politically considered, indeed, the existence of an institution so powerful as the Bank of the United States, may present some inconveniences. The fundamental maxim of the Federal and State constitutions is, that the supreme authority is null and void ; there is no government here in the true sense of the word ; that is, no directing power. Each one is his own master ; it is self-government in all its purity. This anomalous and monstrous development of the individual principle is no evil here, it is even a great good at present ; it is the present stage in the progress of the United States, because self-government is the only form of government to which the

American character, as it is, can accommodate itself. If individuality had not free elbow-room here, this people would fall short of its destiny, which is to extend its conquests rapidly over an immense territory, for the good of the whole human race, to substitute, in the shortest time possible, civilization for the solitude of the primitive forests, over a surface ten times greater than all France, of as great average fertility as that country, and capable, therefore, of accommodating 350 millions of inhabitants.

From these considerations it is clear, that any power whatsoever, if possessed of great influence, and exercising it over a great space, would be inconsistent with the political system of the country ; for this reason the Federal and State governments are in a permanent state of eclipse. And it is furthermore evident, that the Bank, which is met at every turn as an agent in all transactions, which governs credit, regulates the currency, animates or checks at will the activity of commerce by narrowing or widening the channels of circulation, the Bank, which by its numerous branches is, like the fabled polypus, everywhere present, the Bank with its funds, its centralisation, its trusty creatures, is certainly an anomaly, which may become big with danger.   One might, from an abstract, theoretical point of view, imagine cases, in which this financial colossus, seated in the heart of a country absorbed in business, would press with a crushing weight on the liberties of the people. If it were possible that a new Monk should wish to restore the English rule, or that a new Bonaparte, the saviour of the republic in another Marengo, should attempt to make himself dictator, it would also be possible that a conspiracy between the Bank and this Monk, or this Napoleon, might overthrow the liberties of America.   But such an event, possible to be sure in theory, (for in theory nothing is impossible,) is, at present, wholly impracticable in fact.   Yet there are honest and enlightened men, on whom this theoretical danger makes more impression, than the necessity of a regulator amidst the chaos of 500 banks, or of an agent, which, by controlling the currency, should be in financial affairs, what the vast rivers of the country are in the system of internal communication. They fear more, for this land of industry, from the imperceptible tyranny of the Bank, than from a system in which there would be no check on the cupidity of the local banks, and in which they might renew, with their paper money, if not the *assignats* of France, or the Continental money of the Revolution, at least the commercial anarchy which followed the war of 1812.

Unluckily for the United States, it is not on this high ground of foresight, that President Jackson and his friends take their stand in their attack on the Bank. They do not say, that it is possible that it may some time, under a new state of things, become an instrument of oppression; they pretend that it is so already. According to them, it tends to nothing less than the subjugation of the country to its rule. In his last annual message, and in an official paper read to the cabinet on the 18th of September, 1833, the President accuses the Bank :   1. With having intrigued to bring up the question of the renewal of its charter in Congress during the session of 1831–32, in order to reduce him to the alternative of giving his sanction to the bill, or losing the votes of the friends of the Bank in the approaching election, if he refused it. He forgets that he had himself, in his message at the opening of that session, recommended to Congress to settle the business. 2. Of having meddled with politics in opposing his election in 1832, and of having, with this purpose, enlarged its loans and discounts twentyeight and a half millions. The Bank replies that the statement is incorrect ; that its books show, that its available means having been augmented, between January and May, 1831, ten millions, and the requisitions of commerce having increased, it had judged it expedient to extend its credits seventeen and a half millions, so that the actual extension of its operations was only four and a half millions. 3. Of having attempted to corrupt the public press, either by printing a great number of pamphlets, or by gaining over the newspapers. The Bank answers to this charge, that it has a perfect right to defend itself by the press, against the continual attacks upon it to which the press gives currency, that it may certainly be allowed to reprint the speeches delivered in its favor in Congress, or essays in which questions of banking are luminously treated, such as that by the celebrated Mr Gallatin, who was twelve years Secretary of the Treasury, and afterward minister to France. As to the vague imputation of attempting to corrupt a press, which pours forth such a number of journals as the press of the United States, (see *Note* 8, at the end of the volume,) it does not deserve a serious answer.

If a European government, from motives of this character, on facts thus destitute of proof, should attempt to destroy an institution essential to the prosperity of the country, the cry of despotism would be raised on all sides. If the state were itself interested in the institution to the amount of one fifth of its capital (7 millions of dollars), many persons would charge such an attempt not only with violence, but with folly. In the United States the numerical majority, which is the majority of electors, applauded General Jackson's campaign against the Bank almost as enthusiastically as his campaign at New Orleans. The military success of General Jackson, his honesty, his iron firmness, have given him an astonishing popularity. The Bank, on the contrary, in spite of its daily services, (see *Note* 9, at the end of the volume,) is unpopular ; it is so on account of the popular hatred of the Banking System, on account of that jealousy, which, in a land of perfect equality and suspicious democracy, follows in the steps of wealth and pomp; it is so because its extensive privileges shock all republican feelings. In the United States, in spite of the general habits and laws of equality, there is a sort of aristocracy founded on knowledge or on commercial distinction. This aristocracy, somewhat prone to entertain a contempt for the vulgar multitude, causes a strong reaction against itself in the popular mind, and as it supports the Bank by its influence and its writings, this is enough, of itself, to set the pure democracy against the institution. Add to this, that the Bank, irritated by the hostile demonstrations of the administration, has sometimes answered it by angry acts of reprisal, not grave in themselves, but unfortunate in their consequences, and of which its adversaries have adroitly availed themselves to excite the popular passions. Although the Bank has the majority of the Senate in its favor, the chances are now against it. Unless the multitude, which now shouts HURRAH FOR JACKSON! without reflection, shall be led, between this and March, 1836, when its charter expires, to reflect seriously on the matter, it will disappear, until a new experience shall again prove that it is impossible to get along without it.

Thus, at the very moment when the English Reform ministry is renewing the charter and confirming the privileges of the Bank of England, with the approbation of all Europe, here a compact mass, in which, indeed, the enlightened do not form the majority, but in which, notwithstanding, some are included, deals the death-blow to a similar institution, tried and proved by long services. Thus, while one of the greatest, perhaps, in an economical point of view, the very greatest of the benefits which France could receive, would be the establishment of a system of banks, connected with each other as the twenty branches of the Bank of the United States are with the mother bank, America is about to witness, if not the death, at least the suspension of an institution, that has been fruitful of so much good. without the slightest immediate loss of popularity by those who are doing the work of destruction. So goes the world in the United States. The history of this affair shows that the political springs are here wholly different from those that operate in Europe, and that nevertheless, intrigue and petty hate have free course here as well as elsewhere.

LETTER V.

MOVEMENT OF PARTIES. — BANK QUESTION.

PHILADELPHIA, JAN. 5, 1834.

OF all the cities of the Union, the peaceful Philadelphia is the most disturbed by the Bank question, because it is the seat of the mother bank. The State of Pennsylvania also, of all the States, suffers the most from the financial crisis, because it is the most deeply in debt, and is obliged to borrow more, either to finish its canals and railroads, or to pay the interest on its existing debt. Conceive of the situation of a State, whose population amounts to only 1,500,000 souls, loaded with a debt of twenty and a half millions, whose ordinary expenditures are less than 600,000 dollars, but which must raise one million to pay interest already accrued, and nearly two millions and a half, for the next summer, under penalty of seeing her great works, executed at an enormous expense, go to ruin, and who knows not whither to turn. This is not all ; some old loans must be reimbursed next May, or in three months, and, to crown the whole, the capitalists who contracted last year for a loan of three millions, to be employed on the public works, are, in consequence of the present crisis, unable to fulfil their contracts. The local banks, which are bound by their charters to lend the State at the rate of 5 per cent., rather stand in need of assistance themselves. To these public embarrassments is added the private distress, and thus this country, which Cobbett, who always shows talent, and occasionally gleams of good sense, dubs the *Anti-Malthusian*, exhibits for the present the spectacle of a superabundance of labourers. In the manufacturing districts of Pennsylvania, many of the operatives are without work.

The condition of the rest of the country is not, in general, any more favorable. I am very ready to believe that the Anti-Jackson newspapers, for so they call themselves, exaggerate the distress ; but making all due allowance for rhetorical flourishes, it is still undeniable that there is much distress, especially among the commercial class. Bare figures are more eloquent than the best advocates of the Bank, and it is a notorious fact, that excellent paper has been discounted at the rate of 18 per cent. per annum, and at even higher rates, in New York, Philadelphia, and Baltimore. The price currents and the state of the stock-market, show a general fall in prices of 15, 20, 30, and even 40 per cent. Thus far the efforts of the President to fell the hydra of the moneyed aristocracy, the Mammoth, the Monster, have had no other effect than to blast credit and the commercial prosperity of the country ; for the Bank has been administered with so much ability, especially since the presidency of Mr Biddle, one of the most distinguished men in the country, that notwithstanding the abrupt removal of the public deposits, notwithstanding the unexpected and unfair assaults upon some of the branches, particularly that of Savannah*, it is beyond comparison the most solvent and safe of all the financial institutions in the Union. At this critical moment it has as much specie (ten millions) as all the other 500 banks taken together, and I know from good authority, that many Jackson men (this is the epithet adopted by themselves), have been very glad to be sprinkled with a few drops of the *venom* of this dangerous *reptile*.

If what is now taking place in this country were to occur in any European monarchy, those persons who insist upon all nations having a government cast in the republican mould, whatever may be the condition of their territory and population, their wealth and knowledge, their character and manners, would not fail to make it the text of their harangues against monarchical governments ; holding up to view the picture of an unparalleled commercial prosperity, checked of a sudden by the caprice of the sovereign, they would prove that such is one of the unavoidable consequences of an opposition between the interest of the ruler and the welfare of the nation ; they would demonstrate by geometrical syllogisms, that it is the essence of monarchy to place authority in the hands of the weak and the foolish, who, to gratify their personal malice, would not hesitate to hazard the happiness of millions. They would raise the cry of secret influence, of intrigue, which, according to them, is one of the attributes of monarchies. Unluckily for this theory, it is belied by facts under my own eyes, in the most thorough and

---

* The Savannah branch had out only 500,000 dollars in bills. The collector of the port accumulated them, as they were received for customs duties, and one day a broker presented himself at the counter with 380,000 dollars in bills, for which he demanded specie ; but the disappearance of the bills of the branch from circulation had not been unnoticed, and funds had been provided for any exigency. Payment was, therefore, instantly made, and the broker, not knowing what to do with so much specie, was obliged to request the cashier to receive it in deposit.

flourishing republic that has ever existed. The selfishness of royalty, or more correctly speaking of courts, has hitherto begot much mischief and will continue to do so in future ; but it has met with its match in the bosom of republics, and above all under a system of *absolute* equality, which distributes political power in *absolutely* equal quantities to the intelligent and the ignorant, to the most eminent merchant and author, and the brutal and drunken peasant of Ireland, who is but just enrolled in the list of citizens. An *absolute* people, as well as an *absolute* king, may reject for a time the lessons of experience and the councils of wisdom ; a people as well as a king, may have its courtiers. A people on the throne, whose authority is limited by no checks, may blindly and recklessly espouse the quarrels of the minions of the day ; let those who doubt it come here and see it. Ignorance of the true interests of the country is not the exclusive prerogative of monarchies. The official papers of the Federal Executive in the affair of the Bank, so far as concerns a knowledge of the principles of government and the springs of the public welfare, are on a level with the measures of the government of Spain or Rome. And yet this Executive is the creature of the popular choice in the largest sense. It is not merely in monarchies, that a dancer is to be seen in the post that belongs to a mathematician. The camarilla ! Never have I heard it so much talked about, as since I have been in this country. It is here called the *Kitchen Cabinet*, and admitting a fourth of what is said by the opposition to be true, it is difficult not to believe that its influence upon public affairs is greater than that of the ministerial cabinet.

But to return to the Bank. Congress met on the 3d of December ; and most of the State Legislatures are now in session. Every where, and above all in Congress, the great, not to say the only question agitated, is that of the

Bank. The subject of the discussions is the removal of the public deposits, which the President has withdrawn from the Bank after a military fashion, having previously, in the same spirit, removed from office the Secretary of the Treasury, Mr Duane, who, although opposed to the Bank, considered the President's course illegal and rash. Thus far, the manifestations of public opinion and the deliberative assemblies are extremely various and discordant. In New Jersey, a small and unimportant State, the Assembly has adopted, by a large majority, resolutions approving the acts of the administration, and instructing its delegates in Congress to support the President ; notwithstanding which, Mr Southard, one of the Senators from that State, has made an excellent speech on the other side of the question. The Assembly of New York, the first State in wealth and population, has adopted similar resolutions, by a vote of 118 to 9. Some persons to be sure, assert that this is because New York would like to have the Mother Bank.* The youthful State of Ohio, whose growth borders on the miraculous (it now contains eleven hundred thousand inhabitants, although but 50 years ago it had not six thousand), Ohio, the Benjamin of the democracy, has strongly expressed the same wishes. The little State of Maine has done the same. The administration party lately had a brilliant opportunity of displaying its sympathies and its hatred. The 8th of January, the anniversary of the battle of New Orleans, was celebrated by innumerable public dinners, at each of which numerous toasts were drank. President Jackson was the hero, and the Bank was the scape-goat, of the day. It would be impossible to imagine the flood of accusations, insults, and threats, which was

---

* New York is the chief seat of commerce, but Philadelphia is more central, and is, besides, the city of American capitalists. The removal to New York would also require the transference of the mint and some other public offices to that city, at great expense.

poured upon it, mingled with jests in the taste of the
country upon Mr Biddle ; thus, at one of these dinners,
the Bank was toasted, as being *governed by Young Nick
according to the principles of Old Nick.*

But the population of New England, particularly that
of Massachusetts, is opposed to the administration.   In
Virginia the same opinions seems to prevail, and it is the
same with several of the old Southern States.   The merchants and manufacturers of New York, Philadelphia,
Baltimore, Boston, and a hundred other places, have held
meetings and adopted resolutions, strongly censuring the
conduct of the government towards the Bank, and accu-
sing it of having caused the present crisis.   Most of the
Philadelphia Banks have petitioned in favor of the Bank.
Several Banks at Boston and in Virginia have refused to
take the public money in deposit ; those of Charleston
have been unanimous in this measure.   The majority of
persons of intelligence, experience, and moderation, and
most of the merchants and manufacturers, are in favour
of the Bank.   The country, particularly in the Middle
and Western States, and the operatives in the towns, go
for General Jackson.

In Congress the majority of the Senate is friendly to
the Bank, and the majority of the House is on the side of
the Administration.   The superiority in debate belongs
to the defenders of the Bank.   In the Senate, the three
greatest statesmen in the country, Messrs Clay, Webster,
and Calhoun, are on this side of the question, and the
speeches of Messrs Clay and Calhoun have made a strong
impression.   In the House Mr Binney, of Philadelphia,
and Mr McDuffie have pleaded the same cause with
ability.   On the other side there has been more highflown
declamation than reasoning.   I have been struck with the
resemblance between most of the speeches and newspaper
essays directed against the Bank, and our republican tirades

of 1791 and 1792. There are the same declamatory tone, the same swollen style, the same appeal to the popular passions, with this difference, that the allegations made here are vague, empty, and indefinite, while with us fifty years ago the grievances were real. Most generally the pictures presented in these declamations, are fantastical delineations of the moneyed aristocracy overrunning the country with seduction, corruption, and slavery in its train; or of Mr Biddle aiming at the crown. Amidst this swarm of speeches and essays, one hardly ever meets with any indications of serious study or a tolerable knowledge of the subject; but I have been struck with the speech of Mr Cambreleng, who has put forth some prudent suggestions as to the reforms required in the present system of banking. For it must be confessed, that this animosity of the President and the body of the people against the Bank of the United States, blind and unreasonable as it is, is founded on a real necessity, namely, that of a complete reorganization of the banking system. When Congress renewed the charter of the Bank of the United States without modification, in 1832, it committed an error. It should have seized this opportunity to place the currency of the country on a more solid basis; and if General Jackson had abode by the terms of his veto message, in which he declared that he was not opposed in principle to the establishment of a National Bank, but that the present Bank could not be retained without some modification, he might have become the benefactor of his country. He would not, indeed, have received Cobbett's congratulations, but he would have obtained the approbation of all statesmen and men of sense in the Old and the New World. However, whatever his friends may say, as the President did not foresee the distress, which has befallen American commerce, and as nobody can doubt his patriotism, we need need not yet despair of seeing him adopt this wise course.

The present crisis abundantly proves the wretched condition of the currency, for the original cause of it was quite slight ; it was merely the transfer from the vaults of one bank to those of another of ten millions, an inconsiderable sum relatively to the amount of the business of the country.   If the local banks, in spite of the control exercised by the Bank of the United States, had not previously passed all bounds, they would have been able, when the Bank of the United States was obliged to contract its discounts by the withdrawing of the public money, to have enlarged their own in the same proportion, since those same funds were transferred to their vaults.   But the framework of these banks is so badly put together, that it shakes at the slightest breath.   The slight motion in the political and commercial atmosphere caused by the President's blow at the Bank, in removing the public deposits, was enough to make them totter.   They are like a colossus with clay feet, which should have feet of gold, or in other words, specie in their vaults.

The proportion of metals, of which we have an excess in France, is here extremely small.   In many States, among others New York, there is an enormous quantity of bills of one, two, and three dollars.   In South Carolina there are 25 cent, and even 12 1-2 cent bills.   In Pennsylvania, Virginia, and some other States, there are none of less than five dollars.   The Bank of the United States emits none of less than that sum ; but this minimum is too low.   Most political economists, and particularly the English, lay it down as an axiom, that the most perfect money is paper ; this is true, if we suppose a nation in which any disturbance of industry, in consequence or apprehension of war, from foolish speculations, from glut or panic, is impossible.   In such a land of cockayne, such a terrestrial paradise, an unshaken confidence would prevail in all transactions, and consolidate all interests.   The metals would only serve to strike medals and to preserve inscriptions intended to commemorate this ineffable bliss. Paper would there be on a par with gold, and even higher, as some English writers have maintained it should be. I do not know if there will ever be a nation in such a state of heavenly happiness; but I doubt it, because in the world of finance, as well as in the world of passion, I consider the Tender River a fable, and pastorals a sport of fancy; but it is very evident that no such people exists now, or will for some time to come. Now in the United States, the present banking system, like that of England from 1797 to 1821, or even 1825, is founded on this theory of the most perfect money. It is provided, indeed, that the banks shall pay gold for their paper on demand; but by the side of this clause, which tends to keep a certain quantity of the metals in the country, is inserted another, which neutralises it; it is 'the power of emitting bills in any number, and of the sum of 1, 2, 3, or 5 dollars. In prosperous times, the emission of paper is abundant, indefinite; as the necessity of a metallic standard ceases to be felt, in proportion to the confidence which prevails, the metals disappear before the excess of paper; there is scarcely any left in the country. Since I have been in the United States, I have not seen a piece of gold except in the mint. No sooner is it struck off, than the gold is exported to Europe and melted down. When a crisis comes on, the demand for the precious metals increases rapidly, because every one attaches more value to a positive standard than to paper, and the later the application of the remedy for the scarcity of metals, the longer does the crisis last, and the more serious does it become.

In a new country, where capital cannot, of course, be abundant, for capital of all kinds, whether of articles of food or precious metals, is the accumulated produce of labour, it is natural, that the proportion of paper money

should equal and surpass that of metallic money. The
existence of paper money is even a great benefit to any
country. In France we have the enormous sum of 600
million dollars in specie; (see *Note* 10, at the end of the
volume); in the United States 40 millions are sufficient
for all the transactions of a commerce nearly as extensive
as our own. In England the amount of specie at present
does not exceed 220 millions, mostly in gold. Bank notes
in circulation, which constitute the rest of the currency,
amount at this time, in the United States, to 100 million,
that is, two and a half times the amount of specie; in
England to about the same as the specie, which gives for
the whole circulation of

The United States, 140 millions—

Of England,   440 millions.

If we had in France the industrial habits of the English
and Anglo-Americans, 200 millions of circulating medium,
half in paper and half in specie, would probably be sufficient for our operations; but considering our commercial
inferiority, suppose that we should require 300 millions, of
which two thirds should be metallic, and one third paper,
it would follow that we might advantageously employ
400 millions, which are now unproductive in the form of
specie, and which add nothing to our pleasures, our comfort, or our industrial capacity. But if we might expect
great benefit from banks of circulation and the paper which
they would issue, it is evident that the Americans, in the
present stage of their wealth, and considering their actual
capital, would find their advantage in putting some check
upon themselves in this matter. It might then be proper
to raise the minimum of bills of the Bank of the United
States to 10, 15, or 20 dollars, as in England there is no
paper less than the five pound note. The National Bank,
if it were powerful enough, would keep the local banks in
check, and for this reason it is expedient to increase the

capital. There would then be specie enough in the country for all purposes less than the paper minimum, and in case of any disturbance, the currency would be less readily deranged.

Nor is this the only point in which the charter of the Bank of the United States requires modification ; its relations with the Federal government, as well as with the State governments, need to be modified ; and some projects worthy of consideration, in this view, have been broached. It would also, probably, be expedient, as Mr Cambreleng has remarked, to change the rules and regulations relating to private and public deposits, and to provide that in future they should bear interest as they do in the Scotch banks. If this system were adopted by all the American banks, they would gain in solidity, and they would embrace the interest of all classes, and become provident institutions for the general good ; while at present their direct profits, the dividends, fall exclusively to the shareholders, who belong to the wealthier classes ; a fact which contributes not a little to their unpopularity. Finally, it would be proper to consider to what degree the immediate advantages of credit might be extended to mechanics and farmers. In this respect the banks are yet absolutely aristocratical institutions, the Americans having preserved in banking almost all the usages of their ancestors, the English. The American banks are now chiefly devoted to the use of speculators and merchants.

In the midst of so many contradictions, it is difficult to foresee what will be the issue of the struggle. The friends of the Administration maintain that President Jackson and Vice President Van Buren are not only opposed to the Bank as it is, but to any National Bank, and that they will never yield. The Globe, the avowed organ of the President, has told Mr Clay, that unless he *can find a Brutus* (to assassinate General Jackson,) the Bank will neither have the deposits nor a new charter. We may doubt, however, whether the President's mind is so decisively made up, and after all a majority of both houses can set at nought the *veto*. As to the Vice President, whom his opponents call the cunning Van Buren, as he aspires to succeed the President, many persons declare that his object is to gain the vote of the powerful State of New York, by transferring thither the seat of the Mother Bank, but that he is too enlightened seriously to wish the destruction of an institution fraught with so much good to the country.

However this may be, it would be surprising if the present crisis were not followed, sooner or later, by a reaction in favour of the Bank of the United States with suitable modifications, or of another National Bank, which, as Mr Webster observed, would amount to the same thing, if the shareholders of the present Bank are not sacrificed. The jealous democracy of this country has this advantage over other democracies, that in the main it has much good sense ; the recollection of old sufferings caused by the abuses of the banking system, and a jealousy of all pretensions to superiority, have led it to give ear to much noisy declamation about the aristocracy of money, particularly when it has been mixed up with flattery of itself. It may have been led astray for a moment, when its own prerogatives were the subject of discussion, as those sovereigns who assert the divine right of kings, take fire in respect to theirs. Proud of its gigantic labours, it may have been tempted to believe, that to it everything was possible and easy, that it had only to frown to cause the Bank to crumble into the dust at its feet, without being itself shaken by the shock. But facts, positive, inexorable facts now bear witness that it was mistaken, that it has trusted too much to its powers and its star, that the agency of the Bank of the United States is indispensable. The influence of facts has spread step by step even to the country people, who no longer find buyers of their produce. The argument is palpable and effectual; passion cannot long blind men of sense to such facts, for men of sense are those who do not give themselves up implicitly to abstractions, and who admit that every theory which is point blank against fact, is false or incomplete. This is the reason why good sense is worth to the full as much in politics, as talents.

It is worth while to observe here, that all the political difficulties in which the United States have become involved, and which have threatened the existence of the Union itself, have been settled by means of what are here called compromises, and in France *justes-milieux*. Thus was ended the serious dispute on the Missouri question, which had well nigh set the Union in a flame. It was made a question whether Missouri should be received into the Confederacy with a constitution sanctioning the institution of slavery. After a long and ineffectual debate, Mr Clay moved that Missouri should be admitted unconditionally, but that, at the same time, it should be declared that in future no new State lying north of 36° 30′ of latitude, should be admitted into the Union with this institution; this proposition was received with general favour, and the admission of Missouri was carried. In the next session, however, a new quarrel arose between the North and the South, more violent and bitter than the former, in relation to an article in the constitution of Missouri, prohibiting any free man of colour from entering the State. Another compromise, proposed by Mr Clay, finally settled the whole question in 1821, after it had kept the country in a flame for three years. In 1833, another compromise was made in respect to the tariff, the honour of which also belongs to Mr Clay. This question will sooner or later be settled in the same manner; the Union cannot do without a National Bank, and it will have one.

There are some lucky persons who succeed in everything, and there are some lucky nations with whom everything turns out well, even those events which seemed
about to bury them in ruins. The United States is one
of these privileged communities. When Villeroi came
back to Versailles, after his defeat, Louis XIV. said to
him, " Marshal, nobody is lucky at our time of life."
Charles V. also, as he grew old, said that fortune was like
a woman, and preferred young men to old ones. Louis
and Charles were right so far as this, that when a man,
young or old, has finished his mission, foresight, ability,
and perseverance profit him little ; he fails in whatever
he undertakes, whilst he who has a mission yet to fulfil,
takes new strength from the most violent blows. This is
true of nations as well as of individuals. The American
people is a young people, which has a mission to perform ;
nothing less than to redeem a world from savage forests,
panthers, and bears. It moves with mighty strides towards its object, for it has not, like the nations of Europe,
the burden of a heavy past on its shoulders. It may be
checked in its career for a time by the present crisis, but
it will come out of it safe and sound, and more healthy
than when it entered it. It will come out with increased
resources, with a reformed banking system, and according
to all appearances, even with an improved National Bank.
May the nations of Europe not have to wait long for institutions, which have so powerfully assisted England and
America in their progress !

LETTER VI.

PROGRESS OF THE STRUGGLE.—NEW POWERS.

BALTIMORE, MARCH 1, 1834.

FAILURES begin to be frequent in the United States, particularly in New York and Pennsylvania; the great commercial and manufacturing houses are shaking. Meanwhile the Senators and Representatives in Congress are making speeches on the crisis, its causes, and consequences. Three months have already been taken up in discussing the question, whether the Secretary of the Treasury had or had not the right to withdraw the public deposits from the vaults of the Bank, without that institution having given any just cause of complaint, and merely because it was strongly suspected of aristocratical tendencies. The resolutions which have given rise to these debates, have been referred by the Senate to the Committee on Finance, and by the House to the Committee of Ways and Means. Debates will rise on the reports of these committees, on petitions and memorials, and incidental matters, and, I am told, will last two or three months longer. This slowness is at first glance difficult to be understood, among a people, which, above all things, strives to save time, and which is so much given to haste and despatch, that its most suitable emblem would be a locomotive engine or a steamboat, just as the Centaurs were anciently confounded with their horses. From all the large towns of the North, committees appointed by great public meetings, bring to Washington memorials signed by thousands, calling for prompt and efficient measures to put an end to the crisis. On the other hand, the partisans of the Administration find fault with the prolixity of the legislators. The calmness, or rather phlegm, which the Americans have inherited from their English ancestors, is kept undisturbed in both houses of Congress, and the solemn debate goes on. One speaker for example, Mr Benton, occupied four sessions, four whole days, with his speech, which led Mr Calhoun to observe, that the Senator from Missouri took up more time in expressing his opinion on a single fact, than the French people had done in achieving a revolution. But these interminable delays ought not to be too lightly condemned, and for myself I only shrug my shoulders, when I hear some impatient individuals asserting that Congress would be more expeditious, were it not for the eight dollars a day which they receive during the session. This delay may seem irreconcileable with one of the distinctive traits of the American character, but in reality is imperiously demanded by the form and spirit of the government, by the institutions and political habits of the country.

The general discussion in Congress has no other object than to open a full and free public inquest, which enables each and all to make up an opinion. It gives rise to a discussion of the question by the innumerable journals in the United States (where there are 1200 political newspapers), by the twentyfour legislatures, each composed of two houses, and by the public meetings in the cities and towns. It is an animated exchange of arguments of every calibre and every degree, of contradictory resolutions, mixed up with applauses and hisses, of exaggerated eulogies and brutal invectives. A stranger, who finds himself suddenly thrown into the midst of this hubbub, is confounded and stupefied ; he seems to himself to be present in the primeval or the final chaos, or at least at the general breaking up of the Union. But after a certain time some gleams of light break forth from these thick clouds, from the bosom of this confusion,—gleams, which the good sense of the people hails with joy, and which light up the Congress. We see here the realization of the *Forum* on an immense scale, the *Forum* with its tumult, its cries, its pasquinades, but also with its sure instincts, and its flashes of native and untaught genius. It is a spectacle, in its details, occasionally prosaic and repulsive, but, as a whole, imposing as the troubled ocean. In a country like this, it is impossible to avoid these delays; first, because it takes a long time to interchange words between the frontiers of Canada and the Gulf of Mexico, and secondly, because nothing is so dangerous as precipitation in a *Forum*, whether it only covers the narrow space between the *Rostra* and the Tarpeian Rock, or extends from Lake Champlain to the mouth of the Mississippi, and from the Illinois to the Cape of Florida. Unfortunately the session in the *Forum* lasts longer than usual this time. The demagogues have set the popular passions in violent agitation ; the sovereign people has allowed itself to be magnetised by its flatterers, and it will require some time to be able to shake off the trance. The healing beam, which will fix the gaze of the multitude and dissipate the charm that envelopes them, has not yet broke forth from the East, or from the West; meanwhile the merchants and manufacturers, who are stretched upon the coals, writhe in vain ; there is no answer to their cries.

The Bank, meantime, disappears from sight and keeps silence ; it continues to attend to its own business, and prudently confines itself to that alone. Its best policy is to avoid as much as possible making itself the subject of common talk. The demagogues have raised such a cry of monopoly and aristocracy, that the people have come to believe the Bank a colossus of aristocracy, a prop of monopoly. These words *monopoly* and *aristocracy* are here, what the word *Jesuits* was in France a few years ago ; if the enemies of any institution can write on its back this kind of *abracadabra*, it is pointed at, hooted at, and hissed at by the multitude. Such is the magic power of these words, that speculators employ them on all occasions as charms to draw customers. For example, at the head of the advertisements of steamboats you read in staring characters : No MONOPOLY!!! It is pitiful to say that the Bank of the United States has a monopoly, when there are no less than five hundred other banks in the country; by this course of reasoning one might convict the sun of enjoying a monopoly of light. And yet the multitude has believed it, and believes it still. Now the best policy for those against whom such a storm of unpopularity is raised, is to run for port, as the sailors do in a gale of wind. The Bank has twice attempted to strike a blow, by taking advantage of the mistakes of its enemies, and both times the stroke has recoiled on itself.

The first time, the subject of dispute was a draft on the French government, which was sold to the Bank last year by the Federal government, and which France refused to pay ; the draft was, therefore, protested, and then paid by the correspondent of the Bank in Paris in honour of the endorser. In this affair the Executive of the United States committed two faults : 1. It was an act of indiscretion to draw on the French government, before the Chambers had made the necessary appropriation for paying the stipulated indemnity ; 2. Instead of drawing on the French government by a bill of exchange, and selling the bill to the Bank, without knowing whether it would be accepted, the Executive would have conducted itself with more propriety towards France, towards the Bank, and towards itself, if it had authorized the Bank to receive the moneys paid by the French government, in the capacity of its agent or attorney. By the commercial practice of all countries, and of this in particular, the Bank had a right to damages, and it put in its claim. Its object in taking this step, was much more to expose the errors of the Executive, than to pocket the sum of 50,000 or 80,000 dollars. But its adversaries immediately raised the cry, that the Bank was not contented with exacting enormous sums from the sweat of the people to the profit of the stockholders, (observe that the dividends of the Bank are moderate, compared with those of other banking companies in the country, and that the Federal government is itself the largest shareholder); but that it was now attempting, by petty chicanery, to extort a portion of the public revenue, and to bury the *people's money in Biddle's pockets.* To this reasoning, and it passes for demonstration, the multitude answered by imprecations against monopoly and the moneyed aristocracy, and by renewed shouts of HURRAH FOR JACKSON!

A few days since we witnessed another episode of this kind. The Bank is charged, by act of Congress, with the duty of paying the pensions of the old soldiers of the revolution. It performs the service gratuitously, and it is notoriously a troublesome one. It has received several sums of money for this object, and at this moment has about 500,000 dollars in its vaults, intended for the next payments. The Administration, desirous of transferring this agency from the Bank, has demanded the funds, books, and papers connected with it. The Bank replied, that it has been made the depository of this trust by act of Congress, and that it cannot, ought not, and will not surrender it, unless in obedience to an act of Congress. The Bank was right; the refusal was founded in justice; but mark the consequences. Its adversaries express the greatest sympathy for these illustrious relics of the revolution, whom the arrogance of the Bank, as they say, is about to plunge, at the close of their career, into the most dreadful misery; they pour forth the most pathetic lamentations over these glorious defenders of the country, whom a *money-corporation* is about to strip of the provision made for their declining years by the nation's gratitude. You may imagine all the noisy arguments and patriotic harangues, that can be delivered on this text. On the 4th of February, the President sent a message to Congress in the same strain. All this is mere declamation, of the most common-place and the most hypocritical kind; for who will prevent the deliverers of America from duly receiving their pensions, except those who shall refuse them drafts on the Bank, which the Bank would pay at once? But a people under fascination is not influenced by reason, and it is at this moment believed by the multitude that the Bank has determined to kill the noble veterans of Independence by hunger. Once more, then, anathemas against monopoly, hatred to the moneyed aristocracy! HURRAH FOR JACKSON! JACKSON FOREVER!

Whenever, therefore, the Bank has allowed itself to be drawn into a conflict, which is the enemy's country, it is pronounced to be in the wrong, though it were ten times right. On the contrary, when it has kept to its discounts and credits, it has always been able, without opening its mouth, to belie the charges of its enemies, who not only impute to it the atrocious crime of being suspected of aristocracy and monopoly, but attribute to it now the public distress, of which they denied the existence a few months ago, and of which they are themselves the authors. Very lately the Bank came to the relief of several local banks, which were in danger of failing, and a few days since it opened its coffers liberally to Allen & Co., one of the principal houses in the country, who, although having a capital much beyond the amount of their debts, were obliged, by the pressure of the times, to suspend payments; the failure of that house, which has no less than 24 branches, would have involved hundreds of others. This is the only way in which the Bank should assume the offensive;

such acts, without a word of comment, would secure it the favour and the support of all impartial and enlightened men, and the gratitude of the commercial interest, much more completely than the most eloquent protests against the measures of this or that secretary, or the most ingenious and able defence of itself.

I am more and more convinced that the United States will reap advantage from this crisis; sooner or later the reform of the banking system must result from it. Very probably, the National Bank, if it is maintained, and the local banks, will hereafter be less absolutely separated from the Federal and State governments; that is to say, that the Federal and local governments will assume the control of the Banks, and consequently the banks will become a part of the governments. In this way many of the abuses of the banking system will be reformed, and the legitimate and just influence of the banks will be strengthened. It would be easy to cite numerous facts, which go to prove the tendency towards this result; thus in some of the States, the Legislatures have established, or are occupied in establishing banks, in which the State is a shareholder to the amount of one half or two fifths of the capital, appoints a certain number of the directors, and reserves to itself an important control over the operations. There are some States, as for example, Illinois, in which every other kind of bank is expressly forbidden by the constitution.

Republican publicists acknowledge only three classes of powers, the executive, legislative, and judicial; but it will soon be seen in the United States, that there is also a financial power, or at least the banks will form a branch of government quite as efficient as either of the others. The Bank of the United States is more essential to the prosperity of the country than the Executive, as now organized. The latter conducts a little diplomatic inter-

course, well or ill, with the European powers, nominates
and removes some unimportant functionaries, manœuvres
an army of 6,000 men in the western wilderness, adds
now and then some sticks of timber to the dozen ships of
war that are on the stocks at Portsmouth, Boston, New
York, Philadelphia, Washington, Norfolk, and Pensacola.
All this might actually cease to be done without endangering the safety of the country, and without seriously
wounding its prosperity, that is, its industry.   But take
from the country its institutions for the maintenance of
credit, or only that which controls and regulates all the
others, the Bank of the United States, and you plunge it
into a commercial anarchy which would finally result in
political anarchy.

   The word politics cannot have the same meaning in the
United States as in Europe.   The United States, are not
engaged, like the nations of Europe, in territorial combinations and the preservation of the balance of a continent,
nor are they entangled in treaties of Westphalia or Vienna.
They are free from all those difficulties, which in Europe
arise from a difference of origin or religion, or from the
conflict between rival pretensions, between old interests
and new interests.   They have no neighbour, which excites their suspicions.   The policy of the United States
consists in the extension of their commerce, and the occupation by agriculture of the vast domain, which nature
has given them ; in these points is involved the great mass
of their general and individual interests ; these are the
objects which inflame their political and individual passions.
As the Banks are the soul of their commerce, their rising
manufactures, and even their agriculture, it is evident that
the success of their *politics* is intimately and directly connected with the right organization of their banking system.
The real government of the country, that is to say, the
control of its essential interests, is as much in the banks as

in any body or power established by the constitution.
The time is come when this fact should be recognised and
sanctioned. As among a military people the office of marshal or lord-high-constable is the first in the kingdom, so
among a people which has nothing to do with war, and
has only to employ itself with its industry, that of President of the central bank, for example, ought to be a
public charge, *political*, in the sense adapted to the condition and wants of that people,—and one of the first rank
in the country.

From this point of view, it may be said, that what is
now passing in the United States, is a struggle in which
the combatants are, on the one side, the military interest
and the law, which have hitherto divided between them
the control of public affairs, and on the other, the financial
interest, which now claims its share in them ; the two first
have coalesced against the last, and have succeeded for a
time in raising the multitude against it, but they will fail
in the long run, since the multitude has more to gain from it
than from them. It is said, that, when the committee of the
New York merchants went to Washington to present a petition with 10,000 names in favour of the Bank, the President
observed to them, that they declared the grievances of the
brokers, capitalists, and merchants of Wall Street and
Pearl Street, but that Wall Street and Pearl Street were
not the people. I do not know whether the story is
true or not, but I know that such an answer would express
the opinion of the dominant party. There is a school
here, which attempts to eliminate the wealthy classes
from the people, and which is just the reverse of the old
school of European Tories, which reduces the people to
the higher classes, and excludes from that rank the greater
number of the nation. And nothing can be more unjust,
for in order to measure the real importance of the men

of Pearl Street and Wall Street, it is only necessary to consider what New York would be without them.

In fifty years the population of New York has increased tenfold, its wealth probably an hundred fold ; its animating influences have been felt for hundreds of miles around. This unparalleled growth is not the work of lawyers and military men ; the merit belongs chiefly to the industry, the capital, the intelligence, and the enterprise of that, numerically speaking, insignificant minority of Wall Street and Pearl Street. It is very easy to cant about the aristocracy of dollars, and those filthy metals which men call gold and silver. And yet have not those vile metals ceased to be vile, when they are the fruit of the industry and enterprise of those who possess them ? If there is a country in the world where it is preposterous to prate about the aristocracy of dollars, and about the filthy metals, it is this. For here, more than any where else, every body has some employment ; whoever has capital is engaged in turning it to profit, and can neither increase nor even keep it without great activity and vigilance. A man's wealth is, therefore, very generally in the ratio of his importance, and even of his agricultural, manufacturing, or commercial capacity. The merchants are not without their faults ; they are disposed to weigh everything in their doubloon-scales, and a people governed entirely by merchants would certainly be to be pitied. But a people governed by lawyers or by soldiers would be no happier and no freer. The policy of the Hamburg Senate in basely giving up unhappy political fugitives to the English executioner, deserves the contempt of every man of honour ; but would the rule of Russian or even of Napoleon's bayonets, or the babbling anarchy of the Directory, be less loathsome to those whose heart beats with the love of liberty or with feelings of individual and national honour?

The revolutions of ages, which change religion, manners, and customs, modify also the nature of the powers that regulate society. Providence humbles the mighty, when they obstinately shut their eyes to the new spirit of the age, and raises up the lowly, whom this new spirit fires. Four thousand years ago, it was one of the most important dignities in Egypt to have the charge of embalming the sacred birds or of spreading the litter of the bull Apis. In the Eastern empire the post of *protovestiary* was one of the first in the state, and not to go so far back, it was the ambition of many in France, hardly four years ago, to become *gentilhomme de la chambre*, as the *groom of the stole*, or, in other words, the *servant in charge of the wardrobe*, is now one of the grand dignitaries of England. Nobody now-a-days embalms sacred birds, nobody spreads the litter of Apis. No one intrigues for the post of protovestiary or gentleman of the chamber, and from present appearances, I do not think that even the dignity of Groom of the Stole, will long be an object of ambition in England. There are no longer lord-high-constables, or great vassals, or knights-errant, or peers of France in the old sense of the word. The French aristocracy, so brilliant fifty years ago, has fallen like corn before the reaper. The mansions of the old heroes have become factories; the convents have been changed into spinning-works; I have seen Gothic naves in the best style of art transformed into workshops or granaries, and our brave troops have become peaceable labourers on the military roads.

Boards of petty clerks, whom the Castellans had employed to record their sovereign decrees, became in France *parlements*, which braved the kings and assumed to be guardians of the laws of the realm. At present the forge masters of Burgundy and the Nivernais, the distillers of Montpelier, the clothiers of Sedan and Elbeuf, have taken the place of the *parlements*. German princes, who can boast of their fifty quarters, dance attendance in

the imperial, royal, or ministerial antechambers, while their
Majesties or their Excellencies are conversing familiarly
with some banker who has no patent of nobility, and who
even disdains to oblige his royal friends by accepting one.
The East India Company, a company of merchants if
ever there was one, has more subjects than the emperors
of Russia and Austria together.   If in the Old World,
where the old interests had marked every corner of the
land with their stamp, the old interests, the military and
the law, are thus obliged to come to terms with the new
interest of industry, with the power of money, how can it
be possible, that, in the New World, where the past has
never taken deep root, where all thoughts are turned
toward business and wealth, this same power will not force
its way into the political scene, in spite of the opposition
of its adversaries and its envious rivals ?

LETTER VII.

RAILROADS IN AMERICA.

RICHMOND, (VA.) MARCH 15, 1834.

THREE thousand years ago the kings of the earth were
happy ; happy as a king ; but the old proverb is now
become a falsehood. Then no Constantinople was coveted ;
the citadels of Antwerp and Ancona were not built.   No
one troubled himself about the Rhenish frontier ;   the
natural and simple Herodotus told marvellous tales, like
those of the *Arabian Nights*, about the country watered
by the Rhine.   The banks of the Danube were trackless

morasses ; Vienna was not yet, nor of course the Treaty of
Vienna. Peace reigned between the sovereigns, or at least
their contests wereal together academical, philosophical, and
literary. The good king Nectanebus, an enlightened prince,
a patron of the arts, played charades with his neighbours,
the mighty monarchs of Asia ; he guessed all their riddles
without their being able to solve his in turn ; his glory
was unmatched, his people rolled in prosperity. The condition of men of letters and science was, to be sure, somewhat of the meanest ; grammarians and philosophers were
sometimes dragged to market with halters on their necks,
to be sold like cattle, a treatment to which none but
negroes are now subject. But if they were men of genius,
their good star threw them into the hands of the best of
masters, such as Xanthus, the most patient and kind of
men, or good natured princes, like Nectanebus, who knew
how to appreciate true merit. Æsop having become the
property of this good king, soon got to be his counsellor,
friend, and confidant, revised his charades and riddles, and
suggested new ones to the king in such a modest way,
that Nectanebus really believed himself the author of
them. One day Nectanebus, by his advice, proposed to his
rival monarchs this difficult problem ; How would you
build a city in the air ? After they had puzzled their
brains without success, Nectanebus prepared to give a
solution of the question in the presence of the ambassadors of the Asiatic sovereigns solemnly convoked ; Æsop
put some little boys in baskets, which were carried up
into the air by eagles trained for the purpose, and the boys
began to cry out to the astonished ambassadors ; " Give
us stone and mortar, and we will build you a city." This
old story has often occurred to my mind since I have been in
the United States, and I have often said to myself, if Æsop's
boys had been Americans, instead of having been subjects
of king Nectanebus, they would have demanded mate-

rials, not for building a city, but for constructing a railroad. In fact there is a perfect mania in this country on the subject of railroads.

While at Liverpool, I went aboard the Pacific to engage a berth, and Capt. Waite, a very worthy man, who believes in God with all his heart, and is not any the less on that account a very skilful commander, and a most intrepid sailor, offered me the latest American newspapers. The first I opened happened to be the *Railroad Journal.* Soon after sailing I fell sea-sick, and had scarcely a moment's relief till my arrival at New York; of all my recollections of the voyage, the most distinct is that of having heard the word railroad occurring once every ten minutes, in the conversation of the passengers. At New York, I went to visit the docks for building and repairing vessels; after having examined the dry dock and two or three other docks, my guide, himself an enthusiast on the subject of railroads, carried me to the railroad-dock, where the ships are moved along a railway. In Virginia, I found railroads at the bottom of the coal mines, which is not, indeed, new to a European. At Philadelphia I visited the excellent penitentiary, where everything was so neat, quiet, and comfortable, (if that word may be applied to a prison), in comparison with the abominable prisons in France, which are noisy, filthy, unhealthy, cold in winter, and damp in summer. The warden, Mr Wood, who manages the institution with great vigilance and philanthropy, after having shown me the prisoners' cells, the yards in which they take the air, the kitchen where the cooking is done by steam, and allowed me to visit one of the convicts, a poor fellow from Alsace, said to me, just as I was taking my leave; "But you have not seen everything yet, I must show you my railroad;" and in fact there was a railroad in the prison, for the cart in which food was brought to the prisoners.

Some days ago I happened to be in the little city of
Petersburg, which stands at the falls of the Appomattox,
and near which there is an excellent railroad. A merchant of the city took me to a manufactory of tobacco,
in which some peculiar processes were employed. In
these works was manufactured that sort of tobacco which
most Americans chew, and will chew for some time to
come, in spite of the severe, but in this matter just, cen-
sures of English travellers, unless the fashion of vetos
should spread in the United States, and the women should
set theirs on the use of tobacco, with as unyielding a resolution, as the President has shown towards the Bank.
After having wandered about the workshops amidst the
poor little slaves by whom they are filled, I was stopping
to look at some of these blacks, who appeared to me
almost white, and who had not more than one eighth of
African blood in their veins, when my companion said to
me, "As you are interested in railroads, you must see the
one belonging to the works." Accordingly we went to
the room where the tobacco is packed in kegs, and subjected to a powerful pressure. The apparatus for pressing
is a very peculiar contrivance, which I will not now stop
to describe, but of which the most important part is a
moveable railroad, suspended from the ceiling. Thus the
Americans have railroads in the water, in the bowels of
the earth, and in the air. The benefits of the invention
are so palpable to their practical good sense, that they
endeavour to make an application of it everywhere and to
everything, right or wrong, and when they cannot construct a real, profitable railroad across the country from
river to river, from city to city, or from State to State,
they get one up, at least, as a plaything, or until they can
accomplish something better, under the form of a machine.

The distance from Boston to New Orleans is 1600 miles,

or twice the distance from Havre to Marseilles. It is highly probable, that within a few years this immense line will be covered by a series of railroads stretching from bay to bay, from river to river, and offering to the ever-impatient Americans the service of their rapid cars at the points where the steamboats leave their passengers. This is not a castle in the air, like so many of those grand schemes which are projected amidst the fogs of the Seine, the Loire, and the Garonne; it is already half completed. The railroad from Boston to Providence is in active progress; the work goes on à l' Américaine, that is to say, rapidly. From New York to Philadelphia, there will soon be not only one open to travel, but two in competition with each other, the one on the right, the other on the left bank of the Delaware; the passage between the two cities will be made in seven hours, five hours on the railroad, and two in the steamboat, in the beautiful Hudson and the magnificent Bay of New York, which the Americans, who are not afflicted with modesty, compare with the Bay of Naples. From Philadelphia, travellers go to Baltimore by the Delaware and Chesapeake, and by the Newcastle and Frenchtown railroad, in eight hours; from Baltimore to Washington, a railroad has been resolved upon, a company chartered, the shares taken, and the work begun, all within the space of a few months. Between Washington and Blakely, in North Carolina, 60 miles of railroad are completed, from Blakely northwards. A company has just been chartered to complete the remaining space, that is, from Richmond to the Potomac, a distance of 70 miles, and the Potomac bears you to the Federal city by Mt. Vernon, a delightful spot, the patrimony of George Washington, where he passed his honoured old age, and where his body now reposes in a modest tomb. Between Washington and Blakely, those who prefer the steamboats, may take another route; by descending the Chesapeake to Norfolk, they will find another railroad, 70 miles in length, of which two thirds are now finished, and which carries them to Blakely, and even beyond. Blakely is a new town, which you will not find on any map, born of yesterday; it is the eldest, and as yet the only daughter of the Petersburg and Blakely railroad. From Blakely to Charleston the distance is great, but the Americans are enterprising, and there is no region in the world in which railroads can be constructed so easily and so cheaply; the surface has been graded by nature, and the vast forests which cover it, will furnish the wood of which the railroad will be made; for here most of these works have a wooden superstructure. From Charleston, a railroad 137 miles in length, as yet the longest in the world, extends to Augusta, whence to Montgomery, Alabama, there is a long interval to be supplied. From this last town steamboats descend the River Alabama to Mobile, and those who do not wish to pay their respects to the Gulf of Mexico, on their way to New Orleans, will soon find a railroad which will spare them the necessity of offering this act of homage to the memory of the great Cortez.*

Within ten years this whole line will be completed, and traversed by locomotive engines, provided the present crisis terminates promptly and happily, as I hope it will. Ten years is a long time in these days, and a plan, whose execution requires ten years, seems like a romance or a dream. But in respect to railroads, the Americans have already something to show. Pennsylvania, which by the last census, in 1830, contained only 1,348,000 inhabitants, has 325 miles of railroads actually completed, or which will be so within the year, without reckoning 76 miles which the capitalists of Philadelphia have constructed in the little States of New Jersey and Delaware. The total

---

* For observations on these statements see *Letter* XXI., and *the Notes.*

length of all the railroads in France is 95 miles, that is, a little more than what the citizens of Philadelphia, in their liberality, have given to their poor neighbours.   In the State of New York, whose population is the most adventurous and the most successful in their speculations, there are at present only four or five short railroads, but if the sixth part of those which are projected and authorized by the Legislature, are executed, New York will not be behind Pennsylvania in this respect.   The merchants of Baltimore, which at the time of the Declaration of Independence contained 6,000 inhabitants, and which now numbers 100,000, have taken it into their heads to make a railroad between their city and the Ohio, a distance of above 300 miles.   They have begun it with great spirit, and have now finished about one third of the whole road. In almost every section east of the Ohio and the Mississippi, there are railroads projected, in progress, or completed, and on most of them locomotive steam-engines are employed.   There are some in the Alleghanies, whose inclined planes are really terrific, from their great inclination ; these were originally designed only for the transportation of goods, but passenger-cars have been set up on them, at the risk of breaking the necks of travellers. There are here works well constructed and ill constructed ; there are some that have cost dear, (from 40,000 to 50,000 dollars a mile,) and others that have cost little, (from 10,000 to 15,000 dollars a mile).   New Orleans has one, a very modest one to be sure, it being only five miles long, but it will soon have others, and after all, it is before old Orleans, for the latter has yet to wait till its capitalists, seized with some violent fit of patriotism, shall be ready to make the sacrifice of devoting some ten or twelve per cent. of their capital to the construction of a railroad thence to Paris.   Virginia, whose population is nearly the same with that of the Department of the North, and which is inferior in wealth, already has 75 miles of railroad fully completed, and 110 in progress, exclusive of those begun this year. The Department of the North, where it would be quite as easy to construct them, and where they would be more productive, has not a foot completed, or in progress, and hardly a foot projected. Observe, moreover, that I here speak of railroads alone, the rage for which is quite new in America, while that for canals is of very old date (for in this country fifteen years is an age), and has achieved wonders. There are States which contain 500, 800, or 1,000 miles of canals. We in France are of all people the boldest in theory and speculation, and we have made the world tremble by our political experiments ; but during the last twenty years we have shown ourselves the most timid of nations in respect to physical improvements.

LETTER VIII.

THE BANKS. — THE PRESERVATION OF THE UNION.

WASHINGTON, APRIL 10, 1834.

THE drama which has been passing in the United States since the opening of the session, has now reached the end of the first act. The two Houses have had under consideration the subject of the removal of the public deposits from the Bank of the United States to the local banks, by the Executive, and both of them have come to a decision. The Senate has declared, by a majority of 28 to 18, that the reasons alleged by the Secretary of the Treasury in justification of the measure, were neither satisfactory nor sufficient, and, by a majority of 26 to 20, that the conduct of the President in this matter was neither conformable to the constitution nor to the laws. This is the first instance, since the adoption of the Federal constitution, of a censure of the chief magistrate of the nation by the Senate. The House has resolved, on its part, that the charter of the Bank ought not to be renewed, that the public deposits ought not to be restored to it, and that they should remain in the safe-keeping of the local banks. The first resolve passed by a vote of 132 to 92; the majority for the two others was much less, 118 to 103, and 117 to 105. It has been resolved, by a large majority, 171 to 42, that the conduct of the Bank should be made a subject of investigation, but this majority includes many friends of the Bank.

It is to be hoped that the Bank will not be the object of this campaign ; the more vigorously it is defended, the more hateful it becomes to the democracy. Those who feel an interest in their country and its institutions, ought to make an effort to turn the debate toward some other point, for both sides have become heated and exasperated in the struggle, and already violence has been threatened. The most brilliant services have been forgotten, the purest characters trampled under foot. The Globe, the avowed organ of the administration, pours forth the vilest slanders on men, such as Messrs. Clay, Calhoun, and Webster, of whom any country in the world would be proud. It repeated, and unhappily it reiterates still, that the votes of the Senate have been bought by the Bank. On the other hand, General Jackson, to whom it is impossible to deny the possession of eminent qualities, has been himself exposed to the vilest indignities ; the gray hairs of that brave old man have been insulted in the most scandalous manner. Attempts have even been made to throw ridicule on his victory at New Orleans, the most brilliant affair in the American annals, as if his glory were not the common property of the country. Some hot heads have even talked of recurring to violence ; commerce and enterprise have been struck numb ; for want of means, the great works of Pennsylvania have been in danger of being brought to a stand. But at present there appears to be a general wish to bring back a calm ; the failure of a certain number of individuals, and especially that of some banks, have proved a signal of alarm, which has recalled every one to a sense of the common danger, the general ruin that threatened the country. There has been a failure of a bank in Florida, of one in New Jersey, and of two in Maryland, one of which, that of the Bank of Maryland in Baltimore, has caused a great sensation. The leading men of all parties have set themselves in earnest to search out some means of bringing the commercial crisis to an end. There is room to hope, therefore, that the debate will lose its bitterness, and at the same time will take a 'wider range ; instead of quarrelling about the particular question of the Bank, it were to be wished that the higher questions of political economy should be discussed, such as that of a mixed currency, in which there should be the proper mixture of paper and the metals necessary to give it stability, without keeping, as is the case in Europe, a large unproductive capital in the shape of specie ; and that of a system of institutions of credit, banks of loan and discount, of deposit and exchange, powerful enough to serve as a spring and a stay to the industry of the country, and yet so balanced in respect to each other and the powers of the government, as not to be dangerous to the public liberties. A very able speech of Mr Calhoun's has already drawn the general attention to the subject of financial reform, and one of the senators friendly to the administration, Mr Ben-

ton, has embodied some of Mr Calhoun's ideas in the shape
of a bill.

It is now universally agreed, that to obtain a solid and
stable currency, it is necessary to keep a certain quantity of gold and silver in the country ; it is seen that
while there are paper dollars, the silver dollars will disappear, that ten-dollar notes necessarily expel the eagles,
and that half-eagles will not stay where there are five-dol-
lar bills. It is, therefore, proposed to abolish the issue of
notes of less than ten or even twenty dollars, but all that
Congress can do without the aid of a National Bank, is to
prohibit the reception, by the collectors of the customs, of
the bills of any bank which has in circulation notes of less
than ten or twenty dollars ; for Congress has no direct
power over the local banks.   This measure, however,
would be insufficient ; for the amount of money paid for
customs bears a very small proportion to the whole circulation of the country, and consequently would not affect
the circulation in districts remote from the sea coast. The
Administration does not deny the necessity of a police for
controlling and regulating the banks ; it seems disposed to
effect it by means of some of the local banks, which
should act under the direction of the Secretary of the
Treasury, and to which should be granted certain privileges, such as that of being the depositories of the public
money without paying interest.   But this plan has some
disadvantages ; it would invest the Secretary, that is the
President, with a great discretionary power, which is
wholly at war with the political maxims of American government.   It is a received truth in the United States, that
the sword and the purse ought not to be in the same hands.
Beside it is doubtful whether this control would be sufficiently powerful and sufficiently enlightened, and finally
it would be difficult by means of this chain of local banks
to answer one of the most pressing wants of the country,

facility of exchange ; because they are, and must be as slightly connected with each other, as the sovereign States from which they hold their charters. To exterminate small bank-notes the surest agent would be a National Bank, and Congress has the power to establish one. This power, which is disputed because all its powers are disputed, would not be contested, if it were stipulated that the Bank should obtain the consent of each State, before establishing a branch within its limits. It would then be sufficient that the Bank should not receive the bills of any other bank, which issued notes of less than 10 or 20 dollars, or which received the bills of other banks, that issued notes less than the same minimum. In fine, a National Bank is an admirable instrument of exchange, and the most influential friends of the Administration are convinced of the necessity of an institution of the sort. I cannot believe that the President, and especially the Vice-President, are really as much opposed to one, as they have the air of being. As it is possible to conceive of a combination of circumstances, which may reconcile its existence with the interests and views of Mr Van Buren (such would be, for instance, the creation of a Bank of which the seat should be New York, instead of Philadelphia), it may be hoped that sooner or later, under one form or another, Mr Van Buren may yield to the necessity of the case. It is true that out of hatred to the present Bank, the prejudices of the multitude have been excited against the establishment of any bank at all, and it is much more easy to rouse the popular passions than to control them when once let loose ; this kind of game has resulted in the self-murder of many a man's popularity. But in this matter the voice of the public interest and of individual interest will speak so loud, that it would be astonishing if it did not make itself heard by a people, so much more sensible and reflecting than most of the European people.   There is, then, in short, still some chance for a Bank of the United States.

The following are the principal features, in which both parties seem to me to be at present tacitly agreed.   The capital of the Bank to be about 50 millions.   The shares of the present Bank, representing a capital of 35 millions, to be exchanged at par for shares in the new bank ; the rest of the capital to be subscribed by the individual States, thus giving the Bank a more truly national character : The rate of discount to be reduced from 6 to 5 per cent. ; Mr Forsyth, a Senator friendly to the administration, has demanded this modification : The laws relative to public and private deposits to be changed in conformity with the propositions of Mr Cambreleng : The seat of the mother bank to be transferred to New York : The operations of the Bank to be subjected to more strict regulations than those of the old Bank have been : The Bank to be required to keep on hand a larger amount of reserved profits, or some other provision borrowed from the bank of England to be adopted, in order to give more security to the institution.

It would not, probably, be impossible to unite a majority of the two Houses in favour of a plan which should embrace these features.   But there is another subject about which little is said, and upon which no one has yet publicly declared himself, although there are many who have thought much about it, and it will not be easy to reconcile opinions upon it.   How shall the Bank be governed ? What relation shall there be between the administration of the Bank, and the Federal and State governments ? How and by whom shall the President of the Bank be chosen ?   This subject, about which there is a total silence, appears to me to be of so vital importance, that I am convinced that what has occurred in the United States during the last six months, would never have taken place, if the nomination of the President of the Bank had been lodged with the President of the United States. In Europe and particularly in France, the government of the banks is more or less in the hands and under the control of the king and the ministers. In America, conformably with the principles of self-government, the Bank, like all the other industrial and financial institutions, has, up to this time, governed itself. The Federal government, owning one fifth of the shares, names one fifth of the directors ; its powers stop there. The American axiom, which forbids the union of the sword and the purse in the same hand, is opposed to the exercise of a controlling influence over the choice of the President of the Bank by the President of the United States ; and yet I am persuaded that the democratic party will not be willing to hear of a Bank, in the government of which it could not interfere.

The upper classes (*bourgeoisie*) are not here what they are in Europe ; while in Europe they rule, here they are ruled. Democracy takes its revenge in America for the unjust contempt with which it has been so long treated in Europe. Now it is to these upper classes, that the private shareholders of the Bank belong ; it is the merchants, manufacturers, and capitalists, who will always derive the most direct benefit from a National Bank, although all classes must indirectly derive great advantages from it. From the time when the upper classes sanctioned a completely universal suffrage, without making any exception in favour of natural superiority, whether industrial or scientific, from the day when they consented that number should be every thing, and knowledge and capital nothing, they have signed their own abdication. It is too late to agitate the questions, whether this is absolutely a good or an evil, or whether it is well, in the agricultural States, with a scattered population, such as Ohio, Indiana, and

Illinois, and bad in large and populous cities, the seats of
a vast commerce, such as Philadelphia and New York.
This is a matter already settled past recall ; when the sword
is surrendered, the vanquished must submit to take the law
from the victor.   In case, then, of the creation of a new National Bank, the shareholders must consent to receive their
head, either from the President and Senate, as other public functionaries are appointed, or from the House of Representatives alone, or from some other similar source.   If
in a new or a somewhat modified Bank, the Federal and
local governments should be stockholders to a large amount,
this participation of the President or the House of Representatives, or of special delegates chosen by the States, in
the government of the Bank, would appear altogether
natural, even in the eyes of the most exclusive partisans
of self government.   It remains to be seen, whether in
this case, the Bank would not be more likely to become
the instrument of party, a *den of intrigue and corruption*,
a *golden calf*, a *monster*, as it is so often unjustly called,
than in the present state of things.

If this quarrel should be terminated by a compromise,
we may expect that it will be effected on the basis above
stated.   The upper classes will, perhaps, consider the conditions as hard, but they should beware of rejecting them.
It would be a great gain to them to obtain, under any
form, a decisive sanction of a National Bank, connected
with the government, and therefore incorporated with the
interests of the country.   Not only are numbers at present
against the Bank, and numbers give the law here, but the
Opposition is not so well organised as the democratic party.
The Opposition has, indeed, three leaders, who do not
always agree ; the views of Mr Calhoun of South Carolina
do not coincide with those of Messrs. Clay and Webster
on the subjects of the tariff and States' rights ; and Mr
Clay, the son of the west, and Mr Webster, who comes

from Boston, the focus of Federalism, differ on several constitutional questions. The democratic party, on the contrary, is better disciplined; the two heads, General Jackson and Mr Van Buren, present a formidable union of qualities and faculties. The old General is firm, prompt, bold, energetic; Mr Van Buren, who sets up for the American Talleyrand, is mild, conciliating, prudent, and sagacious; his adversaries call him the little magician. While the pretensions of Messrs Clay, Calhoun, and Webster are scarcely to be reconciled with each other, and neither of them is willing to be second, Mr Van Buren is ready to serve under General Jackson for the purpose of becoming his successor in the elections of 1836. Every kingdom divided against itself cannot stand. But, if no compromise can be made, if the democracy is too untractable, and the upper classes persist in claiming more than their position authorises them to do, if the feelings, kept in a state of excitement, become exasperated on both sides, and the contest be too much prolonged, the most frightful consequences may ensue; even the Union may be endangered.

At the close of the war of Independence, the American Confederacy occupied only a narrow strip along the Atlantic. Since that time the wave of an active, enterprising, and rapidly increasing population, has rolled over the Alleghanies, the Ohio, the Mississippi, more recently over the Missouri, the Red River, the Arkansas, and I know not how far. Toward the South it is already sweeping over the Sabine, and covering Texas, while toward the West, it has topped the Rocky Mountains, and is approaching the Pacific shore. Instead of thirteen States, there are twentyfour, and the number will soon be increased to twentysix. By the side of the old Atlantic strip, two other vast tracts with a more fertile soil, have yielded up their riches to civilised man; one, at the west, comprises the great triangle lying between the Ohio, the Mississippi, and the lakes, and the other at the south, includes the fertile regions of Florida and Louisiana, which, under the French and Spanish rule, were a solitary wilderness. The geographical centre of the Union fifty years ago was on the banks of the Potomac, on the spot where the city of Washington—that paper capital—now stands; it is now at Cincinnati, and will soon be near St Louis. In proportion as the territory of the Confederacy has been extended, the Federal bond has been weakened. It was nearly snapped asunder during the Nullification crisis, occasioned by the resistance of South Carolina to the tariff adopted under the influence of New England, in order to protect her growing manufactures. If Congress had not satisfied the demands of South Carolina, Virginia would have made common cause with the latter, and her example would have carried the whole South. The patriotic eloquence of Mr Webster, the moderation of Mr Clay and his prodigies of parliamentary strategy, the efforts of Mr Livingston, then Secretary of State, the firm, and, at the same time, conciliatory conduct of the President, who, for the first time, heard a bold defiance with patience, and the calm attitude of the Northern States, prevented for the moment a general dissolution of the Union; but the germ of mischief remains; the charm is broken; the ear has become familiar with the ominous word SEPARATION. A habit has grown up of thinking, and even of declaring, whenever the interests of the North and the South jar, that the cure-all will be a dissolution of the Union.

South Carolina keeps her militia organised, and exacts from the State officers a special oath of allegiance. Georgia and Alabama contest the validity of treaties concluded between the Federal government and the Cherokee and Creek nations. (See *Note* 11.) Most of the States seek to extend the limits of their individual sovereignty. The

doctrine of State rights has even insinuated itself into the
bosom of orthodox Philadelphia, for I see by the journals,
that a States' rights dinner is announced there.   These
symptoms may become full of danger in a moment of
universal excitement.   When the passions are at the helm,
there is no pause in the course.   What, for instance, would
be the event, if Nullification should find an echo in the
same States of the North, where it has lately been so
firmly rejected?   It is they that have the most direct interest in the establishment of a National Bank ; it is they
that suffer most from the financial combinations of General
Jackson, and from the objections of Southern statesmen
against the constitutionality of a bank.   Although no allu-
sion is made to this danger, it is evident that the solicitude
of many persons has been aroused by it, and it is fortunate
that it is so, for a more general disposition to conciliatory
measures is the consequence.

The principle of separation is engaged in a deadly conflict with the spirit of centralisation or consolidation ;
hardly was the constitution signed, when twelve additional
articles or Amendments were immediately adopted, almost
all of which contained restrictions on the powers and
attributes of the Federal government.   At the same time
the authority of Congress to charter a Bank, and give it
powers within the territories of the States, was contested ;
on this point, however, the principle of union was victorious, and the Bank was established.   Next, the right of
engaging in Internal Improvements was denied to Congress,
which, after a long struggle, has been compelled to resign
its claims ; General Jackson willed it, and it was done.
The National Road, which extends from Washington to
the western wilderness, and for which appropriations have
been annually voted, each professing to be the last, shows
what the Federal government could do and wished to do.
Even the uniform system of weights and measures, seems

to be on the point of being broken up, in spite of the express provisions of the constitution.   Pennsylvania has undertaken, nobody knows why, to establish regulations on this point contrary to the general usage.*   The public debt is now paid ; that is one Federal tie the less.   The Bank, assailed afresh, is on the point of falling ; that is an immense loss to the Federal principle.   The Supreme Court of the United States, one of the bulwarks of the Union, is assaulted.   The vast domain of the West, (see *Note* 12,) the national property, seems in danger of being given up to individual States, for this disposition is one of the favorite topics of the democratic party.

But if centralisation comes off the worse in Federal politics, it has the better within the States.   The principal States are engaged in constructing vast systems of internal communication ; they are establishing for themselves financial systems, and many of them are about to set up great banks, which shall exercise within their respective limits the salutary influence possessed by the Bank of the United States throughout the whole Union.   Thus each State, as it detaches itself from the Federal Union, organises more fully its own powers, and binds more firmly together its imperfectly combined elements.   But, on the other hand, industry and the spirit of enterprise restore to the Union the strength, of which political jealousy and party quarrels tend to deprive it.   There is not a family at the North, that has not a son or a brother in the South ; the community of interests daily grows stronger ; commerce is a centripetal force ; along the whole Atlantic coast there is only one mart, New York ; there is only one of importance on the Gulf of Mexico, New Orleans ; and the relations of New York and New Orleans make these two cities, instead

* An act has been passed by the Pennsylvania legislature, providing that 2,000 pounds shall make a ton.

of rivals, mutual supports. The railroads and the steamboats spread over the country the meshes of a net not easily broken.; great distances vanish ; before long it will be easy to go from Boston to New Orleans in eight days, less time than is generally required to go from Brest to Marseilles. When we reflect on the extent of the Roman empire for ages, we cannot doubt the possibility of maintaining a certain degree of unity on the American territory, immeasurably vast as it appears to an eye accustomed to the divisions of the map of Europe. The Romans had not attained that degree of perfection in the means of intercourse which we possess ; not only had they no knowledge of steamboats and railroads, and the telegraph, but they had few highways, and were unacquainted with the use of carriages hung on springs. The progress of commercial and financial arts, makes it more easy to manage the financial concerns of the universe now, than it was to administer those of a province in the time of Cæsar. I cannot, therefore, make up my mind to believe, that the Union will be broken up into fragments, driven in different directions and dashing one against another.

And yet it is very possible, that the Union will not continue long on its present footing. Are the relations established between the States by the constitution of 1789, the most perfect that can be devised now ? Ought not the unforeseen formation of the two great groups of the West and the Southwest be followed by some modification of those relations ? Would not the subdivision of the general confederacy into three subordinate confederacies, conformable to the three great territorial divisions, the North, the South, and the West, with a more intimate union between the members of each group, have the effect of satisfying the advocates of State rights, without endangering the principle of union ? Would not this arrangement be the means of giving more elasticity to the Union ?

Could not the existence of three partial confederacies be reconciled with that of a central authority, invested with the undisputed powers of the present Federal government, one army, one navy, one diplomatic representation abroad, one common right of citizenship, one Supreme Court, and, as far as possible, one system of customs, and one Bank ? These are questions, which it will, perhaps, be worth while to examine some day, and even at no distant day. But it would be desirable, that they should be approached and discussed with calmness. If they should be unexpectedly raised in a period of irritation and bad feelings, they would be the signal of a deplorable catastrophe. Union gives strength ; North America, once parcelled out into hostile fragments, would be of no more weight in the balance of the world, than the feeble republics of South America.

LETTER IX.

THE FIRST PEOPLE IN THE WORLD.

PHILADELPHIA, APRIL 24, 1834.

WHICH is the first people in the world ? There is no nation which does not make pretensions to this superiority. Who in France has not sung in the words of Béranger, "Queen of the world, oh my country ! oh France !" in the full conviction, that the French nation was predestined to be forever at the head of the human race, to eclipse all others, in peace and in war ? For myself, before I had crossed the frontier, I believed most implicitly,

that we were not only the most generous and chivalric of
people, the most intellectual and ingenious, the first in the
fine arts, the most amiable and brilliant; but also that we
were the most enlightened, the first in political and industrial arts, the most inventive and the most practical, in
short, the pattern-nation, perfect and unrivalled.   Notwithstanding the rains and fogs of Paris, I supposed our climate
the mildest and the most serene in the world; in spite of
the Landes and Champagne, I considered it undeniable,
that our soil was the most fertile, our scenery the most
picturesque, in the world.   Trusting to the reports of our
exhibitions of industrial skill, 1 was ready to swear that
we had left our neighbours of England a hundred leagues
behind, and that their manufacturers, to avoid being reduced to beggary by our competition, would soon be
obliged to come over to learn how to smelt and refine iron,
how to spin cotton, how to manufacture steel, how to
manage the most gigantic establishments in the most
economical manner, how to despatch mountains of merchandise beyond sea most expeditiously.

After having crossed the frontier one gradually lowers
these magnificent pretensions; patriotism becomes purer
and stronger.   In visiting foreign parts one sees what is
wanting to the prosperity and glory of his country, and
how it might be possible to add some jewels to her crown.
Thus it does not require long observation to see, that if
England might borrow much from us, we have not less to
receive from her.   The English are not only more skilful
manufacturers and better merchants than we are, but they
possess in a higher degree than we do, those qualities
which enable men, after having conceived grand projects,
to carry them into execution.   The English have that
practical sagacity and that unbending perseverance, by
which our Titan-like battles of the Revolution and the
Empire, our impetuous and devoted enthusiasm, our un-

paralleled victories, our unmatched triumphs, were reduced to treaties of Vienna, that is to say, were made to result in our own humiliation, and in the enthronement of Great Britain on the apex of the European pyramid. The English have less of the gift of speech, but more capacity for action, than we have. And it is owing to this, that they have found means to extend their colonial possessions, while all other nations were losing theirs; what they lost in the West, they have supplied in the East tenfold. They possess that political sense, to which they owe the peaceful settlement, during the last three years, of questions, that seemed destined to shake the granite foundations of their island and bury it in the sea. They have achieved their Reform; they have abolished the monopoly of the East India Company; they have reconstructed the Bank; they have abolished slavery. During this period, we have been revolving about questions of secondary importance, without being able to make a decision; we do not know how to go to work with monopolies, which, in comparison with the colossal privileges of the East India Company, are grains of sand; we, who have given to the world the most conclusive arguments in favour of liberty of commerce!

If in Paris, we consider ourselves, in all, and for all, and forever, the pattern-people, at London, the opinion is not less exclusively and decidedly in favour of the English. In London, the duke of Wellington is called the conqueror of Napoleon, which, indeed, is true to the letter, but is nevertheless perfectly ridiculous, although Lord Wellington is certainly an extraordinary man. I have seen Englishmen pettishly shake their head, when they were told that the sky of England was foggy; with a little malice, one might drive them to maintain, that they need not envy the climate of Italy, and that even the atmosphere of Manchester, where the sight of the sun is a rarity, has

charms, in spite of the slanders of its detractors, even for
those who have breathed the air of Naples.   At Madrid,
that heroic people, which seems to be awaking at last from
its long lethargy, has not lost the habit of believing in the
supremacy of Spain, and there, they dream that they are
yet in the glorious days of Charles V., when the sun never
sat on the Spanish dominions.   And we can pardon this in
the noble Castilians ; but I verily believe, also, that Don
Pedro and Don Miguel, those interminable pretenders, have
each an official journal which tells them daily, that the
breathless universe has its eyes fixed on their ragged
armies, and that the destinies of the world are settled at
Santarem and Setubal.   At Constantinople, in the capital
of an empire which exists only because the other European powers cannot agree in the division of the spoils,
they call us christian dogs.   In Rome the people still call
themselves Romans, and this ridiculous misnomer really
makes the Transtiberine populace believe, that military
glory is yet the lot of the country, and that the *Romans*
will soon resume the character of lords of the world, mag-
nanimously raising the humble and crushing the pride of
the powerful (*Parcere subjectis*, &c.)!   In Vienna, on the
contrary, everybody thinks that Rome is no longer in
Rome, but that it is, of right and in fact, in the archducal
capital, that the emperor is heir by lineal descent to
Augustus and Trajan.   The devise of an early prince of
the house of Austria (A. E. I. O. U.),* attests that this
pretension is almost as old as the house of Hapsburg.   In
Prussia, meanwhile, the young nobles, proud of having
studied at the great universities of Jena and Berlin, and of
having worn the sword in an army which was once the
great Frederic's, affect an utter disdain for the Austrians.
Elated by the rapid extension of their country, which has

---

* *Austriæ est imperare orbi universo ;* the empire of the world belongs to
Austria.

not, however, yet reached its full growth, the Prussians look upon their sandy land as the cradle of a new civilisation. It seems as if the waters of the Spree had some miraculous qualities, and that whoever has not tasted them, has but four senses instead of five. At St. Petersburg and Moscow, no one doubts, that the sword of the emperor, thrown into the scales of the world's destinies, would at once overbear the opposite balance. Perhaps we of Western Europe have done our part in filling the Russians with these high notions of the influence of the Czar. Thus in Europe, each nation arrogates to itself the first rank, and I do not see why the Americans should be more modest than the people on the other side of the Atlantic. The miracles which they have accomplished in fifty years give them a right to be proud, and they, also, in their turn, are persuaded that they are the first people in the world, and they boast loudly of their preëminence.

The fact is, there is no chosen people, on whom superiority is entailed for ages. The Jewish nation, in which this notion of predestination seemed to be most deeply rooted, has for centuries afforded the most melancholy refutation of the doctrine. Since the age of Richelieu and the Revolution of 1688, that is, since Spain has fallen asleep, France and England have been at the head of civilisation, and have divided the supremacy between themselves ; the one ruling by the theoretical, the other by the practical ; the one giving the tone in politics, the other in taste, the arts, and manners. But what were France and England three centuries ago, in the time of Charles V., when the generals of that emperor and king slew Bayard at Rebecque, made Francis I. prisoner at Pavía, and the Pope in Rome, whilst four thousand miles further west, Cortez was conquering for him the proud empire of Montezuma ? Prussia, who now divides with Austria the dominion of Germany, and who is worthy of that dignity, who is the youthful, the aspiring, the ambitious Germany, full of the future, as Austria is the patriarchal, sober, prudent, conservative Germany, clinging to the past and the old,—what was Prussia three generations ago ?   What shall we all be, French, English, Prussians, and Austrians three centuries hence, or perhaps one hundred years hence ?   Who can say that some northern blast, finding us divided, and enfeebled by our divisions, will not have laid low those who are now so high and haughty ?   Who knows if the vigourous race which is now bursting forth from this virgin soil, will not then have passed us in their turn, as we have outstripped our predecessors ?   Who can foretell, whether the two gigantic figures that are now rising above the horizon, the one in the East with one foot on Moscow and one just ready to fall on Constantinople, the other in the West, as yet half hidden by the vast forests of the New World, whose huge limbs stretch from the mouths of the St. Lawrence to those of the Mississippi ; who can foresee, whether these youthful Titans, who are watching each other across the Atlantic, and already touch hands on the Pacific, will not soon divide the empire of the world ?

Civilisation is a treasure, to which each generation adds something in transmitting it to its heirs, and which passes from hand to hand, from people to people, from country to country.   Setting out from Asia it was four thousand years in reaching the borders of the Atlantic Ocean.   Wo to the nations, that having become depositaries of the treasure, instead of keeping it with watchful care and labouring to increase it, lay it down by the road-side, and waste their time and strength in foolish quarrels ; for they will soon be robbed of their trust !   The Americans are the most enterprising of men, and the most aspiring of people ; if we continue to be swallowed up in our barren disputes, they are the people to snatch from us at unawares the precious charge of the destinies of our race, and to place themselves at the head of its march.

Each people has its qualities, which are developed by education, which at certain moments shine with peculiar brilliancy, like a beacon light towards which the eyes of mankind are directed, and by which its march is guided, and which always command the esteem or love or respect of others. The people of the United States most undenibly have theirs. No people is so peculiarly fitted by its intrinsic character, as well as by the circumstances of the territory and the condition of the population, for democratic institutions. The Americans possess, therefore, in the highest degree, the better features of democracy, and they have also its inseparable defects; but if there is something in them to blame, there is still more to praise. There is much here for a European to learn, who should come to seek, not subjects for fault-finding, satire, and sarcasm (which have become vulgar common-places, since the small coin of Voltaire and Byron has passed through so many hands), but positive facts, which might be imitated in our old countries, with the necessary modifications required by the difference between our circumstances and the condition of America. Almost all English travellers in this country have seen a great deal that was bad and scarcely any thing good ; the portrait they have drawn of America and the Americans, is a caricature, which, like all good caricatures, has some resemblance to the original. The Americans have a right to deny the jurisdiction of the tribunal, for they have a right to be tried by their peers, and it does not belong to the most complete aristocracy in Europe, the English aristocracy, to sit in judgment on a democracy. Yet all the English travellers in America have belonged to the aristocracy by their connexions or their opinions, or were aspiring to it, or aped its habits and judgments, that they might seem to belong to it.

A Yorkshire farmer or a Birmingham mechanic would certainly pass a very different judgment ; they would probably be as exclusively disposed to praise, as the most disdainful tourists have been to blame. And the farmers and mechanics count for something in the numbers of the English population and in the elements of the British prosperity. Suppose an Ohio or Illinois farmer, after having sold his flour and salt pork to advantage, should enact the nabob six months in England, and on his return should describe, with the rude eloquence of the West, the distress of the British operatives, the corn laws, the poor rates, the frightful condition of the Irish peasantry, the impressment of sailors, the sale of military offices, and to complete his picture of manners, should add a boxing match, a scene of the guests at a dinner rolling dead-drunk under the table, and of the sale of a wife by her husband in open market ; if he should give such a picture to his countrymen as a political and moral portrait of England, the English would shrug their shoulders, and with reason. Yet his story would be founded on facts, and could not be said to be actually false in any particular. Now such a 'story would be an exact counterpart of most of the representations of America by English travellers. Do not to others what you would not have others do to you.

There is one thing in the United States that strikes a stranger on stepping ashore, and is of a character to silence his sentiments of national pride, particularly if he is an Englishman ; it is the appearance of general ease in the condition of the people of this country. While European communities are more or less cankered with the sore of pauperism, for which their ablest statesmen have as yet been able to find no healing balm, there are here no paupers, at least not in the Northern and Western States, which have protected themselves from the leprosy of slavery. If a few individuals are seen, they are only an imperceptible minority of dissolute or improvident persons, commonly people of colour, or some newly landed emigrants, who have not been able to adopt industrious habits. Nothing is more easy than to live and to live well by labour. Objects of the first necessity, bread, meat, sugar, tea, coffee, fuel, are in general cheaper here than in France, and wages are double or triple. I happened, a few days ago, to be on the line of a railroad in process of construction, where they were throwing up some embankments. This sort of labour, which merely requires force, without skill, is commonly done in the United States by Irish new-comers, who have no resource but their arm, no quality but muscular strength. These Irish labourers are fed and lodged, and hear their bill of fare ; three meals a day, and at each meal plenty of meat and wheat bread ; coffee and sugar at two meals, and butter* once a day ; in the course of the day, from six to eight glasses of whiskey are given them according to the state of the weather. Beside which they receive in money 40 cents a day under the most unfavourable circumstances, often from 60 to 75 cents. In France the same labour is worth about 24 cents a day the labourers finding themselves.

This positive and undeniable fact of the general ease, is connected with another, which gives it a singular importance in the eyes of a European, who is the friend of progressive reforms, and the enemy of violence ; the prevalence of radicalism in politics. The term *democrat,* which elsewhere would fill even the republicans with terror, is here greeted with acclamations, and the name of *Democratic* is zealously claimed by every party as its exclusive property. But this is the only kind of property which is called in question ; it is true that material property rapidly disappears in this country, unless it is preserved by the

---

* Butter is dearer in the United States than in France.

most constant vigilance, and renewed with untiring industry. But as long as it exists, it is the object of profound
respect, which, I must confess, has rather surprised me.
I should have expected that the social theory would have
borrowed some notions from the predominant political
theory ; but there are those in Europe, who are not there
considered the boldest speculators on this subject, who here
would be looked upon as the most audacious innovators.
From this simple statement, it seems natural to infer, that
valuable lessons are to be learned here by those who seek
to solve the great question that now agitates Europe, the
amelioration of the greatest number. It would be interesting to inquire into the causes of this state of things,
and to examine whether, with certain modifications, it
could not be transferred to Europe, and particularly to
France.

LETTER X.

THE YANKEE AND THE VIRGINIAN.

CHARLESTON, MAY 28, 1834.

THE great flood of civilisation, which has poured over
the vast regions of the West, in the south and the north,
from the great lakes to the Cape of Florida, has flowed
on with a wonderful power and an admirable regularity.
Emigration has taken place, along the whole line of march,
from east to west. The inhabitants of New England,*

---

* The name of Yankee was first applied in derision, but the New Englanders, thinking that they have ennobled it, have adopted it.

after having first spread themselves over their original territory, and founded the States of Maine and Vermont, have thrown themselves into the State of New York; thence, keeping as much as possible along the northern frontier of the United States, they have extended all along the coasts of Lake Ontario and Lake Erie, and overrun the vast delta comprised between the Ohio and the Upper Mississippi, which now contains the States of Ohio, Indiana, and Illinois, and the Territory of Michigan. The New York and Pennsylvania emigrants have spread themselves comparatively little beyond the limits of their own territory, which are very extensive, and were thinly peopled in 1783. They have, however, furnished a small contingent to the great army of emigration from New England, and have helped to occupy the vast tract abovementioned. Virginia, after having settled her western part with her own sons, has given birth to Kentucky, and then, acting the same part in the south as New England in the north, has sent forth to the Gulf of Mexico those numerous swarms that have invaded the southwest. North Carolina has taken part in this task, and has beside a child of her own in Tennessee. Georgia and South Carolina have contributed to create Alabama and Mississippi, and Tennessee and Kentucky have in turn furnished offsets for Missouri and Arkansas.

Thus the States in which there are no slaves, have brought forth a family of truly democratic republics, that is to say, with an essentially farming population, holding no slaves, and, excepting the vine, cultivating all the productions of temperate Europe. These young States are founded on equality and the subdivision of property, for most of the farms do not exceed 80 to 160 acres. The Southern States, on the other hand, have created aristocratical republics, based on slavery and the accumulation of property in a few hands, still more exclusively agricul-

tural than the north-western States, and chiefly occupied in cultivating cotton, a precious commodity, which now furnishes for exportation, inclusive of what is consumed in the North, an annual value of 40 or 50 million dollars.*
Thus amongst all the columns of emigration, two particularly attract attention, and form of themselves the main body of the army, the others are only auxiliaries; these two great masses are the New England and the Virginia columns.

That part of Virginia which was most peopled during the war of Independence has a low and nearly level surface, and a sandy, and in general, very poor soil. Along the rivers there are tracts formerly productive, but even these have been exhausted by the cultivation of tobacco. The proprietors of these estates must have been early led to think of quitting their plantations for the fertile lands of Kentucky, then occupied, or rather overrun, by warlike savages, of whom they were the favourite hunting-ground. Some bold and hardy pioneers, at the head of whom was

---

* Exports of cotton from the United States. (*Doc.* 146, *Ho. of Reps. Sess.* 24 *Cong.*)

Years.	Pounds.	Value.	Years.	Pounds.	Value.
1792	142,000	51,470	1822	144,700,000	24,000,000
1793	500,000	160,000	1823	173,700,000	23,500,000
1794	1,660,000	500,000	1824	142,100,000	21,500,000
Mean	766,600	237,000	Mean	153,700,000	23,000,000
1802	27,500,000	5,250,000	1832	322,250,000	31,750,000
1803	41,100,000	7,750,000	1833	324,500,000	36,000,000
1804	38,100,000	7,750,000	1834	384,750,000	49,500,000
Mean	35,566,000	6,920,000	Mean	343,800,000	39,060,000

The domestic consumption at present amounts to about 250,000 bales, or about 100 million pounds, of the value of about ten millions. The crop of 1835 was 1,350,000 bales or about 500 million pounds, of the value of 60 millions. The yearly value of the wine made in France is about twice that sum, but the value of the export does not exceed thirteen and a half million dollars.

Boon, first ventured across the mountains with their rifles, and bravely sustained a bloody contest with the Indians. After many desperate fights, in which more than one unknown hero fell under the bullet or the tomahawk of some red-skinned Hector, after numerous assaults, in which more than one matron enacted the part of our Jeanne Hachette,* after many alarms and much suffering, the genius of civilisation carried it. At the call of the pioneers, roused by the fame of their exploits, the planters of the coast set out on their pilgrimage ; arriving with their slaves, they cleared and cultivated large tracts, in the midst of which they led a patriarchal life, surrounded by their servants and flocks, following with ardour the chase of wild beasts, and sometimes of Indians, and too often spending the proceeds of their crop in betting on the speed of their horses, of which they are very proud, and whose pedigree is better known to them than their own. More lately, when the demand for cotton had increased, in consequence of the improvements in machinery, and the steamboat had opened the way into the heart of the Mississippi Valley, they have removed southwards, always taking their slaves with them ; a prospect of future wealth and prosperity was thus opened for the south.

The industrious sons of New England likewise bade farewell to the rocky and ungrateful soil of their birthplace ; loading a wagon with a plough, a bed, a barrel of salt meat, the indispensable supply of tea and molasses, a Bible and a wife, and with his axe on his shoulder, the Yankee sets out for the West, without a servant, without an assistant, often without a companion, to build himself a

---

* [This French heroine distinguished herself at the siege of Beauvais, in 1472, when she snatched a standard from the hands of the assailants. Her real name seems to have been Fourquet, that of Hachette (Hatchet) having been probably assumed or given to her, like those of Wat Tyler and Jack Carter, of English history.—TRANS.]

log hut, six hundred miles from his father's roof, and clear away a spot for a farm in the midst of the boundless forest. The first of these wanderers went from Connecticut, *the land of steady habits*, of Puritans among Puritans.

The Virginian and the Yankee have planted themselves in the wilderness, each in a manner conformable to his nature and condition. The part they have taken in founding the new States of the West, explains the fact so often mentioned of fifty or sixty members of Congress being natives of Virginia or Connecticut. In this conquest over nature, Europe has not remained an idle spectator; she has sent forth vigorous labourers, who have co-operated with the sons of New England, for slavery drives them from the men of the South. Many Irish and Scotch, a number of Germans, Swiss, and some French, are now settled in Michigan, Ohio, Indiana, and Illinois. The traveller who descends the Ohio, passes on the way Gallipolis, a French settlement, Vevay, a Swiss village, and Marietta, so called in honour of Marie Antoinette.* The terminations in *burg* are scattered amongst Indian names, Jacksonvilles, Washingtons, and Columbias. But the cooperation of Europeans does not deprive the Yankees of the principal share in the honour of the work; they began it, they have borne and still bear the burden and heat of the day. In comparison with them, the European has been only the eleventh-hour-man, the apprentice, the hireling. The fusion of the European with the Yankee takes place but slowly, even on the new soil of the West; for the Yankee is not a man of promiscuous society; he believes that Adam's oldest son was a Yankee. Enough, however, of foreign blood has been mingled with the

---

* [If the author means to imply that it was so called by French settlers he is in error, as it is well known to have been founded and named by the first New England colony in Ohio. Neither is he correct, if, as seems to be the case, he supposes all the *burgs* to be German towns.—TRANS.]

Yankee blood to modify the primitive character of the New England race, and to form a third American type, that of the West, whose features are not yet sharply defined, but are daily assuming more distinctness; this type is characterised by its athletic forms and ambitious pretensions, and seems destined ultimately to become superior to the others.

The Yankee and the Virginian are very unlike each other; they have no great love for each other, and are often at variance. They are the same men who cut each other's throats in England, under the name of Roundheads and Cavaliers. In England, they patched up a peace by the interposition of a third dynasty, which was neither Stuart nor Cromwell. In America, where there was no power to mediate between them, they would have devoured each other as they did in England, had not Providence thrown them wide apart, one party at the south, the other at the north, leaving between them the territory now occupied by the *justes-milieux* States of New York and Pennsylvania, with their satellites, New Jersey and Delaware.

The Virginian of pure race is frank, hearty, open, cordial in his manners, noble in his sentiments, elevated in his notions, he is a worthy descendant of the English gentleman. Surrounded, from infancy, by his slaves, who relieve him from all personal exertion, he is rather indisposed to activity, and is even indolent. He is generous and profuse; around him, but rather in the new States than in impoverished Virginia, abundance reigns. When the cotton crop has been good and the price is high, he invites everybody, excepting only the slaves that cultivate his fields, to partake in his wealth, without much thought of next year's produce. To him, the practice of hospitality is at once a duty, a pleasure, and a happiness. Like the Eastern patriarchs or Homer's heroes, he spits an ox to regale the guest whom Providence sends him and an old friend recommends to his attention, and to moisten this solid repast, he offers Madeira, of which he is as proud as of his horses, which has been twice to the East Indies, and has been ripening full twenty years. He loves the institutions of his country, yet he shows with pride his family plate, the arms on which, half effaced by time, attest his descent from the first colonists, and prove that his ancestors were of a good family in England. When his mind has been cultivated by study, and a tour in Europe has polished his manners and refined his imagination, there is no place in the world in which he would not appear to advantage, no destiny too high for him to reach ; he is one of those, whom a man is glad to have as a companion, and desires as a friend. Ardent and warm-hearted, he is of the block from which great orators are made. He is better able to command men, than to conquer nature and subdue the soil. When he has a certain degree of the spirit of method, and, I will not say of will, (for he has enough of that), but of that active perseverance so common among his brethren of the North, he has all the qualities needful to form a great statesman.

The Yankee, on the contrary, is reserved, cautious, distrustful ; he is thoughtful and pensive, but equable ; his manners are without grace, modest but dignified, cold, and often unprepossessing ; he is narrow in his ideas, but practical, and possessing the idea of the proper, he never rises to the grand. He has nothing chivalric about him, and yet he is adventurous, and he loves a roving life. His imagination is active and original, producing, however, not poetry, but drollery. The Yankee is the laborious ant ; he is industrious and sober, frugal, and, on the sterile soil of New England, niggardly ; transplanted to the promised land in the West, he continues moderate in his habits, but less inclined to count the cents. In New England he has

a large share of prudence, but once thrown into the midst
of the treasures of the West, he becomes a speculator, a
gambler even, although he has a great horror of cards,
dice, and all games of hazard and even of skill, except the
innocent game at bowls.   He is crafty, sly, always calculating, boasting even of the tricks which he plays upon
the careless or trusting buyer, because he looks upon them
as marks of his superior sagacity, and well provided with
mental reservations to lull his conscience.   With all his
nice subtleties, he is, nevertheless, expeditious in business,
because he knows the value of time.   His house is a sanc-
tuary, which he does not open to the profane ; he is little
given to hospitality, or rather he displays it only on rare occasions, and then he does so on a great scale.   He is a ready
speaker, and a close reasoner, but not a brilliant orator.
For a statesman, he wants that greatness of mind and soul
which enables a man to enter into and love another's nature, and leads him naturally to consult his neighbour's
good, in consulting his own.   He is individualism incarnate ;
in him the spirit of locality and division is carried to the
utmost.*   But if he is not a great statesman, he is an able
administrator, an unrivalled man of business.   If he is not
suited to command men, he has no equal in acting upon
things, in combining, arranging, and giving them a value.
There are nowhere merchants of more consummate ability
than those of Boston.

But it is particularly as the colonist of the wilderness,
that the Yankee is admirable ; fatigue has no hold on him.
He has not, like the Spaniard, the capacity to bear hunger
and thirst, but he has the much superior faculty of finding,
at all times and in all places, something to eat and to drink,

---

* In Massachusetts, with a population of 610,000 souls, the House of
Representatives consists of about 600 members ; the most petty village must
have its Representative.

and of being always able to contrive a shelter from the
cold, first for his wife and children, and afterward for himself. He grapples with nature in close fight, and more
unyielding than she, subdues her at last, obliging her to
surrender at discretion, to yield whatever he wills, and to
take the shape he chooses. Like Hercules, he conquers
the hydra of the pestilential morass, and chains the rivers ;
more daring than Hercules, he extends his dominion not
only over the land, but over the sea ; he is the best sailor
in the world, the ocean is his tributary, and enriches him
with the oil of her whales and with all her lesser fry. More
wise than the hero of the twelve labours, he knows no
Omphale that is able to seduce, no Dejanira, whose poi-
soned gifts can balk his searching glance. In this respect
he is rather a Ulysses, who has his Penelope, counts upon
her faith, and remains steadfastly true to her. He does
not even need to stop his ears, when he passes near the
Syrens, for in him the tenderest passions are deadened by
religious austerity and devotion to his business. Like
Ulysses in another point, he has a bag full of shifts ; over-
taken at night by a storm in the woods, in a half hour,
with no other resource than his knife, he will have made
a shelter for himself and his horse. In winter, caught in
one of those snow-storms, which are unknown among us,
he will construct a sled in the twinkling of an eye, and
keep on his way, like an Indian, by watching the bark of
the trees. Thus to the genius of business, by means of
which he turns to profit whatever the earth yields him, he
joins the genius of industry, which makes her prolific, and
that of mechanical skill, which fashions her produce to his
wants. He is incomparable as a pioneer, unequalled as a
settler of the wilderness.

The Yankee has set his mark on the United States
during the last half century. He has been eclipsed by

Virginia in the counsels of the nation;* but he has in turn had the upper hand throughout the country, and eclipsed her on her own soil; for in order to arouse the Virginian from his southern indolence, it has been necessary that the Yankee should come to set him an example of activity and enterprise at his own door. But for the Yankee, the vast cotton plantations of the South would still be an uncultivated waste. It was a Yankee, Ely Whitney, who, toward the end of the last century, invented the cotton-gin, which has made the fortune of the South. To give a speculation success in the South, some Yankee must have come a thousand miles to suggest the idea to the natives, and carry off the profit before their eyes. New England has given only two Presidents to the Union, both popular on the eve of their election, both unpopular on the morrow, both rejected at the end of their first term, while all the others have been natives of Virginia or South Carolina, and have been rechosen for a second term. But then what a revenge has she taken in business matters, at the North and the South, in the East as well as the West! Here the Yankee is a true Marquis of Carabas. At Baltimore as well as at Boston, in New Orleans as well as at Salem, in New York as well as at Portland, if a merchant is mentioned who has made and kept a large fortune by sagacity and forecast, you will find that he is a Yankee. If you pass a plantation in the South in better order than the others, with finer avenues, with the negroes' cabins better arranged and more comfortable, you will be told, "Oh! that is a Yankee's; he is a *smart man!*" In a village in Missouri, by the side of a

---

* At this time, for instance, ten Senators out of 48 are natives of Virginia. Of seven presidents four have been from Virginia. Many of the members of Congress are natives of New England, and particularly of Connecticut, but they are generally laborious, second-rate men, rather than men of influence and superior abilities.

house with broken windows, dirty in its outward appearance, around the door of which a parcel of ragged children are quarrelling and fighting, you may see another, freshly painted, surrounded by a simple, but neat and nicely white-washed fence, with a dozen of carefully trimmed trees about it, and through the windows in a small room shining with cleanliness, you may espy some nicely combed little boys, and some young girls dressed in almost the last Paris fashion. Both houses belong to farmers, but one of them is from North Carolina, and the other from New England. On the western rivers, you will hear a boat mentioned which never meets with an accident, and in which all travellers and merchants are eager to take their passage ; the master is a Yankee. Along side of the *levée* at New Orleans, you may be struck with the fine appearance of a ship, which all the passers-by stop to admire ; the master is also a Yankee.

The preëminence of the Yankee in the colonisation of the country, has made him the arbiter of manners and customs. It is from him that the country has taken a general hue of austere severity, that is religious and even bigoted ; it is through him that all sorts of amusements, which among us are considered as innocent relaxations, are here proscribed as immoral pleasures. It is he that has introduced the Prison Reform, multiplied schools, founded Temperance Societies (See *Note* 13). It is through his agency, with his money, that the Missionaries are endeavouring silently to found colonies in the South Seas, for the benefit of the Union. If we wished to form a single type, representing the American character of the present moment as a single whole, it would be necessary to take at least three-fourths of the Yankee race, and to mix with it hardly one fourth of the Virginian. The physical labour of colonisation is now nearly brought to an end ; the physical basis of society is laid. On this base it becomes necessary to raise a social structure of yet unknown form, but which, I am fully convinced, will be on a new plan, for all the materials are new ; and besides, neither humanity nor Providence ever repeats itself. Which of the two races is best suited to execute this new task ? I cannot tell ; but it seems to me that the Virginian is now about to take his turn, and that in the phase which the United States are now on the point of entering, the social qualities of the Virginian will obtain the superiority, that naturally belonged to the laborious Yankee in the period of settling the forest. In a word, I believe, that, if the Union lasts, and the West continues to form a united mass from the falls of Niagara to New Orleans, this third type of the west, which is now forming and already aspires to rule over the others, will take a great deal from the Virginian and very little from the Yankee.

It is no small advantage to a people to combine within itself two types with different characteristics, when they unite harmoniously in composing a common national character. A people of which all the individual members are referrible to a single type, is among nations what an unmarried man is among individuals ; it is a sort of hermit, its life is monotonous ; the strongest and sweetest feelings of human nature are dormant in it ; it continues stationaary ; there is nothing to spur it forward. Such was ancient Egypt. A people consisting of two types, on the contrary, when neither has an oppressive superiority over the other, enjoys a complete existence ; its life is a perpetual interchange of ideas and sensations, like that of a married pair. It has the power of reproducing and regenerating itself. Each of the two natures alternately acts and reposes itself, without ever being inactive. By turns each gains the superiority and yields to the other; and thus according to circumstances, different qualities come into play. The two natures mutually support and relieve each other, they stimulate each other, and through this wholesome rivalry, the nation that combines them in itself, reaches high destinies.

History shows that the progress of humanity has been constantly promoted by the reciprocal action and reaction of two natures, or two races, sometimes friends, oftener enemies or rivals. The most general fact in the history of our civilisation is the struggle between the East and the West, from the expedition of the Argonauts and the war of Troy, to the battle of Lepanto and the siege of Vienna by the Turks. In this great drama, it was not merely to shed rivers of blood, that Providence has dashed against each other Europeans and Asiatics, Greeks and Persians, Romans, Carthaginians, and Parthians, Saracens and Franks, Venitians, Turks, and Poles; blows have not been the only thing exchanged between Europe and the Orient. If you wish to know what the West has gained from contact with the East, even when they met sword in hand, look around you ; most of the fruit trees that enrich your fields, the vine which gladdens the heart, the silk and cotton that adorn your houses and your persons, these are the spoils of your Eastern wars ; sugar and coffee, the cultivation of which has changed the political balance of the world, were brought into Europe from the East, the one by yourselves, the other by the Arabs, when they made themselves masters of Spain. The mariner's compass, which has given a new continent to civilisation, and established the dominion of man over the before unconquered deep, was the gift of the East. Your arts and your sciences are of Oriental origin ; the secrets of Algebra were stolen from the Moors of Spain by a monk ; your system of numeration, the basis of all your financial improvements, bears the name of the Arabs ; your chivalry was brought from Asia by the Crusaders. Christianity, the mother of modern Europe, would not have existed in

the West, had not the Roman legions conquered Judea
which contained its germ, had not the Roman empire contained the school of Alexandria in which that germ could
put forth, and had not the Rome of the Cæsars been
raised as a pedestal for the successors of St. Peter, from
which they might rule over the East and the West.

Behold the Roman people ; its noble career was a continual succession of wars, followed by as many incorpora-
tions of the conquered, alliances, real marriages, which
always give it a new vigour. It begins with the double
figure of Romulus and Remus ; then follow the Romans
and Sabines, then Rome and Alba, next Rome and the
Latins, and next Rome and Carthage. It might be called
a young sultan, who carries off a captive at the point of
the sword, and makes her his favourite until he grows
tired of her, or until he finds another more worthy of his
love. It goes on in this way, changing, and daily rising
in the successive subjects of its choice, until it meets with
Greece, which becomes not an object of a passing caprice,
but a favorite sultana. This Union of the Greek and
Roman natures gave its splendour to imperial Rome, and
rest to the world. Its destiny once entwined with that of
Greece, the Roman people paused to enjoy ; and with this
purpose, substituted the rule of the Cæsars for the republican constitution, and Greek rhetoricians and players, and
emperors, voluptuous like the disciples of Epicurus, or
philosophers, like Pericles, for the stern and severe aristocracy of earlier days. What is the history of Greece,
but a continual oscillation between the austere Lacedæ-
mon and the brilliant Athens, between the country of
Lycurgus and Leonidas, and that of Solon, Aspasia, and
Alcibiades. United, they acquired an indomitable energy,
and supported the shock of all Asia. Unfortunately they
had too little feeling of a common nationality, and too
much of local jealousy ; almost perpetually divided, they

never completely extended their sway over Greece itself, and when the Greek race was about to reach its zenith, neither was destined to lead it thither, but Providence raised up a man in the North, before whom *the earth was silent.*

Whilst a nation comprises an indefinite number of types mixed together without order and without rank, it resembles a body not yet in a state of consistency ; it has no definable character, no fixed destination ; it is incapable of achieving any thing great.   Thus from the time of the war of the old German electors against the Holy Empire, and of the treaty of Westphalia, which sanctioned their independence and broke in pieces the former unity of the nation, Germany continued under an eclipse, until the period of the rise of the house of Brandenburg from the midst of the anarchy of the little German States, when a rival was given to the house of Austria and a strong dualism established.   Dualism is not, however, the only mode in which a society can be constituted, at once solid and elastic.   When a third type, whose superiority is admitted by the others, or which partakes sufficiently of the nature of each to serve as a bond and a mediator between them, exists, the social organisation is then in a high degree vigourous ; for then, the harmony between the two primitive types has ceased to be an abstraction, it has become a substance.   In some cases this third personage of the drama becomes so indispensable to the action, that it must be supplied at any rate, and its great prerogatives devolve on a transient actor ; thus in Greece, Thebes played this part during a short period.   Sometimes it has been filled by an aristocracy, which has served as a check to both parties in turn ; an aristocracy worthy of the name is eminently qualified for this task, because it combines the two natures in itself, feels the reaction of their passions influencing itself, and has the energy necessary either to curb or spur them on, as the exigency of the case requires. There is no country in which dualism is more admirably developed than in the United States ; each of the two natures has an open field, each a distinct career of industry ; each possesses in the highest degree the qualities necessary for its peculiar position. Considered in respect to a triple type, the United States are not less favorably situated ; the young giant that is growing up in the West, seems destined to fulfil the prophecy *the last shall be first*, and to bind together the North and the South in his vigourous gripe.

In France we have two distinct types, that of the North and that of the South ; but instead of employing the principle of centralisation as a means of developing the nature of both, and giving them a free and harmonious action, we have endeavoured to confound them in a narrow and sterile unity. We have especially thwarted the most reasonable and legitimate wishes of the South, which has been overborne and crushed by the North. It takes its revenge, indeed, in furnishing us with most of our statesmen, very much as Ireland has the privilege of giving *premiers* to England ; but like Irish ministers in England, our Southern statesmen, ungrateful sons of a neglected mother, govern wholly in the interest of the North, as if France contained towns only, and had no rural population, as if we were chiefly a manufacturing, and but partially an agricultural people, and, what is worse, as if we were a school of philosophers, and not a nation longing for religious faith and political love.

LETTER XI.

L O W E L L .

LOWELL, JUNE 12, 1834.

THE municipal elections which took place in New York
two months ago, and the legislative elections in Virginia,
which occupied the whole month of April, have revealed
to the Opposition its whole strength.   Their success was
unexpected, particularly in New York ; I say success, although the newly elected mayor belongs to the administration party, because the Opposition has the majority in
both houses of the common council, the board of aldermen, and the board of assistants, who govern in reality.
Since that time, the Opposition has continued to gain
ground.   There are some able statesmen in the Senate,
who are also skilful parliamentary tacticians ; they knew
that by irritating the President they might force him to
commit some act of imprudence, and this motive was not
without its weight in the adoption by the Senate of resolutions censuring his conduct in regard to the Bank.   The
old General felt this censure very sensibly, and replied to
it by a protest, which his best friends consider a mistake,
and which the Senate refused to have entered on its journal.   It is a matter of surprise that Mr Van Buren, whose
sagacity all admit, did not interpose his influence to prevent the sending of this message.   One of the fundamental maxims of American politics is, that the sword and
purse should not be united in the same hands ; that is,
that the President, to whom the constitution has entrusted
the military force of the Republic, should not also be the
keeper of the public money.   This is here a universally

received, undisputed maxim ; and the President's protest clashes with this doctrine. It became necessary, therefore, to follow up the protest by an explanatory message, which the Opposition calls a recantation, and which in truth is one. This retractation or explanation has not, however, destroyed the effect of the first message, and the consequence has been a hesitation in the democratic ranks. The Virginia elections, which were then going on, show that they were influenced by it, and some other elections of less importance have turned out unfavorably to the Administration.

In Albany, the head-quarters of Mr Van Buren's friends, the Opposition has carried the municipal elections. The partisans of the Administration have, as if in sport, added fault to fault. A committee of the House of Representatives, appointed to examine into the doings of the Bank, of which the majority were Jackson men, as the administration has the upper hand in that body, committed a series of blunders : there was a paper war between the committee and the directors of the Bank, in which the former were completely unhorsed, and had no better resource than the brutal idea of ordering the President and directors to be taken into custody by the sergeant-at-arms. Such a proposition was revolting to every body ; the majority lately so compact, already exhibits symptoms of disaffection, and several recent votes show that the Opposition is gaining ground. One might say that the prudent, those, to use the words of the great master of diplomacy, *whose watches go faster than those of their neighbours*, are getting ready to desert. Out of the legislative houses, the Opposition is organising energetically for the general elections, which are to take place next autumn ; it is making preparations in the spirit with which they are made, when one feels sure of victory, and is determined that it shall be a decisive one. In New York, for exam-

ple, the common council have removed all the Jackson men
from municipal offices; all have made way for the opponents of the Administration. The mayor will have an
Anti-Jackson secretary, because that officer is chosen by
the common council. These removals are harsh measures,
but the friends of the Administration have no right to
complain, for they have set the example on a larger scale,
by removing hundreds of custom-house officers and postmasters. Without pretending to justify these violent acts,
it should be considered that something more is involved
than merely the removing of an adversary to make way
for a friend. The Opposition wish that the inspectors of
streets should be Anti-Jackson men, because the scavengers, who are in their employ, have a vote; just as the
Administration insists upon all the postmasters being Jackson men, because in the country they have a certain influence.

It is less than a year since General Jackson visited the
great towns of the North. He was received with acclamations such as neither America had ever before witnessed.
Washington never excited half the enthusiasm; neither
Bolivar, Pizarro, nor the great Cortez was ever saluted
with such pompous epithets. It was an apotheosis. It is
not yet a year since, and already abuse has succeeded to
the most extravagant praise. A few days ago, I was
grieved to read some unbecoming pleasantries upon the old
General's scars. What will be held sacred, if honourable
wounds, all received in front, fighting for one's country,
are to become a subject of low jests? The war of the
President on the Bank was certainly unjust and disastrous
to the country; the measures taken in his name against
that institution, were impolitic and unauthorised by law;
the violent passion and imperious temper displayed by him
in the affair, make a strange figure in the seat, that had
been occupied by sages like Washington and his successors.

All this is true ; but when we look back on fifty years of
public services, we are filled with grief and indignation to
think, that at the end of so long a career, outrage and ingratitude will be, perhaps, his only reward. Can he have
been raised so high, only that his fall should be greater ?
Is he destined to furnish another proof of the instability
of popular favour in every age and all countries ? But instead of dwelling on these unpleasant reflections, I will
rather describe the scene now exhibited literally under my
windows.

The town of Lowell dates its origin eleven years ago,
and it now contains 15,000 inhabitants, inclusive of the
suburb of Belvedere. Twelve years ago it was a barren
waste, in which the silence was interrupted only by the
murmur of the little river of Concord, and the noisy dash-
ings of the clear waters of the Merrimac, against the granite
blocks that suddenly obstruct their course. At present,
it is a pile of huge factories, each five, six, or seven stories
high, and capped with a little white belfry, which strongly
contrasts with the red masonry of the building, and is
distinctly projected on the dark hills in the horizon. By
the side of these larger structures rise numerous little
wooden houses, painted white, with green blinds, very
neat, very snug, very nicely carpeted, and with a few
small trees around them, or brick houses in the English
style, that is to say, simple, but tasteful without and comfortable within ; on one side, fancy-goods shops and milli-
ners' rooms without number, for the women* are the
majority in Lowell, and vast hotels in the American style,
very much like barracks (the only barracks in Lowell) ;
on another, canals, water-wheels, water-falls, bridges, banks,
schools, and libraries, for in Lowell reading is the only

---

* The female population of Lowell, between the ages of 15 and 25 years,
corresponds to a total population of from 50,000 to 60,000 souls.

recreation,* and there are no less than seven journals printed here. All around are churches and meeting-houses of every sect, Episcopalian, Baptist, Congregationalist, Methodist, Universalist, Unitarian, &c., and there is also a Roman Catholic chapel. Here are all the edifices of a flourishing town in the Old World, except the prisons, hospitals, and theatres; everywhere is heard the noise of hammers, of spindles, of bells calling the hands to their work, or dismissing them from their tasks, of coaches and six arriving or starting off, of the blowing of rocks to make a mill-race or to level a road; it is the peaceful hum of an industrious population, whose movements are regulated like clockwork; a population not native to the town, and one half of which at least will die elsewhere, after having aided in founding three or four other towns; for the full-blooded American has this in common with the Tartar, that he is *encamped*, not established, on the soil he treads upon.

Massachusetts and the adjoining small States of New England contain several manufacturing towns similar to Lowell, but none of them on so large a scale. An American, well acquainted with the character of his countrymen, gave me the following account of the origin of these towns, and of Lowell in particular. "In 1812," said he, "the United States declared war against Great Britain to defend the honour of their insulted flag. Boston and the rest of New England opposed the war, and thus drew upon themselves the reproaches of their brethren of the Middle and Southern States. The fact is, they were quite

---

* The rigid spirit of Puritanism has been carried to its utmost in Lowell, owing to the great number of young girls collected together in the factories. In 1836, a man was fined by the municipal authorities for exercising the trade of *common fiddler;* he was treated as if he had outraged the public morals, the magistrates fearing that the pleasures of the dance might tend to corruption of manners.

as sensitive as the rest of their countrymen to any insult offered their flag by the mistress of the ocean; the patriotism of the New Englanders is above suspicion; they began the war of Independence, and they supported the principal burden of that war. They were, likewise, resolved to have satisfaction for the outrages committed by England, for it was they who had the greater number of seamen impressed by the English;* but they did not wish to have recourse to the cannon's mouth. A commercial people, they had much to lose and nothing to gain by a maritime war; a clear-sighted race, they saw that the chance of war was on the side that could muster the largest armies and the most numerous navy; in a word, war appeared to them to be a barbarous, old-fashioned means, unworthy of their inventive wit. The Yankees never do anything like other people, but they always have some contrivance in store, that nobody else would have ever thought of. After a careful examination, the Yankee said to himself, the best mode of warfare against the English will be to attack the sources of their wealth; now what is the principal source of the wealth of Great Britain? Its manufactures. Among its manufactures which are the most productive? Why the cotton. Well then, we will set up spinning works and manufactories of cottons; this will be our war on Great Britain. Ten or twelve years were passed in making experiments, in preliminary preparations and attempts to form a class of operatives, and to make machinery. In 1823, the Merrimack corporation began operations at Lowell, where the River Merrimack has a fall of 32 feet, creating a vast motive power, and has been followed by the Hamilton, Appleton,

---

* New England comprises but one sixth part of the whole population of the Union, but she owns one half of the shipping of the country, or 700,000 tons out of a little more than fourteen hundred thousand.

Lowell, Suffolk, Tremont, Lawrence, and other companies in succession.''

Such is Lowell. Its name is derived from that of a Boston merchant, who was one of the first promoters of the cotton-manufacture in the United States. It is not like one of our European towns that was built by some demi-god, a son of Jupiter, or by some hero of the Trojan war, or by the genius of an Alexander or a Cæsar, or by some saint, attracting crowds by his miracles, or by the whim of some great sovereign, like Louis XIV. or Frederic, or by an edict of Peter the Great. It was neither a pious foundation, nor an asylum for fugitives, nor a military post; but it is one of the speculations of the merchants of Boston. The same spirit of enterprise, which a year ago suggested the idea of sending a cargo of ice from Boston to Calcutta round Cape Horn, to cool the drink of Lord William Bentinck and the nabobs of the India company, has led them to build up a town here, wholly at their own expense, with all the buildings required by the wants of a civilised community, in order to be able to manufacture white cottons and calicoes; and they have succeeded, as they always succeed in their speculations. The semi-annual dividends of the manufacturing companies in Lowell, are generally from 5 to 6 per cent.

The cotton manufacture in America, which dates only from the last war with England, is rapidly extending, although the modifications of the tariff, required by the attitude of South Carolina last year, have somewhat tended to check the manufacturing spirit. Boston seems destined, like Liverpool, to have its Lancashire behind it. As water-courses abound in New England, according to the nature of all primary regions, steam-engines may be dispensed with for a long time to come. This part of the country is very unproductive, and it required all the perseverance and obstinacy, even, of the Puritans to introduce

into it the comforts of life. It is rugged, rocky, moun-
tainous, and bleak, consisting in fact of the first ridges of
the Alleghanies, which extend hence to the Gulf of Mexico, continually receding from the Atlantic as they stretch
southwards. The inhabitants have an extraordinary mechanical genius, they are patient, attentive, and inventive,
and they must succeed in manufactures ; or rather they
have already succeeded, and Lowell is a miniature Manchester. About 30,000 bales of cotton, or one sixth of
the whole domestic consumption (see *Note* 14), are consumed in Lowell, besides which there are several manufactories of broadcloths, cassimeres, and carpets. To
strengthen the resemblance between their city and Liverpool, the Boston merchants determined to construct a railroad from Boston to Lowell, the length of which is 26
miles ; there was already a canal, as there is one between
Liverpool and Manchester, but this has been found insufficient, as it was at Liverpool and Manchester. They
would not permit this road to be constructed in the usual
hasty and provisional manner of the American works, but
they determined to have something Roman, and their
engineers have given it to them, and have certainly made
the most solid railroad in the world. They have only
left out the beautiful masonry, the arches of hewn stone,
the columns, and all the monumental architecture, which
makes the Liverpool and Manchester railroad one of the
wonders of modern times ; these magnificent ornaments
yield no dividends. Yet the Boston and Lowell railroad
in its Roman or Cyclopean simplicity, will cost 56,000
dollars a mile.

In travelling through the neighbourhood of Manchester,
one is struck with wonder at the sight of the great spinning works ; in looking at those huge white buildings by
moon-light, projecting themselves on the dark back ground
above the plain, those hundreds of windows from which

stream the brilliant rays of gas-lights, those lofty chimneys, higher than the highest obelisks, one is tempted to think them palaces, abodes of pleasure and joy. Alas! the delusive splendours! alas! the whited sepulchres! All this fairy illusion vanishes, when one crosses their door-sill, sees the haggard looks and ragged clothes of the crowd that fills these vast structures, beholds those poor children whom Parliament vainly strives to protect against their fathers, who are incessantly begetting new competitors, and against the lash of their overseers. On arriving at Lowell, the first impression of pleasure caused by the sight of the town, new and fresh like an opera scene, fades away before the melancholy reflection, will this become like Lancashire? Does this brilliant glare hide the misery and suffering of operatives, and those degrading vices, engendered by poverty in the manufacturing towns, drunkenness and prostitution, popular sedition hanging over the heads of the rich by a frail thread, which an ordinary accident, and slight imprudence, or a breath of the bad passions, would snap asunder? This question I hasten to answer.

LETTER XII.

THE FACTORY GIRLS OF LOWELL.

BOSTON, JUNE 22, 1834.

WAR, the last argument of kings and people, war, in which they put forth their strength with pride, is not, however, the greatest exhibition of human power. A field of battle may excite terror or a feverish enthusiasm, pity or horror; but human strength applied to create is more imposing, than human strength employed in slaughter and destruction. The pyramids or the colossal temples of Thebes, the Colyseum or Saint Peter's of Rome, reveal a higher grandeur than a field of battle covered with desolation and death, were it strown with three hundred thousand bodies, as in those two great fights in which our fathers, under Meroveus and Charles Martel, presented a barrier to the career of the barbarians, and saved the Western world from the encroachments of the East. The power of man, like that of God, is not less visible in small things than in great. There is nothing in the physical order of things of which our race has a better right to boast, than of the mechanical inventions, by means of which man holds in check the irregular vigour, or brings forth the hidden energies, of nature. By the aid of mechanical contrivances, this poor weak creature, reaching out his hands over the immensity of nature, takes possession of the rivers, of the winds of heaven, of the tides of the ocean. By them, he drags forth from the secret bowels of the earth their hidden stores of fuel and of metals, and masters the subterranean waters, which there dispute his dominion. By them, he turns each drop of water into a reservoir of steam,* that is, into a magazine of power, and thus he changes the globe, in comparison with which he seems an atom, into a laborious, untiring, submissive slave, performing the heaviest tasks under the eye of its master. Is there any thing which gives a higher idea of the power of man, than the steam-engine under the form in which it is applied to produce motion on railroads? It is more than a machine, it is almost a living being; it

* In passing into steam, water expands to one thousand seven hundred times its volume.

moves, it runs like a courser at the top of his speed ; more than this, it breathes ; the steam which issues at regular periods from the pipes, and is condensed into a white cloud, resembles the quick breathing of a race-horse. A steam-engine has a complete respiratory apparatus, which acts like our own by expansion and compression ; it wants only a system of circulation to live.

One evening, while in Virginia, I was looking at a distant locomotive engine, approaching along the Petersburg and Roanoke railroad, one of the fine works of which Mr Robinson, the engineer, yet a young man, has executed so many in Virginia and Pennsylvania. The engine came on at its usual rate of speed, through a narrow clearing cut for the road in one of the primitive forests, formerly the domain of the great king Powhatan and his copper-coloured warriors.* The chimney threw out thousands of sparks from its wide, funnel-shaped top ; although yet at a distance, the noise of the quick breathing of the pipes was distinctly heard. In the darkness, in so wild a place, in the bosom of a vast wilderness and the midst of a profound silence, it was necessary either to be acquainted with mechanics, or to be imbued with the incredulity of the age, not to believe this flying, panting, flaming machine, a winged dragon vomiting forth fire. A short time since some Bramins, the fathers of ancient science, seeing a steam-boat stem the current of the sacred Ganges, really believed that it was some strange animal, recently discovered by the English in some distant region.

In our modern societies the improvements of machinery have given us manufactures, which promise to be a source of inexhaustible prosperity and well-being to mankind.

---

* This railroad was constructed for 60 miles through a vast forest of oak and pine, the few houses now found along the line having been erected since the execution of the work.

The English manufactories alone yield about eight hundred million yards of cotton stuffs annually, or about one yard for each inhabitant of the globe. If it were required to produce this amount of cloth without machinery, by the fingers alone, it is probable that each of us would hardly be able to card, spin, and weave his yard a year, so that the whole time of the whole human race would be occupied by a task, which, by the aid of machinery, is accomplished by five hundred thousand arms in Great Britain. From this fact we may conclude, that when the manufacturing system shall be well regulated and completely organised, a moderate amount of labour by a small part of the human race, will be sufficient to produce all the physical comforts for the whole. There can be no doubt, that it will be so, some day or another ; but this beautiful order of things is yet remote. The manufacturing system is a novelty, it is expanding and maturing itself, (see *Note* 15), and as it ripens, it certainly will improve ; the staunchest pessimists cannot deny this, yet we should expose ourselves to the most cruel disappointments, if we imagined that the progress of improvement can be otherwise than slow, step by step. There are seven-leagued boots in fairy-tales, but none in history. Meanwhile the manufacturing system temporarily involves the most disastrous consequences, which it would be useless to enumerate here. Who has not sounded its depths with terror ? Who has not wept over it ? It is the canker of England, a canker so inveterate, that one is sometimes tempted to think, that all the ability displayed of late years by the British statesmen in attempts at domestic reform, will prove a dead loss.

The introduction of the manufacturing system into a new country, under the empire of very different circumstances, is an event worthy of the closest attention. No sooner was I recovered from the sort of giddiness with which I was seized at the sight of this extemporaneous town, hardly had I taken time to touch it, to make sure that it was not a pasteboard town, like those which Potemkin erected for Catherine along the *road to Byzantium*, when I set myself to inquire, how far the creation of manufactures in this country, had given rise to the same dangers in regard to the welfare and morals of the working class, and in regard to the security of the rich and of public order, as in Europe; and through the polite attention of the agents of the two principal companies (the Merrimack and the Lawrence), I was able to satisfy my curiosity.   The cotton manufacture alone employs six thousand persons in Lowell; of this number nearly five thousand are young women from 17 to 24 years of age, the daughters of farmers from the different New England States, and particularly from Massachusetts, New Hampshire, and Vermont; they are here remote from their families, and under their own control.   On seeing them pass through the streets in the morning and evening and at their meal-hours, neatly dressed; on finding their scarfs, and shawls, and green silk hoods which they wear as a shelter from the sun and dust (for Lowell is not yet paved), hanging up in the factories amidst the flowers and shrubs, which they cultivate, I said to myself, this, then, is not like Manchester; and when I was informed of the rate of their wages, I understood that it was not at all like Manchester.   The following are the average weekly wages paid by the Merrimack corporation last May.

For picking and carding, . .	$\begin{cases} 3.00 \text{ Dolls.} \\ 3.10 \\ 2.78 \end{cases}$
For spinning, ...	3.00
For weaving, ...	$\begin{cases} 3.10 \\ 3.12 \end{cases}$

For warping and sizing,   .   . $\left\{\begin{array}{l} 3.45 \text{ Dols.} \\ 4.00 \end{array}\right.$

In the cloth-room (measuring and folding),   3.12

These numbers are averages; the wages of the more skilful hands amounting to five, and sometimes nearly six dollars. Note that last March, in consequence of the crisis occasioned by the President's quarrel with the Bank, there was a general reduction of from 30 to 40 cents a week. You know how much smaller are the wages of women than of men;* there are few women in Europe, out of a few great cities, who can earn more than 20 cents a day or one dollar a week. It must also be remembered, that, in the United States the necessaries of life are not only much cheaper than in England, but even than in France, so that a great many of these girls can save a dollar or a dollar and a half a week. After spending four years in the factories, they may have a little fortune of 250 or 300 dollars, when they often quit work and marry.†

In France, it would be difficult to conceive of a state of things, in which young girls, generally pretty, should be separated from their families, and thrown together, at a distance of 50 or 100 miles from home, in a town in which their parents could have no person to advise and watch over them. It is a fact, however, with the exception of a very small number of cases, which only prove the rule, that this state of things has yet had no bad effects in Lowell. The manners of the English race are totally different from those of us French; all their habits and all their notions wholly unlike ours. The Protestant education, much more than our Catholic discipline, draws round

---

* The wages of a mere labourer in the factories at Lowell are from 5 to 6 dollars a week; of a man who has a trade, as a smith, dyer, 8 to 10 dollars, of the engravers of patterns on the printing cylinders, 17 or 18 dollars.

† Out of one thousand females in the Lawrence mills, only eleven are married women, and nineteen widows.

each individual a line over which it is difficult to step. The consequence is more coldness in the domestic relations, a more or less complete absence of a full and free expression of the stronger feelings of the soul, but, in turn, every one is obliged and accustomed to show more respect for the feelings of others. What amongst us would pass for a youthful imprudence or a pretty trick, is severely frowned upon by the English and Americans, and particularly by the Americans of New England, who are, as has been said, double-distilled English. Nobody in this country, then, is surprised to see the daughters of rural proprietors, after having received a tolerable education, quit their native village and their parents, take up their residence 50 or 100 miles off, in a town where they have no acquaintance, and pass two or three years in this state of isolation and independence; they are under the safeguard of the public faith. All this presupposes an extreme reserve of manners, a vigilant, inexorable, and rigid public opinion, and it must be acknowledged, that, under this rigorous system, there is a sombre hue, an air of listlessness, thrown over society; but, when one reflects on the dangers to which the opposite system exposes the daughters of the poor, who have no guardian to warn and protect them, when one counts its victims, however slight may be his sympathies with the people, it is difficult to deny, that the Anglo-American prudery, all things considered, is fully worth our ease and freedom of manners, whatever may be their attractions.*

---

* Mr H. C. Carey, in his *Essay on Wages* (p. 89), quotes the following letter from the director of one of the factories in Lowell. "There have been in our establishment only three cases of illicit connexions, and in all three instances the parties were married immediately, several months before the birth of the child, so that in fact we have had no case of actual bastardy." Mr Carey adds, that he was informed that there had been no such case at Dover, where there is a very large manufactory. Although I do not believe that such an exemplary degree of purity prevails in all the

The manufacturing companies exercise the most careful supervision over these girls. I have already said, that, twelve years ago, Lowell did not exist; when, therefore, the manufactories were set up, it also became necessary to provide lodgings for the operatives, and each company has built for this purpose a number of houses within its own limits, to be used exclusively as boarding-houses for them. Here they are under the care of the mistress of the house, who is paid by the company at the rate of one dollar and a quarter a week for each boarder, that sum being stopped out of the weekly wages of the girls. These housekeepers, who are generally widows, are each responsible for the conduct of her boarders, and they are themselves subject to the control and supervision of the company, in the management of their little communities. Each company has its rules and regulations, which are not merely paper-laws, but which are carried into execution with all that spirit of vigilant perseverance that characterises the Yankee. I will give you a short summary of one of these codes, for they seem to me to throw great light on some of the most striking peculiarities of this country. I will take those of the Lawrence company, which is the most recently formed; they are a revised and corrected edition of the rules and regulations, of the other companies. They bear date May 21, 1833. Article first of the general rules is as follows: "All persons employed by the Company must devote themselves assiduously to their duty during working-hours. They must be capable of doing the work which they undertake, or use all their efforts to this effect. They must on all occasions, both in their words and in their actions, show that they are

---

manufacturing districts, yet I am convinced that the morals of the manufacturing operatives are in harmony with those of the rest of the population.

penetrated by a laudable love of temperance and virtue, and animated by a sense of their moral and social obligations. The Agent of the Company shall endeavour to set to all a good example in this respect. Every individual who shall be notoriously dissolute, idle, dishonest, or intemperate, who shall be in the practice of absenting himself from divine service, or shall violate the Sabbath, or shall be addicted to gaming, shall be dismissed from the service of the Company. *Art.* 2. " All ardent spirits are banished from the Company's grounds, except when prescribed by a physician. All games of hazard and cards are prohibited within their limits and in the boarding-houses. The articles following from 3 to 13, determine the duties of the agent, assistant agent, foremen, watch and firemen. Article thirteenth directs, that every female employed by the Company shall live in one of the Company's boarding-houses, attend regularly at divine service, and rigidly observe the rules of the Sabbath. Article fourteenth and last, contains an appeal to the operatives, on the necessity of subordination, and on the compatibility of obedience with civil and religious liberty. There is, besides, a special rule relative to boarding-houses ; it recounts, that the Company has built those houses and lets them at a low price, wholly for the good of the hands,* and that the Company, therefore, imposes certain duties on the persons who hire them. It makes them responsible for the neatness and comfortable condition of the houses, the punctuality and good quality of the meals, good order and harmony among the boarders ; it requires that the keepers of the houses shall receive no persons as boarders, who are not employed in the Company's works, and it obliges them

---

* The company gets only 4 per cent. on the capital invested in the boarding-houses, while the average rate of dividends on the manufacturing stock is from 5 to 6 per cent. semi-annually.

to give an account of the behaviour of the girls. It also prescribes that the doors shall be shut at ten, and repeats the injunction of attendance at divine worship.

These regulations, which amongst us would excite a thousand objections and would be in fact impracticable, are here regarded as the most simple and natural thing in the world; they are enforced without opposition or difficulty. Thus in regard to Sunday, for instance, which with us is a holiday, a day of amusement and gaiety, it is here a day of retirement, meditation, silence, and prayer.* This is one of the features in which the French type most strongly contrasts with the Anglo-American. In a moral and religious point of view, there prevail among us a laxity and a toleration, which form a counterpart to the American *let-alone* principle in political matters; whilst the principle of political authority, which has always been established in great vigour among us, under all forms of government, monarchy, empire, or republic, corresponds to the austere reserve of American manners, to their rigid habits of life, and to the religious severity which exists here by the side of the great multiplicity of sects. So true is it, that both order and liberty are essential to human nature, and that it is impossible to establish a society on one of these principles alone! If you abandon a portion of the social institutions exclusively to the spirit of liberty, be assured that the principle of order will take no less exclusive possession of some other portion. Yield up to liberty the whole field of politics, and you are com-

---

* In the United States, the theatres are generally closed on Sunday, out of respect for the rules of the *Sabbath*; the only exception to this custom is among the French population of Louisiana. In New England, religious scruples on this point are carried farther than elsewhere; thus in Boston, a by-law of the city prescribes the shutting up of the theatres on Saturday evening, because, according to some precisians, the *Sabbath* begins at sunset on that day.

pelled to give religion and manners wholly up to order. Leave manners and religion to liberty, and you find yourself obliged to strengthen the principle of order in politics, under pain of suffering society itself to fall into ruins. Such are the general laws of equilibrium which govern the nations and the universe of worlds.

Up to this time, then, the rules of the companies have been observed. Lowell, with its steeple-crowned factories, resembles a Spanish town with its convents; but with this difference, that in Lowell, you meet no rags nor Madonnas, and that the nuns of Lowell, instead of working *sacred hearts*, spin and weave cotton. Lowell is not amusing, but it is neat, decent, peaceable, and sage. Will it always be so? Will it be so long? It would be rash to affirm it; hitherto the life of manufacturing operatives has proved little favorable to the preservation of severe morals. So it has been in France, as well as in England; in Germany and Switzerland, as well as in France. But as there is a close connexion between morality and competence, it may be considered very probable, that while the wages shall continue to be high at Lowell, the influences of a good education, a sense of duty, and the fear of public opinion, will be sufficient to maintain good morals. Will wages, then, continue to be what they are? There are some causes which must tend to reduce them; the rates of the duties which protect American industry are progressively decreasing; on the 1st of July, 1842, they will be reduced to a maximum of 20 per cent. But, on the other hand, the processes become more perfect, the labourers grow more skilful, the capitalists are realising their outlays, and consequently will no longer expect to divide 10 or 12 per cent. A certain diminution of wages is very possible, even after that of last March, because labour is paid in the Lowell factories, better than it is in the surrounding country; but there must be limits to this diminution. In Europe, work is often wanting for the hands ; here, on the other side, hands are wanting for the work. While the Americans have the vast domain in the West, a common fund, from which, by industry, each may draw for himself and by himself, an ample heritage, an extreme fall of wages is not to be apprehended.

In America as in Europe, competition among the head-workmen tends to reduce their wages ; but the tendency is not increased in America, as in Europe, by the competition among the labourers, that is by an excess of hands wanting employ, for the West stands open as a refuge to all who are unemployed. In Europe, a coalition of work-men can only signify one of these two things ; raise our wages or we shall die of hunger with our wives and children, which is an absurdity ; or raise our wages, if you do not, we shall take up arms, which is a civil war ; in Europe, there is no other possible construction to be put upon it. But in America, on the contrary, such a coalition means, raise our wages, or we go to the West. Every coalition which does not amount to this in the minds of the associates, is merely the whim of the moment, an affair of little importance. This is the reason why coalitions, which in Europe are often able to shake the firmest fabric, present no real danger to the public peace in this country, where authority is disarmed. This is the reason why European countries, burdened with an excess of population, need for their safety and welfare a West, into which each may overflow after its own manner. This also is the reason why France is right in keeping Algiers.

LETTER XIII.

THE BANK. — SLAVERY.

ELMINGTON, (VA.) AUG. 24, 1834.

THE elections of members of the House of Representatives will take place in New York, Pennsylvania, and Ohio, the principal States in the Union, next October and November. Although the members then returned will not take their seats until the session which begins in December, 1835, yet great importance is attached to the results of these elections, even in respect to the approaching session of Congress. On both sides preparations are making with the greatest activity; both parties have chosen their text. As the harangues against an aristocracy of money have aroused the prejudices of the labouring classes, who form the majority of electors, against the Bank, the watchword of the Opposition is no longer ostensibly the Bank. But it says to the electors, referring to the late acts of the President directed against the Bank, and the doctrines which on this occasion he has put forth in his messages; " The executive power is guilty of gross usurpation; hasten to the rescue of the constitution from its monstrous encroachments. It is no longer a question about the bank; but our liberties, bought by the blood of our fathers, are at stake, and an audacious soldier, surrounded by a train of servile place-men, has dared to trifle with our dearest rights." This is certainly .the best ground for the Opposition to take; for General Jackson, in the affair of the Bank, as in most other circumstances of his life, has cared little for forms. He has gone straight forward to his object, without stopping to consider where he was placing his foot.

The Administration party, which well knows how unpopular the Bank is with the multitude, since this unpopularity is chiefly its own work, talks Bank and nothing but Bank. " The Opposition," they say, " is mocking you, when it calls upon you to save the Constitution and the laws. What do they care for the Constitution and the laws? It is the Bank that they wish to save. Down with the Bank ! General Jackson, *the Hero of two Wars,* who pushed back the English bayonets from the Union at the peril of his life, wishes to free the soil of the country from this prop of tyranny and corruption. The Bank is nothing but English influence which seeks to enslave you. It is now to be seen, whether you will be freemen or worshippers of the Golden Calf. In spite of the hypocritical protestations of the parasites of the Bank, remember, at the polls, that the question, the only question, the whole question, is Bank or no Bank." At bottom, what the Administration party says, is true ; the Opposision do not give up the cause of the Bank. The question, which is at issue, and which is to bè settled by the elections, is, in fact, the question of the Bank.

But whose fault is it, if the Opposition has a rightful cause to call the citizens to the defence of the Constitution ? Besides, the leaders of the Democratic party felt that their policy, which consisted in setting up the local banks in opposition to to the National Bank, would necessarily fail, and that the financial and commercial interests of the country, comprising the local banks themselves, must, in the long run, rally round the Bank of the United States. The abuse which they had heaped upon the latter, would, therefore, fall directly upon the local banks. It was impossible that the democratic multitude, which had much more just grounds of complaint against the local banks, than against the Bank of the United States, by which nobody had ever lost a dollar, should not perceive this. Accordingly, after having hesitated a long time, the heads of the party seem ready to take the bold stand of openly denouncing all banks. Bank-bills, they say, are nothing but wretched rag-money; the eulogies of the metals, gold and silver, are now become the order of the day. Gold is called *Jackson money;* the United States mint has been actively employed in striking gold coins, half-eagles and quarter-eages. The principal journals of the Jackson party pay the daily wages of their journeymen printers in gold; the warm friends of the Administration affect to carry gold pieces in their pockets, and as paper only is generally used here in business transactions, even of the most trifling amount, you may be certain that a man who is seen with gold in his hands, is a Jacksonman. The President lately made a visit to his seat in Tennessee, and paid his expenses all along the road in gold, and the Globe, his official organ, took care to inform the public of it. At a dinner, given in honour of him, by the citizens of Nashville, he proposed this toast: " *Gold and silver, the only currency recognised by the constitution !*"

This apotheosis of gold and silver, abstractly considered, is all very well; hitherto the metals have made too small a proportion of the currency of the United States; gold, particularly, was never met with. At its last session Congress removed one of the obstacles to gold remaining in the country and taking the place of small bank notes, by raising its legal value. How far this act will effect its object of keeping a certain quantity of gold in the country, I know not; but I am persuaded, that the only prompt and effectual means of sweeping away the small bills, will be a National Bank. The prudent and experienced men of the party will certainly resist a formal declaration of war against all banks; but it is hardly to be avoided, that in the democratic party, the most rash and the most violent should give the law to the men of moderation and expe-

rience.   In this event, Mr Van Buren will have need of all
his address to preserve discipline in the ranks.   He is too
well acquainted with the commercial situation of the
United States, to allow himself to dwell one moment on
such a project as the destruction of the banks.   His creed
is the overthrow of the Bank of the United States, not
because it is a bank, but because, in his view, its existence
is contrary to the constitution.

The tactics of the Opposition have already given it success in some partial and unimportant elections, but even if
they should have the majority in the next Congress, it
would be but an incomplete victory, for the Bank would
not be preserved.   Many persons who have joined the
Opposition because its watchword was the Constitution
and the laws, would have kept aloof, had they seen the
name of the Bank joined with them, so rooted is the jealousy of this useful institution.   Admitting, then, that the
Opposition triumphs in the coming elections, it will be
necessary to set some new springs in motion in order to
save the Bank.   It is easy to refer at present to one on
which the friends of the Bank will not fail to rely.

The Union, homogeneous as it is in regard to language
and general character, is subdivided, as I have already
said, into three groups, daily becoming more and more
strongly marked.   North of the Potomac, the States are
poor in soil, but enriched by commerce* and manufactures ;
there are the great commercial towns, Boston, New York,
Philadelphia, and Baltimore, and the secondary ports of
Salem, Portland, New Bedford, Nantucket, and Providence ; there, also, are almost all the manufactures of the
Union.   These States do not admit slavery, with the ex-

* In 1833, out of 108 millions the ports of the north imported 96 million
dollars.   Deducting the imports of New Orleans, those of all the Southern
States were only of the value of 2,700,000 dollars.   The exports of the
South are much greater than its imports.

ception of Maryland, where the slaves are on the decrease,
and the Lilliputian State of Delaware, where slavery has,
in fact, almost disappeared.   South of the Potomac, between the Atlantic and the Mississippi, are the slave-holding States, wholly agricultural, and the only part of the
country in which cultivation is conducted on a great scale,
producing cotton, rice, sugar, and tobacco, without mechanical industry, and having but little commerce, except the
coasting trade, the foreign trade being in the hands of the
North.   In the West, reaching from the great lakes southwards, and lying on the Ohio and the Mississippi, is a
tract of the highest fertility, in which, since the peace of
1783, have grown up the new States of Ohio, Indiana,
and Illinois, besides Michigan, which is now on the point
of becoming a State.   These are also agricultural States,
producing corn and cattle of all kinds, yielding whiskey
and salted provisions, cultivated by free hands, and in
which property is so far subdivided, that each family has
its own farm.

Of these three groups, the North is most interested in
the existence of a Central Bank ; it is there, also, that the
financial machinery of the Union is most thoroughly understood, and it is most fully perceived, that such a Bank
is one of its most indispensable wheels.   But the North
alone, even with the support of some commercial towns in
the South and West, such as New Orleans and Cincinnati,
does not make up a majority, and in the North itself, in
the rural districts back of New York and Philadelphia, a
jealousy of the commerce of the cities prevails, which is
worse than injustice, for it is ingratitude, and which displays itself by a blind hostility to the Bank.   In a word,
although the question of a National Bank is considered
almost a question of existence by the great commercial
capitals of the North, without whose enterprise that region
would be still little better than a wilderness, yet the North

is far from being unanimous in favour of such an institution, and were it so, would not alone be able to save it.
The North, then, must seek allies in the South or the
West; there are some symptoms of the increase of the
Opposition in the West, but this is only because the question of the Bank has been temporarily left out of view.
The West does not favour the Bank nor the banks. The
hatred of these eminently democratic States to the banking
system is formally proclaimed in the constitutions of Indiana and Illinois, by which banks are expressly prohibited,
unless the State think proper to establish one itself, with
its own funds; a measure which each has already made
preparations to adopt. It is to the South, then, that the
North must look for help.

The inhabitants of the South and the North are very
different from each other in many points (See *Letter* X.),
and in a certain degree there are the same analogies and
the same contrasts between the North and the South, as
between England and France.* The South, like, France,
is most distinguished for the brilliant qualities; the North,
like England, for the solid; great ideas have their origin
rather in the South; good execution belongs rather to the
North. The North is gifted with the English perseverance, at once the pledge and the condition of success;
the South, like us, is easily moved, but easily discouraged;
all ardour at the outset, but disconcerted by a check from
any unforeseen obstacle. It was a matter of general surprise through the Union last year, that the South Caroli-
neans had completed, and completed in a good style of execution, a railroad from Charleston to Augusta; the dis-

---

* I asked a fellow countryman, established at Richmond, whose patriotism had not been cooled by a long absence from France, why he preferred
Richmond to the northern cities, which, in some respects, are more favourable to business; " Because," he replied, " the Virginians are the French of
America."

tance is equal to that from Havre to Paris. From the intermixture of northern with southern men in Congress, we find in that body a spirit of calculation and a practical good sense combined with a lively imagination and large views; the well balanced combination of these opposite qualities explains the union of boldness and wisdom which generally characterises the acts of that body. Until recently, when the West has suddenly loomed up, and taken its stand by the side of these two rivals, the domestic politics of the United States have consisted in maintaining the balance between the North and the South.*

There are important differences in the political views of the North and the South. The North has more respect for the Federal bond, and is disposed to tighten rather than to relax it. The South has the opposite tendency. The South is opposed to the tariff, to the system of internal improvements by the Federal government, to whatever tends to enlarge the influence of the Federal authority. "The lighter is the Federal yoke," says the South, "the more easily it will be borne, the less cause there will be to fear, that any of the members of the confederation will be tempted to shake it off." "By relaxing too much the

---

* It has always been endeavoured to balance the number of non-slave-holding States, as much as possible, by an equal number of slave States; by this means, the Senate would be exactly divided between the two interests. In 1789, six of the thirteen States admitted slavery; in 1792, there were 16 States, equally divided between the two systems; in 1802, out of 17 States, nine did not admit slavery, but in 1812, the admission of Louisiana restored the balance. From 1816 to 1819, four States were admitted, Alabama and Mississippi, slave-holding, Indiana and Illinois, non-slave-holding. In 1820, Maine, without slaves, and in 1821 Missouri with slaves, followed. In 1836 Michigan at the north, and Arkansas at the south, were received into the Union, and next will come the turn of the slave-holding Florida, and the non-slave-holding Wisconsin. It should be observed that Delaware, in which slavery is allowed by law, may be considered a non-slave-holding State, and is often reckoned so. The President has generally been from the South.

Federal bond," says the North, " you destroy it.   If you
go on thus, even for a short time, the Union will be dissolved indeed, and will exist only in name ; the slightest
accident will then be enough to abolish even the name."
In all these quarrels, however, even in that of Nullification, when a part of the South threatened to break the
Federal compact, they have hitherto come to an understanding.   Concessions have been made by both sides, but
more often by the North than by the South, and as they
have so long continued to preserve a Union, there is room
to hope, that they will still be able to live together for a
long time to come.

The general leaning of the South to an interpretation
of the constitution most favourable to the sovereignty of
the States, has led many of the southern politicians to maintain the doctrine of the unconstitutionality of the Bank ;
although in opposition to a formal decision of the Supreme
Court of the United States, the chief-justice of which,
Judge Marshall, is more revered throughout the Union,
than any other southern man, and even more so in the
South than elsewhere.   The Constitution, say the States'
rights puritans, does not give Congress power to establish
a Bank of the United States.   On the other side, if they
are ticklish as to what they call the encroachments of one
branch of the national government, the Congress, they are
not less so as to those of which the Opposition accuses
another branch, that is, the President.   Thus at the same
moment that they combat the Bank, they combat the
President also, on account of his measures against the
Bank.   This third party is numerous in Virginia.   Now
allowing the conclusions of the States' right party relative
to the Bank to be founded on a strict interpretation of the
law, they are none the less inadmissible in practice.   And
as it is impossible in the United States to give currency
to the maxim, *push the colonies rather than principle*, the

North entertains the hope that the States' rights party, after the example of some of its leaders, such as Mr Calhoun and Mr McDuffie, will relax a little of the rigour of their theories. The Administration, on the other hand, is doing its utmost to preserve the theoretical notions of Virginia on the Bank question in all their original purity on their native soil, and Mr Van Buren, who is far-sighted, lately sent the following toast to a 4th of July dinner in that State : " *Unqualified war on the Bank of the United States.*"

The North, fortunately for itself, has a means of acting upon the South, by slavery. This requires some explanation. At the time of the declaration of Independence (1776), slavery existed in all the States. During the war of the Revolution, Pennsylvania, in 1780, adopted a plan which soon exterminated it within her limits ; Massachusetts, in 1781, proclaimed slavery to be incompatible with the laws already existing ; the other States of New England, and finally New York, and the other States north of the Potomac, with the exception of Delaware and Maryland, adopted measures similar to those of Pennsylvania.* This was an easy matter for these States, their slaves not forming more than one twentieth or one fifteenth of the whole population. But it was a very different affair in the South, where the proportion of slaves was six or seven times greater, and where all the rural labour and menial services were performed by slaves ; the institution of slavery was, therefore, permitted to stand, in the South. The acquisition of Louisiana and Florida has enlarged the number of slave States, and by an oversight, which will one day be bitterly rued, slavery has been authorised in some of the new States, such as Missouri, where it would

* They consisted in declaring all persons born after a certain period free, the children of a slave to remain in the service of her owner during a certain number of years.

be easy to do without the blacks.* In 1790, there were 660,000 slaves† distributed in six States, one Territory, and the Federal District; in 1830 there were 2,000,000, in twelve States, two Territories, and the Federal District. The white population of the slave section, in 1790, was 1,250,000, or as 190 to 100; in 1830, it was 3,760,000, or as 186 to 100. The proportional increase of the slave population would appear still greater if we added the free blacks, and struck out the States of Delaware and Maryland. In 1830, the number of slaves in Louisiana and South Carolina was greater than that of the whites.

In our days, slavery is a scourge to all the countries in which it exists; of this the people of the United States, in the South as well as in the North, are convinced; but how to put an end to it? The bloody experiment of St. Domingo and its fatal consequences to the majority of the blacks themselves, offer no encouragement to immediate emancipation. The great experiment just making by the English government in its colonies,‡ is not yet advanced enough to afford any light. Besides, the English colonies contain only about one third of the number of slaves now in the United States. And supposing the slaves once emancipated, what shall be done with them? This question is the most embarrassing of all, to one who is acquainted with the wretched condition of the free blacks in the United States. (See *Note* 16.) On the other hand, the difficulties increase with the progress of time, and the Southern States are, or think they are, obliged to adopt

---

* At the time of its admission into the Union, Missouri contained only ten or eleven thousand slaves, which might have been easily sold in the neighbouring slave-holding States.

† Deducting those in the Northern States.

‡ The indemnity allowed to the owners amounts to about 125 dollars a head, which for 2,500,000, the present number in the United States, would amount to about 312 millions.

measures in regard to the black population, which may be defended by the plea of necessity, but which are nevertheless excessively harsh.*

In spite of all the precautions against an insurrection of the blacks, the solicitude of the Southern States continually increases; from the first of this month the blacks in the English West Indies, which are within three days' sail of the United States, are partially free. Between those islands and the southern and northern ports, there is an active commerce, and the communication is frequent. Finally, religious proselytism, which has carried the measure of emancipation in England, has its organs in the United States. There are not wanting philanthropists in Boston, Philadelphia, and Ohio, who are always ready to facilitate the escape of runaway slaves. Last winter, while I was at Richmond, 40 or 50 slaves disappeared, and there is no doubt that the fanatics of Philadelphia or New England furnished them the means of flight. The question of slavery, then, is, of all others, the most deeply interesting and alarming to the Southern States. Whenever it has been raised, even indirectly and secondarily, they have vehemently remonstrated; the moment it

---

* Some are surprised, that the slave and the free black are more severely dealt with by the laws of the Southern States, than by those of a colony belonging to an absolute monarchy, Cuba for instance, and that, for example, it should be prohibited, under pain of fine and imprisonment, to teach them to read or write. The contrary would be much more surprising. In a country where there is perfect liberty for the free class, it would be impossible to sustain slavery unless by the severest legislation. If the slave should read in your constitutions and bills of right, "that all men are born free and equal," how can it be that he would not be in a standing conspiracy against you? It is just to observe that, in the United States, the slaves, though intellectually and morally degraded, are humanely treated in a physical point of view. They are less severely tasked, better fed, and better taken care of, than most of the peasants of Europe. Their rapid increase attests their easy condition.

is touched, their voice is heard; this is ·their weak side; here the North has a hold upon them.

In regard to slavery, the Northern States have never departed from the policy of concession. This conduct of the North may even appear like culpable connivance, to Europeans not aware that the most precious treasure of North America, that is to say, the Union, has been at stake. The Northern States have written in their laws all that the South has demanded; they have granted to the south- ern master the right to claim his runaway slave before their own courts, so that the republican soil of the North does not enjoy the privilege which belongs to some of the monarchical countries of Europe, that of giving liberty to whoever sets his foot upon it. The North has permitted slavery to be maintained in the Federal District, in Wash- ington, at the foot of the Capitol steps. The North, see- ing the South in a flame on the Missouri question, stifled its just repugnance to her admission. The North, which has an interest in the recognition of Hayti, has yielded that point, because the South declares that it would be an encouragement to the slaves to revolt. Thus to main- tain harmony in the Union, the North has pushed its con- cessions even to silencing its religious feelings, its princi- ples of liberty, its commercial interests. As the Union promotes the good of all, all ought to be ready to make sacrifices to preserve it, and it would be just, that the South should renounce its theories about the constitution- ality of a National Bank, theories which are belied by long practice, and which have been formally condemned by judges, of whom the South itself is proud.

Some months ago the public clamour imposed silence on the Abolition Societies in the North, whose object is the abolition of slavery in the South. The newspapers contain details of the devastation and pillage committed by a handful of people on the poor, inoffensive blacks, during three consecutive nights of July, in New York, and during the same number in Philadelphia, about a week ago. Far be it from me to accuse the Opposition, which has the majority in these two cities, of having been an accomplice of these wretches! Yet I believe I state a fact when I say, that those terrible riots, in which houses, schools, and churches were plundered and pulled down every evening by the dozen, and in which peaceable persons of colour were robbed and personally abused, would have been more promptly repressed, had not the North, above all things else, been eager to punish the Abolitionists, and to show to the South that it had nothing in common with them. The North, in a word, has given and continues to give to the South every conceivable guarantee on the subject of slavery. The South, which may one day need, not merely the passive forbearance, but the active aid of the North against insurrection, should consider if the North exacts too much in return, in asking toleration for an institution indispensable to the North, and from which the South itself has received nothing but favours.

LETTER XIV.

THE ELECTIONS.

NEW YORK, Nov. 11, 1834.

THE autumnal elections have taken place in most of the States, and have resulted favourably to the democratic party and the President. Last April the mayor of New York, who is a Jackson man, was chosen by the small majority of 181 votes out of 35,147, and the Opposition

prevailed in the Common Council.   The majority in favour
of General Jackson is now 2,400; several causes have
contributed to produce this result.

The name of the Bank, whose cause is closely connected with that of the Opposition, sounds more and more
odious to the ears of the multitude; this is unjust, but it
is, nevertheless, true, and some of the late measures of the
Bank have redoubled the animosity of the democratical
party towards it.   It refused to show its books to the committee of inquiry appointed by the House of Representatives, unless in the presence of the officers of the Bank,
and its enemies have persuaded the multitude, that the
Monster dared not reveal the secrets of its den to the
representatives of the people.*   The Bank persists, conformably to the custom of merchants, in demanding damages on account of the protest by the French government
of the bill of exchange sold to the Bank by the Administration, and has withheld the dividends due the United
States on their stock.   The purpose is merely, say the
officers of the Bank, to bring the question of damages before the proper tribunal.   But the democratic party takes
this act as the text for its tirades against the Bank.   " Behold it," they say, " setting itself above the laws, taking
the execution of justice into its own hands, and under
false pretences, laying hold of the public money."   In
both these cases it is quite possible that the right was
wholly on the side of the Bank, but appearances are
against it, and nothing can be more injurious to it in a country governed by universal suffrage.   Many of its friends,
admitting that the course of the Bank has been strictly
legal, would have preferred that a more prudent policy
had been adopted, both for the interest of the Bank itself
and of the Opposition.

---

* The reason given for this refusal was the indiscreet use by a former
committee of inquiry, of notes made during a similar examination.

The silence of the principal speakers in Congress, who are almost all in the ranks of the Opposition, has no less contributed to swell its losses since the close of the session. The friends of the Administration in Congress, and more especially in the Senate, were beaten in debate, they felt it themselves, and their whole appearance was a formal confession of defeat; the whole party was disconcerted by this hesitation and embarrassment of the leaders. Since the 30th of June, the party, generals and soldiers, has had time to rally; they have restored their ranks beyond the reach of the fire of Messrs Clay, Calhoun, and Webster, and they have gained a victory, which four months ago they could not have hoped for. The revival of business in the country has also turned to the disadvantage of the Opposition. During the April elections in New York, the community was just recovering from a crisis, all classes had suffered and were still suffering. It was difficult to deny, that the distress had been caused by the President's attack on the Bank, in what he himself called an experiment. Commerce is now active again, the autumn business has been good, and every thing encourages the expectation of a not less favourable state of the spring-trade. General Jackson's experiment seems then to have succeeded; and a great number of persons who belong to the democratic party as their natural element, and who had quitted it in the spring, have very naturally fallen back into its ranks.

But it is proper to explain the real extent of this victory of the Administration; the Opposition has not actually been driven from its former positions, but the Jackson party has maintained the greater number of those it before occupied, and has particularly stood firm in Pennsylvania and New York. In a word, to judge by the elections that have already taken place, the House of Representatives in the session that begins at the close of 1835, will be, like the present House, composed of a majority of Jackson men. The Opposition, however, has gained rather than lost. It has carried the State of Maryland by a considerable majority, and has even gained the democratic State of Ohio, upon which it hardly calculated; ten Representatives out of nineteen from that State, belong to the Opposition, and although the Governor is of the Jackson party, the majority of the State legislature is Anti-Jackson, an important circumstance because the legislatures elect the Senators in Congress.

The elections in Pennsylvania, where the Opposition has lost two representatives, have surprised no one, but those in New York have disappointed all calculations. I know that some well-informed Jackson men, who had formed correct anticipations in regard to former elections, did not expect a majority of more than three or four hundred in the city, and, as I have before observed, they had one of 2,400. The Opposition thought itself able to contest the possession of the State, and relied upon carrying the city. It is certainly extraordinary, that the commercial interest should be beaten in the first commercial city in the New World, and such a result does no honour to the system which has caused it. The unexpected triumph of the Opposition in Ohio had redoubled their confidence in New York; they had celebrated with great display the junction of the young giant of the West with the Anti-Jackson forces. One of the magnificent steamboats belonging to the New York and Albany line, and called the Ohio, had been sent up the river with cannon, and the roar of its guns had been mingled with the shout of the towns and villages on the Hudson. The little frigate Constitution, the palladium of the opposition in New York,*

---

* This is a miniature frigate that takes its name from a favorite ship in the American navy, which covered herself with glory in the last war under the command of Hull, Bainbridge, and Stewart.

had been publicly paraded before the eyes of the multitude. A packet-boat had been sent up the canal from Albany, and made the new and flourishing towns, which at once give to and take from that great artery of the State, life, activity, and wealth, to resound with salvos of artillery in honor of Ohio. But now the cannon of the Opposition is silent, and that of Tammany Hall only is heard. The little frigate, which during the elections was hung up before the head-quarters of the Opposition, no longer displays the coloured lights with which her rigging was then illuminated. The streets of New York, which do not indeed require it, receive no additional light, except from the Jackson processions, which parade them nightly by torch-light.

The New York elections are not only important in their results, but also on account of the order which prevailed while they were going on. During the last six months, the spirit of anarchy had raised its head in the United States in such a manner as to inspire serious alarm, even among those not prone to be timid. You know what happened in New York during the April elections ; several months later, in July, the city became the theatre of a series of outrages against the poor blacks, which were repeated several nights. In August the same excesses were committed in Philadelphia, under the same pretext, and with no less audacity and perseverance : then came the brutal assault on the convent in Charlestown, when the retreat of peaceful nuns devoted to the education of young girls was attacked, plundered, and burnt down, without the Selectmen of the town having the power or the courage to make head against the rioters, and without the well-disposed citizens, taken by surprise by this act of savage intolerance, venturing to interfere. (See *Note* 17). Hardly a month since, there was also an incendiary conflagration at Philadelphia on the evening of the election ;

six houses were burnt, and the fire-men were driven off by the rioters, as at Charlestown, by main force. The same evening, an event of a more grave character occurred; several muskets were discharged by some of the Opposition whom the mob had assailed with stones, several persons were wounded, and one or two killed. A week before, during the preparatory elections, an obscure and peaceable individual was killed by a stab with a dagger.

A repetition of these scenes of disorder was feared in New York; but nothing of the sort occurred. Nearly 36,000 voters exercised their right of suffrage without any disturbance, although both parties were highly excited. The merit of this wise conduct is wholly due to the people; the Common Council had, indeed, taken extraordinary measures for the preservation of the peace, but what is here considered extraordinary, hardly comes up to the ordinary police in Europe. If the multitude in the United States abstain from acts of violence, it is because they choose to do so; if they preserve order, it is because they` love order. Three hundred constables more or less, in a city of 260,000 souls, like New York, could do nothing. Some persons, however, attribute this moderation of the democracy wholly to its confidence in success, and insist, that, if there had been any symptoms of the elections going the other way, the streets would have been thronged, as in April, by bodies of men armed with clubs.

The fate of the Bank has been decided by these elections. In fifteen months its charter expires, and the Bank will die, to be revived ere long under a new form, when a new series of commercial disasters, shall have proved to the conviction of the most incredulous, that they cannot get along without it. It is worthy of note, that it falls by the hands of the two States that owe it the most, New York and Pennsylvania. The blindness of Pennsylvania in particular is inexplicable. Who would expect this stupid fury in drying up the sources of its own prosperity ? For without the Philadelphia capital, the interior districts of the State would yet be a wilderness ; its one thousand miles of canals and railroads, its innumerable bridges, the finest wooden structures in the world, its numerous roads, its manufactures and mines which now enrich it, would not exist. Some persons assert, that Pennsylvania, which begins with perhaps the most enlightened and refined city in the United States, ends with a rural population of German origin, the most ignorant and stupid in North America. The conduct of the Pennsylvanians in regard to the Bank is not calculated to change the opinion of these severe judges.* As for the New York electors, it may be supposed, that, if the seat of the Mother Bank were in their capital, the votes of the town and the State would have resulted very differently.

The only chance left for the Bank is, that the portion of the South which is under the influence of Virginia, should condescend to lend it a helping hand. Such an act of generous compassion on the part of the South is not probable, but it is not absolutely impossible. I have often been present at discussions between men of the South and the North, in which the latter have said to the former : " Without us you would be at the mercy of your slaves ; it is our union with you which will prevent them from rising and cutting your throats." The Southerners answered : " We will take it upon ourselves to keep down our slaves ; we shall have no need of your help against any attempts at insurrection for a long time to come. All we ask of you is, not to stir them up to revolt. But as for you, why you are yourselves overwhelmed by a flood of ultra-dem-

---

* The able Correa, for some time Portuguese minister to the United States, used to say, that this State reminded him of the Sphinx, *which had the head of an angel, and the body of a beast.* This saying is often quoted in the United States.

ocracy. Your workmen give you the law. Before long
you will be glad to get the aid of the South to restore the
balance which your universal suffrage has destroyed." The
South has now a fine opportunity to exercise in the North
this moderating power of which it boasts the possession.

Frederic the Great, having gained a victory over the
Imperialists just after the battle of Fontenoy, wrote to
Louis XV. : " I have just paid the draft which your
majesty drew on me at Fontenoy." General Jackson has
honoured the bill drawn on him by the New York electors
more promptly.   A circular has been directed by the Secretary of the Treasury to the receivers of the public money, prohibiting the reception of certain drafts on the
branch banks.   These drafts were issued, merely because
it was physically impossible for the president and cashier
of the Mother Bank to sign five and ten dollar notes, fast
enough to supply the place of those that were worn out
or torn in the course of circulation.   They have the same
form with the Bank-notes, and pass like them, although the
charter of the Bank makes no mention of them.   This act
of the Administration will, however, do no injury to the
Bank ; for if it is obliged to withdraw all these drafts,
amounting to seven millions, from circulation, there is
nothing to prevent its issuing bills to the same amount.
The Bank is prepared for every event ; the amount of its
bills in circulation comprising the drafts on the branches,
does not exceed 17 millions, and its means in specie, or
other property that can be realised at a moment's warning,
exceed 20 millions.   It will merely be necessary for the
president, Mr Biddle, and the cashier, Mr Jaudon, who
were already crowded with business, to devote three or
four hours a day to signing bills ; for the branch drafts
were only designed to relieve them from this duty.   The
order of the Secretary of the Treasury amounts, therefore,
merely to a task inflicted on those gentlemen.

On both sides of the Atlantic, there is at present a reaction against the aristocracy of money. Whilst here the
eternal chorus of No BANK! DOWN WITH THE BANK!
No RAG-MONEY! is forever displayed on the liberty-poles
and the flags of the democracy, amongst us the bankers
are denounced from the national tribune by our most able
speakers. Do those who hope that industry will soon
raise itself to political influence and dignity, deceive themselves then? Or are not rather the industrial classes
themselves, and particularly those who are at their head,
the financial class, yet unconscious of their future destiny,
and too slow to shake off the bad habits which they contracted when the sword was law, and work was the lot of
slaves and serfs? Do not these Princes of Industry pay
too little regard to those lofty and noble sentiments which
are well worth letters of nobility, and without which no
supremacy could ever be sustained? To engage in public
affairs with dignity, the hands must be clean, the public
good must be prized above the money bags; and yet, such
is the state of commercial dealings in our day, that, without inheriting a double share of generosity and patriotism,
it is difficult to escape from them without becoming con-
taminated and callous. How many honorable men are
there not in the industrial ranks, who groan over the customs to which they are obliged to conform, over the examples which they are obliged to imitate? The Bank of
the United States must pay the penalty of the vices,
which even in our day degrade commerce, but which are
henceforth to belong only to history. It is punished for
the sins of others, for this great institution has not itself
deserved the reproach of cupidity; the services it has
rendered to the country are immense; those which it has
rendered itself, that is to say, its profits, have been moderate.

I must, however, do America the justice to observe,

that, although the desire to make money is universal, yet
in the principal and older commercial centres, there is
more honesty and less illiberality than amongst us.
American selfishness is less contracted than ours ; it does
not stoop to petty meannesses ; it operates on a more
liberal scale.   There are certainly wild speculators, blind
and desperate gamblers here also : but the objects of their
schemes are almost always enterprises of public utility.
The spirit of speculation in the United States has strown
this vast country with useful works, canals, railroads,
turnpike-roads, with manufactories, farms, villages, and
towns ; amongst us it has been more rash, wild, and foolish, and much less productive in useful results.   It is with
us mere stock-jobbing, without any good influence on
the prosperity of the country ; it is a game in which the
dice are loaded, in which the credulous lose the earnings
of years in a fever-fit of a moment.   Its only results are
ruin and despair, and if it contributes to people any thing,
it is the cells of the mad-house.   These are sad truths, but
truths which it may be useful to utter.

LETTER XV.

PITTSBURG.

PITTSBURG, NOVEMBER 24, 1834.

SEVENTYSIX years ago this day, a handful of Frenchmen sorrowfully evacuated a fort, which stood on the
point of land where the Alleghany and Monongahela
mingle their waters to form the Ohio.   The French,
with their faithful allies the Indians, had made a vigour-

ous resistance; they had defeated the expedition sent against them in 1754, and compelled Washington, then a lieutenant-colonel in the Virginia militia, to surrender Fort Necessity. They had routed the troops of the boastful Braddock, and spread terror, of which the memory is not yet effaced, through the English colonies. But the destiny of France was then in the hands of him, who of all her kings will be most severely judged by the tribunal of history. Under that most dissolute and selfish prince, France, sacrificed to the paltry intrigues of the bed-chamber, humbled at home, could not triumph abroad. The French were, therefore, obliged to abandon Fort Duquesne; on that day, November 24, 1758, one of the most magnificent schemes ever projected, was annihilated.

France had then possession of Canada and Louisiana; we were then masters of the two finest rivers, the two largest and richest basins of North America, that of the St. Lawrence and that of the Mississippi.* Between these two basins nature has raised no barrier, so that in the rainy seasons, canoes can pass from Lake Michigan into the bed of the Illinois, and continue their course thence without any obstruction to the Gulf of Mexico. The plan of our heroic pioneers, priests, sailors, and soldiers, had been to found the empire of New France in this great valley. It is beyond a doubt, that this idea had attracted the attention of Louis XIV., and that its execution was already begun by the erection of a chain of posts, the sites of which were admirably chosen. There is no country in the world which comprises such an amount of so highly fertile land; none which offers natural routes of communication comparable to the net-work of navigable

---

* The valley of the Mississippi with a small part of that of the St. Lawrence belonging to the United States, is six times larger than all France. A large tract in the extreme west is sterile; but the most fertile portion, already occupied by States and Territories, is three times as large as France.

rivers and streams spread over this great region. There is
none more healthy, for with the exception of a few points
or tracts subject to autumnal fevers, but which rapidly
lose this character when brought under cultivation, there
are only two infected spots, New Orleans and Natchez, in
which the yellow fever occasionally makes its appearance,
during a few months in the year. The sums swallowed up
by one of the foolish wars of Louis XV., would probably
have been amply sufficient to accomplish this noble project.   But the enterprise, although pushed forward by the
local agents with admirable zeal and sagacity, encountered
only indifference from the ministers at home, the great
point of whose policy was to know, who was to be the
favourite mistress of his Most Christian Majesty on the
morrow.   The capture of Fort Duquesne was soon followed by the conquest of all Canada by the English ; and
in 1763, by the treaty of Paris (these treaties of Paris
never bode us any good), France, exhibiting an example of
that complete submission and flat despair, of which our
annals exhibit so many instances, and the English so few,
ceded the basin of the St. Lawrence and the left bank of
the Mississippi to England, with one hand, and the right
bank of that great river to Spain, with the other.

Thus it came to pass, that the empire of New France,
like so many other magnificent schemes conceived in our
country, existed only on paper, or in the visions of youthful officers, full of sagacity and boldness, and intrepid missionaries, heroes alike without a name, whose memory is
honoured only in the wigwam of some poor exiled Sa-
chem.   Fort Duquesne is now become Pittsburg ; in vain
did I piously search for some relics of the French fortress ;
there is no longer a stone, a brick, on the Ohio, to attest
that France bore sway here.*

* At Kingston, (U. C.) the site of Fort Frontenac, I found the remains of
a wall built by La Salle, or one of his successors, in the barrack yard of one
of the English regiments.

Pittsburg is at present essentially pacific; if cannon and balls are seen here, it is because a trading people make it a rule to supply the market with whatever is wanted. The cannon are new, fresh from the mould, and equally at the disposition of the Sultan Mahmoud, or the Emperor of Morocco, or the government of the States, whichever will pay for them. Pittsburg is a manufacturing town, which will one day become the Birmingham of America; one of its suburbs has already received that name. It is surrounded, like Birmingham and Manchester, with a dense, black smoke, which, bursting forth in volumes from the founderies, forges, glass-houses, and the chimneys of all the manufactories and houses, falls in flakes of soot upon the dwellings and persons of the inhabitants; it is, therefore, the dirtiest town in the United States. Pittsburg is far from being as populous as Birmingham, but it exhibits proportionally a greater activity. Nowhere in the world is everybody so regularly and continually busy as in Pittsburg; I do not believe there is on the face of the earth, including the United States, where in general very little time is given to pleasure, a single town in which the idea of amusement so seldom enters the heads of the inhabitants. Pittsburg is, therefore, one of the least amusing cities in the world; there is no interruption of business for six days in the week, except during the three meals, the longest of which occupies hardly ten minutes, and Sunday in the United States, instead of being, as with us, a day of recreation and gaiety, is, according to the English custom, carried to a greater degree of rigour by the Anglo-Americans, consecrated to prayer, meditation, and retirement. By means of this energetic assiduity in work, which is common to all ages and classes, and by the aid of numerous steam-engines which labour like humble slaves, the inhabitants of Pittsburg create an amount of products, altogether disproportioned to their number. The nature, bulk, and weight of the articles make this disproportion more striking ; for, whether it be that American art, yet a novice, cannot give the finish required for articles of luxury and ornament, or that the Americans have the good sense to discern at a glance, that the manufacture of objects of the first necessity or of essential use, is more profitable than that of the trinkets with which civilisation seeks to adorn herself wherever there is wealth, and even where there is none, only the ruder and coarser kinds of work are done in Pittsburg.

Although Pittsburg is at this moment the first manufacturing town in the Union, it is yet far from what it is destined one day to become. It stands in the midst of an extensive coal-formation, the beds of which are very easily worked. The district east of Pittsburg furnishes much pig-iron, which is brought hither to be converted into malleable iron, or into all kinds of machines, tools, and utensils. Pittsburg has then coal and iron within reach ; that is to say, power, and the lever by which the power is to be applied. The vent for its wares is still more vast than its means, for the whole basin of the Mississippi, with all its lateral valleys, which on our continent would be basins of the first class, lies open to it. The population, which improves in its condition, as rapidly as it increases in numbers,* creates an indefinite demand for the engines and machines, hollow-ware, nails, horse-shoes, glass, tools and implements, pottery, and stuffs of Pittsburg. It needs axes to fell the primitive forests, saws to convert the trees into boards, plough-shares and spades to turn up

---

* The valley of the Mississippi contained, exclusive of Indians,

In 1762 about	100,000 inhabitants,	In 1810	1,365,000
In 1790	150,000	In 1820	2,625,000
In 1800	580,000	In 1830	4,232,000

The Indians, now mostly removed to the west of the Mississippi, number only about 300,000 souls.

the soil once cleared. It requires steam-engines for the
fleet of steamers, which throng the western waters. It
must have nails, hinges, latches, and other kinds of hard-
ware for houses ; it must have white lead to paint them,
glass to light them ; and all these new households must
have furniture and bed linen, for here every one makes
himself comfortable.

Thus Pittsburg is beginning to be what Birmingham
and St Etienne are, and what several places in the departments of the Aveyron and Gard will become, when we
become more enterprising, and use the proper exertions to
develop all the resources now buried in the bowels of our
belle France, for so it is called everywhere abroad. Pittsburg is beside and must be a commercial city, a great mart.
Standing at the head of steam navigation on the Ohio, it
is, directly or indirectly, that is through the medium of
the more central cities of Cincinnati and Louisville, the
natural *entrepot* between the upper and lower country, the
North and the South. Pennsylvania has spared no pains
to secure and extend the advantages resulting from this
situation. It has made Pittsburg one of the pivots of its
great system of internal improvements, which was undertaken with such boldness, and has been pursued with such
perseverance. Pittsburg is connected with Philadelphia
by a line of railroads and canals nearly four hundred miles
in length, and the numerous branches of the Pennsylvania
Canal give it a communication with all the most important points in the State. A direct communication with
Lake Erie is, indeed, wanting, but it will soon have a
double and triple one. A railroad, 300 miles in length is
projected between Baltimore and the Ohio, and one third
of the distance is already completed ; the legislature of
Pennsylvania have made it a condition that the western
terminus of this work shall be at Pittsburg. A canal, for
which the plans and drawings were furnished by General

Bernard, is to connect Chesapeake Bay by the way of Washington with the Ohio, and the same condition in favour of Pittsburg has been prescribed in this case.

Pittsburg is one of the few American towns, which owe their birth to war; it was at first one of the chain of French forts, and was afterward occupied by the English as a frontier post against the savages. In 1781, Pittsburg consisted of a few houses under the protection of the cannon of Fort Pitt. The origin of Cincinnati was similar; both commenced with a fortress, but more fortunate than some of our great commercial towns, such as Havre, which is stifled in the embrace of its fortifications, Pittsburg and Cincinnati have caused all traces of their original destination to disappear. Of Fort Pitt, which the English constructed just above the site of Fort Duquesne, nothing remains but a small magazine which has been converted into a dwelling house; another trace of the martial epoch (which here forms the mythological ages), is the name of Redoubt Alley, which is taken from a battery once erected there, to sweep the Monongahela. At Cincinnati, Fort Washington has been razed, and on its site now stands a bazaar built by Mrs Trollope. Not one of the least singular changes that have taken place in America within a half century, is the difference between the old mode of founding a town, and the manner in which they are at present made to rise out of the ground.

Some weeks ago I visited the anthracite coal district in Pennsylvania (see *Note* 18); the Anthracite, the most convenient kind of fuel, is at present in general use all along the Atlantic coast from Washington to Boston, and its introduction has made a revolution in household matters. Six or seven years since, when the demand for it was suddenly very much increased, the district which contains the coal-beds became the subject of speculation, at first prudently conducted, but finally growing wild and extravagant. The speculators vied with each other in tracing out town-plots; I have seen detailed plans, with straight streets and fine public squares scrupulously reserved, of cities which do not actually consist of a single street, of towns which hardly contain three houses. This frenzy gave birth, however, to one town of 3,000 inhabitants, Potts-ville, to ten or twelve railroads, great and small, to several canals, basins, and mining explorations, that have proved pretty successful. As for the great cities, several of them have really become flourishing villages, although the dreams of their founders have not proved true.

In this anthracite region, in the manufacturing districts of the North East, along the New York canals, and in all parts of the West, a traveller often has an opportunity of seeing the process of building towns. First rises a huge hotel with a wooden colonnade, a real barrack, in which all the movements, rising, breakfasting, dining, and supping, are regulated by the sound of a bell with military precision, uniformity, and rapidity, the landlord being, as a matter of course, a general or, at least, a colonel of the militia. The bar-room is at once the exchange, where hundreds of bargains are made under the influence of a glass of whiskey or gin, and the club-room, which resounds with political debate, and is the theatre of preparations for civil and military elections. At about the same time a post-office is established; at first the landlord commonly exercising the functions of postmaster. As soon as there are any dwelling-houses built, a church or meeting-house is erected at the charge of the rising community; then follow a school-house and a printing press with a newspaper, and soon after appears a bank, to complete the three-fold representation of religion, learning, and industry.

A European of continental Europe, in whose mind the existence of a bank is intimately associated with that of a great capital, is very much surprised even for the hundredth time, at finding one of these institutions in spots yet in an intermediate state between a village and the primitive forest inhabited by bears and rattle-snakes. On the banks of the Schuylkill, which has lately been canalled, and which, flowing from the coal-region, empties itself into the Delaware near Philadelphia, may be seen the beginnings of a town, built during the time of the mining speculations, at the head of navigation. Port Carbon, for that is its name, consists of about thirty houses standing on the declivity of a valley, and disposed according to the plan of the embryo city. Such was the haste in which the houses were built, that there was no time to remove the stumps of the trees that covered the spot; the standing trees were partially burnt and then felled with the axe, and their long, charred trunks still cumber the ground. Some of them have been converted into piles for supporting the railroads that bring down the coal to the boats; the blackened stumps, four or five feet high, are still standing, and you make your way from one house to another by leaping over the prostrate trunks and winding round the standing stumps. In the midst of this strange scene, appears a large building with the words, OFFICE OF DE-POSIT AND DISCOUNT. SCHUYLKILL BANK. The existence of a bank amidst the stumps of Port Carbon, surprised me as much as the universal neatness and elegance of the peaceful Philadelphia, or the vast fleet which is constantly receiving and discharging at the quays of New York, the products of all parts of the world.

I return to the triple emblem of the church, the school with the printing-press, and the bank. A society which is formed by accretion around such a nucleus, must differ more and more from the present European society, which was formed chiefly under the auspices of war, and by a succession of conquests, following one upon another. American society, taking for its point of departure labour, based upon a condition of general ease on one side, and on a system of common elementary education on the other, and moving forward with the religious principle for its lode-star, seems destined to reach a degree of prosperity, power, and happiness, much superior to what we have attained with our semi-feudal organisation, and our fixed antipathy against all moral rule and all authority. It presents, doubtless, especially in the newer States, many imperfections, and it will have to submit to various modifications; this is the lot of all unfinished works, even when God himself is the maker. But a few errors and follies are of little import in the eyes of those whose thoughts are occupied with the great interests of the future rather than with the paltry troubles of the present hour. Of little moment are the disgust and disappointment that a European of delicate nerves may have to encounter, if, for the purpose of killing time, he ventures upon a western steamboat, or into a western tavern; so much the worse for him, if he has fallen into a country where there is no place for an idle tourist, seeking only for amusement! Let the foreigner smile at the simplicity and extravagance of national vanity. That patriotic pride, rendered excusable by brilliant success, will be moderated; the errors and the follies are daily correcting themselves; the unavoidable rudeness of the backwoodsman will be softened, as soon as there are no more forests to fell, no more swamps to drain, no more wild beasts to destroy. The evil will pass away, and is passing away; the good remains and grows and spreads, like a grain of mustard.

LETTER XVI.

GENERAL JACKSON.

LOUISVILLE, (KY.), DECEMBER 15, 1834.

You must have been astonished in France at the President's Message; here the sharp and reckless tone of a portion of the press had prepared the public mind for some energetic demonstration; but the Message has exceeded the hopes of those who wished to assume an attitude of defiance in regard to France, and the fears of those who dreaded some imprudent step. Had such a paper come from any former President,—from Washington to John Quincy Adams,—it would have been looked upon as an expression of the sentiments of a majority of the American people. Neither of them would have been willing thus to commit the United States, without being sure that the national will really required it. Their rule of action would have been to let themselves be pushed on by the nation, rather than to draw it after them, or to go beyond it; and this, in fact, is more conformable to notions of self-government. They would have had the question profoundly discussed by the cabinet, not only orally, but in writing, as Washington did at the time of the establishment of the first bank in 1791. They would have consulted individually some of the leading statesmen of the country of all parties and all interests. They would have listened patiently to the representations of those upon whom the heavy burden of war would have most directly fallen, the merchants of Boston, New York, Philadelphia, Baltimore, Charleston, New Orleans, and other large ports; and finally, after having weighed all objections, measured all difficulties, if they had been convinced that the interest and honour of their country absolutely required the appeal to the last argument, they would have reluctantly addressed the challenge to their oldest ally and friend, to the firmest stay of liberty and improvement in the Old World.

General Jackson has changed all this; the rules of conduct and the policy of his administration are no longer those adopted by the wisdom of his predecessors. Some may maintain that this change is for the better; on this point, the future, and no distant future, will decide; but the fact of a change is undeniable. General Jackson possesses in the highest degree the qualities necessary for conducting a partisan warfare. Bold, indefatigable, vigilant, quick-sighted, with an iron will and a frame of adamant, devoted to his friends, harsh and terrible to his enemies, making light of obstacles, passionately fond of danger, his campaigns against the Creeks and Seminoles were marked by the most brilliant success, and his resistance to the English army under Packenham, at New Orleans, was heroic. By these exploits and the enthusiasm which military services excite in all countries, General Jackson found himself the most popular man in the Union, when the founders of the national independence disappeared, and naturally became the candidate for the presidential chair. Objections were made to his unbending temper, the impatience of contradiction which he had shown throughout his whole career, his obstinacy in following his own impulses, in spite of the provisions of the laws, and his disposition to use the sword of Alexander, rather than to conform himself to the delays of constitutional forms. His natural propensities, strengthened by the habits of military command, and by the peculiarities of that kind of warfare in which he had been engaged, must, it was urged, have become ungovernable; and it would be impossible for him to acquire that moderation, which is necessary in the exercise of civil authority. It was predicted that in politics, as in war, he would be zealous for his friends, implacable towards his adversaries, violent against whoever should attempt to check his course ; that, instead of being above party-quarrels, he would come down into the arena in person. His arrest of a judge in New Orleans, the execution of the militia men, and of the two Englishmen, Arbuthnot and Ambristier, his invasion and conquest of Florida in time of peace, his anger and threats when Congress was deliberating upon charges founded on these summary acts, were all dwelt upon.

But his chivalric character, his lofty integrity, and ardent patriotism, seemed sufficient guarantees for his conduct, and from reasons of domestic policy, which it would take too much time to explain, many enlightened men, who had at first treated the idea of supporting him for the presidency with ridicule, gave into the plan, trusting that they should be able to exercise a salutary influence over him. His fiery temper seemed in fact to be calmed by his elevation ; the recollection of his professions, which, at the moment they were made, were made in good faith, was yet fresh ; he had conscientiously resolved to observe the principles consecrated by Washington, Jefferson, and and the other patriarchs of America, to keep himself scrupulously within the narrow limits of prerogative, as he had traced them or allowed them to be traced out for him ; to follow the current of public opinion, without seeking to bar its course or divert it from its regular channels ; to be moderate, patient, and calm. During his first term, he continued pretty faithful to his resolution, to his professed principles, and to the advice of those who raised him to his seat. But this state of constraint was insupportable to him ; it is too late to reform at the age of sixty years.

Besides, it is not all temperaments, or, I should rather say, the distinctive qualities of all men, that can adapt themselves to that high sphere of serenity, in which he who governs others should move. Such a conformity was even more difficult for General Jackson than for any other man ; the turbulence and impetuosity of youth had not been tempered in him either by age or by the fatigues of war. And in a country where universal suffrage prevails, political disputes are of a character to exhaust the patience of an angel. Step by step, then, the stormy propensities of the Tennessee planter were seen returning. The character of the bold, daring, restless, obstinate, fiery, indomitable partisan chief, of the conqueror of the Creeks and Seminoles, gradually broke through the veil of reserve, caution, gravity, and universal good-will which had covered it, and tore in pieces the constitutional mantle in which his friends had taken so much pains to wrap him.

At length, in 1832, South Carolina furnished a natural occasion for giving the rein to his warlike propensities, which had now been curbed for four years. That State had, on its own individual authority, declared the tariff act of Congress null and void, and had armed its militia to sustain its nullification Ordinance. The President immediately began preparations for war, retaining, however, the language of moderation, and obtained an act of Congress (the Force Bill) authorising him to employ all means to maintain the laws of the United States ; when this storm was laid (see *Note* 5), General Jackson was proclaimed the saviour of the Constitution ; and perhaps sufficient care was not taken to prevent a very natural mistake of an old soldier, and to make him sensible that the congratulations of a grateful people were addressed less to his warlike attitude, than to the pacific measures taken under his auspices. In the heat of debate and the shout of acclamation that followed the restoration of order, the old military leaven began to ferment in the President's heart, and without a pause, he rushed into a vigourous campaign against the Bank. This was a war almost without provocation, certainly without a just cause, and for some time it appeared that the General would be worsted. But he held his own, and neither bent nor broke. In this affair he was the same OLD HICKORY that the Indians had found always and everywhere on their trail, whom they could neither tire nor surprise, and upon whom they could get no hold, either by force or fraud. The last elections of Representatives assure him the victory, and the Bank is condemned to the fate of the Creeks and Seminoles, of Mr Clay and Mr Calhoun, of the Spanish government of Florida, and of the English General Packenham (see *Note* 19.)

The intoxication of success seems to have restored all the fire of his youth, and at an age when other men look only towards repose, he requires new perils and new fatigues. Last winter, Mr Clay declared in the Senate, that, if phrenology were a true science, President Jackson must certainly have the bump of combativeness, for his life had been nothing but the perpetual exercise of that appetite; at fourteen years of age, against the English, then against his neighbours the first settlers of Tennessee, not a very tractable race, and who handled the knife, the sword, the pistol, and the rifle, with as much promptness as himself; next against the Indians, the English, the Indians again, and the inoffensive Spaniards; then against Mr Clay, Mr Calhoun, and South Carolina, and finally, for want of other adversaries, he was engaged in a bout with the Bank. The General seems, in fact, to be possessed with the demon of war; for no sooner had he put his foot on the throat of the Bank, than he required a new enemy, and finding in America none but vanquished adversaries, or objects unworthy of his anger, he flings down the glove to France. Thus far the defiance thrown out to France is merely the expression of General Jackson's humour. But, unluckily, this act of an individual emanates from a man who is President of the United States until the 4th of March, 1837, and who is even more pertinacious in his enmities than in his friendships. Unluckily too, the defiance has been inserted in a solemn document, which is looked upon in Europe as the faithful exhibition of the sentiments of the American people. And finally, the man who has set the United States in this posture, has just made an experiment which shows the degree to which he can lead the people to espouse his personal quarrels.

His tactics in politics, as well as in war, is to throw himself forward with the cry of, *comrades, follow me!* and this bold stroke has succeeded admirably in the case of the Bank. If he had recommended to Congress to withdraw the public deposites from that institution, he would certainly have failed; Congress would have declared against it. He, therefore, boldly took the first step himself, and ordered the removal, in opposition to the advice of the majority of his cabinet, two months before the meeting of Congress, without the slightest possible pretence of the urgency of the measure. *I will take the responsibility*, he said. The Secretary of the Treasury refused to execute the order, because he considered it a fatal abuse of power, and he was dismissed. The majority of the House of Representatives, and in the last elections, of the people, have sanctioned those dictatorial acts. General Jackson has, indeed, lost most of his friends in the enlightened classes and among the merchants, but he cares little for individuals, however distinguished ; by virtue of universal suffrage, it is numbers that rule here.

Will the bold policy by which he carried the multitude against the Bank, be as successful now that he attempts to edge them on against France ? It may be compared to one of those feats of strength, in which one may succeed the first and even the second time, but will break his back the third. General Jackson may be considered to possess that sort of popularity which is irresistible for a short time ; but the duration and solidity of which are in the inverse ratio of its intensity and brilliancy ; this, however, is a mere conjecture. One thing is certain, that the General has the majority in the House of Representatives, and from what is known of the composition of the next Congress, there is every appearance that he will keep it during the term of his Presidency ; whilst the Opposition, which now has the majority in the Senate, may lose it after the present session. Besides, it is not plain to me, that the Opposition will be unanimous in censuring the measures of General Jackson in regard to France. The opponents of General Jackson, as well as his friends, are obliged to court their common sovereign, the people. Now in all countries the multitude are very far from being cosmopolites ; their patriotism is more lively and warm, but it is also more brutal, more unjust, and more arrogant, than that of the higher classes. In France, they cry with enthusiasm, *Our country before all things!* Here the word is, *Our country, right or wrong!* which is the perfection of national selfishness.

As General Jackson is not, however, a madman or a fool, it is difficult to imagine, that he wishes the United States to pass at once from a close friendship to a state of hostility with France. If he thinks that France has exceeded all reasonable bounds of delay, that she has exhausted all the patience she had a right to expect from an old ally, from a nation whose independence was bought with our blood and our treasure, why is he not content with proposing measures of commercial restriction? A duty upon our goods would also be a means of paying the twentyfive millions. He knows, that, if France has more to lose than the United States in a war of tariffs, the United States, whose commerce and navigation are much more extensive than ours, have more to lose in a war of cannon, of which the sea would naturally be the theatre. But which class in the United States will suffer most by a war? The commercial, certainly. Who own the vessels and the goods? Oh! the merchants and ship-owners who vote against the General and his friends, his adversaries whom he detests and despises; the traders of Boston, who beheaded his statue on the bows of the Constitution frigate; those of New York, who have had caricature medals struck at Birmingham, holding up his government to hatred and contempt; the capitalists of Philadelphia, friends of Mr Biddle and admirers of Mr Clay. General Jackson troubles himself very little about the interest of such fellows as these.

On the contrary, an increase of the customs duties, whatever should be the motive of it, would be particularly hurtful to the Southern States, and would be very unwelcome to them. As it is the South that produces cotton, the principal article of export from the United States to France, the reprisals which the French government would not fail to make, would fall chiefly upon the South. Now the democratic party at present needs the support of the South, and is courting Virginia in particular, the most influential of the Southern States. The success of the plans of the democratic party, that is to say, the election of Mr Van Buren to the presidency, depends much upon the attitude taken by Virginia, not in 1836, the year of the election, but the present year, not tomorrow but to-day. Public opinion is yet undecided in Virginia; it is desirable, at any price, to prevent it from leaning in any degree to the side of the Opposition, and it is well understood that

Virginia will not consent to laying any especial burdens on the South. The Virginia legislature is now in session, and one of its first acts will be the choice of a Senator in Congress. If Mr Leigh, the present Senator, is chosen, then it will be committed in favour of the Opposition, and perhaps lost to the democratic party. The loss of the legislature may involve that of the State; the loss of Virginia may involve that of the South. Considerations of this kind have much more weight here than would be imagined in Europe. In the midst of the changing institutions of this country, politicians live only from hand to mouth.

It sometimes happens that European governments are clogged in their foreign policy by domestic difficulties. General Jackson would have been more cautious, if he had not thought that such is the position of the French government at this moment. But be assured, that he also has his domestic embarrassments, which affect his measures. This is more peculiarly the case with him than with any other President, because he is more a man of party, more entangled in party meshes, than any of his predecessors. Congressional intrigues and sectional interests create the same difficulties here, particularly for an administration like his, which amongst us result from an ill-balanced population, and the burden of the past. The French government may be confident of this, and ought to act conformably.

LETTER XVII.

PUBLIC OPINION.

LOUISVILLE, DECEMBER 22, 1834.

THE first impression produced in the United States by General Jackson's Message, was astonishment, as the tone was wholly unexpected to every one. In Europe, I suppose that it will have excited more than surprise, and it will be a matter of wonder, how a measure so rash and reckless could have emanated from a government, which, from its origin, has been characterised by address and prudence. I have already attempted to give an explanation of this mystery, and I have stated, that this *quasi* declaration of war was altogether an individual affair of General Jackson, that in this, as in every thing else, he has acted from his own impulse. The enlightened statesmen, who surrounded him in the beginning of his government, and whose wise counsels repressed his ardour, no longer have any influence. One after another has been separated from him, and several, such as Mr Calhoun, who, during his first term, was Vice-President, are now become his irreconcileable enemies. His position, as the head of the democratic party, obliges him, therefore, to supply some fuel for the furious passions, which the late contests had kindled.

It would be a mistake to judge of the reception of a document of this character in this country, by what would take place under similar circumstances in Europe. Public opinion has not the same arbiters here as in European societies; what is called public opinion in Europe, is the generally current opinion among the middling and higher classes, that of the merchants, manufacturers, men of let-

ters, and statesmen, of those who, having inherited a competency, devote their time to study, the fine arts, and, unfortunately too often, to idleness.   These are the persons,
who govern public opinion in Europe, who have seats in
the chambers, fill public offices, and manage or direct the
most powerful organs of the press.   They are the polite
and cultivated, who are accustomed to self-control, more
inclined to scepticism than fanaticism, and on their guard
against the impulses of enthusiasm ; to whose feelings all
violence is repugnant, all rudeness and all brutality offensive ; who cherish moderation often even to excess, and
prefer compromises and half-measures.   Among persons like
these, General Jackson's message would have met with
universal condemnation, or rather if General Jackson had
derived his ideas from such a medium, he would never
have dictated such a message.

The minority, which in Europe decides public opinion,
and by this means is sovereign, is here deposed, and
having been successively driven from post to post, has
come to influence opinion only in a few saloons in the
large cities, and to be itself under as strict guardianship as
minors, women, and idiots.   Until the accession of General
Jackson, it had, however, exercised some influence over
all the Presidents, who were generally scholars, and all of
whom, aside from their party connections, were attached
to it by family and social relations, and by their habits of
life.   Up to the present time, this class had also preserved
some influence over the two houses; but it has now completely broken with the President, or rather the President
has broken with it ; it has no longer any credit, except
with one of the Houses, because the Senate still consists
of men whom it may claim as belonging to it by their
superior intelligence, education, and property.   The democracy does not fail, therefore, to stigmatise the Senate as
an aristocratic body, and to call it the House of Lords.

The mass, which in Europe bears the pack and receives the law, has here put the pack on the back of the enlightened and cultivated class, which among us on the other hand, has the upper hand. The farmer and the mechanic are the lords of the New World ; public opinion is *their* opinion ; the public will is *their* will ; the President is *their* choice, *their* agent, *their* servant. If it is true that the depositaries of power in Europe have been too much disposed to use it in promoting their own interests, without consulting the wishes and the welfare of the mass beneath them, it is no less true that the classes which wield the sceptre in America are equally tainted with selfishness, and that they take less pains to diguise it. In a word, North America is Europe with its head down and its feet up. European society, in London and Paris as well as at St. Petersburg, in the Swiss republic as well as in the Austrian empire, is aristocratical in this sense, that, even after all the great changes of the last fifty years, it is still founded more or less absolutely on the principle of inequality or a difference of ranks. American society is essentially and radically a democracy, not in name merely but in deed. In the United States the democratic spirit is infused into all the national habits, and all the customs of society ; it besets and startles at every step the foreigner, who, before landing in the country, had no suspicion to what a degree every nerve and fibre had been steeped in aristocracy by a European education. It has effaced all distinctions, except that of colour ; for here a shade in the hue of the skin separates men more widely than in any other country in the world. It pervades all places, one only excepted, and that the very one which in Catholic Europe is consecrated to equality, the church ; here all whites are equal, every where, except in the presence of Him, in whose eyes, the distinctions of this world are vanity and nothingness.* Strange inconsistency! Or rather solemn protest, attesting that the principle of rank is firmly seated in the human heart by the side of the principle of equality, that it must have its place in all countries and under all circumstances!

Democracy everywhere has no soft words, no suppleness of forms; it has little address, little of management; it is apt to confound moderation with weakness, violence with heroism. Little used to self-control, it gives itself unreservedly to its friends, and sets them up as idols to whom it burns incense; it utters its indignation and its suspicions against those of whom it thinks that it has cause for complaint, rudely, and in a tone of anger and menace. It is intolerant towards foreign nations; the American democracy in particular, bred up in the belief that the nations of Europe groan ignobly under the yoke of absolute despots, looks upon them with a mixture of pity and contempt. When it throws a glance beyond the Atlantic, it affects the superior air of a freeman looking upon a herd of slaves. Its pride kindles at the idea of humbling the

---

* In Roman Catholic countries, the churches, vast structures, are open to all without distinction; each takes his seat where he pleases; all ranks are confounded. In the United States the churches are very numerous and very small, being built by joint-stock companies. They are appropriated to the exclusive use of the proprietors, with the exception of one free-seat for the poor, each one's share of property being designated by an enclosed space or a pew. The whole floor of the church is thus occupied by pews, and the gallery is generally divided in the same manner, though a part of the latter is generally open and free to all. Each pew is sold and transferred like any other property; the price varies according to the town, the sect, or the situation. The proprietors pay an annual tax for the support of public worship, lighting, and warming the church, and the minister's salary, the amount of the tax being proportioned to the value of the pew. Sometimes the church itself owns the pews, and the rent covers the expenses of the public worship. According to this system, the place occupied by the worshippers depends on their wealth, or, at least, on the price they are able or willing to pay for their pews.

monarchical principle in the person of the "tyrants who tread Europe under foot."

It may, then, be expected, that public opinion here will approve the Message, both as to its manner and matter, that it will consider it full of moderation and propriety. It is probable, that most of the men and the journals of the Opposition will fear to censure it openly and boldly. Not that the Jackson men themselves are unanimous in its favour; but that the speakers and writers of the Opposition consider themselves and are, bound to pay homage to the sovereign people, that they are all obliged to court the multitude, which is not very manageable in regard to points of national dignity and vanity. A certain number of journals and of political men have expressed their views as to the occasion and the consequences of a declaration of war with independence, and have been able to reconcile their patriotism with a lofty courtesy toward the oldest and the most faithful ally of America; but these are exceptions to the general rule. Some of the best informed and most influential of the Opposition journals have, to the general astonishment, suddenly turned right-about-face, and welcomed the part of the Message relative to France with acclamations. Thus they appear more democratic than the democracy, furious upon a point of honour, ready to sacrifice every thing in order to obtain redress for an outrage, to which, after twenty years, they have now first become sensible. He, who yesterday was a peaceful and reasonable writer, is to-day a thunderbolt of war, can talk of nothing but the violated national dignity, thinks only of blowing up the flame. The cause of this sudden change is this; if the United States were at war, they would spend a great deal of money, and a Bank then would be indispensable to the Federal government. Now *a* Bank and *the* Bank is at bottom all one. This is what is called po-

licy, cleverness, but it remains to be seen if the democratic party will be the dupe of such arts, and if those
who are most interested in the existence of the Bank, that
is, the merchants of New York, Boston, and New Orleans,
and even those of Philadelphia, wish to have a Bank at
any price.

Happily for the peace of the world, the majority of the
Senate of the United States consists of men eminent for
their experience, their ability, and their patriotism, who
judge the interests of their country on grounds of high
policy, and who, among other questions, will not fail to
consider this ; whether it would not be the worst of all
means of securing the liberty of the seas, an object which
they have at heart, for the French and American navies
to destroy each other. They do not hesitate, when circumstances require it, to take a stand above the demands of
an ephemeral popularity, and to meet the difficulties face
to face. A handful of firm and eloquent men in this illustrious assembly, was sufficient last winter to sustain the
shock of the popular masses, and to check and bear them
back. The Senate has only to continue equal to itself, to
deserve well of its country and of mankind.

LETTER XVIII.

CINCINNATI.

MEMPHIS, (TENN.), JAN. 1, 1835.

CINCINNATI has been made famous by Mrs Trollope,
whose aristocratic feelings were offended by the pork-trade,
which is here carried on on a great scale. From her accounts

many persons have thought that every body in Cincinnati
was a pork merchant, and the city a mere slaughter-house.
The fact is that Cincinnati is a large and beautiful town,
charmingly situated in one of those bends which the Ohio
makes, as if unwilling to leave the spot.   The hills which
border the *Belle Rivière* (Beautiful River, the French
name of the Ohio) through its whole course, seem here to
have receded from the river bank, in order to form a lofty
plain, to which they serve as walls, whenever the Ohio
does not serve as a foss, and on which man might
build a town above the reach of the terrible floods
of the river.   Geologists, who have no faith in the favours
of the fabled Oreads, will merely attribute this table-land
to the washing away of the mountains, in the diluvian
period, by the River Licking, now a modest little stream,
which, descending from the highlands of Kentucky,
empties itself into the Ohio opposite Cincinnati.   However this may be, there is not, in the whole course of the
river, a single spot which offers such attractions to the
founders of a town.

    The architectural appearance of Cincinnati is very near-
ly the same with that of the new quarters of the English
towns.   The houses are generally of brick, most commonly three stories high, with the windows shining with
cleanliness, calculated each for a single family, and regularly placed along well paved and spacious streets, sixty
feet in width.   Here and there the prevailing uniformity is
interrupted by some more imposing edifice, and there are
some houses of hewn stone in very good taste, real palaces
in miniature, with neat porticoes, inhabited by the aristocratical portion of Mrs Trollope's hog-merchants, and several very pretty mansions surrounded with gardens and
terraces.   Then there are the common school-houses,
where girls and boys together learn reading, writing,
cyphering, and geography, under the simultaneous direc-

tion of a master and mistress.* In another direction you
see a small, plain church, without sculpture or paintings,
without coloured glass or gothic arches, but snug, well
carpeted, and well-warmed by stoves. In Cincinnati, as
everywhere else in the United States, there is a great number
of churches ; each sect has its own, from Anglican Episcopalianism, which enlists under its banner the wealth of
the country, to the Baptist and Methodist sects, the religion of the labourers and negroes. On another side,
stands a huge hotel, which from its exterior you would
take for a royal residence, but in which, as I can testify,
you will not experience a princely hospitality ; or a museum, which is merely a private speculation, as all American
museums are, and which consists of some few crystals,
some mammoth-bones, which are very abundant in the
United States, an Egyptian mummy, some Indian wea-
pons and dresses, and a half-dozen wax-figures, representing, for instance, Washington, General Jackson, and the
Indian Chiefs, Black Hawk and Tecumseh, a figure of
Napoleon afoot or on horseback, a French cuirass from
Waterloo, a collection of portraits of distinguished Americans, comprising Lafayette and some of the leading men
of the town, another of stuffed birds, snakes preserved in
spirits, and particularly a large living snake, a boa con-
strictor, or an anaconda. One of these museums in Cincinnati is remarkable for its collection of Indian antiqui-
ties, derived from the huge caves of Kentucky, or from

* According to the official report of the Trustees and visiters of the common schools, dated July 30, 1833, there were then in Cincinnati 6,000 children between the ages of 6 and 16 years, exclusive of 230 children of colour
for whom there is a separate school. About 2,300 children attended the
common schools and 1,700 private schools. The number of common
schools is 18, under the care of 12 masters and 5 asssitants, 6 mistresses and 7 assistant mistresses. The masters receive 400 dollars a year,
and the assistants 250 ; the school mistresses 216, and the assistants 168.
These salaries are thought to be too low.

the numerous mounds on the banks of the Ohio, of which there were several on the site of Cincinnati.*

As for the banks they are modestly lodged at Cincinnati, but a plan of a handsome edifice, worthy of their high fortune, and sufficient to accommodate them all, is at present under consideration. The founderies for casting steam-engines, the yards for building steamboats, the noisy, unwholesome, or unpleasant work-shops, are in the adjoining village of Fulton, in Covington or Newport on the Kentucky bank of the river, or in the country. As to the enormous slaughter of hogs, about 150,000 annually, and the preparation of the lard, which follows, the town is not in the least incommoded by it; the whole process takes place on the banks of a little stream called Deer Creek, which has received the nickname of the Bloody Run, from the colour of its waters during the season of the massacre, or near the basins of the great canal, which extends from Cincinnati towards the Maumee of Lake Erie. Cincinnati has, however, no squares planted with trees in the English taste, no parks nor walks, no fountains, although it would be very easy to have them. It is necessary to wait for the ornamental, until the taste for it prevails among the inhabitants; at present the useful occupies all thoughts. Besides, all improvements require an increase of taxes, and in the United States it is not easy to persuade the people to submit to this. (See *Note* 20.) Cincinnati also stands in need of some public provision for lighting the streets, which this repugnance to taxes has hitherto prevented.

---

* This museum has one show which I never saw anywhere else ; it is a representation of the Infernal Regions, to which the young Cincinnati girls resort in quest of that excitement which a comfortable and peaceful, but cold and monotonous manner of life denies them. This strange spectacle seems to afford a delicious agitation to their nerves, and is the principal source of revenue to the museum.

Cincinnati has had water-works, for supplying the inhabitants with water, for about 20 years; for an annual rate, which amounts to about 8 or 12 dollars for a family, each has a quantity amply sufficient for all its wants. A steam-engine on the banks of the river raises the water to a reservoir on one of the hills near the city, 300 feet high, whence it is conducted in iron pipes in every direction. The height of the reservoir is such that the water rises to the top of every house, and fire-plugs are placed at intervals along the streets to supply the engines in case of fire. Several of the new towns in the United States have water-works, and Philadelphia, among the older cities, has an admirable system of works, which, owing to a series of unsuccessful experiments, have cost a large sum.* At this moment, a plan for supplying Boston with water is under discussion, which will cost several millions, because the water must be brought from a distance. New York is also engaged in a similar work, the expense of which will be about five millions. The Cincinnati water-works have not cost much above 150,000 dollars, although they have been several times completely reconstructed. It is generally thought in the United States, that the water-works ought to be owned by the towns, but those in Cincinnati belong to a company, and the water-rate is, therefore, higher than in Philadelphia and Pittsburg. The city has three times been in negociation for the purchase of the works, and has always declined buying on advantageous terms; the first time the establishment was offered for 35,000 dollars, and the second time for 80,000; the

---

* The water used in Philadelphia is supplied by the Schuylkill, a fall in which is made to drive the pumps, by which the reservoirs are filled. The Fairmount works are arranged and ornamented with much taste, and at very little expense; the ornamental part, strictly speaking, merely consists of some lawns, wooden balustrades, and two wretched statues; yet the effect is very elegant.

third time, 125,000 dollars were demanded, and 300,000 or 400,000 will finally be paid for it. In this case, as in regard to lighting the streets, the principal cause of the refusal of the city to buy was the unwillingness to lay new taxes.

The appearance of Cincinnati as it is approached from the water, is imposing, and it is still more so when it is viewed from one of the neighbouring hills. The eye takes in the windings of the Ohio and the course of the Licking, which enters the former at right angles, the steamboats that fill the port, the basin of the Miami canal, with the warehouses that line it and the locks that connect it with the river, the white-washed spinning works of Newport and Covington with their tall chimnies, the Federal arsenal, above which floats the starry banner, and the numerous wooden spires that crown the churches. On all sides the view is terminated by ranges of hills, forming an amphitheatre yet covered with the vigorous growth of the primitive forest. This rich verdure is here and there interrupted by country houses surrounded by colonnades, which are furnished by the forest. The population which occupies this amphitheatre, lives in the midst of plenty; it is industrious, sober, frugal, thirsting after knowledge, and if, with a very few exceptions, it is entirely a stranger to the delicate pleasures and elegant manners of the refined society of our European capitals, it is equally ignorant of its vices, dissipation, and follies.

At the first glance one does not perceive any difference between the right and left bank of the river; from a distance, the prosperity of Cincinnati seems to extend to the opposite shore. This is an illusion; on the right bank, that is, in Ohio, there are none but freemen; slavery exists on the other side. You may descend the river hundreds of miles, with slavery on the left and liberty on the right, although it is the same soil, and equally capable of being

cultivated by the white man.   When you enter the Mississippi you have slavery on both sides of you.   A blind
carelessness, or rather a fatal weakness in the rulers, and a
deplorable selfishness in the people, have allowed this
plague to become fixed in a country where there was no
need of tolerating its existence.   Who can tell when and
how, and through what sufferings, it will be possible to
eradicate it?

I met with one incident in Cincinnati, which I shall
long remember.   I had observed at the hotel table a man
of about the medium height, stout and muscular, and of
about the age of sixty years, yet with the active step and
lively air of youth.   I had been struck with his open and
cheerful expression, the amenity of his manners, and a
certain air of command, which appeared through his plain
dress.   " That is," said my friend, " General Harrison,
clerk of the Cincinnati Court of Common Pleas"—" What!
General Harrison of the Tippecanoe and the Thames?"
" The same; the ex-general, the conqueror of Tecumseh
and Proctor; the avenger of our disasters on the Raisin
and at Detroit; the ex-governor of the Territory of Indiana, the ex-senator in Congress, the ex-minister of the
United States to one of the South American republics.
He has grown old in the service of his country, he has
passed twenty years of his life in those fierce wars with
the Indians, in which there was less glory to be won, but
more dangers to be encountered, than at Rivoli and Aus-
terlitz.   He is now poor, with a numerous family, neglected by the Federal government, although yet vigorous,
because he has the independence to think for himself.   As
the Opposition is in the majority here, his friends have bethought themselves of coming to his relief by removing
the clerk of the court of Common Pleas, who was a Jackson man, and giving him the place, which is a lucrative
one, as a sort of retiring pension.   His friends in the East

talk of making him President of the United States. Meanwhile we have made him clerk of an inferior court." After a pause my informant added, " At this wretched table you may see another candidate for the presidency, who seems to have a better chance than General Harrison ; it is Mr McLean, now one of the judges of the Supreme Court of the United States."

Examples of this abandonment of men, whose career has been in the highest degree honourable, are not rare in the United States. I had already seen the illustrious Gallatin at New York, who, after having grown old in the service of the republic, after having been for forty years a legislator, a member of the cabinet, a minister abroad, after having taken an active part in every wise and good measure of the Federal government, was dismissed without any provision, and would have terminated his laborious career in poverty, had not his friends offered him the place of president of one of the banks in New York. The distress of President Jefferson in his old age is well known, and that he was reduced to the necessity of asking permission of the Virginia legislature to dispose of his estate by lottery ; while President Munroe, still more destitute, after having spent his patrimony in the service of the State, was constrained to implore the compassion of Congress ; and these are the men to whom their country owes the invaluable acquisitions of Louisiana and Florida. The system of retiring pensions is unknown in the United States. No provision is made for the old age of eminent men who accept the highest offices in the State, although it is impossible for them to lay up anything out of their comparatively moderate salaries, and several of them have seen their fortunes disappear with their health in the public service. The public functionaries are treated like menial servants ; the system of domestic life is such in the United States, that every American, in private life, treats the

humblest of his white domestics with more respect, than
most of them show, in public life, to officers of the highest
rank.   On every occasion and in a thousand forms, the
latter are reminded, that they are nothing but dust, and
that a frown of the people can annihilate them.

This treatment of their public officers by the Americans
is the mathematical consequence of the principle of popular sovereignty; but I consider it as consistent neither
with reason nor justice.   If it is true, that nations have
an imprescriptible right to regulate the conduct of the
depositaries of power conformably to their own interests,
it is equally true, that men of superior abilities and worth
have a natural and sacred right to be invested with high
powers and functions.   If it is criminal to sport with the
welfare of the mass, it is no less so to trample under foot
the wise and good.   And if those whom talents and zeal
for the public good call to important posts, are repulsed by
the prospect of ingratitude and contempt, to what hands
shall the care of the commonwealth be confided?   What
will then be the fate of the sovereign people?   There is
no less despotism in a people, who, impatient of all superiority, repays the services of illustrious citizens only with
neglect, and capriciously throws them aside, like so much
garbage, than in an Asiatic prince, who reduces all to the
same level of servitude, treats all with the same insolence
and brutality, and considers virtue and genius overpaid by
the honour of being permitted to kneel on the steps of his
throne.

In conformity with the prevailing ideas on the subject
of offices and officers, no sort of provision has been made
for the protection of the latter.   They are removeable
without any kind of pretence or formality, without being
informed of the ground of their removal, and without any
reason being given to the public.   In this way a terrible
rod of tyranny hangs over them, although under the mild

and moderate administration of former Presidents little use was made of it; but, since the accession of General Jackson, a regular system of removal from office has been sanctioned, and office has become the reward of party-services ; it has been publicly declared, that the *spoils of victory belong to the conquerors.* President Jackson has filled all the custom-houses and post offices with his creatures, and this policy has gained over some States, counties, and towns ; at every change of opinion, the State changes its executive officers; the legislators change their secretaries, printers, and even their messengers ; the courts, their clerks ; the towns, their treasurers, their inspectors of markets, weights and measures, and even their scavengers and watchmen. Men in office now understand, that the preservation of their places and the bread of their families are hazarded at every municipal, State, or Federal election, according as they hold of the town, State, or general government. Formerly they took no part in election manœuvres, the Presidents having expressly forbidden the officers of the Federal government to meddle with them ; at present, they are the most active agents in them. The President has now at his command an army of 60,000 voters,* dependent on his will, whose interests are bound up in his, and who are his forlorn hope. So true is it that extremes meet, and that, by pushing to excess a single principle, however true, we shall come to conclusions, which, practically speaking, amount to the overthrow of the principle itself. Thus by drawing out too fine the

---

* In a report on executive patronage lately made to the Senate by Mr Calhoun, the following statement of the number of persons employed by the Federal government is given :

Administrative and financial agents	12,144	Naval affairs 6,499
Military Service and Indian affairs	9,643	Post Office 31,917

Total   60,203

principle of the popular sovereignty, we may come nearer
and nearer to tyranny and the oppression of the people.
Is not this a proof that logic is not always reason, and
that truth is often, if not always, to be found in the harmonious combinations of seemingly contradictory principles?

LETTER XIX.

CINCINNATI.

NATCHEZ, (MISS.) JAN. 4, 1835.

CINCINNATI contains about 40,000 inhabitants, inclusive
of the adjoining villages; although founded 40 years ago,
its rapid growth dates only about 30 years back.   It seems
to be the rendezvous of all nations; the Germans and
Irish are very numerous, and there are some Alsacians;
I have often heard the harsh accents of the Rhenish French
in the streets.   But the bulk of the population, which
gives its tone to all the rest, is of New England origin.
What makes the progress of Cincinnati more surprising is,
that the city is the daughter of its own works.   Other
towns, which have sprung up in the United States in the
same rapid manner, have been built on shares, so to speak.
Lowell, for example, is an enterprise of Boston merchants,
who, after having raised the necessary funds, have collected
workmen and told them, "Build us a town."   Cincinnati
has been gradually extended and embellished, almost
wholly without foreign aid, by its inhabitants, who have
for the most part arrived on the spot poor.   The founders
of Cincinnati brought with them nothing but sharp-sighted,

wakeful, untiring industry, the only patrimony which they inherited from their New England fathers, and the other inhabitants have scrupulously followed their example and adopted their habits.   They seem to have chosen Franklin for their patron-saint, and to have adopted Poor Richard's maxims as a fifth gospel.

I have said that Cincinnati was admirably situated ; this is true in respect of its geographical position, but, if you follow the courses of the rivers on the map, and consider the natural resources of the district, you will find that there are several points on the long line of the rivers of the West as advantageously placed, both for trade and manufactures, and that there are some which are even more favoured in these respects.   Pittsburg, which has within reach both coal and iron, that is to say, the daily bread of industry, which stands at the head of the Ohio, at the starting point of steam-navigation, at the confluence of the Monongahela and the Alleghany, coming the one from the south and the other from the north ; Pittsburg, which is near the great chain of lakes, appears as the pivot of a vast system of roads, railroads, and canals, several of which are already completed.   Pittsburg was marked out by nature at once for a great manufacturing centre and a great mart of trade.   Louisville, built at the falls of the Ohio, at the head of navigation for the largest class of boats, is a natural medium between the commerce of the upper Ohio and that of the Mississippi and its tributaries. In respect to manufacturing resources, Louisville is as well provided as Cincinnati, and the latter, setting aside its enchanting situation, seemed destined merely to become the market of the fertile strip between the Great and Little Miami.

But the power of men, when they agree in willing anything and in willing it perseveringly, is sufficient to overbear and conquer that of nature.   In spite of the superior

advantages of Louisville as an *entrepôt*, in spite of the
manufacturing resources of Pittsburg, Cincinnati is able to
maintain a population twice that of Louisville and half as
large again as that of Pittsburg in a state of competence,
which equals, if it does not surpass, the average condition
of that of each of the others. The inhabitants of Cincinnati have fixed this prosperity among them, by one of those
instinctive views with which the sons of New England
are inspired by their eminently practical and calculating
genius. A half-word, they say, is enough for the wise,
but cleverer than the wisest, the Yankees understand each
other without speaking, and by a tacit consent direct their
common efforts toward the same point. To work Boston
fashion means, in the United States, to do anything with
perfect precision and without words. The object which
the Cincinnatians have had in view, almost from the origin
of their city, has been nothing less than to make it the
capital, or great interior mart of the West. The indirect
means which they have employed, have been to secure
the manufacture of certain articles, which, though of little
value separately considered, form an important aggregate
when taken together, and getting the start of their neighbours, with that spirit of diligence that characterises the
Yankees, they have accordingly distributed the manufacture of these articles among themselves. This plan has
succeeded.

Thus with the exception of the pork trade, one is surprised not to see any branch of industry carried on on the
great scale of the manufacturing towns of England and
France. The Cincinnatians make a variety of household
furniture and utensils, agricultural and mechanical implements and machines, wooden clocks, and a thousand
objects of daily use and consumption, soap, candles, paper,
leather, &c., for which there is an indefinite demand
throughout the flourishing and rapidly growing States of

the West, and also in the new States of the Southwest, which are wholly devoted to agriculture, and in which, on account of the existence of slavery, manufactures cannot be carried on.   Most of these articles are of ordinary quality; the furniture, for instance, is rarely such as would be approved by Parisian taste, but it is cheap and neat, just what is wanted in a new country, where, with the exception of a part of the South, there is a general ease and but little wealth, and where plenty and comfort are more generally known than the little luxuries of a more refined society.   The prosperity of Cincinnati, therefore, rests upon the sure basis of the prosperity of the West, upon the supply of articles of the first necessity to the bulk of the community; a much more solid foundation than the caprice of fashion, upon which, nevertheless, the branches of industry most in favour with us, depend. The intellectual also receives a share of attention; in the first place, there is a large type-foundery in Cincinnati, which supplies the demand of the whole West, and of that army of newspapers that is printed in it.   According to the usual English or American mode of proceeding, the place of human labour is supplied as much as possible by machinery, and I have seen several little contrivances here, that are not probably to be found in the establishments of the Royal Press or of the Didots.   Then the printing-presses are numerous, and they issue nothing but publications in general demand, such as school-books, and religious books, and newspapers.   By means of this variety of manufactures, which, taken separately appear of little consequence, Cincinnati has taken a stand, from which it will be very difficult to remove her, for, in this matter, priority of occupation is no trifling advantage.   The country trader, who keeps an assortment of everything vendible, is sure to find almost everything he wants in Cincinnati, and he, therefore, goes thither in preference to any other place in order to lay in his stock of goods. Cincinnati is thus in fact the great central mart of the West ; a great quantity and variety of produce and manufactured articles find a vent here, notwithstanding the natural superiority of several other sites, either in regard to the extent of water-communication or mineral resources.

M. Fourrier has characterised the spirit of the 19th century by the term *industrial feudalism.* The human race, according to some, has thrown off one yoke only to bear another, less burdensome perhaps, but also less noble. The warlike lords of the Middle Ages have passed away, but the industrial lords have come to take their place, the princes of manufactures, banks, and commerce. These new masters will embitter the life of the poor with less distress and privation, but they will also shed less glory upon it. They will increase the body's pittance, but diminish the soul's. At the sight of the great manufactories of England and some of those of the European continent, of those which are multiplying so rapidly in New England, in that wonderful creation the city of Lowell, one is tempted to think that the industrial feudalism is already established in the former, and is creeping beneath the democratic institutions, like the snake under the grass, in the latter. Those who do not believe that the human race can go backward, and who prefer to rock themselves in the cradle of hope, rather than to yield to flat despair, while they admit the existence of this tendency of the age, console themselves by the contemplation of its other characteristic features, at the head of which they place the general spirit of emancipation, which breaks down all obstacles in its way. If in England, for instance, there are, in the factories, a thousand germs of despotism, there are, in the working classes, a thousand germs of resistance, in the population a thousand germs of liberalism ; there are Trades' Unions, there are radicals : neither of these opposite forces alone will decide the destinies of the future. From their opposing impulses will result a single force, different from both, yet partaking of both. The force of emancipation will make what to some seems about to become feudalism, simply patronage.

Patronage has not finished its career upon the earth ; it will endure while Providence shall continue to cast men in different moulds ; it will subsist for the good of the weak and the poor, and for that of the class of men, so numerous in southern Europe, for example, who require the support of somebody more powerful than themselves. But it will be modified in character, growing successively less and less violent, and more and more mild. The inferior has been a slave, a serf, a paid freeman ; he may in time become an associate or partner without ceasing to be an inferior. However this may be, there is no germ of industrial feudalism in Cincinnati, there are no great factories or work-shops. Mechanical industry is subdivided there, pretty much as the soil is amongst us ; each head of a family, with his sons and some newly arrived emigrants as assistants and servants, has his domain in this great field. Cincinnati is, therefore, as republican in its industrial organisation, as in its political. This subdivision of manufactures has hitherto been attended with no inconvenience, because in the vast West, whose growth is visible to the eye, the production cannot at present keep pace with the consumption. But how will it be in a century, or perhaps in fifty years ? Will not the condition of mechanical industry undergo some great change, or rather will not the whole of this vast region undergo a complete change of character and condition, which will involve a reorganisation of the industrial system ?

The moral aspect of Cincinnati is delightful in the eyes of him who prefers work to every thing else, and with whom work can take the place of every thing else. But whoever has a taste for pleasure and display, whoever needs occasional relaxation from business, in gaiety and amusement, would find this beautiful city, with its picturesque environs, an insupportable residence. It would be still more so for a man of leisure, desirous of devoting a large part of his time to the cultivation of the fine arts and the rest to pleasure. For such a man, indeed, it would not be possible to live here ; he would find himself denounced irom political considerations, because men of leisure are looked upon in the United States as so many stepping-stones to aristocracy, and anathematised by religion, for the various sects, however much they may differ on other points, all agree in condemning pleasure, luxury, gallantry, the fine arts themselves. Now the United States are not like some countries in Europe, particularly France, where religion and the pulpit can be braved with impunity. Hemmed in by the laborious habits of the country, by political notions, and by religion, a man must either resign himself to the same mode of life with the mass, or seek a soil less unfriendly to his tastes in the great cities of New York, Philadelphia, or New Orleans, or even in Europe. There is, therefore, no such thing in Cincinnati as a class of men of leisure, living without any regular profession on their patrimony, or on the wealth acquired by their own enterprise in early life, although there are many persons of opulence, having one hundred thousand dollars and upwards. I met a young man there, the future heir of a large fortune, who, after having been educated at West Point and received a commission, had retired from the service in order to live at home. Wearied out with his solitary leisure, burdened with the weight of his own person, he could find no other relief than to open a fancy-goods shop.

Every where in the United States where there are no slaves, and out of the large towns of the sea-coast, a strict watch is kept up in regard to persons of leisure, obliging those who might be seduced by a taste for this kind of life to fall into the ranks and work, at least until age makes repose necessary. Public opinion is on the lookout to banish any habits of dissipation, however innocent, that might get a footing in society, and make a life of leisure tolerable. Religious and philanthropical societies, instituted under various names, take upon themselves the task of enforcing the decrees of public opinion ; like vigilant sentinels, they compel a rigid observance of the austerities, or if you choose the *ennuis*, of Sunday, labour to suppress intemperance and gaming, the spirit of which, if once diffused among a people so wholly devoted to money-making, might lead to the most fatal consequences. These societies and committees pursue their task with a more than British perseverance, and sometimes with a puritanical fanaticism. When Mr John Quincy Adams became President, he had a billiard-table placed in the President's House, and such is here the real or affected abhorrence of every thing called a game, that this billiard-table was actually one of the arguments against the re-election of Mr Adams. " It is a scandal, the abomination of desolation," was the general cry. Mr Adams, whose private character is above suspicion, was, if we must believe the Opposition journals of the day, a teacher of immorality, because he had a billiard-table in his house, and General Jackson has doubtless caused that scandalous piece of furniture to be broken up and burnt, since he has become master of the White House. Any where else this rigour would be called intolerance, inquisition ; here it is submitted to without a murmur, and few persons are really annoyed by it, or show that they are. The American can support a constant and unrelaxing devotion to labour ; he does not feel the need of amusement and recreation. The silence and retirement of his Sunday seem to be a more effectual relaxation for him, than the noisy gaiety of our festivals ; one might even say that he was destitute of the sense of pleasure. All his faculties and energies are admirably and vigorously combined for production ; he wants those without which pleasure is not enjoyment, and amusement is but a painful effort ; and, between these two kinds of work, he would of course prefer that which is gainful, to that which is expensive.

Such a social organisation is the very best for a pioneer people. Without this devotion to business, without this constant direction of the energies of the mind to useful enterprises, without this indifference to pleasure, without those political and religious notions which imperiously repress all passions but those whose objects are business, production, and gain, can any one suppose that the Americans would ever have achieved their great industrial conquests ? With any other less exclusive system, they would yet, perhaps, be meditating the passage over the Alleghanies. Instead of having that great domain of the West, immense in its extent and resources, already cleared and cultivated, furrowed with roads and dotted over with farms, they would probably be still confined to the sandy strip that borders the Atlantic. It must be allowed that this ardent and entire devotion to business gives the nation a strange aspect in the eyes of a European : And this explains the fact that the Americans have found so little favour with most foreigners who have visited their country. But, in return, they are sure of the gratitude of that innumerable posterity for whom they are preparing with such energy and sagacity an abode of plenty, a land of promise. This posterity, it is said, will change the habits of their fathers, will adopt new tastes, and even new institutions. So be it ! It is of little consequence whether the Americans of the 20th or 21st century, shall retain the national character, customs, and laws of the Americans of the 19th.

But the more interesting consideration is, whether the Americans of our day do not fulfil, as perfectly as human nature is capable of doing, the mission which Providence has entrusted to them, that of acting as a nation of pioneers and subduers of the forest; and if they do not deserve to be excused, like all nations and individuals, for having the defects inherent in their good qualities. The question thus stated will be easily answered by every one who sets any value on the interests and welfare of the future.

LETTER XX.

WESTERN STEAMBOATS.

NEW ORLEANS, JAN. 8, 1835.

ONE of the points in which modern society differs most from the ancient, is, certainly, the facility of travelling. Formerly it was possible only for a patrician to travel; it was necessary to be rich even to travel like a philosopher. Merchants moved in caravans, paying tribute to the Bedoweens of the desert, to the Tartars of the steppes, to the chieftains perched, like eagles, in castles built in the mountain passes. Instead of the English stage-coach, or the post-chaise, rattling at high speed over the paved road, they had the old Asiatic litter or palanquin, still preserved in Spanish America, or the camel, the ship of the desert, or four bullocks yoked to the slow wagon, or for the common citizens or the iron warriors, the horse; and instead of those sumptuous steam-packets, genuine floating palaces, the small and frail bark, pursued by robbers on the rivers

and by pirates by sea, the sight of which extorted from
the Epicurean Horace the exclamation of terror,

Illi robur et æs triplex—Circa pectus erat.

The roads were then rough and narrow paths, rendered
dangerous by the violence of men, or by the monsters of
the forest, or by precipices. A long train of luggage, provisions, servants, and guards, was necessary, and from time
to time the traveller reposed himself with some hereditary
friend of his family, for there were then no comfortable
hotels, in which he can now procure all he needs for
money, and command the attentive services of officious
attendants. If there were any place of shelter, it was
some filthy den, like the caravanserais of the East, wretched, naked, and comfortless, where he found nothing but
water and a roof, or like the inns of Spain and South
America, which are a happy mean between a caravanserai
and a stable. The great bulk of mankind, slaves in fact
and in name, were then attached to the glebe, chained to
the soil by the difficulty of locomotion.

To improve the means of communication, then, is to
promote a real, positive, and practical liberty; it is to extend to all the members of the human family the power
of traversing and turning to account the globe, which has
been given to them as their patrimony; it is to increase
the rights and privileges of the greatest number, as truly
and as amply as could be done by electoral laws; I go
further, it is to establish equality and democracy. The
effect of the most perfect system of transportation is to
reduce the distance not only between different places, but
between different classes. Where the rich and the great
travel only with a pompous retinue, while the poor man,
who goes to the next village, drags himself singly along
in mud and sand, over rocks and through thickets, the
word equality is a mockery and a falsehood, and aristocracy

stares you in the face. In India and China, in the Mahometan countries, in half-Arabian Spain and her former American colonies, it matters little whether the government is called republic, empire, or limited monarchy ; the peasant and the labourer cannot there persuade himself that he is the equal of the soldier, the brahmin, the mandarin, the pacha, or the noble, whose retinue runs over him, or covers him with mud. Spite of himself, he is filled with awe at its approach, and servilely bends before it as it passes him. In Great Britain, on the contrary, in spite of the wealth and the great privileges of the nobility, the mechanic and the labourer, who can go to the office and get a ticket for the railroad cars, if they have a few shillings in their pockets, and who have the right, if they will pay for it, of sitting in the same vehicle, on the same seat with the baronet or the peer and duke, feel their dignity as men, and touch, as it were, the fact, that there is not an impassable gulf between them and the nobility.

These considerations would make me slow to believe in the tyrannical projects of a government which should devote itself zealously to the task of opening roads through the country, and diminishing the time and expense of transportation. Is it not true that ideas, as well as goods, circulate along the great highways, the canals, and the rivers, and that every travelling clerk is more or less a missionary ? Those who are possessed with the retrograde spirit, are fully convinced of this fact ; they favour no projects of internal improvement ; they fear an engineer almost as much as they do a publisher of Voltaire. As it is undeniable that one of the first railroads in Europe was constructed in the Austrian empire, as the imperial government has opened many fine roads from one end of its possessions to the other, and as it is encouraging the introduction of steamboats on the Danube, I may venture to conclude that Von Metternich deserves a better reputation than he enjoys, on this side the Rhine. You know, on the other hand, that during the short ministry of M. de Labourdonnaye, in 1829, the surveys and plans of various roads in Vendée disappeared from the archives, and have never since been found. Only a few months ago, in Puebla, one of the free and sovereign States of the Mexican confederacy, which, however, enjoys a very high reputation for ignorance and bigotry, the representatives of the people, animated with a holy wrath against those ruthless unbelievers (mostly foreigners), who have pushed the sacrilegious spirit of innovation so far as to set up a line of stage-coaches betewen Vera Cruz and Mexico, and to repair the great road between the two cities, imposed an annual tax of 135,000 dollars upon them, and prohibited their taking any tolls within the limits of the State.

There is a region where, by simply perfecting the means of water-transportation, a revolution has been produced, the consequences of which on the balance of power in the New World are incalculable. It is the great Valley of the Mississippi, which had, indeed, been conquered from the wild beasts and Red Skins previous to the invention of Fulton, but which, without the labours of his genius, would never have been covered with rich and populous States. After the conquest of Canada had put an end to the brilliant but sterile exploits of the French on the Ohio and the Mississippi, the Anglo-Americans, then subjects of the king of Great Brirain, began to spread themselves over the Valley. The first settlers seated themselves in Kentucky, and occupied the soil for agricultural purposes. In a short time they had effaced from its surface the slight traces, which the French, almost exclusively engaged in hunting, had left of their passage. Instead of the little and restless, but indolent race produced by a cross of French with Indian blood, the new comers, avoiding all mixture with the natives, produced a laborious and energetic population, which, on this fertile soil, and like its natural productions, acquired those gigantic proportions, which characterise the Western-Virginian, the Kentuckian, and the Tennesseean, no less than the trees of their forests. Without ever laying aside their rifles, which forty years ago were carried to divine service in Cincinnati itself, they cleared and brought under the plough, the fertile tracts, which were converted into fine farms for themselves and their rapidly multiplying families. They had to pass days of terrour and distress, and in many an encounter with the Indians, from whom they conquered the wilderness, more than one husband, and more than one father, fell under the balls of the Red men, were dragged into the most wretched captivity, or underwent the horrid torments of the stake. The name of Blue Licks still sounds in the ears of Kentucky, like that of Waterloo in ours. Before the decisive victory of the Fallen Timber, gained by General Wayne, two American armies, under the command of Generals Harmer and Saint Clair, were successively defeated with great slaughter. The story of this long struggle between the whites and the Red men is still repeated in the bar-rooms of the West.

In 1811, although the formidable Tecumseh and his brother the Prophet, had not yet been conquered by General Harrison, the American had extended his undisputed empire over the most fertile districts of the West. Here and there villages had been built ; and the forest every where showed *clearings*, in the midst of which stood the log-house of some squatter or some more legal proprietor. On the left bank of the Ohio, Kentucky and Tennessee had been erected into States, and Western Virginia had been settled. A current of emigration had transported the industrious sons of New England upon the right bank of the river, and by their energy the State of Ohio had been founded, and already contained nearly 250,000 inhabitants. Indiana and Illinois, then mere Territories, gave fair promise of the future. The treaty of 1803 had added to the Union our Louisiana, in which one State and several Territories, with a total population of 160,000 souls had already been organised. The whole West, at that time, had a population of nearly a million and a half: Pittsburg and Cincinnati were considerable towns. The West had, then, made a rapid progress, but separated as it was from the Gulf of Mexico by the circuitous windings and the gloomy swamps of the Mississippi, from the eastern cities by the seven or eight ridges that form the Alleghany Mountains, destitute of outlets and markets, its further progress seemed to be arrested. The embryo could grow but slowly and painfully, for want of the proper channels through which the sources of life might circulate.

At present, routes of communication have been made or are making from all sides, connecting the rivers of the West with the Eastern coast, on which stand the great marts, Boston, New York, Philadelphia, Baltimore, Richmond, and Charleston. At that time, there was not one which was practicable through the whole year, and there was not capital enough to undertake one. All the commerce of the West was carried on by the Ohio and the Mississippi, which is, indeed, still, and, probably, always will be, the most economical route for bulky objects. The western boatmen descended the rivers with their corn and salt-meat in flat boats, like the Seine coal-boats; the goods of Europe and the produce of the Antilles, were slowly transported up the rivers by the aid of the oar and the sail, the voyage consuming at the least one hundred days, and sometimes two hundred. One hundred days is nearly the length of a voyage from New York by the Cape of Good Hope to Canton; in the same space of time France was twice conquered, once by the allies and once by Napoleon. The commerce of the West, was, therefore, necessarily very limited, and the inhabitants, separated from the rest of the world, had all the rudeness of the forest. It was in this period and this state of manners, that the popular saying, which describes the Kentuckian as half horse, half alligator, had its origin. The number of boats, which made the voyage up and down once a year, did not exceed ten, measuring on an average about 100 tons; other small boats, averaging about 30 tons measurement, carried on the trade between different points on the rivers, beside which there were numerous flat boats, which did not make a return voyage. Freight from New Orleans to Louisville or Cincinnati was six, seven, and even nine cents a pound. At present the passage from Louisville to New Orleans is made in about 8 or 9 days, and the return voyage in 10 or 12, and freight is often less than half a cent a pound from the latter to the former.

In 1811, the first steamboat in the West, built by Fulton, started from Pittsburg for New Orleans; it bore the name of the latter city. But such are the difficulties in the navigation of the Ohio and Mississippi, and such was the imperfection of the first boats, that it was nearly six years before a steamboat ascended from New Orleans, and then not to Pittsburg, but to Louisville, 600 miles below it. The first voyage was made in twentyfive days, and it caused a great stir in the West; a public dinner was given to Captain Shreve, who had solved the problem. Then and not before, was the revolution completed in the condition of the West, and the hundred-day boats were supplanted. In 1818, the number of steamboats was 20, making an aggregate of 3,642 tons; in 1819 the whole number that had been built was 40, of which 33 were still running; in 1821, there were 72 in actual service. In that year the Car of Commerce, Captain Pierce, made the passage from New Orleans to Shawneetown, a little below Louisville, in 10 days. In 1825, after fourteen years of trials and experiments, the proper proportion between the machinery and the boats was finally settled (See *Note* 21). In 1827, the Tecumseh ascended from New Orleans to Louisville in eight days and two hours. In 1829, the number of boats was 200, with a total tonnage of 35,000 tons; in 1832, there were 220 boats making an aggregage of 40,000 tons, and at present there are 240, measuring 64,000 tons. According to statements made to me by experienced and well-informed persons, the whole amount of merchandise annually transported by them between New Orleans and the upper country, is at least 140,000 tons. The trade between the basins of the Ohio, the Tennessee, and the Upper Mississippi, not included in this amount, forms another considerable mass. To have an idea of the whole extent of the commerce on the western waters, we must also add from 160,000 to 180,000 tons of provisions and various objects, which go down in flat-boats. This amount is, indeed, enormous, and yet it is probably but a trifle compared with what will be transported on the rivers of the West in 20 years from this time ; for on the Erie canal, which, compared with the Mississippi is a line of but secondary importance, and at a single point, Utica, 420,000 tons passed in a period of seven months and a half.

Such is the influence of routes of communication on which cheapness is combined with dispatch.* In Mexico, where nature has done so much, and where, in return, man has done so little, in those countries where natural resources are, perhaps, tenfold greater than those of the United States, but where man is a hundred fold less active

---

* Freight on our canals is only about half as high as in the United States ; but this advantage is counterbalanced by the excessive slowness of our movements.

and industrious, transportation is effected wholly on the backs of mules or men, even in the plain country. The annual amount of the transportation from Vera Cruz, the principal port, to Mexico, the capital of the country, does not, therefore, amount to 6,000 tons, and the descending freight is much less. The western steamboats look very much like the Vigier baths on the Seine; they are huge houses of two stories.* Two large chimneys of columnar form vomit forth torrents of smoke and thousands of sparks; from a third a whitish cloud breaks forth with a loud noise; this is the steam-pipe. In the interior they have that coquettish air that characterises American vessels in general; the cabins are showily furnished, and make a very pretty appearance. The little green blinds and the snugly fitted windows, pleasingly contrasting with the white walls, would have made Jean-Jacques sigh with envy.

The more ordinary capacity is from 200 to 300 tons, but many of them measure from 500 to 600; their length varies from 100 to 150 feet. Notwithstanding their dimensions and the elegance with which they are fitted up, they cost but little, the largest boats being built for about 40,000 dollars, including their engines and furniture.† A very nice boat 100 feet long, of the legal measurement of 100 tons but carrying 150, only costs from 7,000 to 8,000 dollars. It is estimated that the large boats cost about 100 dollars a ton, legal measurement, and the small ones, 80 dollars. But if these elegant craft cost little, they do not

---

* The Homer, a noted boat built by Mr Beckwith of Louisville, one of the most skilful builders in the West, has a third story.

† A boat of the same dimensions would cost nearly 100,000 dollars in France; this is owing to the low price of the timber, the coarseness of the steam-engines, which, on account of the cheapness of fuel, there would be no advantage in making with more nicety, and the skill of the mechanics; the Americans excel in working in wood.

last long ; whatever care is taken in the choice of materials and for the preservation ef the boat, it is rare that they wear more than four or five years. An old captain, lately giving me an account of a boat about the construction of which he had taken great pains, told me, with a deep sigh, that "she died at three years." The magnificent vegetation of the West, those thrifty, tall, straight trees, by the side of which our European oaks would appear like dwarfs, growing rapidly on the thick layer of soil deposited by the great rivers of the West in the diluvian period of geologists, last just in proportion to the time occupied by their growth. And in this case, as in regard to human glory and the splendour of empires, the rule holds good, that time respects only what he has himself founded.

The number of passengers which these boats carry, is very considerable ; they are almost always crowded, although there are some which have two hundred beds. I have myself been in one of these boats which could accommodate only 30 cabin passengers, with 72. A river voyage was formerly equivalent to an Argonautic expedition, at present it is one of the easiest things in the world. The rate of fare is low ; you go from Pittsburg to New Orleans for 50 dollars, all found, and from Louisville to New Orleans for 25 dollars. It is still lower for the boatmen; who run down the river in flat boats and return by the steamers ; there are sometimes 500 or 600 of them in a separate part of the boat, where they have a shelter, a berth, and fire, and pay from 4 to 6 dollars for the passage from New Orleans to Louisville ; they are, however, obliged to help take in wood. The rapidity with which these men return, has contributed not a little to the extension of the commerce of the West ; they can now make three or four trips a year instead of one, an important consideration in a country where there is a deficiency of hands. On the downward voyage, their place is occupied by horses and cattle, which are sent to the South for sale, and by slaves, human cattle destined to enrich the soil of the South with their sweat, to supply the loss of hands on the sugar plantations of Louisiana, or to make the fortune of some cotton planters. Virginia is the principal seat of this traffic, "the native land of Washington, Jefferson and Madison, having become," as one of her sons sorrowfully observed to me, "the Guinea of the United States."

Excellent as these boats are, great as is the service they render America, when the first feeling of curiosity is once satisfied, a long confinement in one of them has little that is attractive for a person of a cultivated mind and refined manners. There are few Europeans of the polished classes of society, and even few Americans of the higher class in the Eastern cities, who, on escaping from one of these floating barracks, would not feel disposed, under the first impulse of ill humour, to attest the correctness of Mrs Trollope's views of western society. There is in the West a real equality, not merely an equality to talk about, an equality on paper; everybody that has on a decent coat is a gentleman; every gentleman is as good as any other, and does not conceive that he should incommode himself to oblige his equal. He is occupied entirely with himself, and cares nothing for others; he expects no attention from his neighbour, and does not suspect that his neighbour can desire any from him. In this rudeness, however, there is not a grain of malice; there is on the contrary an appearance of good humour that disarms you. The man of the West is rude, but not sullen or quarrelsome. He is sensitive, proud of himself, proud of his country, and he is so to excess, but without silliness or affectation. Remove the veil of vanity in which he wraps himself, and you will find him ready to oblige you and even generous. He is a great calculator, and yet he is not cold, and he is capable of enthusiasm. He loves money passionately, yet he

is not avaricious; he is often prodigal. He is rough because he has not had time to soften his voice, and cultivate
the graces of manner. But if he appears ill-bred, it is not
from choice, for he aspires to be considered a man of breed-
ing; but he has been obliged to occupy himself much
more with the cultivation of the earth, than of himself.
It is perfectly natural that the first generation in the West
should bear the impress of the severe labours it has so
energetically and perseveringly pursued. If these reflections, however, are consoling for the future, they cannot
give to a life aboard the Ohio and Mississippi steamboats any
charms for him who sets value on amiable and engaging
manners.

Besides, the voyage on the Mississippi is more dangerous
than a passage across the ocean; I do not mean merely
from the United States to Europe, but from Europe to
China. In the former, you are exposed to the risk of explosions, and of fire, and in ascending, to that of running
against snags and planters. Then there is the danger of
your boat falling afoul of another, running in an opposite
direction, in a fog, to say nothing of the inconvenience of
getting aground on sand-bars. Add to these things the
monotonous aspect of the country on the river, the solitude of its flat and muddy banks, the filthy appearance of
its yellow and turbid waters, the strange habits of most of
the travellers crowded into the same cage with yourself,
and you may conceive, that, in course of time, such a
situation becomes extremely unpleasant. The Louisiana
planters, therefore, who go North in the hot season in
search of a fresher and purer air than that of New Orleans,
make their annual migrations by sea, aboard the fine
packet-ships, which run regularly between that city and
New York. Explosions of the boilers are frequent, either
on account of the ignorance and want of skill of the engineers, or on account of the defective nature of the boilers

themselves, and they are always attended with serious injury, because the boats are so much crowded with passengers. A few days ago, sixty persons were killed and wounded aboard a single boat, but these accidents do not occur in well managed boats, in which no unseasonable economy has been practised in the purchase of the machinery and the wages of the engineers.* Some law containing provisions similar to those in force in France, is required here, but in order to be practicable, it should be made to apply to the whole Valley, which would only be the case with an act of Congress. Public opinion, however, would not permit Congress to meddle with the matter, and the cry of Federal encroachment on State rights would be raised at once. One State only, Louisiana, has passed a law on the subject, but it is very defective, and I do not suppose that it is enforced. Preventive measures are what is wanted, inspection of the machinery and licensing of competent engineers, while the law of Louisiana only provides for the punishment of the captain on board whose boat an accident happens, with a special penalty in case he should be engaged in any game of hazard, at the time of the accident.

There have been many accidents by fire in the steamers, and many persons have perished in this way, although the river is not very wide. The Brandywine was burnt near Memphis, in 1832, and every soul on board, to the number of 110, was lost. The Americans show a singular indifference in regard to fires, not only in the steamboats, but also in their houses; they smoke without the least concern in the midst of the half open cotton-bales, with which a boat is loaded; they ship gunpowder with no more precaution than if it were so much maize or salt pork, and

---

* A good engineer gets about 100 dollars a month in the large boats, and there are two to a boat. In France the wages of the same man would be from 20 to 25 dollars a month.

leave objects packed up in straw right in the torrent of sparks that issue from the chimneys. The accidents caused by the trunks of trees in the bed of the river, called logs, snags, sawyers, or planters, according to their position, have been very numerous ; attempts have been made to prevent this class of disasters, by strengthening the bows, and by bulk-heads which double the hull in that part. The Federal government has two snag-boats, constructed with great ingenuity, which are employed in removing these obstructions from the rivers, but the bordering States, whose taxes are very light, have contributed nothing towards these objects. The machinery of the Heliopolis and Archimedes, contrived by Captain Shreve, has done much toward clearing the channel, but there is still much to be done.

The chances of accident might be diminished in various ways, by well-directed measures, and at a moderate expense. The character of the river is now well understood, and there are many engineers in the United States, who can manage the Great Father of Waters. Unluckily the Federal government, which does not know what to do with its money, (for it has now on hand a surplus of eleven millions,) is checked by a doctrine with which, one cannot tell why, the democratic party have become possessed, and which forbids the general government from engaging in public works within the limits of the individual States. Thus, although the whole Union is interested in the improvement of the navigation of the western rivers, the Federal government does not venture to undertake it with energy and on a liberal scale. General Jackson's predecessor, Mr Adams, was a warm friend to the action of the government in internal improvements. He thought, like Mr Clay and other men of superior abilities, that the progress of the young States of the West would be very much accelerated, to the advantage of the whole Union, if the central government would undertake to execute, in whole or in part, a system of public works of general interest. But one of the watchwords of the opponents of Mr Adams was, *No Internal Improvements!* and the very States which would have been most immediately benefited by it, rallied to this cry. So utterly can party spirit blind the most clear-sighted of men !

If accidents of so serious a nature succeeded each other with such frequency in Europe, there would be a general outcry. The police and the legislative power would vie with each other in their efforts to put a stop to them. Steamboats would become the terror of travellers, the public would abandon them, and they would be left deserted on the rivers. The effect would be the same, in a degree, around the large eastern cities, because society there is beginning to be regularly organised, and a man's life counts for something. In the West, the flood of emigrants, descending from the Alleghanies, rolls swelling and eddying over the plains, sweeping before it the Indian, the buffalo, and the bear. At its approach the gigantic forests bow themselves before it, as the dry grass of the prairies disappears before the flames. It is for civilisation, what the hosts of Ghengis Khan and Attila were for barbarism ; it is an invading army, and its law is the law of armies. The mass is everything, the individual nothing. Wo to him who trips and falls ! he is trampled down and crushed under foot. Wo to him who finds himself on the edge of a precipice ! The impatient crowd, eager to push forward, throngs him, forces him over, and he is at once forgotten, without even a half-suppressed sigh for his funeral oration. *Help yourself!* is the watchword. The life of the genuine American is the soldier's life ; like the soldier he is encamped, and that, in a flying camp, here to-day, fifteen hundred miles off in a month. It is a life of vigilance and strong excitement ; as in a camp, quarrels are settled

in the west, summarily and on the spot, by a duel fought
with rifles, or knives, or with pistols at arm's length.
It is a life of sudden vicissitudes, of successes and reverses ; destitute to-day, rich to-morrow, and poor the day
after, the individual is blown about with every wind of
speculation, but the country goes on increasing in wealth
and resources.   Like the soldier, the American of the
West takes for his motto, *Victory or death !* But to him, victory is to make money, to get the dollars, to make a fortune out of nothing, to buy *lots* at Chicago, Cleveland, or
St. Louis, and sell them a year afterward at an advance
of 1000 per cent. ; to carry cotton to New Orleans when
it is worth 20 cents a pound.   So much the worse for the
conquered ; so much the worse for those who perish in the
steamboats !   The essential point is not to save some individuals or even some hundreds ; but, in respect to steamers, that they should be numerous ; staunch or not, well
commanded or not, it matters little, if they move at a
rapid rate, and are navigated at little expense.   The circulation of steamboats is as necessary to the West, as that
of the blood is to the human ·system.   The West will
beware of checking and fettering it by regulations and
restrictions of any sort.   The time is not yet come, but it
will come hereafter.

　There are certain feelings in the human heart that must
show themselves in some form or another, and if repressed
in one point, will break out in another.   Respect for the
depositaries of authority, which until the time of our revolution, had so firmly eemented European society together,
has constantly been on the wane on this side of the
Atlantic, and in the West is totally obscured.   There the
authorities, for so they are called, have as little power as
pay ; there are governors who govern nothing, judges who
are very liable to be brought to judgment themselves.
The chief magistrate is pompously styled in the constitu-

tions of these new States commander-in-chief of the army
and navy of the State.   Pure mockery ! for it is at the
same time provided, except in time of war; and even in
time of peace, he has hardly the power of appointing a
corporal.   Yet the feeling of discipline and obedience
subsists, and it is instinctively transferred to those men
who are in fact the generals of the great migration.   If
little concern is felt in regard to the Governor of the State,
every body is docile and obedient to the innkeeper, the
driver of the coach, and the captain of the steamboat ;
with them no one ventures to maintain the principles of
self-government.   All rise, breakfast, dine, sup, when the
landlord or his lieutenant-general, the bar-keeper, thinks
fit to ring the bell, or beat the gong ; it is just as it is in a
camp.   They eat what is placed before them, without
ever allowing themselves to make any remark about it.
They stop at the pleasure of the driver and the captain,
without showing the least symptom of impatience ; they
allow themselves to be overturned and their ribs to be
broken by the one, they suffer themselves to be drowned
or burnt up by the other, without uttering a complaint or
a reproach ; the discipline is even more complete than in
the camp.   It has been said that the life of founders of
empires, from the times of Romulus to that of the buca-
neers, consists of a mixture of absolute independence and
passive obedience.   The society which is now founding
itself in the West, has not escaped the common law.

This part of the United States, which was a mere wilderness at the time of the Declaration of Independence,
and on which no one spent a thought, when the capital
was fixed at Washington, will be the most powerful of
the three great sections of the Union, at the taking of
the next census.   Before long, it will singly be superior
to the two others taken together, it will have the majority
in Congress, it will govern the New World.   Already

the old division into North and South is becoming of
secondary moment, and the great division of the Union
will soon be into the East and the West; the present
President is a man of the West. The democratic party
have just held a convention at Baltimore to agree upon the
selection of candidates for the next presidential election.
Mr Van Buren, who is from the East, has been chosen,
but although he had the unanimous vote of the convention, he seems about to find a formidable competitor in the
bosom of his own party, in the person of Mr White of
Tennessee. On the subject of the Vice-Presidency there
was an animated debate in the convention itself; some
proposed Mr Rives from the South, others Mr Johnson
from the West. Mr Rives passes for a man in every respect superior to his antagonist, his diplomatic services have
been highly esteemed by his countrymen. Mr Johnson
is honest, indeed, but there is great doubt, or rather there
is no doubt at all, about his abilities. The only claim set
up by his friends is, a *strong suspicion* that he killed
the celebrated Indian chief Tecumseh, in the battle of the
Thames. But then Mr Johnson is from the West, and
he has been preferred to his rival, even at the risk of
offending Virginia, whose influence in the South is
acknowledged to be commanding. Mr Van Buren has
yielded to this arrangement or probably he has concerted
it, because he would rather risk the loss of the South than
of the West. This, then, the West is already become ;
and when we reflect that the only visible instrument of
this progress is the steamboat, we shall not wonder that
the whole political system of some men is comprised in
physical improvements, and the interests connected with
them.

LETTER XXI.

INTERCOMMUNICATION.

BUFFALO, (N. Y.) JULY 9, 1835.

THE territory of the United States consists; 1. of the two great inland basins of the Mississippi and the St. Lawrence, which run, the former from north to south towards the Gulf of Mexico, the latter from south to north toward the gulf to which it gives its own name : 2. on the eastern side, of a group of smaller basins, which empty their waters into the Atlantic ocean, and of which the principal are those of the rivers Connecticut, Hudson, Delaware, Susquehanna, Potomac, James, Roanoke, Santee, Savannah, and Alatamaha. The Alleghany Mountains, which, from their lying in the direction of the length of the continent, are called the back-bone of the United States, form a natural water-shed, dividing the great inland basins from the eastern group of small basins. On the west, the valleys of the St. Lawrence and Mississippi are bounded by the Mexican Cordilleras, which here take the name of Rocky Mountains. At the foot of this chain spreads out a wide desert, bare of vegetation, and which, excepting some oases, can never, it is said, be peopled by man.

Almost the whole English-American population is as yet on the left of the Mississippi. On the right bank there is only one State, and that one of the least important of the confederacy, and one Territory, that of Arkansas, which will soon become one of the members of the Union.*

---

* Arkansas became a State in 1836. [It is a strange oversight of the author to say, that Missouri is the only State west of the Mississippi, when

The Alleghany chain does not reach a great height ; being hardly as lofty as the Vosges, while the Rocky Mountains exceed in elevation the Pyrenees and even the Alps.

The Alleghany system, although of no great height, rises from a very wide base, of which the breadth is nearly 150 miles by an air-line. Viewed as a whole, it consists of a number of cavities separated by as many ridges or crests, and stretching with great uniformity, nearly from one end of the chain to the other, from the shores of New England, where the mountains are washed by the sea, to the Gulf of Mexico, in the neighbourhood of which they gradually sink down. These alternations of the ridges and cavities form a series of parallel furrows, which may be traced on the surface, with some breaks, through a distance of 1200 or 1500 miles. The geological formations are arranged very nearly in conformity with these furrows, through great distances ; there are, however, exceptions from this rule, for sometimes the same layer is seen to pass from one furrow to another, always cutting the former at a very acute angle.

Notwithstanding this general character of regularity, these cavities are not hydrographical basins or river valleys. But the rivers, instead of hollowing out beds between two successive ridges, and thus passing off to the sea, frequently pass from one furrow to another, breaking through the weak points of the ridges. These openings or gaps, as they are here called, are highly useful as routes for roads, canals, and railroads, enabling the engineer, by

nearly the whole of Louisiana is on its right bank. Neither is it correct to say, that Missouri is one of the least important States. In point of territorial extent, geographical position, agricultural resources, and mineral wealth, she is one of the most important, and even in point of population, which is increasing with great rapidity, is little behind many of her sisters. The Territory of Iowa, established in 1837, on the north of Missouri, has now about 30,000 inhabitants, and is rapidly filling with settlers.—TRANSL.]

following the course of the rivers, to flank heights, which it would have been almost impossible to top. Of all these openings the most interesting is that made by the Potomac through the Blue Ridge, at Harper's Ferry, which Jefferson, in his Virginian enthusiasm, said was worth a voyage across the Atlantic.

The United States may then be divided hydrographically into two distinct regions, the one to the east, the other to the west, of the Alleghanies; or into three, as under: 1. the Mississippi valley: 2. the valley of the St. Lawrence with the great lakes: 3. the Atlantic coast. This vast country may also be divided into the North and the South, and it has two commercial capitals, New York and New Orleans, which are, as it were, the two lungs of this great body, the two galvanic poles of the system. Between these two divisions, the North and the South, there are radical differences, both in a political and an industrial point of view. The social frame in the South is founded on slavery; in the North, on universal suffrage. The South is a great cotton-plantation, yielding also some subsidiary articles, such as tobacco, sugar, and rice. The North acts as factor or agent for the South, selling the productions of the latter, and furnishing her in return with those of Europe; as a sailor, carrying her cotton beyond sea; as an artisan, making all her household utensils and farming tools, her cotton-gins, her sugar-mills, her furniture, wearing apparel, and all other articles of daily use, and finding her also in corn and salted provisions.

From these views it appears that the great public works in the United States must have the following objects: 1. To connect the Atlantic coast-region with the region beyond the Alleghanies; that is, to unite the rivers of the former, such as the Hudson, the Susquehanna, the Potomac, the James, or its bays, such as the Delaware and the Chesapeake, either with the Mississippi or its tributary the

Ohio, or with the St. Lawrence, or the great lakes Erie and Ontario, whose waters are carried by the St. Lawrence to the Ocean : 2. To form communications between the Mississippi Valley and that of the St. Lawrence, that is, between one of the great tributaries of the Mississippi, such as the Ohio, the Illinois, or the Wabash, and Lake Erie or Lake Michigan, which, of all the great lakes of the St. Lawrence basin, reach the furthest southwards. 3. To connect together the northern and southern poles of the Union, New York and New Orleans.

Independently of these three new systems of public works, which are in fact, in progress, and even in part completed, there are numerous secondary lines, intended to make the access to the centres of consumption more easy, or to open outlets from certain centres of production, whence arise two new classes of works ; the one including the various canals and railroads, which, starting from the great cities as centres, radiate from them in all directions, and the other, comprising the similar works executed for the transportation of coal from the coal-regions.

Sect. I. Lines Extending Across the Alleghanies.

The works which have hitherto almost wholly occupied, and still chiefly occupy, the attention of statesmen and business men in the United States, are those designed to form communications between the East and the West. There are on the Atlantic coast four principal towns, which long strove with each other for the supremacy ; namely, Boston, New York, Philadelphia, and Baltimore. All four aimed to secure the command of the commerce of the new States which are springing up in the fertile regions of the West ; and they have sustained the struggle with different degrees of success, but always with a rare spirit of intelligence. They have not, however, been equally favoured in respect to natural advantages. Boston is too far north ; she has no river which permits her to stretch her arms far toward the West, and she is surrounded by a hilly country, which throws great obstacles in the way of rapid communication, and makes all works designed to promote it expensive. Philadelphia and Baltimore are shut up by ice almost every winter, and this obstruction is, on the part of the latter,* a drawback from the other advantages of her position, her greater nearness to the Ohio, her more central latitude, and the beauty of her bay, which is above 250 miles in length, and receives numberless streams, as the Susquehanna, Potomac, Patuxent, Rappahannock, &c. Philadelphia is badly placed ; Penn was led astray by the beauty of the Schuylkill and the Delaware ; he thought that the broad plain spread out between their waters to the width of nearly three miles, would afford an admirable site for a city, whose streets should be run with regularity, and whose warehouses, easy of access, would permit thousands of vessels to load and unload at once. He forgot to secure for his city a great hyurographical basin, capable of consuming the merchandise which it should import, and of sending it in return the products of its own labour, and he neglected to make an examination of the Delaware, which he took for a great river, but which, unluckily is not so. If he had founded the city of Brotherly Love on the banks of the Susquehanna, it might have maintained a long struggle against New York.

New York is, then, the queen of the Atlantic coast. This city stands on a long, narrow island, between two rivers (the North River and the East River) ; ships of any burden and in any numbers may lie at the wharves ; the harbour is very rarely closed by ice ; it can be entered by small vessels with all winds, and by the largest ships at

---

* This difficulty is almost wholly, if not quite, remedied by ice-boats.

all times except when the wind is from the northwest.
New York has beside the invaluable advantage of standing upon a river for which some great flood has dug out a
bed through the primitive mountains, uniformly deep,
without rocks, without rapids, almost without a slope, and
cutting through the most solid mass of the Alleghanies at
right angles.   The tide, slight as it is on this coast, flows
up the Hudson to Troy, 160 miles from its mouth ; and
such is the nature of its bed, that whale-ships are fitted
out at Poughkeepsie and Hudson, of which the former is
75 and the latter 116 miles above New York, and that,
except in the lowest stage of the water, vessels of 9 feet
draft can go up to Albany and Troy, in any tide.

New York possesses in addition great advantages in respect to the character of its population.   Originally a Dutch
colony, conquered by the English, and lying in the neigh-
borhood of New England, she presents a mixture of the
solid qualities of the Saxon race, of the Dutch phlegm,
and the enterprising shrewdness of the Puritans.   This
mixed breed understands admirably how to turn to account all the advantages which nature has bestowed on
the city.

Hardly was the war of independence at an end, when
the great men whose patriotism and courage had brought
it to a happy close, filled with ideas of the wealth yet
buried in the bosom of the then uninhabited West, began to
form plans for rendering it accessible by canals.   If it is
true, that Prussia, in the time of Voltaire, resembled two
garters stretched out over Germany, the United States in
the time of Washington and Franklin, and it is only fifty
years since, might be likened to a narrow riband thrown
upon the sandy shore of the Atlantic.   Washington at
that time projected the canal which has since been begun
according to the plans of Gen. Bernard, and which seeks
the West by following up the Potomac ; but from want of

capital and experienced engineers, what in our day has become a long and fine canal, was then merely a series of side-cuts around the Little Falls and Great Falls of the Potomac. At the same time, the Pennsylvanians made some unsuccessful efforts and spent considerable sums, in ineffectual attempts to render the Schuylkill navigable, and to connect it with the Susquehanna. In the State of New York, some short cuts, some locks and sluices, were then the only prelude to greater schemes.* The works undertaken at that time and during the fifteen first years of the present century could not be completed, or failed in the expected results. One work only was successfully executed, the Middlesex Canal, which extends from Boston to the River Merrimack at Chelmsford, a distance of 27 miles.†

The war of 1812 found the United States without canals, and almost without good roads ; their only means of intercourse were the sea, their bays, and the rivers that flow into them. Once blockaded by the English fleets, not only could they hold no communication with Europe and India, but they could not keep up an intercourse among themselves, between State and State, and between city and city, between New York and Philadelphia for instance. Their commerce was annihilated, and the sources of their capital dried up. Bankruptcy smote them like a destroying angel, sparing not a family.

First Line. Erie Canal.

The lesson was hard, but it was not lost. The Ameri-

---

* In 1792 the New York legislature incorporated two companies, the Western and the Northern Inland Lock Navigation companies, which, however, did nothing of importance, the former with authority to connect the Hudson by the Mohawk with Seneca Lake and Lake Ontario, the latter to form a junction between the Hudson and Lake Champlain.

† By Mr Baldwin, father of the late Loammi Baldwin, who constructed the dry docks at Charlestown and Gosport.

cans, to do them justice, know how to profit by the teach-
ings of Providence, especially if they pay dear for them.
The project of a canal between New York and Lake Erie,
which had already been discussed before the war, was
eagerly taken up again after the peace. De Witt Clinton,
a statesman whose memory will be ever hallowed in the
United States, succeeded in inspiring his countrymen with
his own noble confidence in his country's great destiny,
and the first stroke of the spade was made on the 4th of
July, 1817. In spite of the evil forebodings of men distinguished for their sagacity and public services; in spite
of the opinion of the venerated patriarch of democracy,
of Jefferson himself, who declared it necessary to wait a
century longer before undertaking such a work; in spite
of the remonstrances of the illustrious Madison, who wrote
that it would be an act of folly on the part of the State
of New York to attempt, with its own resources only, the
execution of a work for which all the wealth of the Union
would be insufficient; notwithstanding all opposition,
this State, which did not then contain a population of
1,300,000 inhabitants, began a canal 428 miles in length,
and in eight years it had completed it at a cost of 8,400,000
dollars. Since that time it has continued to add numerous branches, covering almost every part of the State, as
with net-work. In 1836, the State had completed 656
miles of canal including slack-water navigation, at the
expense of 11,962,712. dollars, or 18,235 dollars per
mile.*

The results of this work have surpassed all expectations; it opened an outlet for the fertile districts of the

---

* The official statements of the Canal Board, Feb. 23, 1837, are here given
instead of those of M. Chevalier. The statement in the text does not include the Black River Canal and the Genesee Valley Canal, begun in 1837,
with a total length of 168 miles, exclusive of 40 miles of improved navigation in the Black River; estimated cost, 3,000,000 dollars.—TRANSL.

western part of the State, which had before been cut off
from a communication with the sea and the rest of the
world. The shores of Lake Erie and Ontario were at
once covered with fine farms and flourishing towns. The
stillness of the old forest was broken by the axe of New
York and New England settlers, to the head of Lake
Michigan. The State of Ohio, which is washed by Lake
Erie, and which had hitherto had no connection with
the sea except by the long southern route down the Mississippi, had now a short and easy communication with
the Atlantic by way of New York. The territory of Michigan was peopled, and it now contains 100,000 inhabitants,
and will soon take its rank among the States.* The transportation on the Erie Canal exceeded 400,000 tons in 1834,
and it must nearly reach 500,000 tons in 1835. The annual
amount of tolls from the canals, and at moderate rates, is
about one million and a half dollars. The population of
the city of New York increased in the ten years, from
1820 to 1830, 80,000 souls.† New York is become the
third, if not the second port in the world, and the most
populous city of the western hemisphere. The illustrious
Clinton lived long enough to see the success of his plans,
but not to receive the brilliant reward which the gratitude
of his countrymen intended for him. He died, February
11, 1828, at the age of 59 years, and but for this premature death, he would probably have been chosen President
of the United States.

The Erie Canal is no longer sufficient for the commerce
which throngs it. In vain do the lock-masters attend
night and day to the signal horn of the boatmen, and per-

---

* Michigan became a State in 1837, at which time it had a population of
175,000 souls.—TRANSL.

† The increase of the population has since been at a still more rapid rate ;
from 1830 to 1835, the number of inhabitants increased from 203,000 to
270,000, or including Brooklyn, from 218,000 to 294,000.—TRANSL.

form the process of locking with a quickness that puts to shame the slowness of our own ; there is no longer room enough in the canal, whose dimensions however are rather limited.* The impatience of commerce, with whom time is money, is not satisfied with a rate of speed about four-fold that which is common on our canals. Merchandise of all sorts, as well as travellers, flows in at every point in such quantities, that railroads have been constructed along the borders of the canal, to rival the packet-boats in the transportation of passengers only. There is one from Albany to Schenectady, 15 miles in length, which, though not well built, cost about 550,000 dollars. A second, which will be finished in 1836, runs from Schenectady to Utica, and is 78 miles in length.† A third railroad is in progress from Rochester to Buffalo by way of Batavia and Attica, about 80 miles in length, and it is probable that before long the line will be completed from one end of the canal to the other.‡

A still greater undertaking is already in train ; a company was chartered in 1832, which will begin next spring the construction of a railroad from New York city to Lake Erie, through the southern counties of the State ; on account of the circuitous route made necessary by the uneven nature of the ground, the length of this road will

---

* It is 40 feet wide on the surface and 4 feet deep ; the locks are 95 feet long and 15 wide. The Languedoc Canal is 90 feet wide, and 6 1-2 feet deep, with locks 115 feet long, 36 feet wide in the centre, and 18 at each end. The English Canals are generally of about the dimensions of the Erie Canal.

† The legislature incorporated the company on the express condition that they should transport only travellers and their baggage. Notwithstanding this provision, when the books were opened, seven times the amount of capital needed was subscribed ; the sum required was 2,000,000 dollars; the amount of subscriptions 14,000,000.

‡ Several links in this chain between Auburn and Utica on one side, and Rochester on the other, are already completed.—Transl.

be about 340 miles.* Meanwhile the Canal Commissioners have not slept ; in July, the Canal Board, in compliance with an act of the Legislature, directed the construction of a double set of lift locks on the whole line, in order that there may be as little delay as possible in the passage of boats, and the enlargement of the canal so that the width shall be 70 feet and the depth 6 feet, with a corresponding increase in the dimension of the locks ; larger boats may then be used the speed may be increased, and perhaps it will be practicable to use steam tow-boats. The cost of this work is estimated at about 12,500,000 dollars.

Finally, to make herself more entirely mistress of the commerce of the West, and to penetrate her own territory more completely, the State of New York is about to commence a new branch of the Erie canal (if we may call a work of which the entire length will be 120 miles, a branch), which will form an immediate connection with the River Ohio. This canal is to run from Rochester, the flourishing city of millers, following up the course of the Genesee, with a rise of 979 feet to the summit level, and a fall of 78 feet thence to Olean, on the River Alleghany, 270 miles from its junction with the Monongahela at Pittsburg. The main canal from Rochester to Olean is only 107 miles in length, but there is a branch to Danville. The Alleghany, in its natural state, is navigable only during a few months in the year ; the total distance from New York to Pittsburg by this route is 800 miles.

When there could no longer be a doubt of the speedy completion of the Erie Canal, Philadelphia and Baltimore

---

* In the session of 1836, the legislature authorised a loan of the credit of the State for the sum of 3,000,000 dollars to the company ; the estimated cost of the road is 6,000,000. This road terminates at Tappan Sloat on the Hudson.

felt that New York was going to become the capital of
the Union. The spirit of competition aroused in them a
spirit of enterprise. They wished also to have their
routes to the West ; but both had great natural obstacles
to overcome. By means of the Hudson, which had
forced a passage through the heart of the mountains, New
York was freed from the greatest difficulty in the way of
effecting a communication between the East and the
West, that of topping the crest of the Alleghanies. Between Albany, where the Erie canal begins, and Buffalo,
where it meets the lake, there are no high mountains.
Baltimore could not look for a similar service to the
Patapsco, nor Philadelphia to the Delaware ; neither of
these cities can approach the west by the basin of the
great lakes, unless by a very circuitous route ; they are
too far off. It became necessary for them, therefore, to
climb the loftiest heights, and thence to descend to the
level of the Ohio with their works.

Second Line. Pennsylvania Canal.

What is called the Pennsylvania canal is a long line of
400 miles, starting from Philadelphia, and ending at Pittsburg on the Ohio. It was begun simultaneously with
several other works, at the expense of the state of Pennsylvania, in 1826. It is not entirely a canal; from Philadelphia a railroad 81 miles in length, extends to the
Susquehanna at Columbia. To the Columbia railroad,
succeeds a canal, 172 miles in length, which ascends the
Susquehanna and the Juniata to the foot of the mountains
at Holidaysburg. Thence the Portage railroad passes
over the mountain to Johnstown, a distance of 37 miles,
by means of several inclined planes constructed on a
grand scale, with an inclination sometimes exceeding one
tenth, which does not, however, deter travellers from going

over them.* From Johnstown a second canal goes to Pittsburg, 104 miles. This route is subject to the inconvenience of three transhipments, one at Columbia at the end of the railroad from Philadelphia, and the others at the ends of the Portage railroad, one of these may be avoided by means of two canals constructed by incorporated companies, namely, the Schuylkill canal, which extends up the river of that name, and the Union canal, which forms a junction between the upper Schuylkill and the Susquehanna. The distance from Philadelphia to Pittsburg by this route is 435 miles, or 35 miles more than by the other route.

The Pennsylvania canal, begun in 1826, was finished in 1834. The State has connected with this work a general system of canalization, which embraces all the principal rivers, and especially the Susquehanna, with its two great branches (the North Branch and the West Branch), and also works preparatory to a canal connecting Pittsburg with Lake Erie, at Erie, a town founded by our Canadian countrymen, and by them called Presqu'île. Pennsylvania has executed, then, in all about 820 miles of canals and railroads, of which 118 are railroads, at a cost of about 25,000,000 dollars, exclusive of sums paid for interest. Average cost per mile, 35,000 dollars ; average cost per mile, of canals, 32,500 ; average cost per mile of railroads, 48,000.

This is much more than the cost of the New York works, although the dimensions of the works are the same, and the natural difficulties were not greater in one case than in the other ; it is owing to bad management in

---

* The maximum of inclination allowed by our *Administration des Ponts-et-Chaussées* (board of public works) is $\frac{1}{200}$; in the great lines executed at the expense of government, the inclination has generally been kept below $\frac{1}{333}$, which is the maximum adopted in the fine railroad from London to Birmingham.

Pennsylvania.   The Pennsylvanians had no Clinton to guide them.   An unwise economy, forced upon the Canal Commissioners by the legislature, prevented them from securing the services of able engineers, and for the sake of saving some thousands of dollars in salaries, they have been obliged to spend millions in repairing what was badly done, or in doing badly what more able hands would have executed well at less cost.

THIRD LINE. BALTIMORE AND OHIO RAILROAD.

Still less than Philadelphia, could Baltimore think of a continuous canal to the Ohio.   Wishing to avoid the transhipments which are necessary on the Pennsylvania line, the Baltimoreans decided on the construction of a railroad extending from their city to Pittsburg or Wheeling, the whole length of which would be about 360 miles.   It is now finished as far as Harper's Ferry on the Potomac, a distance of 80 miles, and the company seem to have given up the design of carrying it further.   It will here be connected with the Chesapeake and Ohio Canal, of which I shall speak below, as the Columbia railroad is connected with the Pennsylvania canal.   It is probable, that, on approaching the crest of the Alleghanies, the canal will in turn give away to a railroad across the mountains, and thus the Maryland works will be similar to the Pennsylvania line.*

* In 1836 the Maryland legislature voted the sum of 8,000,000 dollars in aid of public works, of which 3,000,000 were appropriated to the Baltimore and Ohio railroad, and 3,000,000 to the Chesapeake and Ohio Canal, and rest is divided between several works, one of which is intended to connect Annapolis, the capital, with the Potomac. Baltimore has also subscribed 3,000,000 dollars towards aiding the completion of the railroad. [Virginia and Wheeling have also subscribed 1,000,000 each for the same object, and so far from being come to a stand, the Baltimore and Ohio railroad is now pushed on with great vigour towards Cumberland.—TRANSL.]

FOURTH LINE. CHESAPEAKE AND OHIO CANAL.

The plan, which had been cherished by Washington, of making a lateral canal along the Potomac which should one day be extended across the mountains to the Ohio, was resumed when New York had taught the country that it was now ripe for the boldest enterprises of this kind. John Quincy Adams, then President of the United States, favoured the project with all his might. At that time it was not a settled principle, that the Federal government had no right to engage in internal improvements. The old idea, which Washington had cherished, of making the political capital of the Union a great city, was not less to the taste of Mr Adams and his friends. It was, therefore, resolved to undertake the Chesapeake and Ohio Canal, and a company was incorporated for this purpose. Congress voted a subscription of 1,000,000 dollars; the city of Washington without commerce, without manufactures, with its population of 16,000 souls, subscribed the same sum; the other little cities of the Federal District, Georgetown and Alexandria, having both together a population of about 10,000, furnished a half million; Virginia contributed 250,000, and Maryland 500,000 dollars; and 600,000 dollars were raised by individual subscriptions. The work was begun July 4, 1828. Next year, by aid of a loan of 3,000,000 from Maryland, this great work will be carried to the coal-beds of Cumberland at the foot of the mountains; the length of this division is 185 miles, the estimated cost 8,500,000 dollars, or 46,000 dollars per mile. The execution is on a bold scale, and superior to that of the works before-mentioned; its dimensions exceed those generally adopted in the proportion of 3 to 2, which gives a larger section in the ratio of 9 to 4.

FIFTH LINE. JAMES RIVER AND KANAWHA COMMUNICATION.

Virginia, formerly the first State in the confederacy, but now fallen to the fourth in rank, and already outstripped by Ohio, which was not in being during the war of Independence, is at length roused to action, and has determined to profit by the lessons, which have come to her from the North. A company, whose means consist of little more than the subscriptions of the State and of the capital, Richmond, is about to open a canal from the East to the West. James River, which flows into Chesapeake Bay, is navigable for vessels of 200 tons to the foot of the table-land, on which Richmond stands in so charming a situation. On the east of the mountains, the canal, starting from Richmond, will follow the course of James River, and on the West it will descend the Kanawha, one of the tributaries of the Ohio, to Charleston, at the head of steamboat navigation. The Alleghany crest will be passed by a railroad, 150 miles in length ; the canal itself will be about 250 miles long.

South Carolina, stirred up by the example of Virginia, is engaged in a great railroad from Charleston to Cincinnati on the Ohio ; and the surveys are at present actively going on. The people of Cincinnati are enthusiastically interested in this scheme.* Georgia is also dreaming of a great railroad from the Savannah to the Mississippi, at Memphis ; but this project has not assumed a substantial

---

* In 1836, the construction of this road has been authorised by the legis latures of Kentucky, Tennessee, North Carolina, and South Carolina. The surveys have been completed, the route fixed upon, and a board organised for pushing the work with vigour. Mr Hayne, late a Senator in Congress, and since governor of South Carolina, and one of the most highly respected men in the country, is president. Including the two branches, one to Louisville, and one to Maysville, the whole length of the road will be 700 miles ; the estimated cost is 11,870,000 dollars.

shape. North Carolina does nothing, and projects nothing. If she ever becomes rich, it will not be because she has seized fortune by the forelock, but because fortune has come to her bedside.*

Sixth Line. Richelieu Canal.

The Canadians are constructing a canal which will form another communication between the East and the West, that is, between the Hudson and the St. Lawrence, between New York and Quebec. The great fissure, which forms so fine a bed for the Hudson between New York and Troy, does not end here, but stretches on towards the north to the St. Lawrence, constituting the basin of Lake Champlain, which is a long and narrow cavity in the midst of the mountains, and the bed of the River Richelieu. Between Lake Champlain and the Hudson, there is only a ridge 54 feet above the level of the former, and 134 above that of the latter. The River Richelieu, which issues from the northern end of the lake and flows into the St Lawrence, is broken by rapids, and a lateral canal, 12 miles in length, and of sufficient dimensions to receive

---

* [Two great works are now actively pushed on in Georgia, which will form another connection between the Mississippi Valley and the Atlantic ; these are the Central railroad from Savannah to Decatur, 285 miles, and the Georgia railroad from Augusta to the same place, 160 miles in length ; the Main Trunk of the Atlantic and Western railroad is the common continuation of these two roads from Decatur to the Tennessee, a distance of 120 miles. These works are already in a state of forwardness, and a third, the Brunswick and Florida railroad, now under survey, will extend from Brunswick to the head of the Appalachicola, and connect the southernmost part of the western valley with the Atlantic. In North Carolina, beside the Raleigh and Gaston railroad, the railroad from the Roanoke to Wilmington is now nearly completed. As steam-packets run from Wilmington to Charleston, and the Chattahoochee is already connected with Montgomery, which stands at the head of steamboat navigation on the Alabama, the continuation of the Central railroad from Decatur to the Chattahoochee, a distance of 80 miles, is all that is wanted to complete the communication between Boston and New Orleans by railroads and steamboats.—TRANSL.]

the lake-craft, will be opened here in the course of a year; the cost will be 350,000 dollars ; the distance from New York to Quebec by the canals, rivers, and lakes, is 540 miles. The railroad from St. John, where the rapids of the Richelieu begin, to Laprairie, on the St. Lawrence, opposite to Montreal, a distance of 16 miles, effects for Montreal what the canal does for Quebec ; it cost about 160,000 dollars, or 10,500 dollars per mile. The distance from Montreal to New York is 360 miles.

SECTION II. LINES OF COMMUNICATION BETWEEN THE MISSISSIPPI VALLEY AND THAT OF THE ST. LAWRENCE.

There is no mountain chain between these two valleys ; the basin of the great lakes, whose united waters form the St. Lawrence, is separated from the valley of the Mississippi only by a spur of the Alleghany system, not exceeding 450 feet in height, and sinking rapidly down toward the west, so as to be elevated but a few feet above the surface of Lake Michigan. During the rainy season, when the streams are swollen and the marshes of the water-shed are flooded, our Canadian countrymen were wont to pass in boats from Lake Michigan into the Illinois, by the Des Plaines. The breadth of this dividing spur is more considerable than its height. It is not a ridge or crest, but rather a table-land, which imperceptibly merges by gentle slopes into the plains that surround it. Its level summit is filled with marshes, and therefore offers great facilities for feeding the canals which traverse it; further west, where it is scarcely higher than the rest of the country, it is often as dry as the surrounding prairies.

FIRST LINE. OHIO CANAL.

Only one work connecting the two valleys is as yet completed, this is the Ohio canal, which traverses that State from North to South, extending from Portsmouth, on the Ohio, to the little city of Cleaveland, which has sprung up on the shore of the lake since the canal was made. It is 334 miles in length, and cost nearly 4,500,000 dollars, or about 13,500 dollars per mile. This is low, yet the locks are all of hewn stone ; the ground, however, was very favorable. The work was executed at the expense of the State, and was undertaken at the same time that Pennsylvania and Baltimore, on the traces of New York, started in the course of internal improvements. This young State, with a population of farmers, not having a single engineer within her limits, and none of whose citizens had ever seen any other canal than those of New York, has thus, with the aid of some second rate engineers borrowed from that State, constructed a canal longer than any in France, with more skill and intelligence than was displayed by Pennsylvania, in spite of the scientific lights of Philadelphia. This farming population of Ohio, almost wholly of New England origin, has a business instinct, a practical shrewdness, and a readiness to exercise all trades without having learned them, that would be sought in vain in the Anglo-German population of Pennsylvania. The legislators, under whose direction the public works were executed in both States, were, as is usual in the United States, a perfect copy of the mass of their constituents, with all its good and bad qualities. The Ohio canal commissioners added to a noble disinterestedness an admirable good sense, and to them is due the greater part of the glory of having planned and executed it. They were farmers and lawyers, who set themselves about making canals, naturally, easily, and without even a suspicion that in Europe no one dares to undertake such a work without long preparation and scientific studies. Now it is no longer an art in that State to plan and construct canals, but a mere trade ; the science of canalling is there become quite an affair of the common people. The first-comer in a bar-room will explain to you, over his glass of whiskey, how to feed the summit level and how to construct a lock. All our mysteries in civil engineering are here fallen into the hands of the public, very much as the methods of descriptive geometry are to be found in the workshops, where they had been handed down by tradition, ages before Monge gave them the sanction of theory.

I have before said that Ohio, Indiana, and Illinois form a great triangle, wholly comprised within the Mississippi valley, with the exception of a narrow strip along the lakes, belonging, of course, to the St. Lawrence basin. The general slope of the surface is from north to south ; the streams run mostly in that direction ; this is especially true of the great tributaries of the Ohio. This arrangement of the secondary valleys is no less favourable to the construction of canals between the lakes, on the one side, and the Ohio and Mississippi on the other, than the configuration and humidity of the dividing table-land.

Second Line. Miami Canal.

Ohio has constructed another canal, which, starting from Cincinnati on the Ohio, runs north to Dayton, and is called the Miami canal. It is 65 miles in length, and cost nearly 1,000,000 dollars, or 15,400 dollars a mile. By the aid of a grant of land from Congress, and the State's resources, its prolongation is now in progress to Defiance, on the river Maumee, the site of a fortress of that name built by Gen. Wayne after his celebrated victory over the Indians. The Maumee, which was called by the French the Miami of the Lakes, is one of the principal tributaries of Lake Erie, and is to be canalled by the State. The distance from Dayton to Defiance is 125 miles ; estimated cost 2,750,000 dollars, or 22,000 dollars per mile.

Third Line. Wabash and Erie Canal.

Ohio and Indiana, with the aid of a grant of land* from Congress, have undertaken in concert a canal, which will connect the Wabash, one of the tributaries of the Ohio, with the Maumee. The greater part of the canal will be parallel to the two rivers, or in their beds; the length of the whole work will be 382 miles, of which 195 are in Indiana, and 87 in Ohio. The greater portion of the Indiana section lateral to the Wabash has been completed, but Ohio has not yet been able to commence her portion, because, owing to an absurd system of establishing boundaries, the mouth of the Maumee, whose whole course is in Ohio, will fall within Michigan.† Ohio protests against this arrangement, Michigan stands firm to her claims; both sides have voted the sums needful for war, and both have taken arms; hostilities have even been begun, but the interference of the Federal government has led the parties to consent to an armistice. In this quarrel, Ohio has reason on her side, but Michigan appeals to the letter of the laws as favourable to her. It is probable that in creating Michigan a State, Congress will attach this strip to Ohio, to whom it is so important.‡ In this unsettled

---

* These grants of land are generally made so that every other section (of six miles square) along the line of the work is retained by Congress, and the rest are given to the State or company constructing the canal. Sometimes, however, a certain number of acres in some other quarter is granted outright.

† No one can look at a map of the United States without being struck by the appearance of the right lines, constituting the frontiers of most of the States; this method of bounding a territory by meridians and parallels of latitude is absurd, since it requires an infinite number of geodesic operations, which have not been executed, and cannot be so for a long time. Meridians and parallels do very well for the divisions of the heavens; but for the earth, there are no suitable boundaries but the beds of rivers, or water-sheds in the mountain chains.

‡ By the act establishing the State of Michigan (1836), Congress has annexed this disputed belt to Ohio. [The whole line of this great work is now nearly completed.—Transl.]

state of things, Ohio has suspended the execution of her part of a work, which will give new importance to the mouth of the Maumee.

Fourth Line. Illinois and Michigan Canal.

The project of a canal from the Chicago, at the southern end of Lake Michigan, to the head of steam navigation, that is, to the foot of the falls, in the River Illinois, has long been discussed. It is said to be of very easy construction; and that by means of a cut of the maximum depth of 26 feet, the summit level can be reduced to the level of Lake Michigan, so that the lake can be used as a feeder. It will be 96 miles in length, and will traverse a level or slightly undulating country, bare of trees, and still known by the name given it by the French Canadians, *Prairie.* It is proposed to construct this canal of larger dimensions than is common in the United States, so as to make it navigable by the lake-craft and steamboats. It is one of the most useful works ever undertaken in the world.*

Fifth Line. Western Pennsylvania Canal.

The canal which has been commenced by Pennsylvania between the Ohio and the town of Erie, 112 miles in length, and for feeding which extensive works have already been constructed around Lake Conneaut, will make another and a short line of water communication between the basins of the Mississippi and the St. Lawrence.

---

* The work was begun on the canal, July 4, 1836; it is six feet deep, and 60 feet wide at top; estimated cost 8,654,300 dollars. [The progress of population in that region within the last two years has given rise to new and very important projects. One of these is a canal connecting the Rock River with Lake Michigan, at Milwaukie, and the other is the junction of the Wisconsin with the Fox River of Green Bay, thus adding two links to the chain of communication between the Mississippi and St. Lawrence valleys. —Transl.]

Different Lines.

Lastly, two canals are about to be undertaken, which will connect the Pennsylvania works with those of Ohio, and of consequence, form new connections between the Mississippi and the St. Lawrence. One of these is the Sandy and Beaver canal, which, beginning at the confluence of the Big Beaver with the Ohio, follows the latter to the mouth of the Little Beaver, ascends the valley of this stream, and passes down that of the Sandy River to the Ohio canal at Bolivar; the length will be 90 miles. From Bolivar to New York by the Ohio canal, Lake Erie, Erie canal, and the Hudson, the distance is 785 miles; by the new canal the distance from Bolivar to Philadelphia, that is, to the ocean, is only 512. The Mahoning canal leaves the Ohio canal at Akron, following the valleys of the Little Cuyahoga, the Mahoning, a tributary of the Big Beaver, and the Big Beaver, to the Ohio; it is about 90 miles in length; the distance from Akron to the river Ohio is 115 miles.

The generally level character of the surface of Ohio, Indiana, and Illinois is not less favourable to the construction of railroads than to that of canals. But as capital is scarce in this new country, which is as yet but imperfectly brought under cultivation, but few enterprises of much importance have hitherto been undertaken. The financial companies and institutions, which have always preceded the introduction of canals and railroads, have, however, been already established and are prosperous, and their success is the omen of the approach of the latter. In the absence of companies, the States are ready to adopt the most extensive schemes of public works; for the American of the West is not a whit behind the American of the East in enterprise. At present, I know of but a single railroad actually in process of construction beyond the

Ohio, and that does not seem to be pushed forward with much activity ; it is the° Mad River railroad, which is to extend from Dayton, on the Miami canal, to Sandusky, on the bay of that name in Lake Erie ; the length will be 153 miles.   Many others have been projected in this region, and Indiana has caused surveys to be made for a railroad extending across the State from north to south, or from New Albany on the Ohio to some point on Lake Michigan.*

WORKS FOR IMPROVING THE NAVIGATION OF THE OHIO, MISSISSIPPI, AND ST. LAWRENCE.

To this head belong the works executed in the beds of the rivers themselves.   The Mississippi is the *beau idéal* of rivers in regard to navigable facilities.   From St. Louis to New Orleans, a distance of nearly 1200 miles, there is

---

* In 1836, the legislature of Indiana adopted a general system of public works, for the execution of which it authorised a loan of 10,000,000 dollars. The system embraces the canalisation of the Wabash and White River, the connection of the Wabash with the Maumee, and of Lake Michigan with the same river by canals, and a canal across the centre of the State from Evansville by Indianapolis to the Wabash and Erie canal. Appropriations were made by the same law for railroads from Madison and Jeffersonville on the Ohio to the Wabash canal, and in aid of the Lawrenceburg and Indianapolis railroad which has been undertaken by a company. [The State of Illinois has also made provision for a series of public works on an equally liberal scale ; an act of 1837 establishes a Board of Public Works and an Internal Improvement Fund, and provides for the construction of a railroad across the State from north to south, reaching from the junction of the Ohio and Mississippi by Vandalia and Peru to Galena, being about 460 miles in length ; of four roads crossing the State from east to west, namely, from Shawneetown on the Ohio to Alton on the Mississippi, from Mt. Carmel on the Wabash to Alton, from Terre Haute on the Wabash to Alton, and from Covington on the Wabash to Quincy on the Mississippi, and of another cross road from Bloomington, in the centre of the State to Warsaw on the Mississippi. These works are now in active progress, as are also some works for improving the navigation of the Illinois, Rock River, Kaskaskia and Little Wabash. The youthful State of Michigan has followed the example of these elder sisters, by establishing a Board of Public

water enough for steamers of 300 tons throughout the year. Its yellow and muddy waters flow in a deep, although very circuitous channel, and its general breadth is from 800 to 1,000 yards, in places where it is not expanded to a much greater width by low, flat islands, thickly covered with trees. There are no sand-banks in this part of the channel, yet there are formidable dangers in the way of the inexperienced navigator; these are the trunks of trees, that have been carried away from the banks, as has been before mentioned, and in the removal of which the Federal government keeps steam *snag-boats*, the Heliopolis and Archimedes, employed; these boats are provided with a peculiar machinery by means of which they drag the trees up from the bed, and saw them into pieces of an inconsiderable length.

Captain Shreves, who has the command of these boats, and who invented the machinery, is also employed in constructing sunk dams of loose stones in the Ohio, which have the effect of increasing the depth of water in the dry season. He is at present engaged with a flotilla of steamboats in opening the bed of Red River, one of the great tributaries of the Mississippi, which the drift timber has choaked up and covered over through a distance of 165 miles.* At Louisville, the Ohio, whose bed has generally a very slight inclination, has a descent of 22 feet in the distance of two miles, so as to be impassable for steam-

Works, and directing the construction of three railroads across the peninsula, from Monroe, Detroit, and Huron to Lake Michigan, and a canal from the river Saginaw of Lake Huron to the Grand River of Lake Michigan. There are also several railroads executed by companies in Michigan.— TRANSL.]

* [This work was completed in the spring of 1838, at which time several steamboats passed wholly through the place formerly occupied by the raft. The removal of that obstruction, has extended the navigation by steamboats 750 miles on the Red River, exclusive of 600 miles on several branches.— TRANSL.]

boats, except during the season of high water. The Louisville and Portland canal has been constructed by a company to avoid this obstruction; it is nearly one mile and three fourths in length, and cost 750,000 dollars.* It receives the largest boats at a rate of toll which for the Henry Clay amounts to 175 dollars, and for the Uncle Sam 190 dollars. It has been proposed that Congress should buy this canal, and make the passage toll-free; and the importance of the navigation of the Ohio would justify the measure.

The St. Lawrence differs essentially from the Mississippi; instead of an expanse of muddy waters, it presents to the eye a clear blue surface. The Mississippi traverses a low, uninhabited, and uninhabitable region, of which the soil consists entirely of sand, or rather of mud deposited by the river-floods; not a stone as large as the fist is to be found, and only a few bluff points are met with which are above the reach of high water, and on which the pale inhabitants struggle unsuccessfully with the pestilential emanations of the surrounding swamps. The St. Lawrence flows through a broken, hilly, and sometimes rugged country, with a fertile soil, everywhere healthful, sprinkled with flourishing villages, which attract the eye of the traveller from a distance by their houses newly white-washed every year, and their churches built in the French style with their spires covered with tin. The Mississippi, like the Nile, has its annual overflow, or rather it has two in each year, but the spring-floods are much the most considerable. The St. Lawrence, owing to the vast extent of the lakes which serve as a reservoir and feeder to it, always preserves the same level, the extreme range of its rise and fall being only about 20 inches. The St. Lawrence, from

---

* It is 50 feet wide at bottom and 200 feet at top, and has four locks, 170 feet long by 50 wide.

the beauty of its waters, from their prodigious volume, from the country which it waters, and from the groups of isles scattered over it, would be one of the first rivers in the world in the eyes of the artist, but in those of the merchant, it is of quite a secondary importance. Its transparent waters hardly hide the numerous rocks; the navigation is interrupted first by the Falls of Niagara, and after it leaves Lake Ontario by numerous rapids, cataracts, or rocks between that lake and Montreal, and none but an Indian or a French Canadian, would dare to descend these points in that portion of the river in a canoe; at several points, the most powerful steamer would be unable to make head against the current.

The spirit of emulation which has prevailed among the States of the Union, has extended to the British Provinces, to the English population, which, leaving the lower part of the river to the French, has occupied Upper Canada. The inhabitants of this Province have embraced the opinion, that if the chain of communication which is broken by the cataracts and rapids, could be made whole, much of the produce, which now finds its way to the Mississippi, or to the Pennsylvania and New York canals, would seek a more convenient vent by the St. Lawrence, and that the British manufactures would take the same route up the river, through the ports of Quebec and Montreal, to the Western States. One canal has, therefore, already been executed around the falls of the Niagara, which forms a communication between Lakes Erie and Ontario; the Welland canal is 28 miles in length, exclusive of 20 miles of slack-water navigation. It is navigable by lake-craft of 120 tons, and has cost 2,000,000 dollars, nearly the whole of which was furnished by the upper Province, Lower Canada and the mother country having contributed a very trifling sum.

Since that work has been completed, the river below

Lake Ontario has been surveyed, and it has been found that the aggregate length of the points not passable by steamboats of ten feet draft is only 30 miles, pretty equally divided between the two provinces. Upper Canada, which contains hardly 250,000 inhabitants, with no large towns and with little capital, has begun her portion of the work along the rapids within her limits. This work will be large enough to admit the passage of steamboats drawing nine feet water, and of the burden of 500 tons. I saw the labourers at work along the Long Saut Rapids at Cornwall, where there will be a cut of 13 miles in length ; the estimated cost of this section is 1,250,000 dollars. The French population of Lower Canada, swallowed up in political quarrels, the result of which cannot be foreseen, neglects its essential interests in pursuit of the imaginary interests of national pride. It has done nothing towards continuing, within its limits, the great work, which has been begun by the poorer province of Upper Canada.

Sect. III. Lines of Communication along the Atlantic.

First Line. Inland Channels by the Sounds and Bays along the Atlantic.

Upon examining the coast of the United States from Boston to Florida, it will be seen that there is almost a continuous line of inland navigation, extending from north-east to southwest in a direction parallel to that of the coast, formed, in the north by a series of bays and rivers, and in the south, by a number of long sounds, or by the narrow passes between the mainland and the chain of low islands that lie in front of the former. The necks of land that separate these bays, rivers, and lagoons, are all flat and of inconsiderable breadth. From Providence (42 miles south of Boston) to New York are Narragansett Bay and Long Island Sound, together 180 miles in length.

Thence to reach to the Delaware you go to New Brunswick at the head of the Raritan Bay, where you encounter the New Jersey isthmus, a level tract, not more than 40 feet above the level of the sea, or than 35 to 40 miles in width. This neck is now cut across by the Raritan and Delaware Canal, a fine work, navigable by the small coasting craft, and 43 miles in length, exclusive of a navigable feeder 24 miles, all lately executed by a company, in less than three years, at a cost of about 2,500,000 dollars.*

This canal terminates at Bordentown, on the Delaware. Hence the navigation is continued to Delaware City, 70 miles below Bordentown, and 40 below Philadelphia. There, the isthmus which divides the Delaware from the Chesapeake, is cut through by a canal, of which the summit level is only 12 feet above the surface of the sea ; this is the Chesapeake and Delaware canal, like the last mentioned of dimensions suited to coasting vessels. The cost was very great, about 2,600,000 dollars ; length 13 1-2 miles. Having entered the Chesapeake, the voyage may be continued to Norfolk about 200 miles. Thence, to the series of sounds and inland channels on the coast of North Carolina, South Carolina, and Georgia, extends the Dismal Swamp Canal, whose length is 20 miles, and whose summit level is only 10 feet above the level of the sea ; this is also adapted for coasting vessels. The works intended to continue the navigation beyond the sounds connected with the Dismal Swamp canal, have not been completed, and to the south of the Chesapeake the line is, therefore, imperfect ; but steamboats run from Charleston to Savannah, by the channels and lagoons between the mainland and the low islands which yield the famous long-staple cotton.

---

* It is from 65 to 75 feet wide at top, and 7 feet deep. The locks are well constructed, and very expeditiously worked.

SECOND LINE. COMMUNICATION BETWEEN THE NORTH AND SOUTH
BY THE MARITIME CAPITALS.

Parallel to the preceding line which is designed for the
transportation of bulky articles, is another further inland
for the use of travellers, and the lighter and more valuable
merchandise, on which steam is becoming the only motive
power, both by land and by water; by land on railways,
and by water in steamboats. You go from Boston to
Providence by a railroad, 42 miles in length, which cost
1,500,000 dollars, or 33,000 dollars a mile. From Providence to New York, passengers are carried by the steamboats in from 14 to 18 hours; some boats have made the
passage in 12 hours. In passing from Narragansett Bay
to the Sound, it is necessary to double Point Judith, where
there is commonly a rough sea, to avoid which a railway
is now in progress from Providence to Stonington, a distance of 47 miles. A third railroad, of which the utility
seems questionable (since the boats in the Sound move at
the rate of 15 miles an hour), is projected from a point on
Long Island opposite Stonington to Brooklyn, a distance
of 88 miles.

Between New York and Philadelphia, you go by steamboat to South Amboy on Raritan Bay, 28 miles, whence
a railroad extends across the peninsula to Bordentown,
and down along the Delaware to Camden, opposite Philadelphia. In summer a steamboat is taken at Bordentown,
but in winter the Delaware is frozen over, and the railway is then used through the whole distance to transport
the crowd that is always going and coming between the
commercial and financial capitals of the United States,
between the great mart and the exchange of the Union,
between the North and the South. An ice-boat lands the
traveller in Philadelphia, a few minutes after he has left
the cars at Camden. This railroad is 61 miles in length,
and cost 2,300,000 dollars, or 38,000 dollars a mile. It

has but one track most of the way. I met many persons at Philadelphia, who remembered having been two, and sometimes three long days on the road to New York; it is now an affair of seven hours, which will soon be reduced to six. Two railroads belonging to a different group, of which one is completed, and the other nearly so, will form, with the exception of an interval of several miles, a second line across the peninsula, from New York to Philadelphia. The one extends from Philadelphia to Trenton, 26 miles; the other from Jersey City, opposite New York to New Brunswick, 30 miles; if, therefore, rails were laid between New Brunswick and Trenton, a distance of 28 miles, over a perfectly level plain, the land communication between New York and Philadelphia would be complete; but the State of New Jersey has hitherto refused to authorise this connection, because it received a considerable sum from the Camden and Amboy company for the monopoly of the travel.*

From Philadelphia to Baltimore, the route is continued by a steamboat to Newcastle, and a railroad from thence to Frenchtown, across the peninsula, 16 1-4 miles long, whence another steamboat takes the traveller to Baltimore, in 8 or 9 hours after starting from Philadelphia. The Newcastle and Frenchtown railroad cost 400,000 dollars, or 24,500 dollars a mile. The navigation of the Chesapeake and Delaware is sometimes interrupted by ice, and it has, therefore, been thought that it would be useful to have a continuous railroad from Philadelphia; there would also be a saving of time, for the present route is somewhat circuitous. Different companies have undertaken different portions of this work, which will pass by Wilmington and Havre de Grace, at the mouth of the Sus-

---

* [The link between New Brunswick and Trenton has since been authorised by the State and constructed.—Transl.]

quehanna. The whole distance by this route is only 93 miles, instead of 118, the distance by the present line, and the passage will occupy five or six hours, instead of eight or nine. From Baltimore southwardly two routes offer themselves ; you may take the steamboat to Norfolk, a distance of 200 miles, which is accomplished in 18 or 20 hours, whence another boat ascends the James River to Richmond still more rapidly, the distance of about 135 miles being passed over in 10 hours ; or you may go from Norfolk to Weldon on the Roanoke by a railroad 77 miles in length, of which two thirds are completed.*

From Baltimore you may also go to Washington, by a branch of the Baltimore and Ohio railroad, and thence by steamboat down the Potomac to a little village, 15 miles from Fredericksburg, from which a railroad is now in progress to Richmond. It will be 58 miles in length, and will cost but 12,000 dollars a mile, including the engines, cars, and depots. From Petersburg, 20 miles from Richmond, a railroad extends to Blakely on the Roanoke, 60 miles, and the interval between Petersburg and Richmond will soon be filled up. The Petersburg and Roanoke railroad, which is shorter than the post-road, follows with very little deviation an old Indian trail, a remarkable fact, which was told me by the able engineer Mr Moncure Robinson. It extends, almost entirely on the surface of the ground and without embankments, through the sandy, uncultivated plains, intersected by pools of stagnant water, which uniformly border the sea from the Chesapeake to Cape Florida, and are annually infested by the fever of the country. The whole region is most admirably adapted for railroads, which are constructed almost wholly of wood. The surface is graded by nature, and the sandy

---

* [The Baltimore and Philadelphia, Fredericksburg and Roanoke, and Portsmouth and Roanoke railroads have since been completed.—TRANSL.]

soil offers an excellent foundation for the wooden frame on which the rails are placed. The still virgin forests, consisting of pine and oak, afford an inexhaustible supply of timber for the construction of the railways, free to whoever wishes to use it. But if the nature of the country is well suited to this object, the condition of the population is far from being so. In this sterile tract, the inhabitants are thinly scattered over the surface, and there are only a few villages here and there on the rivers. Large towns, in which alone the necessary capital would be found, do not exist, and the aid of Northern capitalists has been necessarily resorted to. Philadelphia capital has been largely employed in the construction of the Petersburg and Richmond railroads, and without it, the great line between the South and the North, will not be continued across North Carolina, one of the poorest States in the confederacy, and connected with the works completed or in progress in Georgia and South Carolina.

There is, therefore, a great void of 325 miles, between the Roanoke and Charleston, the chief city of South Carolina, or rather of 275 miles between the Roanoke and Columbia, the capital of that State.* From Charleston, a railroad 136 miles in length, extends through the uncultivated and feverish zone of sand and pine-barrens to the cotton-region; it terminates at Hamburg, on the River Savannah, opposite Augusta, which is the principal interior cotton-market; the cost of this work was only about 9,500 dollars a mile including some cars, &c. Its construction is peculiar in this respect, that where its level is above that of the surface, recourse has been had to piles

---

* It will be easy to construct a branch from the Charleston and Augusta railroad to Columbia, and the route has been surveyed. [This branch is now in progress, and as the Raleigh and Gaston railroad, from the Roanoke to Raleigh, is also nearly completed, there remains only the link between Raleigh and Columbia not yet undertaken.—TRANSL.]

instead of embankments ; the railway, thus perched upon stilts from 15 to 25 feet high, certainly leaves something to be desired in regard to the safety of travellers, but it was necessary to construct it, and to do so with a very small capital, and in this respect it has been successful. The receipts have already been sufficiently large to permit the company gradually to substitute embankments of earth for the frail props on which it formerly rested. Another singular circumstance about it is, that it was constructed almost entirely by slaves. This road was undertaken with the purpose of diverting the cotton, which descended the river Savannah to the town of the same name, from that place to Charleston, and it has fully answered the expectations of its projectors.

From Augusta, the Georgia railroad has lately been begun, and will traverse some of the most fertile cotton districts in the State ; it will extend to Athens, a distance of 115 miles. To continue the line from North to South, or from Boston to New Orleans, it would be necessary that this railroad should be prolonged in the direction of Montgomery, Alabama, whence a steamer takes the traveller to Mobile, on the River Alabama.* Between Mobile and New Orleans, there are regular lines of steamboats running through Mobile Bay, Pascagoula Sound, and Lakes Borgne and Pontchartain. The four last miles, between the latter lake and New Orleans, are passed over in a quarter of an hour on a railroad, which the Louisiana legislature calls in its bad French *chemin à coulisses.* Such is the line between the North and South, of which the execution is the most advanced ; it will not be the

---

* [A prolongation of the Georgia railroad to Decatur, 160 miles from Augusta, is already in progress, and the Montgomery and Chattahoochee railroad, extending from West Point on the latter to the river Alabama, forms another link in the chain between Boston or rather Bangor and New Orleans.—Transl.]

only one, but as civilisation establishes itself further west
and capital multiplies, several new routes will be formed,
receding more and more from the coast.

The Baltimore and Ohio railroad is connected at Harper's Ferry with the Winchester railroad, 30 miles in
length, which runs up the bed of one of those long valleys that separate the successive ridges of the Alleghany
Mountains from each other. That in which Winchester
stands, is one of the most regular and fertile of these great
basins, and is celebrated under the name of the Virginia
Valley. Although, therefore, the Winchester railroad was
constructed only for the purpose of giving the produce of
Winchester and its vicinity an easy access to the market
of Baltimore, yet it may one day become a link in the
great chain of communication extending through the
Valley from north to south. A company has already been
chartered for continuing the work to Staunton, a distance
of 96 miles. Another line from the South to the North,
which will, perhaps, be connected with that of the great
Valley, has been projected at New Orleans, and authorised
by the legislatures of Louisiana and the other States through
which it will pass; it is a railroad from New Orleans to
Nashville, the capital of Tennessee, and I am assured that
the work will soon be commenced. This line aspires to
nothing less than a competition with the magnificent
river lines of the Ohio and the Mississippi, in the transportation of passengers and cotton.

Sect. IV. Lines Radiating around the Large Towns.

First Centre. Boston.

Three railroads extend from Boston in different directions; the first, 26 miles in length, to the manufacturing
city of Lowell, which is thus become a suburb of Boston,
and the second, 44 miles in length, to Worcester, the cen-

tre of an important agricultural district.   The former cost
60,000 dollars a miles, the latter 32,000.   The third road
is the Providence railroad, already mentioned above as one
of the links in the great chain from north to south.   The
Lowell railroad enters into competition with the Middlesex canal; the Worcester road is to be continued to the
River Hudson, where it will terminate opposite Albany.
It will also be connected with the city of Hudson, 30
miles below Albany, by a railroad extending from West
Stockbridge.   It will thus become to Boston a Western
Railroad, which name it has in fact received.   A company
has been authorised to execute the portion between Worcester and Springfield, a distance of 54 miles, the whole
distance from Boston to Albany being 160 miles.*   The
Eastern railroad, a fourth work is about to be undertaken,
passing through Lynn, famous for its boots and shoes,
Salem, a little city which carries on an extensive trade
with China, Ipswich, Beverly, and Newburyport towards
Portland, the principal town in the northern extremity of
the Union.

SECOND CENTRE.   NEW YORK.

Radiating from New York are, 1. The railroad to Pater-
son, an important manufacturing town at the falls of the
Passaic, 16 miles in length ; 2. The New Brunswick rail-

---

* During the session of 1836 the legislature of Massachusetts subscribed
1,000,000 in aid of the Western Railroad; this measure was the first step
taken by the State in the promotion of public works, and indicates a complete revolution in its policy on this point.   [This act was immediately followed by similar acts in aid of the several other railroads now in progress
in the State, and in 1838, by a further grant of the credit of the State to the
Western Railroad to the amount of 1,200,000 dollars.   That work will be
completed to Springfield in October (1839), and the section between Springfield and West Stockbridge is already far advanced towards its completion.
The Lowell railroad has been extended to Nashua, and an eastern branch
is now completed to Haverhill, of which a continuation towards Exeter is
now in progress.—TRANSL.]

road already mentioned, which serves as a route of communication with several important points, especially Newark, and for the transportation of provisions for the New-York market from a portion of New Jersey ; 3. The Harlæm railroad, almost exclusively for passengers ; and 4. The Brooklyn and Jamaica railroad, on Long Island, 12 miles in length, and designed both for pleasure excursions, and for transporting articles of consumption to the markets of New York.*

THIRD CENTRE. PHILADELPHIA.

Around Philadelphia, in addition to the great works extending to Columbia, Amboy, and Baltimore, already mentioned, are 1. The Trenton railroad ; 2. The Norristown and Germantown road, designed for passengers and for the accommodation of some manufacturing villages, such as Manayunk, 16 miles in length ; and 3. That of West Chester, a branch of the Columbia railroad, 9 miles in length, designed for the supply of the markets of the city. There are also several railroads running through the city, of which the rails are laid on the level of the street, and on which horse-cars only are used.

FOURTH CENTRE. BALTIMORE.

Beside the Baltimore and Ohio railroad with its Washington branch, Baltimore is also about to have a railroad through York, to the Susquehanna, opposite to Columbia, the length of which will be 73 miles. The object of this road is to contest with Philadelphia the commerce of the valley of the Susquehanna. The Pennsylvania canal

* [To these should be added the railroads from Newark to Morristown, and from Elizabethtown to Somerville, both intersecting the New Brunswick railroad, and extending into a fine farming country. The Brooklyn railroad has also been continued about 20 miles beyond Jamaica.—TRANSL.]

with its various branches forms a canalisation of this river and its tributaries above Columbia. But below Columbia, there are several rapids and shoals which interrupt the navigation of the river, except for downward-bound boats in the highest stages of the water. The Philadelphia merchants, fearing that all the works executed at a great expense by Pennsylvania, would turn out much less advantageously for them than for the Baltimoreans, as these last have, indeed, openly boasted, opposed for a long time both the canalisation of the Susquehanna from Columbia to its mouth, and the permission to construct that section of a railroad from Baltimore to Columbia, which would lie within the limits of Pennsylvania. Their opposition has, however, been at last overcome, and charters have been granted authorising the construction of both works. The railroad company, to which Maryland has just made a loan of 1,000,000 dollars, is pushing on the railway with great activity.

Fifth Centre. Charleston.

Some short canals have been cut to facilitate the access to Charleston from the interior, but they are in a bad state, and are of little importance.

Sixth Centre. New Orleans.

Independently of the short railway of five miles from Lake Pontchartain to New Orleans, there are several other works, such as the Carrolton railroad, which is a little longer, and two short canals extending from the city to the lake. Some cuts have also been made between the lagoons and marshes of the lower Mississippi. These canals, dug in a wet and muddy soil, have presented serious difficulties in their construction ; but they are of no interest in regard to extent or importance.

Seventh Centre. Saratoga.

Saratoga Springs in New York are visited for two or three months in the summer, by crowds of persons who throng thither in shoals. There is not a master of a family of Philadelphia, New York, and Baltimore, in easy circumstances, who does not feel obliged to pass 24 or 48 hours with his wife and daughters, amidst this crowd in their Sunday's best, and to visit the field where the English army under General Burgoyne surrendered its arms. There are at present two railroads to Saratoga; one from Schenectady, 22 miles in length, a branch of the Albany and Schenectady road, and another from Troy on the Hudson, 25 miles in length. After the season is over they serve for the transportation of fuel and timber.

Section V. Works Connected with Coal-mines.

The bituminous coal-mines of Chesterfield, near Richmond, are connected with the river James by a short railway adapted only for horses, which is 12 miles long, and cost 15,000 dollars a mile, inclusive of the cars, depots, &c. Once delivered at the river, the coal is easily transported along the whole coast, where it comes into competition with the English and Nova Scotia coals.

The anthracite beds of Pennsylvania have caused the construction of a much more extensive series of works. At present hardly any other fuel is consumed on the coast for domestic and manufacturing purposes than the anthracite, which is found only in a small section of Pennsylvania, lying between the Susquehanna and the Delaware. It gives a more intense and sustained heat than wood, which had also become very dear, and is much better suited to the rigorous winters, which are experienced in the United States, under the latitude of Naples. It is also much preferable to the bituminous coal, which is the only sort of coal in use with us ; it makes no smoke, and is much more cleanly, not soiling the carpets and drapery. The fire is very easily kept up, and a grate needs to be filled only two or three times during the whole twentyfour hours, to maintain a fire night and day. The servants, whom it spares a great deal of trouble, prefer it, and on this point, as on several others, their opinion is more important than that of their masters. The only inconvenience attending it is, that it sometimes diffuses a sulphurous smell. It is also beginning to take the place of wood in the steam-boats. The anthracite trade has, therefore, become considerable, and several canals and railroads have been made or are making, to transport the fuel from the mines to the points of consumption.

The principal of these lines are the following : 1. The Schuylkill canal, which extends from Philadelphia to the vicinity of the mines about the head of the Schuyl-kill. Its length from Philadelphia to Port Carbon, is 108 miles ; it cost, inclusive of the double locks, 3,000,000 dollars, or 28,000 dollars a mile, and yields a net income of 20 to 25 per cent. ; 400,000 tons of coal are annually brought down upon it. 2. The Lehigh canal runs from the Delaware to the mines near the heads of the Lehigh ; it is 46 miles long, and cost 1,560,000 dollars, or 34,000 dollars a mile. 3. The lateral canal along the Delaware starts from Easton, at the mouth of the Lehigh, and ends at Bristol, the head of navigation for sea-vessels. It transports to Philadelphia, the coal that is brought down the Lehigh canal ; it is 60 miles long, and cost 1,238,000 dollars, or 20,600 dollars a mile. This work was executed by the State of Pennsylvania, and has been before enumerated among the State works. 4. The Morris canal starts from Easton, and ends at Jersey City, opposite New York. It serves to supply the New York market with coal. The change of level is here for the most part effected, not by locks, but by inclined planes, the operation of which is very simple; the length of this work is 102 miles, cost 2,650,000 dollars, or 25,000 dollars a mile. 5. The Delaware and Hudson canal extends from the Round-out creek on the Hudson, near Kingston, 90 miles above New York, to the anthracite mines near the upper Delaware. The coal is brought down to the canal, at Honesdale, from the mountains, at Carbondale, on a railroad 16 miles in length; the canal is 109 miles long, and cost 2,250,000 dollars or 20,000 dollars a mile; the railroad cost 300,000 dollars or 17,500 dollars a mile. 6. The Pottsville and Sunbury railroad is designed to bring down to the Schuylkill the products of the mines lying in the heart of the mountains between the Susquehanna and the heads of the Schuylkill. It is remarkable for the boldness of the inclined planes, some of which have an inclination of 25 and 33 per cent., and which are worked by very ingenious and economical contrivances. It is 45 miles in length, and cost 1,120,000 dollars, or 25,000 dollars a mile. 7. The Philadelphia and Reading railroad, now in progress, will enter into competition with the Schuylkill canal; it is 56 miles in length, and cost, including the necessary apparatus, 26,300 dollars a mile. It is proposed to continue it to Pottsville, 35 miles from Reading; there would then be a continuous railroad from Philadelphia to the centre of the Susquehanna valley.

Beside these seven great lines, several mining companies have constructed various railways of less importance, which branch from them in different directions. At the end of 1834, there were 165 miles of these smaller works, constructed at an expense of about 1,125,000 dollars, which, added to the 542 miles, and 13,280,000 of the seven works above enumerated, gives a total of 707 miles and 14,400,000 dollars, or deducting the Delaware canal, which has been before reckoned, of 647 miles and

13,162,000 dollars. The aggregate length of all the works which I have already enumerated, including only those that are finished or far advanced, is 3,025 miles of canal, and 1,825 miles of railroad, made at a cost of above 112 millions. If we add several detached works, such as the Ithaca and Owego, the Lexington and Louisville, the Tuscumbia and Decatur (Alabama) railroads, and various canals in New England, Pennsylvania, Georgia, &c., we shall have a total of 3,250 miles of canal, and 2,000 miles of railroad, constructed at an expense of upwards of 120 million dollars. (See *Note* 22.) The impulse is, therefore, given, the movement goes on with increasing speed, the whole country is becoming covered with works in every direction. If I were to attempt to enumerate all the railroads, of which the routes are under survey, which have been or are on the point of being authorised by charters from the several legislatures, for which the subscription is about to be opened, or has already been filled up, I should be obliged to mention all the towns in the Union. A town of 10,000 inhabitants, which has not its railroad, looks upon itself with that feeling of shame, which our first parents experienced in the terrestrial paradise, when, after having eaten of the fruit of the tree of knowledge, they saw that they were naked.

I have here spoken of the more perfect means of intercommunication, canals and railroads, and not of common roads. If I had undertaken to speak of these, I should have mentioned at their head, the great work called the National or Cumberland road, which, starting from Washington, or strictly speaking, from Cumberland, on the Potomac, strikes the Ohio at Wheeling, and extends westwards, across the centre of Ohio, Indiana, and Illinois, to the Mississippi; it has been constructed wholly at the expense of the Federal government, and up to the present time there have been expended upon it 5,400,000 dollars.

It was begun in 1806, and is now nearly finished to Vandalia in Illinois. A dispute between Illinois and Missouri in respect to its termination, has delayed the completion of the last division. From Washington to Vandalia, the distance is 800 miles, and from Cumberland to Vandalia, 675 miles. The doctrine of the unconstitutionality of Congress engaging in internal improvements having prevailed since the accession of General Jackson to the presidency, Congress has offered the National Road to the States within which it lies, and they have accepted it on condition of its being first put in a state of perfect repair. Several of the States have also spent considerable sums in improving the condition of their roads; South Carolina, for instance, has devoted about a million and a half to this object.

The public works of the United States are generally managed with economy, as the statements above made testify; for the cost has been much less than that of similar works in Europe, although the wages of labour are two or three times higher than on the old continent. The canals constructed by the States are, nevertheless, pretty well finished; their dimensions are less that those of our canals, but greater than those of England; the locks are almost always of hewn stone.* The bridges, viaducts, and aqueducts are generally wooden superstructures resting on abutments and piers of common masonry. The river-dams are always of wood. The railroads constructed by the States, those of Pennsylvania in particular, have been built at a great expense; they have a double track with stone viaducts and some tunnels; the rails are wholly of iron, resting on stone blocks or sleepers. The Lowell

---

* On some of the canals the locks are partly of wood and partly of stone; these composite locks are economical and easily kept in repair, and deserve to be introduced in other countries. On many canals the locks are wholly of wood.

railroad company also wished to have their road constructed
in the most solid manner, and have displayed a luxury of
granite, which, if not injurious, is certainly superfluous.
The Baltimore and Ohio railroad has two tracks, but except
for a short distance is on wood. In the Northern States
and near the large towns most of the railroads have an
iron edge rail and a roadway prepared for two tracks, but
with only one track laid. Such are the Worcester, Providence, and Amboy railways, and such will be the Philadelphia and Reading road ; but the rails rest upon wooden
cross-pieces, which, independently of their cheapness, have
some advantage over the stone sleepers, in regard to
wear of the cars, superior ease of motion, and greater facility of repairs. Those railroads in the North on which
there is less travel, and which are more remote from the
large towns, and all those of the South, have but a single
track, with no preparation for a second, and consist of an
iron bar, about two inches wide and half an inch thick,
resting on longitudinal sleepers.

On most of the American railroads, the inclinations are
much greater than what in Europe are usually considered
the *maxima*. A rise of 35 feet to the mile, for instance,
seems moderate to American engineers, and even 50 feet
does not frighten them. Experience has shown that these
inclinations, the latter of which is double of the *maximum*
established by our engineers, do not endanger the safety
of travellers. They do, indeed, diminish the rate of speed,
unless additional power is applied at certain points, to
increase the force of traction ; but the Americans think
that these inconveniences are more than overborne by the
reduction of the first cost of construction. The curves
are also greater ; on the Baltimore and Ohio railroad, on
which locomotives are used, there are several with a radius
of 400 or 500 feet, but the consequence is, that on this
road the mean rate of speed does not exceed 12 or 13 miles

an hour, only half as great as that on the Liverpool railroad, but twice as great as that of a coach on an ordinary road. In general, however, the American engineers endeavour to avoid curves of less than 1000 feet radius. In France the Board of Public Works (*Ponts et chaussées*), in their surveys and plans, have fixed upon 2,700 feet as the *minimum*.

On some of the American railroads, however, even the rules of European science have been exceeded; on the Lowell railroad the *minimum* radius is 3,000 feet; on the Boston and Providence railroad there is no curve of a less radius than 6,000 feet. The rate of velocity on the American railroads is as various as the manner of their construction, and the amount of their inclinations and curvatures. On the Boston and Lowell road the rate is nearly 25 miles an hour, on the Boston and Providence and Worcester roads it is about 20 miles; on the Camden and Amboy railroad the mean velocity has been reduced to 15 miles; on the Charleston and Augusta road, it is only about 12, and it is still less on the Baltimore and Ohio railway.

One of the chief means of economy in the construction of these works in this country, is the use of wood for bridges. The Americans are unequalled in the art of constructing wooden bridges; those of Switzerland, about which so much as been said, are clumsy and heavy compared with theirs. The American bridges have arches of 100 and 200 feet span,* and they are not less remarkable for their cheapness, than for their boldness. The bridge over the Susquehanna at Columbia is 6,000 feet long and cost 130,000 dollars; it is roofed over, has two carriage-

---

* The bridge over the Schuylkill at Philadelphia consists of a single arch of 300 feet span. [This beautiful structure has lately been destroyed by fire.—TRANSL.]

ways and two side-ways for foot passengers. In general the wooden superstructure of a covered bridge, with a double carriage way, may be built at the rate of 8,000 to 14,000 dollars, according to the locality and the character of the work, per 600 feet; a similar structure with us would be built of hewn stone, and would cost at least 200,000 to 300,000 dollars. The masonry is generally of uncut stonè, or of undressed hewn stone, and is not, therefore, expensive. Three different plans are followed in the construction of bridges; one is that of a carpenter Burr, a second that of Col. Long, and the third, which is the newest, most interesting, and most suitable for railroads, on account of its firmness, is that of Mr Town; they are all remarkable for requiring scarcely any iron. There are, however, some bridges of hewn stone on the American railroads; such is the Thomas Viaduct over the Patapsco, on the Baltimore and Ohio railroad, wholly of fine granite; it is 700 feet long, and cost only 120,000 dollars, although it has two road-ways, and is 60 feet high.

The greatest difficulty which the Americans encountered in the execution of their public works, was not to procure the necessary capital, but to find men capable of directing operations. In this respect also, New York has done the Union signal service; the engineers, who were formed by the construction of the Erie canal, have diffused the benefits of the experience acquired in that work, over the whole country. Mr Wright, the most eminent among them, and still the most active of American engineers, notwithstanding his advanced age, has been engaged in the superintendence of an inconceivable number of undertakings.* His name is associated with the construction

---

* At this very time, Mr Wright, in spite of his 60 years, is directing in person the Harlæm railroad, the great New York and Erie road, the great work of connecting the James and Kanawha, by a railroad and canal, the works going on along the St. Lawrence in Upper Canada, 750 miles further

of canals from the Chesapeake to the Ohio, from the Delaware to the Chesapeake, from the Hudson to the Delaware, from the James to the Kanawha, on the St. Lawrence, and even on the Welland, as well as with those of the railroads just mentioned. Within the last ten years the number of able engineers in the United States has become considerable, and they have written the records of their skill and science on the soil of their country. General Bernard contributed not a little to this result, by carrying with him into the New World the most improved processes of European art, and setting an example of their application. Mr Moncure Robinson, also a pupil of the French schools of science, who excels in the art of combining great economy with great solidity and neatness of execution, has constructed the inclined planes of the Portage Railroad over the Alleghany, and has built the Chesterfield, Petersburg and Roanoke, the Little Schuylkill, and the Winchester railroads; he is, at present, engaged on the Pottsville and Sunbury, the Philadelphia and Reading, and the Fredericksburg and Richmond roads. Major McNeil has just finished the Boston and Providence railway, and is engaged on the Stonington and the Baltimore and Susquehanna roads. Mr Douglass, after having completed the Morris canal, and the Brooklyn and Jamaica railroad, is preparing, for the coming season, the operations on the New York water-works. Mr Fessenden, who has executed the Worcester railroad, is now engaged on the Eastern and Western railroads on the right and left of Boston. Mr Knight, the principal engineer of the Baltimore and Ohio railroad, is occupied in devising plans for topping the Alle-

---

north, and the railway from Havana to Guines in the islands of Cuba. The aggregate length of all these works is 870 miles. The most eminent engineers have always several works under their direction at once; it is understood, of course, that they are aided by skilful and intelligent assistants, who do most of the work.

ghanies. The late Mr Canvass White assisted in the construction of the Louisville and Portland canal, and had finished the fine canal from the Raritan to the Delaware, not long before his death. Mr Allen has built the Charleston and Augusta railroad. Mr Jervis, who is now directing a part of the great works of canalisation in New York, constructed the Carbondale and Honesdale road.

To supply the want of men of science, demanded by the spirit of enterprise, the Federal government authorises the officers of the engineer corps and of the topographical engineers to enter into the service of the companies. It also employs them itself, in surveying routes and preparing plans, or constructing works on its own account. General Gratiot, the chief engineer, therefore, performs the duties of president of a board of public works (*directeur-général des ponts et chaussées*). Cols. Albert and Kearney of the topographical engineers, take an active part in the construction of the great canal from the Chesapeake to the Ohio, of which 'the Federal government is the principal shareholder. Capt. Turnbull superintends the canal from Georgetown to Alexandria ; Capt. Delafield the works on the National Road, and Capt. Talcott the improvements of the navigation of the Hudson. Col. Long passes from route to route, and conducts at one time the surveys from Memphis to Savannah, at another those from Portland to Montreal and Quebec. On the other hand, architects become engineers, and Mr Strickland of Philadelphia, and Mr Latrobe of Baltimore, superintend the construction of the railroad between these two cities ; and even simple merchants take upon themselves the responsibility of great works, as in the case of Mr Jackson of Boston, who is in fact, chief engineer of the Lowell railroad.

The spectacle of a young people, executing, in the short space of fifteen years, a series of works, which the most powerful States of Europe with a population three or four times as great, would have shrunk from undertaking, is in truth a noble sight. The advantages which result from these enterprises to the public prosperity are incalculable, and the political effects are not less important. These numerous routes, which are traversed with so much ease and speed, will contribute to the maintenance of the Union more than a regularly balanced national representation. When New York shall be only six or eight days from New Orleans, not merely for a class of the rich and privileged, but for every citizen, every labourer, a separation will be impossible. Distance will be annihilated, and this colossus, ten times greater than France, will preserve its unity without an effort.*

It is impossible not to turn back my thoughts to Europe, and to make a comparison by no means favorable to the great kingdoms which occupy it. The partisans of the monarchical principle maintain, that it is as powerful in promoting the greatness and welfare of peoples, and the progress of the human race, as the principle of independence and self-government, which prevails on this side the Atlantic. For myself, I believe them to be in the right ; but it is necessary that some tangible proofs of the correctness of their opinion should be given, if we do not wish that the contrary doctrine should make proselytes. It is by the fruits that the tree must be judged. Now the European governments dispose of the property and the

---

* The lowest rate of speed on a railroad can be hardly less than 15 miles an hour, or about three times greater than the ordinary speed of the stagecoaches in France and America. At this rate, a country with railroads, nine times larger than France, would be on the same footing in respect to intercommunication, as France without railroads ; supposing a velocity of 25 miles an hour, or five times greater than that of the coaches, the proportion would then stand as one to twentyfive, and a territory four and a half times greater than western Europe, or five times greater than that included within the limits of the 27 States, would be as easily and as promptly administered as France is at present.

persons of more than 250 millions of men, that is, of a population twenty times more numerous than that of the United States at the time these great works were begun. The extent of territory which demands their care, is not quite four times as great as that at present occupied by the States and the organised Territories. The millions which the European nations raise so easily for war, that is to say, to destroy and slaughter each other, would not certainly be wanting to their princes for the execution of useful enterprises. The latter have only to will it, and all the peoples of Europe will be so completely blended together in interests, feelings, and opinions, that the whole continent would be like a single state, and a European war would be looked upon as no less sacrilegious than a civil war. By putting off the day of these useful works, do not the sovereigns give countenance to the reasonings of those, who assert that the cause of kings is irreconcileable with the cause of nations ?

LETTER XXII.

LABOUR.

LANCASTER, (PENNSYLVANIA,) JULY 20, 1835.

THERE can be no success without special devotion to some one end ; individual or nation, to be successful and prosperous, beware of attempting every thing. Human nature is finite, and, like it, you must set some bounds to your wishes and efforts. Learn how to check yourself and to be content, is the precept of wisdom. If it is a wise rule, then are the Americans, at least partially, wise, for they practise it partially. In general, the American is little disposed to be contented ; his idea of equality is to be inferior to none, but he endeavours to rise only in one direction. His only means, and the object of his whole thought, is to subdue the material world, or, in other words, it is industry in its various branches, business, speculation, work, action. To this sole object every thing is made subordinate, education, politics, private and public life. Every thing in American society, from religion and morals to domestic usages and daily habits of life, is bent in the direction of this common aim of each and all. If there are some exceptions to this general rule, they are few, and may be referred to two causes ; first, American society, exclusive as it is, is not destined to remain forever imprisoned in this narrow circle, and it already contains the germs of its future condition ages hence, whatever that may be ; and secondly, human nature, although bounded, is not exclusive, and no force in the world can stifle its eternal protest against exclusiveness in taste, institutions, and manners. Speculation and business, work and action, these, then, under various forms, make the exclusive object to which the Americans have devoted themselves, with a zeal that amounts to fanaticism ; this was marked out for them by the finger of Providence, in order that a continent should be brought under the dominion of civilisation with the least possible delay.

I cannot reflect without sorrow, that at one moment France seem called to take part in this great mission with the two nations, between whom God has placed it, not less morally in regard to character and institutions, than physically in respect to geographical position ; namely the English and Spaniards. Whilst Spain, then queen of the world, grasped South America and the vast empire of Mexico, civilised, sword in hand, the native tribes, and built those monumental cities, which will bear witness to its genius and its power, ages after the calumnies of its slanderers shall have been forgotten, whilst England was planting some insignificant colonies on the barren shore of North America, France was exploring the vast basin of the Father of Waters, and taking possession of the St. Lawrence, compared with which our Rhine, *tranquille et fier*, is but a modest rivulet : we were crowning with fortifications the steep rock of Quebec, building Montreal, founding New Orleans and St. Louis, and here and there subduing the rich plains of Illinois. At that time, we were occupying the most fertile, best watered, and finest portion of North America, the part best suited to become the seat of a magnificent empire, in harmony with our notions of unity. Our engineers, with a sagacity for which the Americans now express the greatest admiration, had marked out by fortresses, the sites most suitable for large towns. Our flag floated over Pittsbug, then Fort Duquesne, Detroit, Chicago, Erie, then Presqu'île, Kingston, then Fort Frontenac, Michillimackinac, Ticonderoga, Vincennes, Fort Charters, Peoria, and St. John, as well as over the capitals of Canada, and Louisiana. Then our language might have set up its claim to be the universal language ; the French name bade fair to become the first, not only in the world of ideas, by art and letters, like the Greek ; but also in the material and political world, by the number of individuals who would take pride in bearing it, by the immensity of the territory over which its dominion stretched, like the Roman. Louis XIV. in the days of his deification, in the Olympus which he had built himself, meditated this noble destiny for his people and his race. With a lofty pride, he seemed to read their future triumphs on the pages of fate. But there is left to us, who are separated from him only by a single century, there is left, alas ! nought but vain and impotent regrets. The English have driven us forever, not only from America, but also from the East Indies, where that great prince had given us a footing. The descendants of our fathers in Canada and Louisiana struggle in vain against the British flood that swallows them up ; our language is whelmed in the same deluge ; even our names for the cities we founded and the regions we discovered, are corrupted in the harsh throats of our fortunate rivals, and are too Saxonised to be any longer recognised. We have ourselves forgotten, that there was ever a time when we could have claimed to rule the New World ; we no longer remember the generous men who devoted themselves, that they might secure the dominion to us. To preserve the name of the heroic La Salle from oblivion, it has become necessary that the American Congress should raise a monument to his memory in the rotunda of the Capital, between those to William Penn and John Smith. We have had no stone for him among all our innumerable sculptures ; our painters have covered miles of canvass with their colours, but have not drawn a line in honour of him.

Meanwhile, the gigantic upstarts of Europe defy us, elbow us, and crowd us in. In vain did the genius of the the second Charlemagne restore to us the capital of the first Frank Kaisar, and the finest provinces of Clovis ; capital and provinces have been snatched from us almost immediately. One step more downward, and we should have been forever forced back among the secondary states, the worn out and decrepit nations, with no successors to receive and sustain with honor the inheritance of our fathers' glories. What is it that has thus degraded a great people, and robbed it of its well-earned future ? In an absolute monarchy like ours, it was enough, that we should be ridden by such a prince as Louis XV., who had inherited nothing from his great ancestor but his vices ; it was enough, that during fifty years, France was the play-thing

of his infamous selfishness, and of the shameful imbecili-
ty of his creatures. Absolute governments may sometimes produce wonders in a short space of time, but they
are exposed to cruel reverses. Had we been the conquerors in America, instead of having been conquered by the
English, what would have been the consequences? To
judge what the people of New France would have been, by
what the Canadians and the Creoles of Louisiana are, the
boldness and rapidity of the progress of civilisation would
have been much less than it has been. When it is proposed to conquer nations on the field of battle, France
may enter the lists with confidence ; but when it is proposed to subdue nature, the Englishman is our superior.
He has firmer sinews and more vigorous muscle; physically he is better made for labour ; he carries it on with
more perseverance and method ; he becomes interested in
it, and obstinately bent upon it. If he meets any obstacle
in his task, he attacks it with the devouring passion which
a Frenchman can feel only in the presence of an adversary
in a human form.

With what zeal and devotion has the Anglo-American
fulfilled his mission as a pioneer in a new continent ! Behold how he makes his way over the rocks and precipices ;
see how he struggles in close fight with the rivers, with
the swamps, with the primeval forests ; see how he slaugh-
ters the wolf and the bear, how he exterminates the Indian,
who in his eyes is only another wild beast ! In this conflict with the external world, with the land and the
waters, with mountains and pestilential marshes, he appears
full of that impetuosity with which Greece flung itself
into Asia at the voice of Alexander ; of that fanatical daring with which Mahomet inspired his Arabs for the conquest of the Eastern Empire ; of that delirious courage
which animated our fathers forty years ago, when they
threw themselves upon Europe. On the same rivers,

therefore, on which our colonists floated, carelessly sing-
ing, in the bark canoe of the savage, they have launched
fleets of superb steamers. Where we fraternised with the
Red Skins, sleeping with them in the forests, living like
them on the chase, travelling, in their manner, through
rugged trails afoot, the persevering American has felled the
aged trees, guided the plough, inclosed the fields, substituted the best breeds of English cattle for the wild deer,
created farms, flourishing villages, and opulent cities, dug
canals, and made roads. Those waterfalls which we admired as lovers of the picturesque, and the height of
which our officers measured at the risk of their lives, he
has shut up for the use of his mills and factories, regardless of the scenery. If these countries had continued to
belong to the French, the population would certainly have
been more gay than the present American race; it would
have enjoyed more highly, whatever it should have possessed, but it would have had less of comfort and wealth,
and ages would have passed away, before man had become
master of those regions, which have been reclaimed in
less than fifty years by the Americans.

If we examine the acts passed by the local legislatures
at each session, we shall find that at least three-fourths
relate to the banks, which give credit to the working
men; to the establishment of new religious societies and
churches, which are the citadels where the guardians of
industry keep watch; to routes and means of communication, roads, canals, railways, bridges, and steamboats,
which facilitate the access of the producer to the markets;
to primary instruction for the use of the mechanic and the
labourer; to various commercial regulations; or to the incorporation of towns and villages, the work of these hardy
pioneers. There is no mention of an army; the fine arts
are not so much as named; literary institutions and the
higher scientific studies are rarely honoured with notice.

The tendency of the laws is above all to promote industry, material labour, the task of the moment. In the older States, they always profess the greatest respect for property, because the legislature feels that the greatest encouragement to industry is to respect its fruits. They are especially conservative of landed property, either from a lingering remembrance of the feudal laws of the mother country, or because they are anxious to preserve some element of stability in the midst of the general change ; yet the laws generally pay less regard to the rights of property than is the case in Europe. Wo to whatever is inactive and unproductive, if it can be accused, on however slight a foundation, of resting upon monopoly and privilege ! The rights of industry here have the precedence of all others, efface all others, and it is on this account, that, except in in the affair of public credit, in which the towns and States pique themselves on the most scrupulous exactness in fulfilling their engagements, in every dispute between the capitalists and the producer, the latter has almost always the better.

Every thing is here arranged to facilitate industry ; the towns are built on the English plan ; men of business, instead of being scattered over the town, occupy a particular quarter, which is devoted exclusively to them, in which there is not a building used as a dwelling-house, and nothing but offices and ware-houses are to be seen. The brokers, bankers, and lawyers here have their cells, the merchants their counting-rooms ; here the banks, insurance offices, and other companies, have their chambers, and other buildings are filled from cellar to garret with articles of merchandise. At any hour, one merchant has but a few steps to go after any other, after a broker or a lawyer. This, it will be seen, is not according to the Paris fashion, by which a great deal of precious time is lost by men of business in running after one another ; in this respect, Paris is the worst arranged commercial city in the world. New York is, however inferior in this particular to London or Liverpool ; it has nothing like the great docks and the Commercial House.

The manners and customs are altogether those of a working, busy society. At the age of fifteen years, a man is engaged in business ; at twentyone he is established, he has his farm, his workshop, his counting-room, or his office, in a word his employment, whatever it may be. He now also takes a wife, and at twentytwo is the father of a family, and consequently has a powerful stimulus to excite him to industry. A man who has no profession, and, which is nearly the same thing, who is not married, enjoys little consideration ; he, who is an active and useful member of society, who contributes his share to augment the national wealth and increase the numbers of the population, he only is looked upon with respect and favour. The American is educated with the idea that he will have some particular occupation, that he is to be a farmer, artisan, manufacturer, merchant, speculator, lawyer, physician, or minister, perhaps all in succession, and that, if he is active and intelligent, he will make his fortune. He has no conception of living without a profession, even when his family is rich, for he sees nobody about him, not engaged in business. The man of leisure is a variety of the human species, of which the Yankee does not suspect the existence, and he knows that if rich to-day, his father may be ruined tomorrow. Besides the father himself is engaged in business, according to custom, and does not think of dispossessing himself of his fortune ; if the son wishes to have one at present, let him make it himself !

The habits of life are those of an exclusively working people. From the moment he gets up, the American is at his work, and he is engaged in it till the hour of sleep. Pleasure is never permitted to interrupt his business ; public affairs only have the right to occupy a few moments. Even meal-time is not for him a period of relaxation, in which his wearied mind seeks repose in the bosom of his friends ; it is only a disagreeable interruption of business, an interruption to which he yields because it cannot be avoided, but which he abridges as much as possible. In the evening, if no political meeting requires his attendance, if he does not go to discuss some question of public interest, or to a religious meeting, he sits at home, thoughtful and absorbed in his meditations, whether on the transactions of the day or the projects of the morrow. He refrains from business on Sunday, because his religion commands it, but it also requires him to abstain from all amusement and recreation, music, cards, dice, or billiards, under penalty of sacrilege. On Sunday an American would not venture to receive his friends ; his servants would not consent to it, and he can hardly secure their services for himself, at their own hour, on that day. A few days since, the mayor of New York was *accused* by one of the newspapers of having entertained on Sunday some English noblemen, who came out in their own yacht to give the American democracy a strange idea of British tastes. The mayor hastened to declare publicly, that he was too well acquainted with his duties as a Christian to entertain his friends on the *Sabbath*. Nothing is therefore, more melancholy than the seventh day in this country ; after such a Sunday, the labour of Monday is a delightful pastime.

Approach an English merchant in his counting-room in the morning, and you will find him stiff and dry, answering you only by monosyllables ; accost him at the hour of closing the mails, he will be at no pains to conceal his impatience ; he will dismiss you without always taking care to do it politely. The same man, in his drawing-room in the evening, or at his country-house in summer, will be full of courtesy and attention towards you. The Englishman divides his time, and does but one thing at once; in the morning he is wholly absorbed in business; in the evening he plays the man of leisure, reposing and enjoying life; he is a gentleman, having before his eyes, in the English aristocracy, a perfect model to form his manners, and to teach him how to spend his fortune with dignity and grace. The modern Frenchman is a confused mixture of the Englishman of the evening and the Englishman of the morning; in the morning a little of the former, in the evening a little of the latter. The old French model was the former, or rather, to do each one justice, was the original after which the English aristocracy has formed itself. The American of the North and the Northwest, whose character now gives the tone in the United States, is permanently a man of business, he is always the Englishman of the morning. You find many of the Englishmen of the evening on the plantations of the South, and some are beginning to be met with in the great cities of the North.

Tall, slender, and light of figure, the American seems built expressly for labour; he has no equal for despatch of business. Nobody also can conform so easily to new situations and circumstances; he is always ready to adopt new processes and implements, or to change his occupation. He is a mechanic by nature; among us there is not a schoolboy who has not made a *vaudeville*, a ballad, or a republican or monarchial constitution; in Massachusetts and Connecticut, there is not a labourer who has not invented a machine or a tool. There is not a man of much consideration, who has not his scheme for a railroad, a project for a village or a town, or who has not *in petto* some grand speculation in the drowned lands of Red River, in the cotton lands of the Yazoo, or in the corn fields of Illinois. Eminently a pioneer, the American who is not more or less Europeanised, the pure Yankee, in a word, is not only a working man, but he is a migratory one. He has no root in the soil, he has no feeling of reverence, and love for the natal spot and the paternal roof; he is always disposed to emigrate, always ready to start in the first steamer that comes along, from the place where he had but just now landed. He is devoured with a passion for locomotion, he cannot stay in one place; he must go and come, he must stretch his limbs and keep his muscles in play. When his feet are not in motion, his fingers must be in action, he must be whittling a piece of wood, cutting the back of his chair, or notching the edge of the table, or his jaws must be at work grinding tobacco. Whether it be that a continual competition has given him the habit, or that he has an exaggerated estimate of the value of time, or that the unsettled state of everything around him, keeps his nervous system in a state of perpetual agitation, or that he has come thus from the hands of nature, he always has something to be done, he is always in a terrible hurry. He is fit for all sorts of work, except those which require slow and minute processes. The idea of these fills him with horror; it is his hell. "We are born in haste," says an American writer, "we finish our education on the run; we marry on the wing; we make a fortune at a stroke, and lose it in the same manner, to make and lose it again ten times over, in the twinkling of an eye. Our body is a locomotive, going at the rate of twentyfive miles an hour; our soul, a high-pressure engine; our life is like a shooting star, and death overtakes us at last like a flash of lightning."*

---

* In the hotels and on board the steamboats, the door of the eating-room is beset by a crowd on the approach of a meal-time. As soon as the bell sounds, there is a general rush into the room, and in less than ten minutes every place is occupied. In a quarter of an hour, out of 300 persons, 200 have left the table, and in ten minutes more not an individual is to be seen.

"Work," says American society to the poor man; "work, and at eighteen years of age, although a mere workman, you shall get more than a captain in Europe. You shall live in plenty, be well-clothed, well-lodged, and be able to lay up a part of your earnings. Be attentive to your work, be sober and religious, and you will find a devoted and submissive partner of your fortunes; you shall have a more comfortable home, than many of the higher classes of the commonalty in Europe. From a journeyman, you will become a master; you will have apprentices and dependents under you in turn; you shall have credit without stint; you shall become a manufacturer or agriculturist on a great scale; you shall speculate and become rich; you shall found a town and give it your own name; you shall be a member of the legislature of the State, or alderman of the city, and finally member of Congress; your son will have as good a chance to be made President as the son of the President himself. Work, and if the fortune of business should be against you, and you fall, you will soon be able to rise again; for a failure is nothing but a wound in battle; it will not deprive you of the esteem or confidence of any one, if you have always been prudent and temperate, a good christian and a faithful husband."

On my passage from Baltimore to Norfolk, in the winter of 1834, I found that, notwithstanding the cold, three fourths of the passengers had risen at 4 o'clock, and at six, being almost the only person left abed, and feeling sure that we must be near our port, I got up and went upon deck; but it was not until eight o'clock, that we came in sight of Norfolk. On mentioning the fact afterward to an American, a man of sense, who was on board at the same time, and who, wiser than I, had lain abed till after sunrise; "Ah, sir," said he, "if you knew my countrymen better, you wouldn't be at all surprised at their getting up at four o'clock, with the intention of arriving at nine. An American is always on the lookout lest any of his neighbours should get the start of him. If one hundred Americans were going to be shot, they would contend for the priority, so strong is their habit of competition."

" Work," it says to the rich, " work, and do not stop to think of enjoying your wealth. You shall increase your income without increasing your expenses; you shall enlarge you fortune, but it will be only to increase the sources of labour for the poor, and to extend your power over the material world. Be simple and severe in your exterior, but at home you may have the richest carpets, plate in abundance, the finest linens of Ireland and Saxony; externally your house shall be on the same model with all the others of the town; you shall have neither livery nor equipage; you shall not patronise the theatre, which tends to relax morals; you shall avoid play; you shall sign the articles and pledges of the Temperance Society; you shall not even indulge in good cheer; you shall set an example of constant attendance at church; you shall always show the most profound respect for morals and religion, for the farmer and mechanic around you have their eyes fixed upon you; they take you for their pattern, they still acknowledge you to be the arbiter of manners and customs, although they have taken from you the political sceptre. If you give yourself up to pleasure, to parade, to amusement, to dissipation and luxury, they also will give the reins to their gross appetites and their violent passions. Your country will be ruined, and you will be ruined with it."

It is possible to imagine various social systems differently organised but equally favourable, theoretically, to the promotion of industry. We may imagine a society organised for labour under the influence of the principle of authority; that is, a society composed of a gradation of ranks; we may conceive another constituted under the auspices of the principle of liberty or independence. To organise *a priori*, for purposes of industry, any given people, it is necessary, under penalty of engendering a Utopian scheme, to consult the circumstances of its origin and the condition of its territory, to know whence and how it has come, and whither it is going. With the people of the United States, a scion of the English stock, and thoroughly imbued with Protestantism, the principle of independence, of individualism, of competition, in fine, could not but be successful. The iron hearts of the Puritans, the *Ultras* of Protestantism, could not fail to find this principle congenial to them. It is owing to this course that the sons of New England, which was peopled by the *Pilgrims*, have played the chief part in the occupation of the great valley of the Mississippi.

The civilisation of the West* has sprung from the secret and silent coöperation of two or three hundred thousand young farmers, who started, each on his own account, from New England, often alone, sometimes with a small company of friends. This system would not have succeeded with Frenchmen. The Yankee alone in the woods, with no companion but his wife, is all-sufficient for himself. The Frenchman is eminently social; he could not bear the solitude in which the Yankee would feel at his ease. The latter, although solitary, becomes excited by his own plans and eager to accomplish them. The Frenchman cannot become interested in any industrial enterprise except in connection with others, whose concurrence with him is evident and palpable, or rather he rarely becomes interested in any material task, for he reserves his affections and sympathies for living objects. It is quite impossible for him to fall in love with a *clearing*, to feel the same transports at the success of a manufacture as for the safety of a friend or the happiness of a mistress; but he is capable of applying himself to the task with ardour, if his characteristic passions, his thirst

* I allude particularly to the Northwest, or that portion of the West in which slavery does not exist.

for glory and his spirit of emulation, are brought into play by contact with human beings. If it were proposed, then, to settle colonies with Frenchmen, it would be necessary to put little reliance on individual efforts. In all things, as well as in a line of battle, a Frenchman must feel his neighbour's elbow. Americans might be thrown separately upon a new land, they would form little centres round which constantly expanding circles of population and cultivation would grow up. But if the new settlers were Frenchmen, it would be necessary to carry with them a society ready constituted, social bonds already binding them in, or at least a regular social framework, and bolts to which the social bonds are to be attached ; that is, they must have, at starting, the great circle with its centre strongly marked.

Canada is almost the only colony that has been founded exclusively by Frenchmen,* and a complete social organisation was carried thither. The country once explored, the royal fleet landed the *seigneurs*, who had received fiefs from royal grants, and who were followed by vassals transplanted from Normandy and Brittany, among whom the lands were distributed. At the same time an endowed regular and secular clergy, with ample domains and the right of collecting the tithe, was brought to the St. Lawrence. Next came traders and companies, to whom was given the monopoly of the fur-trade and the commerce of the colony. In a word the three orders, the clergy, nobility, and third estate, were imported ready made from Old France into New. The only thing which the colonists left behind them, was the poverty of the greatest number. The system was a good one for that period ; the principle of order and of ranks, which prevailed under the only form

---

* In Louisiana, St Domingo, and the other islands, the mass of the population consisted of blacks.

then practicable, was in keeping with the character of the people. The proof of this is to be found in the fact, that Canada has flourished under this system in which the English conquerors have made no changes, and the population has increased in the bosom of general ease. I have seen nothing which more completely realised the *aurea mediocritas*, than the pretty villages on the banks of the St. Lawrence. They do not exhibit the ambitious prosperity of those of the United States ; they are much more modest than those of the republic ; but if there is less show, there is also more content and happiness. Canada reminded me of Switzerland ; it is the same aspect of calm contentment and quiet happiness. It would be a subject of admiration were it not by the side of the American colossus ; its rapid growth would attract attention, were it not for the miraculous expansion of the United States. Neither would it be right to assert that the progress of Canada has been in spite of the colonial system ; the dispute about the *because* and the *although* is easily settled in this case. All that was burdensome about the original system remains untouched, and there is no complaint against it. The seignorial dues, the tithe, the seignorial mill, and the *four banal*, still exist in full vigour ; and do not appear in the interminable list of ninetythree grievances, lately drawn up by the Canadians.

LETTER XXIII.

M O N E Y.

SUNBURY, (PENNSYLVANIA,) JULY 31, 1835.

IN a society devoted to production and traffic, money must be regarded with other eyes, than among a people of military spirit, or nourished in classical studies and scientific speculations. Among the latter, it must be looked upon, theoretically at least, as vile metal. With them honour and glory are more powerful and more common motives of action than interest; they are the coin with which many persons are content, the only coin which many persons are ambitious to acquire. In an industrious society, on the other hand, money, the fruit and object of labour, is not to be despised; a man's wealth is the measure of his capacity and of his consideration among his fellow-citizens. Whatever may be the cause, the fact is certain, that money is not the same thing here that it is with us; that it weighs here where with us it has no weight; that it appears openly here, where with us it would hide itself. When I was in England, I was surprised at the number of notices in the docks, threatening, for instance, a fine for certain offences, with a promise of half to the informer. If a prefect of the police should offer such a premium to informers among us, our blood would boil with indignation. In this country the same practice prevails, and seems to be still more frequent. When a crime is committed, the authorities offer a reward of 100 or 200 dollars to whoever will make known or deliver up the criminal. In Philadelphia, I saw the governor of the State and the mayor of the city endeavouring to outbid each other in promises; a murder had been committed during one of the preliminary elections, and those officers, who were of different parties, endeavoured to prove by the greatness of their offers, that the opposite party was guilty of the act. In some cases of incendiarism or poisoning, a reward of 1000 dollars has been offered. It should be observed, however, that in England, out of London, and in this country, there is no organised police like ours, and it, therefore, becomes necessary that the citizens themselves should act as a police.

The maxim here is that everything is to be paid for. Museums and institutions for higher instruction to which admission is gratuitous, are here unknown. Nor are those unpaid offices, which take a citizen from his business, and would make it impossible for him to provide for the support of his family, if he discharged them faithfully, known here. The municipal offices in the country have no pay attached to them, because they take up little time and require little attention, and because a man in the country has more leisure than the busy inhabitant of the city. But in the cities all officers are paid, as soon as their functions come to occupy much of their time. The custom of paying by the day, which prevails in England, is very general here. Members of Congress are paid at the rate of eight dollars a day, and if a legislative committee prolongs its sessions beyond those of the legislative body, the pay is continued on the same footing. All the State legislatures are paid by the day. Canal commissioners, who are generally men of some distinction, that is, rich men, are generally paid in the same way, an account being kept of the number of days they are employed in the public service; for them the pay amounts merely to the payment of their expenses. Those, however, who are permanently occupied, receive an annual salary. In some offices, the incumbents are paid by fees for each affair in which they become engaged; this is generally the case with the

States' Attorneys and the Justices of Peace, and with the Aldermen in some of the cities. The public officers who are regularly employed, such as the Governors· of the States, and the Mayors of the principal cities have a fixed annual salary. It is a settled principle here that all work should stand on the same footing with industrial labour, and be paid in the same manner. Intellectual merchandise and material merchandise, capital and talent, dollars and science, are here placed on the same level ; this practice puts every one at his ease, and facilitates, abridges, and simplifies all operations. No one feels the least embarrassment in asking for a service, which he knows will be paid for. Everything is settled plainly and easily, because in an industrious and prosperous society every one has the power to be liberal.

Money is also made an instrument of punishment, as well as of reward. It is well known that, in England, a conviction for adultery enriches the wronged husband at the expense of the guilty paramour, and the same practice would prevail here, if the crime were not extremely rare. The American law is very sparing of bodily punishments for simple misdemeanours, but it makes very free use of fines. On most bridges, there are notices forbidding the passing with horses at any other pace than a walk, under penalty of a fine of 2, 3, or 5 dollars. When a man is suspected or even accused of a crime, such as forgery, arson, or murder, it is not his person, but his purse that is secured ; that is, instead of being arrested, he is obliged to give bail in a sum which is left to the discretion of the Judicial authority. Last year, while a convention for revising the constitution of Tennessee was in session in Nashville, one of the members, a militia general, of whom there are thousands in the country, a man of large property, and therefore very respectable, got into a quarrel with an editor of a newspaper, and uttered violent threats against him. Some days afterward, in company with another violent fellow, he actually discharged a pistol at his adversary in·the bar-room of a hotel, and wounded him dangerously. The affair was brought before the proper authorities, and the assassin was admitted to bail, being thus left at full liberty on depositing some thousand dollars, continuing to sit in the Convention and to assist in the formation of the new constitution of the State.* So much tenderdess towards an assassin, and similar proceedings which I have witnessed relative to incendiaries and persons guilty of forgery, recall to mind those times of barbarism, in which criminals were redeemed at a price. It will be readily imagined, after what has been said, that imprisonment for debt is very abhorrent from American ideas ; in fact, a general clamour has been raised against it ; most of the States have already abolished it, and others will not long delay to follow the example.

Money, is therefore, the sanction of the laws and of the most simple police regulations. If a magistrate has good reason for believing that an individual has intentions to break the peace, instead of taking him into custody as a measure of prevention, he requires him to give bail for his good behaviour. It is by money-penalties, also, that chartered companies are obliged to conform to the provisions of their charters. It is by fines, that even the magistrates are punished for neglect of duty. To remedy the inconveniences arising from the minute subdivision and dispersion of administrative authority in the New England States, resort is also had to money. In that part of the Union, the repair of roads is left to the care of the towns, and it is plain that the travel through a whole State might be seriously

---

* This man was finally condemned in light damages, and this was his only punishment. The object of assault survived the attempted assassination.

incommoded by the neglect of one town. It is, therefore,
provided by law, that every town shall be responsible for
any accidents to travellers within its limits, which may be
owing to the bad state of the roads ; it is not uncommon
to read accounts in the newspapers of a town being condemned to pay a traveller, who has been overturned on its
roads or bridges, 500 or 1000 dollars damages. The city
of Lowell was very lately condemned to pay 6,000 dollars
to two travellers, who had broken their legs by such an
accident. The judge charged that the plaintiffs should
not only be reimbursed for the expenses of the cure, but
also for the estimated probable earnings of their industry
during their confinement.

Amongst us, it is not money, but honour, that occupies
the most conspicuous place, and if it be admitted that the
sentiment of honour lies at the foundation of monarchies,
and if every thing turn upon this one principle, this is very
well. The principle of honour is quite as good in every
view, whether logically, morally or practically considered,
as the principle of money. It is, indeed, more congenial
to the generosity of the French character ; but then it is
necessary that the honour should be something real, that
the consideration it gives, should be incontestable ; it
is necessary that the authority which is the source of honour, should be itself respected. If the supreme authority
is insulted and despised, public functions become not a
source of consideration, but of contempt. If jealousy and
suspicion of power are admitted and consecrated by the
modern spirit of legislation and administration, is it not
true that your pretended recompense of public service by
the consideration and dignity they confer, is a mockery, and
and that your whole system is founded upon a contradiction ? If royalty still sat all-powerful on the magnificent
throne of Versailles, amidst its guards glittering with steel
and gold, surrounded by the most brilliant court of which

history preserves the record, and by the fascinations with which the homage of the arts invested it ; or if the prince were a saviour of his country, raised on the buckler by his victories, and dating his decrees from the palace of vassal kings, or from the Schœnbrunn of the conquered Kaisars; if he crowned and uncrowned kings, as our ministers now make and unmake sub-prefects ; if at a breath of his mouth, victorious veterans calmly met death ; if the world did him homage ; if he were the anointed of the Lord, the choice and idol of the people; if you had yet the monarchy of Louis XIV., or of Napoleon, you would be welcome to speak of consideration and honour ! It was then distinction enough to be noticed by a royal look. The favour of the sovereign then secured the confidence, or at least the outward homage of the people. The point of precedence was worthy of being a subject of envy in the days of the splendour of Versailles, or when one might lose oneself in the crowd of kings in the Tuileries. But what does it signify now-a-days, when royalty has lost its poetical attributes, when public ceremonies are abolished, when there is no longer a court or court-dress ? Titles have been profaned and degraded by the ignorance and stupidity of those who ought to have supported their dignity, or sullied by the jealousy of the commons. As for your ribbands you have been obliged to scatter them under the hoofs of horses. The system of honour is, therefore, gone by ; to restore it, a revolution would be necessary ; not a revolution like that of July, but a revolution like that which was going on during the three centuries between Luther and Mirabeau, and which, ripe at last, has been shaking both worlds during the last fifty years ; a revolution in the name of authority, like that which our fathers accomplished in the name of liberty.

Among the sayings attributed to M. de Talleyrand, the following is often quoted ; " I don't know an American that hasn't sold his horse or dog." It is certain that the Americans are an exaggeration of the English, whom Napoleon used to call a nation of shop-keepers. The American is always bargaining ; he always has one bargain afoot, another just finished, and several more in meditation. All that he has, all that he sees, is merchandise in his eyes. The poetical associations which invest particular spots or objects with a character of sanctity, have no place in his mind.   The spire of his village church is no more than any other spire to him, and the finest in his view, is the newest, the most freshly painted.   To him a cataract is a motive power for his machinery, *a mill privilege ;* an old building is a quarry of bricks and stones, which he works without the least remorse.   The Yankee will sell his father's house, like old clothes or rags.   In his character of pioneer, it is his destiny to attach himself to nothing, to no place, edifice, object, or person, except his wife, to whom he is indissolubly bound night and day, from the moment of marriage till death parts them.

At the bottom, then, of all that an American does, is money ; beneath every word, money.   But it would be a mistake to suppose that he is not capable of making pecuniary sacrifices ; he is in the habit of subscribing to all useful objects, and he does so without reluctance or regret, oftener than we are accustomed to do, and more liberally also ; but his munificence and his donations are systematic and calculated.   It is neither enthusiasm nor passion that unties his purse strings, but motives of policy or considerations of propriety, views of utility and regard for the public good, in which he feels his own private interests to be involved.   The American, therefore, admits some exceptions to his general commercial rule of conduct.   He gives money, he attends committee-meetings, he draws up in haste a report or an opinion ; he even goes in person, at high speed, to Washington, in order to present a set of resolutions to the President, or he hastens to a neighbouring city to attend a public dinner, and returns in equal haste ; but he requires in this case that the exception to the general rule should be sharply defined and the cause strongly marked, that the public interest should be at stake. And he particularly insists that the sacrifice should be of money only, once for all, and that his time should be respected. To everything of a private nature, to everything that takes up his time and demands his attention, he applies the mercantile principle, nothing for nothing. He pays the services of others with dollars, and he expects others to do the same by him, because he looks upon compliments as too hollow and light to be put in the scale against labour, and because distinctions, such for instance as precedence, are unknown and incomprehensible to him. With him it is an indisputable maxim, that the labourer is worthy of his hire. The ideas of service and salary are so inseparably connected in his mind, that in American almanacs it is common to see the rate of pay annexed to the lists of public officers. He is of opinion that nobody can live on a dry crust and glory ; he thinks of the welfare of his wife and children, of a provision for his old age, and if he were told that there is a country in which these considerations are disregarded, for the purpose of obliging a neighbour or paying a courtesy to a magistrate, such a thing would appear absurd to him.

High pay is not, however, consonant with the spirit of democracy, because it is incapable of discerning its propriety. The mechanic who makes 500 dollars a year, thinks himself generous towards a public officer to whom he gives 1,500 or 2,000; just as our citizens of the middling class in Paris, who have an income of 10,000 francs, cannot see why a public functionary should not be content with 12,000. The Americans thought that among them, as elsewhere, there would be two kinds of coin, money

and public consideration, and they were persuaded, on the
authority of Franklin, that it would be easy to find able
public officers, whose salary should chiefly consist in the
honour of public station. But they were mistaken; for
office is here no title to respect, but quite the contrary;
and as public services are neither paid by dollars nor consideration, only a Hobson's choice is left to the people.
With the exception of a very small number of places,
which the delights of power still cause to be sought after,
notwithstanding the cost of the pleasure of commanding
and having dependents or subordinates, office is generally
sought for only by the floating part of the population, which
has been unsuccessful in business, and tried one occupation
after another in vain. It is not even, strictly speaking, a
profession, but rather the temporary resort of persons who
have no settled pursuit, who, as soon as they find a more
eligible employment in industry or speculation, take leave
of the State. The West Point Academy sends out about
forty lieutenants for the army annually; about one third
of these resign their commissions before two or three years
of service, because the pay of the officers, although much
higher than with us, is very inconsiderable compared with
the profits of a merchant or the salary of an engineer.

The duties of a public officer are generally less difficult
in the United States than in France. Among us every
question that arises, embraces a great complication of interests, and requires more knowledge. The powers and
duties of the government in France are much more extensive and more various, and more care is exacted of persons
in the public employ among us, than in this country. Yet
the average of salaries here is much greater than with us.
When the Congress and the States shall stand in need of
able men for functionaries, they will do as the American
merchants do to their clerks, they will pay them. Congress, having lately become sensible of the importance of

securing the services of good naval officers, has just raised the pay of that corps.* It may even be said that the number of office-holders who are treated with illiberality, is very small.† Out of 158 persons employed in the service of the Treasury department at Washington, there are only 5 who receive less than 1,000 dollars, and there are only two who receive more than 2,000 ; this is the application of the principle of equality to pay. As the price of common objects of consumption, that is, bread, meat, coffee, tea, sugar, and fuel, is generally lower in the United States than in France, and especially in Paris, a salary of 1,500 or 2,000 dollars is sufficient in most cases to support

---

* PAY OF OFFICERS OF THE FRENCH AND AMERICAN NAVIES.

French Navy.		American Navy.	
Vice Admiral, - - - -	$7,525		
Rear Admiral, - - - -	6,000		
		Senior Captain, - - - -	$4,500
		Capt. Com. a Squadron, -	4,000
Captain of Ship of the Line,			
1st class, - - -	2,750	Captain, - - - - - -	3,500
2nd class, - - -	2,700		
of Frigate, - - -	2,170	Commander, - - - - -	3,500
of Corvette, - -	1,650		
Lieut. Command. - - - -	1,150	Lieut. Command. - - - -	1,800
Lieut. - - - - - - -	600	Lieut. - - - - - -	1,500
Lieut. of Frigate, - - - -	500	Passed Midship. - - - -	750
Midshipman, 1st class, - -	220	Midshipman, - - - - -	400
2d class, - -	160		

The gunners, boatswain, sail-makers, and carpenters receive,

In a ship of the line, 750 dollars,
For a Frigate, - - 600 "
On other duty, - - 500 "

In the French navy the pay of corresponding officers is from 400 to 200 dollars.

† They are the governors of most of the States, and the heads of the executive departments at Washington. These last receive only 6,000 dollars, and they are obliged to keep up a certain style of living. It is singular that some subaltern officers are permitted to receive enormous fees. Thus the inspector of flour in New York received in 1835, 10,000 dollars, the inspector of potash 20,000, and the inspector of tobacco 34,500.

a family in comfort and abundance. An officer of the
government, who receives from 400 to 600 dollars in
Paris, lives only by practising the strictest economy if he
is a bachelor, and suffers great privations if he is a married
man. At Washington he would receive from 1,000 to
1,200 dollars, and would live in abundance and comfort,
if not in style and luxury. Nor would he here, as with
us, be condemned to the punishment of Tantalus, for the
pomp and splendour of the privileged classes in the
European capitals is unknown in the United States.
In Paris, the *employé* is bespattered with mud by the equipage of a man who spends his 20,000 dollars a year ; in
the streets of Philadelphia, he would elbow a rich capi-
talist who kept no coach because he would not know what
to do with it, and who, with a revenue of 30,000 or
60,000 dollars, cannot spend more than 8,000 or 10,000
at the most. The ratio of conditions, which in Paris is
as one to forty, is here not more than one to eight.

Here the condition of the richest merchant, and that of
a mechanic and a farmer, are not essentially different ; the
difference is merely in degree and not in kind. All have
similar houses, built on a similar plan ; only that one has
a front five or six feet wider, and is one or two stories
higher than another ; the distribution of apartments, and
the furniture are similar. All have carpets from the cellar
to the garret, all sleep in large high-post bedsteads very
much like each other, projecting out into a chamber without closets, alcoves, or double door, and with bare walls ;
only the carpets of the one are coarse, and those of the other
are fine, the bedstead of the rich is of mahogany, and
that of the mechanic of cherry or walnut. In general
the table is served much alike ; there is the same number
of meals, and there is nearly the same number of dishes.
This is so much the case, that, if my French palate had to
decide between the dinner of a great city hotel (excepting

those of Boston, New York, Philadelphia, and Baltimore), and that of a country inn, at which I should sit by the side of the blacksmith of the place, with sooty visage and with sleeves rolled up, I think that I should really pronounce in favour of the latter. This is especially the case in the North, and particularly in New England, the land of the Yankees. In the South, the condition of the planter on his estate gains all that is taken from the mass of the population, or the slaves. And even at the North, of late years, commerce, which has collected men into large cities, has also accumulated capital in single hands, and created great fortunes. The inequality of condition is, therefore, beginning to manifest itself; the style of the new houses in Chesnut Street, Philadelphia, with their first story of white marble, is a blow at equality. The same innovation is creeping in in New York; the anti-democratical tendency of commerce is revealing itself.*

It might be expected that among a people so deeply absorbed in material pursuits, misers would abound; but it is not so. There is never any niggardliness in a Southerner; it is sometimes found in the Yankee, but nowhere do you see specimens of that sordid avarice, of which examples are so common among us. The American has too high a notion of the dignity of human nature, to be wil-

---

* If the rich in the large towns of the North spend eight or ten times as much as the clerk, it is not that they keep up much style, or even that they have an equipage. When would the husband, always immersed in business, or the wife, occupied with her household cares be able to use the coach? Suppose they had time to use it, and the public opinion would not be offended by it, what could one do with an equipage in the streets of Philadelphia? The principal difference in the expenditure of the two classes, is that the rich man now and then gives a ball, and piques himself on his parade, which the indulgent democracy pardons for one day; this sort of luxury is much more expensive here than with us, and it does not require a very brilliant rout, in small houses, in which the company is received in two rooms 20 feet by 25, to cost 700 or 800 dollars.

ling to deprive himself and his children of those comforts which soften the asperities of life ; he respects his own person too much not to surround it with a certain degree of decency.   Harpagon is never to be met with in the United States, and yet Harpagon is not by a great deal the most wretchedly degraded miser, that European society exhibits.   The American is devoured with a passion for money, not because he finds a pleasure in hoarding it up, but because wealth is power, because it is the lever by which he governs nature.   I ought also to do the Americans justice on another point.   I have said that with them every thing was an affair of money, and yet there is one thing, which among us, a people of lively affections, prone to love, and generous by nature, takes the mercantile character very decidedly, and which among them has nothing of this character ; I mean marriage.   We buy a woman with our fortune, or we sell ourselves to her for her dower.   The American chooses her, or rather offers himself to her, for her beauty, her intelligence, or her amiable qualities, and asks no other portion.   Thus, whilst we make a traffic of what is most sacred, these shop-keepers exhibit a delicacy and loftiness of feeling, which would have done honor to the most perfect models of chivalry.   It is to industry that they are indebted for this superiority.   Our idle cits, not being able to increase their patrimony, are obliged in taking a wife to calculate her portion, in order to decide if their joint income will be enough to support a family.   The American, having the taste and the habits of industry, is sure of being able to provide amply for his household, and is therefore, free from the necessity of making this melancholy calculation. Is it possible to doubt, that a race of men, which thus combines in a high degree the most contradictory qualities, is reserved for lofty destinies ?

LETTER XXIV.

S P E C U L A T I O N S .

JOHNSTOWN, (PENN.) AUG. 4, 1835.

THE present aspect of this country is, in a high degree, calculated to encourage the friends of peace in their hopes and wishes with respect to a rupture with France. The Americans of all parties conduct themselves in their private affairs like men who are convinced that business will experience no interruption from that quarter. A person who landed at New York, Boston, or Philadelphia, on the day that news was received of the effect produced in France by the President's message, and had since played Epimenides, would not now recognise the United States ; the most unlimited confidence has succeeded to the general anxiety. Every body is speculating, and every thing has become an object of speculation. The most daring enterprises find encouragement ; all projects find subscribers. From Maine to the Red River, the whole country has become an immense *rue Quincampoix*. Thus far every one has made money, as is always the case when speculation is in the ascendant. And as soon-come soon goes, consumption is enormously increased, and Lyons feels the effect. I said that every thing has become an object of speculation ; I was mistaken. The American, essentially practical in his views, will never speculate in tulips, even at New York, although the inhabitants of that city have Dutch blood in their veins. The principal objects of speculation are those subjects which chiefly occupy the calculating minds of the Americans, that is to say, cotton, land, city and town lots, banks, railroads.

The amateurs in land at the north, dispute with each

other the acquisition of the valuable timber-lands of that region ; at the southern extremity, the Mississippi swamps, and the Alabama and the Red River cotton lands, are the subject of competition, and in the West, the corn fields and pastures of Illinois and Michigan. The unparalleled growth of some new towns has turned the heads of the nation, and there is a general rush upon all points advantageously situated ; as if, before ten years, three or four Londons, as many Parises, and a dozen Liverpools, were about to display their streets and edifices, their quays crowded with warehouses, and their harbours bristling with masts, in the American wilderness. In New York building-ing lots* have been sold sufficient for a population of two million souls, and at New Orleans, for at least a million. Pestilential marshes and naked precipices of rock have been bought and sold for this purpose. In Louisiana, the quagmires, the bottomless haunts of alligators, the lakes and cypress-swamps, with ten feet of water or slime, and in the North, the bed of the Hudson with 20, 30, or 50 feet of water, have found numerous purchasers.

Take the map of the United States ; place yourself on the shore of Lake Erie, which twenty years ago was a solitary wilderness ; ascend it to its head ; pass thence to Lake St. Clair, and from that lake push on towards the north, across Lake Huron : go forward still, thread your way through Lake Michigan, and advance southwards till the water fails you ; here you will find a little town by the name of Chicago, one of the out-posts of our indefati-gable countrymen when they had possession of America. Chicago seems destined, at some future period, to enjoy an extensive trade ; it will occupy the head of a canal, which is to connect the Mississippi with the lakes and the St. Lawrence ; but at present it hardly numbers two or

---

* A *lot* is generally from 22 to 25 feet front, and from 80 to 100 deep.

three thousand inhabitants. Chicago has in its rear a country of amazing fertility ; but this country is yet an uncultivated wild. Nevertheless the land for ten leagues round has been sold, resold, and sold again in small sections, not, however, at Chicago, but at New York, which, by the route actually travelled, is 2,000 miles distant. There you may find plans of Chicago lots numerous enough for 300,000 inhabitants ; this is more than any city of the New World at present contains. More than one buyer will, probably, esteem himself fortunate, if, on examination, he shall find not more than six feet of water on his purchase.

Speculations in railroads have hardly been less wild than those in land. The American has a perfect passion for railroads ; he loves them, to use Camille Desmoulins' expression in reference to Mirabeau, as a lover loves his mistress. It is not merely because his supreme happiness consists in that speed which annihilates time and space ; is also because he perceives, for the American always reasons, that this mode of communication is admirably adapted to the vast extent of his country, to its great maritime plain, and to the level surface of the Mississippi valley, and because he sees all around him in the native forest, abundance of materials for executing these works at a cheap rate. This is the reason, why railroads are multiplied in such profusion, competing not only with each other, but entering into a rivalry with the rivers and canals. If the works now in process of construction are completed (and I think that they will be,) there will be, within two years, three distinct routes between Philadelphia and Baltimore, exclusive of the old post-route ; namely, two lines consisting wholly of railroads, and a third consisting in part of steamboats, and in part of railroad. The line that has the advantage of half an hour over its rivals, will be sure to crush them.

The manner of establishing banks here is this ; an act

authorising the opening of books in a public place, for subscription of stock, is obtained from the legislature, and all
persons have the right to subscribe on payment of a certain sum, say five, ten, or twenty per cent. on the amount
of stock taken by them respectively. The affair of opening the books becomes a matter of the greatest moment.
In France, we form lanes (*on fait queue*) round the doors
of the theatres ; but in the United States, during the last
year, the doors of the sanctuaries in which the books for
registering the subscriptions for bank-stock have been deposited, have been thronged with the most intense solicitude. In Baltimore, the books were opened for a new
bank, the Merchants' Bank, with a capital of two millions ;
the amount subscribed was nearly fifty million. At
Charleston, for a bank of the same capital, ninety millions
were subscribed, and as the act in this instance required
the advance of 25 per cent., the sum actually paid in, in
paper money to be sure, but yet in current bills at par,
amounted to twentytwo and a half millions, or more than
eleven times the capital required. This rage for bank-
stock is easily explained. Most of the banks here are, in
fact, irresponsible establishments, which have the privilege
of coining money from paper. The share-holders, by
means of a series of ingenious contrivances, realise 8, 9,
10, and 12 per cent. interest on capital, which they do not
actually hold ; and this in a country where the five per
cents. of Pennsylvania and New York, and the six per
cents. of Ohio are at 110 to 115. The Ohio sixes !
What would the heroes of Fort Duquesne think of that,
if they should come back ?

Most of these speculations are imprudent, many of them
are foolish. The high prices of to-day may and needs
must be followed by a crisis tomorrow. Great fortunes,
and many of them too, have sprung out of the earth since
the spring ; others will, perhaps, return to it before the fall

of the leaf. The American concerns himself little about that ; violent sensations are necessary to stir his vigorous nerves. Public opinion and the pulpit forbid sensual gratifications, wine, women, and the display of a princely luxury ; cards and dice are equally prohibited ; the American, therefore, has recourse to business for the strong emotions which he requires to make him feel life. He launches with delight into the ever-moving sea of speculation. One day, the wave raises him to the clouds ; he enjoys in haste the moment of triumph. The next day he disappears between the crests of the billows ; he is little troubled by the reverse, he bides his time coolly, and consoles himself with the hope of better fortune. In the midst of all this speculation, whilst some enrich and some ruin themselves, banks spring up and diffuse credit, railroads and canals extend themselves over the country, steamboats are launched into the rivers, the lakes, and the sea ; the career of the speculators is ever enlarging, the field for railroads, canals, steamers, and banks goes on expanding. Some individuals lose, but the country is a gainer ; the country is peopled, cleared, cultivated ; its resources are unfolded, its wealth increased. *Go ahead !*

If movement and the quick succession of sensations and ideas constitute life, here one lives a hundred fold more than elsewhere ; all is here circulation, motion, and boiling agitation. Experiment follows experiment ; enterprise succeeds to enterprise. Riches and poverty follow on each other's traces, and each in turn occupies the place of the other. Whilst the great men of one day dethrone those of the past, they are already half overturned themselves by those of the morrow. Fortunes last for a season ; reputations, during the twinkling of an eye. An irresistible current sweeps away everything, grinds everything to powder, and deposits it again under new forms. Men change their houses, their climate, their trade, their condition, their party, their sect ;* the States change their laws, their officers, their constitutions. The soil itself, or at least the houses, partake in the universal instability.† The existence of social order, in the bosom of this whirlpool seems a miracle, an inexplicable anomaly. One is tempted to think, that such a society, formed of heterogeneous elements, brought together by chance, and following each its own orbit according to the impulse of its own caprice or interest,—one would think, that after rising for one moment to the heavens, like a water-spout, such a society would inevitably fall flat in ruins the next ; such is not, however, its destiny. In the midst of this general change, there is one fixed point ; it is the domestic fire-side, or, to speak more correctly, the conjugal bed. An austere watchman, sometimes harsh even to fanaticism, wards off from this sacred spot everything that can disturb its stability ; that guardian is the religious sentiment. Whilst that fixed point shall continue invariable, whilst that sentinel shall persist in his vigilant watch over it, the social system may make new somersets, and undergo new changes without serious risk ; it may be pelted by the storm, but while it

---

* The causes of religious changes are various. It is not rare to see Americans, on becoming rich, abandon their former sect for Episcopalianism, for instance, which is the most fashionable. The change, however, from one sect to another is less considerable than is supposed in Catholic countries ; for the different Protestant sects differ less from each other, than a Jansenist from a Molinist, or a Jesuit from a Gallican. But we must except from this remark the Anglican church, which has a peculiar character, discipline, and liturgy, and the two not very numerous sects of Unitarians, who deny the divinity of Christ, and Universalists, who reject the doctrine of reprobation.

† The American houses are low and slight ; the walls are generally only a brick and a half, sometimes only one in thickness ; when, therefore, the course of the street is changed, as is often the case in New York, they are set forward or back with little difficulty, and they are often even raised bodily. In the country, the houses are mostly of wood, and are often transported a considerable distance on wheels. Between Albany and Troy, I was stopped on the road by a house of more than forty feet front, which was travelling in this manner.

is made fast to that hold, it will neither split nor sink. It may even be divided into separate and independent masses, but it will still grow in energy, in resources, in extent.

The influence of the democracy is so universal in this country, that it was quite natural for it to raise its head amidst the speculators. There have, therefore, been strikes on the part of the workmen, who wish to have a share in the profits of speculation, and who have demanded higher wages and less work. The former demand was just, for all provisions, all articles of consumption have risen in price. These coalitions are by no means timid in this country; for the English practice of haranguing in public and getting up processions prevails here, and the working class here feels its strength, is conscious of its power, and knows how to make use of it. The different traders have held their meetings in Philadelphia, New York, and other places, discussed their affairs publicly, and set forth their demands. The women have had their meeting as well as the men. That of the seamstresses of Philadelphia attracted notice; Matthew Carey, known as a political writer, presided, assisted by two clergymen. Among the demands of the trades, that of the journeymen bakers, who, by virtue of the rights of man and the sanctity of the seventh day, would not make bread Sundays, is worthy of attention. The principal trades have decided that all work shall be suspended until the masters,* if this name can be applied here except in derision, have acceded to their *ultimatum.* That every one may know this, they have caused their resolutions to be published in the newspapers, signed by the president and secretaries of the meeting. These resolutions declare that those workmen, who shall refuse to conform to their

---

* This word is not used here; that of employers is substituted for it.

provisions, will have to abide the *consequences* of their refusal. The *consequences* have been, that those refractory workmen, who persisted in their labours, have been driven, with stones and clubs, from their workshops, without any interference on the part of the magistrates. The *consequence* is, that at this very moment, a handful of boatmen on the Schuylkill canal, prevent the coal boats from descending to the sea, lay an embargo upon them, and thus interrupt one of the most lucrative branches of the Pennsylvania trade, deprive the mariners and ship-owners, who transport the coal to all parts of the coast, of wages and freights, and expose the miners to the danger of being dismissed from the mines. Meanwhile the militia looks on ; the sheriff stands with folded arms. If this minority of the boatmen, for these acts of disorder are the work of a small minority, persists in their plans, a fight between them and the miners is to be apprehended.* In Philadelphia, the *consequence* has been, that the carpenters, in order to reduce some contractors to terms, have set fire to several houses, which these latter were building. In this case, the authorities at length interfered, the mayor issued a proclamation, reciting that, whereas there is reason to believe these fires to be the work of some evil-minded persons, he offers 1000 dollars reward to whoever shall disclose the authors of the same. But it is too late. The municipal authorities, for the purpose, it is said of gaining a few votes on the side of the Opposition, instead of interposing their power between the workmen and the masters, hastened, from the first, to comply with all the de-

---

* The citizens of Pottsville have put an end to these outrages, by repairing with a sheriff's mandate to the spot where the boatmen were assembled, and seizing the ringleaders, whom they conducted to prison. This courage of simple citizens, who in time of need convert themselves into an armed force, is one of the surest guarantees of American liberty ; but it is relaxing in the cities.

mands of the former who were employed on the municipal works.

The philosopher, in whose eyes the present is but a point, may find reason to rejoice in considering these facts. Workmen and domestics in Europe live in a state of absolute dependence, which is favourable only to him who commands. Legitimists, republicans, the *juste-milieu*, all comport themselves toward the operative whom they employ, or the domestic who is in their service, as if he were a being of an inferior nature, who owes his master all his zeal and all his efforts, but who has no claim for any return beyond a miserable pittance of wages. One may be permitted to wish for the establishment of a juster scale of rights and duties. In the United States, the absolute principle of the popular sovereignty having been applied to the relations of master and servant, of employer and operative, the manufacturer and the contractor, to whom the workmen give the law, endeavour to dispense with their aid as much as possible, by substituting more and more machinery for human force ; thus the most painful processes in the arts become less burdensome to the human race. The master, whose domestics obey him when they please, and who pays dear* for being badly and ungraciously served, favours, to the extent of his power, the introduction of mechanical contrivances for simplifying work, in order to spare himself the inconveniences of such a dependence.

It would be worth while to study not only the great manufacturing machinery, but the common hand tools and domestic utensils, in this country. These utensils, tools, and machines exert a powerful influence upon the practical liberty of the greatest number ; it is by means of them,

---

* In most of the provinces in France servants' wages are from 12 to 15 dollars a year; here they are from 10 to 12 dollars a month, and one servant in France does the work of two in this country.

that the most numerous class of society gradually frees
itself from the yoke which tends to crush and abase it.
In this point of view, the present relations between the
employer and the employed, between the master and the
servant, in this country, tend to hasten the coming of a
future, which every friend of humanity must hail with joy.
But if the philosophical satisfaction is ample, present, physical comfort is almost absolutely wanting.   But whoever
is neither operative nor domestic, whoever, especially, has
tasted and enjoyed the life of the cultivated classes in
Europe, he will find the actual practical life in America,
the mere bone and muscle, as it were, of life, to consist of
a series of jars, disappointments, mortifications, I had almost
said, of humiliations.   The independence of the operatives
is sometimes the ruin of the masters ; the independence
of servants involves the dependence of the women, condemns them to household labours little consonant with the
finished education which many of them have received,
and nails them to the kitchen and the nursery from the
day of their marriage to the day of their death.

When the innovating force, acting without check or
balance, operates with an excess of energy, all classes suffer equally from the derangement.   Not only what in
Europe are called the higher classes, (but which here must
take another name,) are deprived of a thousand little en-
joyments, which it is a matter of convention to despise in
books and set speeches, although every one sets a high
value on them in practice ; but the whole social machine
gets out of order, discomfort becomes general, and the extravagant claims of the lower classes, to speak as a European,
recoil violently on themselves.   At this very moment, for
example, the Sybarites of Philadelphia, whose hearts are set
upon having fresh bread on Sunday, are not the only persons who suffer or are threatened with suffering.   If the
exaggerated pretensions of the working classes are persisted

in, they will lose their custom, there will be no demand for labour. Speculations, if not made solid by labour, will burst like soap-bubbles, and if a reaction comes, the operative, who is little used to economise, will feel it more sensibly than others.

LETTER XXV.

BEDFORD SPRINGS.

BEDFORD SPRINGS, (PA.) AUG. 7, 1835.

HERE I am at Bedford, one of the American watering-places ; it is hardly three days since I arrived, and I am already in haste to quit it. The Americans, and, still more especially, the American women, must be desperately list-less at home, to be willing to exchange its quiet comfort for the stupid bustle, and dull wretchedness of such a residence. It would seem that in a country truly democratic, as is the case here in the Northern States, nothing like our water-ing-places can exist ; and you will see that in proportion as Europe grows democratic, if such is its destiny, your delightful summer resorts will lose their charm. Man is naturally exclusive ; there are few pleasures, which do not cease to be such, the moment they become accessible to all, and for that reason only. At Saratoga or at Bedford, the American soon grows weary, because he sees that there are twenty thousand heads of families in Philadelphia and New York, who can, as well as he, if the notion seizes them, and it actually does seize them, have the satisfaction of bringing their wives and daughters to the same place, and, once there, of gaping on a chair in the piazza the whole day ; of going, arms in hand (I mean the knife and fork,) to secure their share of a wretched dinner ; of being stifled in the crowd of the ball-room during the evening, and of sleeping, if it is possible, in the midst of such a hubbub, upon a miserable pallet in a cell echoing one's tread from its floor of pine boards. The American passes through the magnificent landscapes on the Hudson without noticing them, because he is one of six hundred or a thousand on board the steamer. And to confess the truth, I have become an American myself in this respect, and I admired the panorama of West Point and the Highlands, only when I found myself alone in my boat on the river.

Democracy is too new a comer upon the earth, to have been able as yet to organise its pleasures and its amusements. In Europe, our pleasures are essentially exclusive, they are aristocratic like Europe itself, and cannot, therefore, be at the command and for the use of the multitude. In this matter, then, as in politics, the American democracy has yet to create every thing afresh. The problem is difficult, but it is not insoluble, for it was once resolved among us. The religious festivals of the Catholic church were eminently democratic ; all were called to them, all took part in them. To what transports of joy did not all Europe, great and small, nobles, burgesses, and serfs, give itself up in the time of the crusades, when the victory of Antioch or the capture of Jerusalem was celebrated by processions and *Te Deums ?* Even to this day, in our southern provinces, where faith is not yet extinct, there are ceremonies truly popular ; such are the festival of Easter with the representations of the Passion exhibited in the churches, and the processions with banners and crosses, the brotherhoods of penitents with their quaint frocks and flowing robes, and their long files of women and children ; with the effigies of the saints in full dress, and their relics piously carried about ; and, finally, with the military and civil pomp, which, notwithstanding the atheism of the law, is mingled with the show. This is the poor man's spectacle, and one which leaves on his mind better and more vivid recollections, than the atrocious dramas of the *boulevard* and the fire-works of the Barrier of the Throne, leave to the suburban of Paris.

Already democracy, especially in the Western States, is beginning to have its festivals, which thrill its fibres, and stir it with agreeable emotions. There are religious festivals, the Methodist camp-meetings, to which the people press with eager delight, in spite of the philosophical remonstrances of the more refined sects, who find fault with their heated zeal and noisy ranting, and in spite, or rather in consequence, of the convulsionary and hysterical scenes of the *anxious bench*. In the older States of the North, there are political processions, for the most part mere party exhibitions, but which are interesting in this respect, that the democracy has a share in them ; for it is the democratic party that gets up the most brilliant and animated. Beside the camp-meetings, the political processions are the only things in this country, which bear any resemblance to festivals. The party dinners, with their speeches and deluge of toasts, are frigid, if not repulsive ; and I have never seen a more miserable affair, than the dinner given by the Opposition, that is to say, by the middle class, at Powelton, in the neighbourhood of Philadelphia. But I stopped involuntarily at the sight of the gigantic hickory-poles which made their solemn entry on eight wheels, for the purpose of being planted by the democracy on the eve of the election. I remember one of these poles, with its top still crowned with green foliage, which came on to the sound of fifes and drums, and was preceded by ranks of democrats, bearing no other badge than a twig of the sacred tree in their hats. It was drawn by eight horses, decorated with ribbands and mottoes ; Astride on the tree itself, were a dozen Jackson men of the first water, waving flags with an air of anticipated triumph, and shouting, *Hurrah for Jackson !*

But this entry of the hickory was but a by-matter compared with the procession I witnessed in New York. It was in the night after the closing of the polls, when victory had pronounced in favour of the democratic party. (See *Letter XV.*). The procession was nearly a mile long ; the democrats marched in good order to the glare of torches ; the banners were more numerous than I had ever seen them in any religious festival ; all were in transparency, on account of the darkness. On some were inscribed the names of the democratic societies or sections ; *Democratic young men of the ninth* or *eleventh ward ;* others bore imprecations against the Bank of the United States ; *Nick Biddle* and *Old Nick* here figured largely, and formed the pendant of our *libera nos a malo.* Then came portraits of General Jackson afoot and on horseback ; there was one in the uniform of a general, and another in the person of the Tennessee farmer, with the famous hickory cane in his hand. Those of Washington and Jefferson, surrounded with democratic mottoes, were mingled with emblems in all tastes and of all colours. Among these figured an eagle, not a painting, but a real live eagle, tied by the legs, surrounded by a wreath of leaves, and hoisted upon a pole, after the manner of the Roman standards. The imperial bird was carried by a stout sailor, more pleased than ever was a sergeant permitted to hold one of the strings of the canopy, in a catholic ceremony. From further than the eye could reach, came marching on the democrats. I was struck with the resemblance of their air to the train that escorts the *viaticum* in Mexico or Puebla. The American standard-bearers were as grave as the Mexican Indians who bore the sacred tapers. The democratic procession, also, like the Catholic procession, had its halting places; it stopped before the houses of the Jackson men to fill the air with cheers, and halted at the doors of the leaders of the Opposition, to give three, six, or nine groans. If these scenes were to find a painter, they would be admired at a distance, not less than the triumphs and sacrificial pomps, which the ancients have left us delineated in marble and brass; for they are not mere grotesques after the manner of Rembrandt, they belong to history, they partake of the grand; they are the episodes of a wondrous epic which will bequeath a lasting memory to posterity; that of the coming of democracy.

Yet as festivals and spectacles, these processions are much inferior to revivals, which take place in the camp-meetings. All festivals and ceremonies in which woman does not take part, are incomplete. Why is it that our constitutional ceremonies are so entirely devoid of interest? It is not because the actors are merely commoners, very respectable citizens surely, but very prosaic, and that the pomp of costumes and the fascination of the arts, are banished from them; it is rather because women do not and cannot have a place in them. A wit has said that women are not poets, but they are poetry itself.

I remember what made the charm and the attraction of the processions in my provincial city. We opened our eyes with wonder at the red robe of the chief president; we gazed with delight at the epaulets and gold lace of the general, and more than one youth was inspired with military ardour at that show; we stretched forward with impatience to catch a glimpse of the episcopal train; we threw ourselves on our knees mechanically, on the approach of the canopy with its escort of priests, and the venerable bishop, crowned with the mitre, and bearing the host in his hands; we envied the glory of those boys, who

had the privilege of enacting St. Mark or St. Peter for the
day; more than one tall stripling was glad to sink his fifteen years, in which he prided himself, for the sake of
taking the character of St. John, clad in a sheepskin; but
the whole multitude held their breath, when, beneath the
forest of banners, through the peaked frocks of the penitents and the bayonets of the garrison, amidst the surplices
and albs of the priests, there appeared in sight one of those
young girls in white robes, who represented the holy women and the Mother of the seven woes; or she, who in
the person of St. Veronica, displayed the handkerchief,
with which the sweat was wiped from the Saviour's brow
as he ascended Mount Calvary; or she, who, loaded with
gold chains, ribands, and pearls, represented the empress
at the side of the emperor;* or those who had just been
confirmed by my lord bishop, and still bore the traces of
the emotions excited by that solemn act. So it is because
there are women in the camp-meetings, and because they
take a not less active part in them than the most rousing
preachers, and it is on this account only, that the American
democracy throngs to these assemblages. The camp-
meetings with their raving Pythonissas have made the
fortune of the Methodists, and attracted to their church in
America a more numerous body of adherents than is numbered by any of the English sects in Europe.

Take women from the tournaments, and they become
nothing more than a fencing-bout; from camp-meetings
take away the *anxious bench*, remove those women who
fall into convulsions, shriek, and roll on the ground, who,
pale, dishevelled, and haggard, cling to the minister from
whom they inhale the holy spirit, or seize the hardened
sinner at the door of the tent, or in the passage-way, and

* This is one of the recollections of the Roman empire, which has left
deep impressions in the South of France.

strive to melt his stony heart ; it will be in vain, that a majestic forest overshadows the scene, of a beautiful summer's night, under a sky that need not fear a comparison with a Grecian heavens ; in vain, will you be surrounded with tents and numberless chariots, that recall to mind the long train of Israel fleeing from Egypt ; in vain the distant fires, gleaming amongst the trees, will reveal the forms of the preachers gesticulating above the crowd ; in vain, will the echo of the woods fling back the tones of their voice ; you will be weary of the spectacle in an hour. But the camp-meetings, as they are now conducted, have the power of holding the people of the West for whole weeks ; some have lasted a month.

I allow that the camp-meetings and political processions are as yet only exceptions in America. A people has not a complete national character, until it has its peculiar and appropriate amusements, national festivals, poetry. In this respect, it will not be easy to create American nationality ; the American has no past from which to draw inspiration. On quitting the old soil of Europe, on breaking off from England, his fathers left behind them the national chronicles, the traditions, the legends, all that constitutes country, that country which is not carried about on the soles of one's feet. The American, then, has become poor in ideality, in proportion as he has become rich in material wealth. But a democracy always has some resource, so far as imagination is concerned. I cannot pretend to decide how the American democracy will supply the want of a past and of old recollections, any more than I can undertake to pronounce, in what manner it will bridle itself, and curb its own humours. But I am sure that America will have her festivals, her ceremonies, and her art, as I am that society in America will assume a regular organisation ; for I believe in the future of American society, or, to speak more correctly, of the beginnings of society, whose growth is visible on the east and still more on the west of the Alleghanies.

In France we have been for more than a century struggling against ourselves, in the attempt to lay aside our national originality. We are striving to become reasonable according to what we imagine to be the English pattern ; and after our example the Southern Europeans are endeavouring to torture themselves into a parliamentary and calculating demeanour. Imagination is treated as a lunatic. Noble sentiments, enthusiasm, chivalric loftiness of soul, all that made the glory of France, and gave Spain half the world, is regarded with contempt and derision. The public festivals and popular ceremonies have become the laughing-stock of the free thinkers. Love of the fine arts is nothing more than a frivolous passion. We make the most desperate efforts to starve the heart and soul, conformably to the prescriptions of our religious and political Sangrados. To strip life of the last vestige of taste and art, we have gone so far as to exchange the majestic elegance of the costume, which we borrowed from the Spaniards when they ruled Europe, for the undress of the English, which may be described in one word, as suited to the climate of Great Britain. This could be borne, if we had merely flung away our tournaments, our carousals, our jubilees, our religious festivals, our elegance of garb. But unhappily we have gone to the sources of all national and social poetry, to religion itself, and tried to dry them up. Our manners and customs scarcely retain the slightest tincture of their boasted grace. Politics is abandoned to the dryest matter of fact. The national genius would have to be given over as past cure, did not now and then some gleams and outbursts prove that it is not dead but sleeps, and that the holy fire is yet smouldering beneath the ashes.

France, and the peoples of Southern Europe, of whom

she is the coryphæus, certainly owe much to the philosophy of the 18th century; for that was our Protest, that raised the standard of liberty amongst us, opened a career for the progress of mind, and established individuality. But it must be confessed that it is inferior to German, English, and American Protestantism, because it is irreligious. The writings of the Apostles of that great revolution will survive as literary monuments, but not as lessons of morality; for whatever is irreligious, can have but a transient social value. Place the remains of Voltaire and Montesquieu, of Rousseau and Diderot, in the Pantheon; but on their monuments deposit their works veiled under a shroud. Teach the people to bless their memory; but do not teach it their doctrines, and do not permit it to learn them from servile followers, whom those great writers would disavow, if they could return to the earth; for men like them belong to the present or a future age, but never to the past.

In return for all that has been taken from us, we have received the representative system. This, it has been supposed, would satisfy all our wants, would meet all our wishes in moral and intellectual, as well as in physical things. Far be it from me to undervalue the representative system! I believe in its permanency, although I doubt whether we have yet discovered the form, under which it is suited to the character of the French and the Southern Europeans; but whatever may be its political value, it cannot be denied that it does not, that it never can, of itself alone, make good the place of all that the reformers have robbed us of. It has its ceremonies and its festivals; but these smell too much of the parchment not to disgust our senses. It has, to a certain degree, its dogmas and its mysteries, but it has no hold on the imagination. Art has no sympathy with it; it has not the power to move the heart; and it embraces, therefore, but one fourth of our existence.

I can conceive how representative government should

here be made the keystone of the social arch. An American of fifteen years of age is as reasonable as a Frenchman of forty. Then society here is wholly masculine; woman, who in all countries has little of the spirit of the representative system, here possesses no authority; there are no saloons in the United States. But even here the system no longer exists in its primitive purity except on paper. The field of religion, although much narrowed, it is true, still remains open here, and the imagination still finds food, however meagre, within its limits. But among us, it would be sheer fanaticism to set up the representative system as the pivot of social life. All of us, God be thanked, have a period of youth! Among us, women have a real power, although not enumerated in the articles of the Charter; and our national character has many feminine, I will not say effeminate, features. In vain would you decimate France, and leave only the burghers of forty years, who have the senses calmed, the mind clear of illusions, that is to say, unpoetical and dry; you would hardly then have a community that would be satisfied with constitutional emotions.

This is the cause why France is the theatre of a perpetual struggle between the old and the middle-aged on one side, and the young, who find their bounds too narrow, on the other. Youth accuses age of narrow views, of timidity, of selfishness; the old complain of the greedy ambition which devours the young, and of their ungovernable turbulence. That is the only good government, which satisfies at once the demands for order, regularity, stability and physical prosperity on the part of those of riper years, and fills the longings of the young, and of that portion of society which always continues youthful, for lively sensations, brilliant schemes, and lofty aspirations. By the side of their parliament, the English have their vast colonies, by which this spirit finds vent, over the remotest seas.

The Anglo-Americans have the West, and also, like Great Britain, the ocean. This double invasion of the East by the fathers, and of the West by the emancipated sons, is a spectacle of gigantic magnitude and sublime interest. To suppose that we, who stand in need of some vast enterprise, in which some may play a part before the eyes of the world, and others may enjoy the spectacle of their prowess,—to suppose that we shall be content to be forever imprisoned within our own territory, with no other occupation than that of watching or turning the wheels of the representative machine, would be to wish that a man of taste, confined to this paltry hamlet of Bedford, should imagine himself in paradise.

LETTER XXVI.

POWER AND LIBERTY.

RICHMOND, AUG. 16, 1835.

RICHMOND stands in an admirable situation on the slope of a hill whose base is bathed by the James River. Its Capitol, with its brick columns covered with plaster, with its cornice and architrave of painted wood, produces an effect, at a distance, which even the Parthenon, in the days of Pericles, could not have surpassed ; for the sky of Virginia, when it is not darkened by a storm, or veiled with snow, is as beautiful as that of Attica. Richmond has its port nearer than the Piræus was to Athens, while, at the same time it stands upon the falls of James River. Richmond enchanted me from the first by its charming situation and the cordiality of its inhabitants ; and it pleases me by its ambition, for it aspires to be a metropolis, and it is making the due preparations to assume that character by the great works which it is executing or aiding to execute, canals, railroads, water-works, huge mills, work-shops, for which the fall in the river affords an almost un-limited motive power.   Here I also found some country-men, whose love for their country had not been chilled by fifty years of absence and eighty years of age, and who have preserved, amidst the simplicity of American man-ners, that fine flower of courtesy, of which the germ is daily disappearing amongst us.   I went yesterday, for the second time, to visit the cannon and mortars, given to America during her struggle for independence, by Louis XVI.   In the Capitol, by the side of the statue of Wash-ington, I found the bust of Lafayette.   I heard the names of Rochambeau and d'Estaing pronounced, as if they were old friends who had left but yesterday.   I seem to myself, at times to have been miraculously transported, not into France, but on the frontiers.

My admiration of Richmond is not, however, blind ; the founders of the new city have plotted out streets one hundred feet wide, like the highways in the style of Louis XIV. ; but in our great roads, between the quagmires on the right and left, there is at least a strip of passable pave-ment or roadway.   The streets of new Richmond have neither pavement nor light.   In the rainy season, they are dangerous bogs, in which, I am told, that several cows, who are here allowed by the municipal authorities to go at large, have met with the fate of the master of Ravens-worth in the Kelpie.   Richmond has, also, something of the aspect of Washington ; with the exception of the busi-ness part of the town, it is neither city nor country ; the houses are scattered about on an imaginary plan, and it is almost impossible to find any lines to guide you, or to re-

cognise the street K, F, or D, to which you are referred ;
for the alphabet has furnished the names here, as the
arithmetic has done at Washington. The plot of Richmond has, however, this advantage over that of Washington, that it is on a smaller scale and will be more speedily
filled up ; whilst Washington with its arrangements for a
million inhabitants, will not, perhaps, have fifty thousand,
twenty years hence.

There is something in Richmond which offends me
more than its bottomless mudholes, and shocks me more
than the rudeness of the western Virginians,* whom I met
here during the session of the legislature ; it is slavery.
Half of the population is black or mulatto ; physically,
the negroes are well used in Virginia, partly from motives
of humanity, and partly, because they are so much live
stock raised for exportation to Louisiana; morally, they
are treated as if they did not belong to the human race.
Free or slave, the black is here denied all that can give
him the dignity of man. The law forbids the instruction
of the slave or the free man of colour in the simplest ru-
diments of learning, under the severest penalties ; the
slave has no family ; he has no civil rights ; he holds no

---

* When the assembly is in session, Richmond is full of country gentlemen from Western Virginia, real giants, taller, stouter, and broader than the
giants who are exhibited among us for money. When I found myself surrounded by these men, with their loud voices and Herculean frame, I experienced the same feeling with the companions of Magellan, when they
found themselves alone amidst a crowd of Patagonians. These good people, to testify their good will, lavish upon you the same weighty caresses, as
those which the Spaniards at first took for blows, and when you feel their
heavy hands fall like a sledge upon your European shoulders, nothing less
than the frank smile that lights up their broad faces, would convince you of
their friendly disposition. The first time I was in Richmond, I occupied the
chamber, that had just been left by one of these gentlemen ; wishing to
consult some of the papers of the session, I sought in vain for any thing like
his library. His whole parliamentary outfit consisted of a mass of empty
bottles, a barrel of biscuit, a case of liquors, and the fragments of a huge
cheese.

property. The white man knows that the slave has opened his ear to the word which every thing here proclaims aloud, liberty ; he knows that in secret the negro broods over hopes and schemes of vengeance, and that the exploits and martyrdom of Gabriel, the leader of an old conspiracy, and of Turner, the hero of a more recent insurrection, are still related in the negro cabins.* The precautionary measures which this knowledge has induced the whites to adopt, are such as freeze the heart of a stranger with horror.

Richmond is noted for its tobacco and flour market. The Richmond flour is prized at Rio Janeiro as much as at New York, at Lima as well as at Havana. The largest flour-mill in the world is at Richmond, running twenty pair of stones, containing a great variety of accessory machinery, and capable of manufacturing 600 barrels of flour a day. The reputation of the Richmond flour in foreign markets, like that of the American flour in general, depends upon a system of inspection peculiar to the country, which contravenes, indeed, the theory of absolute commercial freedom, but is essential to the prosperity of American commerce, and has never, that I have heard of, been a subject of complaint. The flour is inspected previous to its being exported. The weight of each barrel and the quality of of the flour are ascertained by the inspector, and branded on the barrel-head. The superior qualities only can be exported ; the inspection is real and thorough, and is performed at the expense of the holder. The Havana, Brasilian, or Peruvian merchant is thus perfectly sure of the quality of the merchandise he buys ; both the buyer and the seller find their advantage in it.

---

* A gang of negroes rose against their masters in Southampton in 1831, and murdered several white families, without distinction of age or sex, and the alarm became general through the country. The murderers were soon captured and executed.

Commerce can no more dispense with confidence in the market than with credit in the counting-house.

Tobacco is subjected to the same system of inspection, and in general, all the coast States, all those from which produce is exported to foreign parts, have established this system, and applied it to almost all articles in which frauds can be committed. Thus in New York wheat-flour and Indian corn-meal, beef, pork, salt fish, potash, whale oil, lumber, staves, flax-seed, leather, tobacco, hops, spirits, are all inspected. In regard to flour, the law is more rigourous than in respect to other articles. The inspector brands with the word *light* those barrels which are not of the legal weight, and the exportation of which is also prohibited, and with the word *bad* those which are of poor quality. As for Indian corn, it is required that the grain shall have been kiln-dried before grinding. Flour from other States cannot be sold in the city of New York, even for local consumption, unless it has been inspected the same as if for exportation. Every inspector has the right to search vessels in which he suspects that there is flour that has not been inspected, and to seize what has been so shipped, or what it has been attempted to ship. There are beside various other provisions and penalties to prevent fraud.

If the necessity of these inspections were not sufficiently proved by their good effects and by long experience, it would be by the abuses that prevail in those articles of commerce which are not subjected to the system. Complaints have already been made in Liverpool, that bales of cotton are often made up of an inferior article concealed beneath an outer layer of good quality. From a report addressed to the Chamber of American Commerce in this metropolis of the cotton trade, by the principal cotton-brokers, it appears that this has not been confined to two or three bales, amidst large quantities, but that whole lots of one or two hundred bales have been found thus deficient.

What! it will be said, is there not, then, freedom of commerce in this classic land of liberty? No! the foreign commerce is not free in the United States, because the American people is not willing to expose the industry and commerce of a whole country to be ruined by the first rogue that comes along. The people of this country is eminently a working people; every one is at liberty to work, to choose his profession, and to change it twenty times; every one has the right to go and come on his business, at pleasure, and to transport his person and his industry from the centre to the circumference, and from the circumference to the centre. If the country does not enjoy the political advantages of administrative unity, neither is it hampered in the most petty details of industry by excessive centralisation. No man is obliged to go six hundred miles to solicit the license and personal signature of a minister, overloaded with business, and harassed by parliamentary solicitudes. But American liberty is not a mystical, undefined liberty; it is a practical liberty, in harmony with the peculiar genius of the people and its peculiar destiny; it is a liberty of action and motion, of which the American avails himself to spread himself over the vast territory that Providence has given him, and to subdue it to his uses. The liberty of locomotion is almost absolute with the exception of some restraints imposed by the observance of the Sabbath. The liberty, or rather independence, in matters of industry is also ample; but if it is abused by some individuals, the general tendency is to restrain them by law or by dictatorial measures, or by the influence of public opinion, sometimes expressed in the shape of mobs.

The restraints on internal trade are few; there are, however, some restrictions upon hawkers and pedlers who impose on the credulity of the country people. If no effective bankrupt-law has yet been enacted, severe penalties are provided against false pretences. If stock-jobbing has not been prohibited, it is not from want of will on the part of the legislators, for they are fully alive to the evils of unproductive speculation, which diverts from industry the needful capital ; but because they do not see how it is to be effectually prevented. Besides, it is not easy to commit frauds in the United States, in the home trade ; for here every body knows every body else, and every one is on the watch against others; and it is not difficult to ascend to the sources of a fraud. In respect to articles designed for the foreign trade, detection is not so easy. There is also here a sort of patriotism, which is by no means at war with the real interests of the parties, and which operates with the fear of public opinion, in keeping up a certain degree of honesty in domestic transactions, and a tone of morality, which, if not wholly above reproach, is certainly far superior to what prevails amongst us ; whilst, to many persons, all is fair in dealings with foreigners, whom they look upon as a kind of barbarians.

Previous to 1789, we had numerous restrictions not only on foreign commerce, but on domestic industry, in France. These were all blown away by the Revolution ; and certainly the destruction of most of them, which had become antiquated and inapplicable to the existing state of things, was a great gain ; but we have run into the contrary extreme, and abolished not only the burdensome restraints, but the most salutary checks, and among them the inspection of exported articles. Yet on the whole we have gained in respect to domestic industry, by sweeping away those often cumbersome regulations; but in regard to our foreign trade, the evil has certainly overborne the good, as the decline of our maritime commerce fully proves.

On the peace of 1814, when the sea was again opened to our vessels, our foreign commerce fell into the hands of petty traffickers, whose cupidity exhausted the vocabulary of fraud. During the first years after the Restoration, the French name became discredited in all the markets of the Old and the New World. The Levant trade, of which we had the monopoly, passed into the hands of the English and Austrians. The stuffs, with which we formerly supplied the East, being no longer subject to inspection on exportation, fell short in measure and were inferior in quality. Formerly packages of our goods changed hands without distrust and without search; but it became necessary to submit them to a rigourous examination, for their contents often turned out to be quite different from the invoice. South America was the great theatre of these frauds; water was actually sold for Burgundy, rolls of wood for rolls of ribands. The Bordelese, who, not without reason, charge the prohibitive system with the decline of their prosperity, cannot be blind to the fact, that their own unscrupulous rapacity contributed pretty largely to this result.

As customers could no longer be found to deal with us, these frauds have necessarily been checked. Our foreign trade has gradually fallen into the hands of a few great houses, and this concentration, which has powerfully contributed to the prevalence of honorable dealings in English commerce, has done something towards reviving ours. The small dealers have been driven out of the field; and it is to this cause that we have to attribute the good condition of our trade with the United States. But let us not deceive ourselves; some sleights of hand are still played off; Bordeaux is not yet wholly purged of the infection; French commerce abroad is yet cankered by foul sores. It must be confessed, that, if our public policy has been marked by a good faith and a spirit of disinterestedness, that give us a right to denounce the Punic faith of *perfidious Albion,* the English race can proudly oppose the bold and honourable spirit of its commercial dealings to the pusillanimity and unworthy shifts of our own. Let us confess our shame, and submit to the necessary diet for the cure of so loathsome a leprosy.

The United States constitute a society which moves under the impulse and by the guidance of instinct, rather than according to any premeditated plan; it does not know itself. It rejects the tyranny of a past, which is exclusively military in its character, and yet it is deeply imbued with the sentiment of order. It has been nurtured in the hatred of the old political systems of Europe; but a feeling of the necessity of self-restraint runs through its veins. It is divided between its instinctive perceptions of the future and its aversion to the past; between its thirst after freedom, and its hunger for social order; between its religious veneration of experience, and its horror of the violence of past ages. Hence the apparent contradictions which appear in its tastes and its tendencies; but the confusion is only apparent.

In each State there are two authorities, distinct in their composition and their attributes. The one corresponds to the government in the European social system, to the old Cæsar. At its head is a magistrate who bears the old name of Governor,* with the pompous title of commander-

---

* The respect of the Americans for old names and titles is shown in their retaining most of those that were in use under the English rule. Thus the States are divided into counties, and there are in several towns, for instance, in Charleston, a King's Street and a Queen's Street. In Virginia, there are Prince Edward's, Prince George's, King's and Queen's, King George's and King William's Counties. Georgia retained its name, even when at war with the monarch in honour of whom it bore it. I was very much surprised to hear a court of justice in Pennsylvania opened with the old French word *oyez! oyez! oyez!* repeated by the crier, without his understanding the meaning. The English received it from the Normans, and the Americans have retained it, because they received it from their fathers. In France we not only changed the name of Choisy-le-Roi into Choisy-le-Peuple, but we even suppressed the prefix of Saint, in the names of the Streets.

in-chief of the sea and land forces. This authority is reduced to a shadow. In the new States of the West,
which have come into the world since the establishment
of Independence, its attributes have been gradually suppressed, or rather the citizens have reserved the exercise of
them to themselves. Thus the people itself appoint most
of the public officers. The management of funds is rarely
confided to the Governor, but is generally entrusted to a
special board of Commissioners. The Governor has not the
control of the forces of the State ; strictly speaking, indeed,
there are none ; but in case of necessity, the Sheriff has
the right to summon the *posse comitatus*, and to oblige all
bystanders, armed or not, to render him assistance, and to
act as police officers. There is no regular police, there
are no passports ; but nobody can stop at an inn without
entering his name and residence on the register. This
register is open to the examination of all in the bar-room,
which is a necessary appendage of every public place, and
there it remains at all times to be turned over by all. The
bar-keeper fills, in fact, the post of commissioner of police,
and the crowd that assembles in the bar-room to read the
newspapers, smoke, drink whiskey, and talk politics, that
is to say all travellers, would, in case of necessity, be ready
to act the part of constables. This is real self-government ; these are the obligations and responsibilities, that
every citizen takes upon himself when he disarms authority. The power of the Governor, who was formerly
the representative of royalty, the brilliant reflexion of the
omnipotence of the proud monarchs of Europe, is crumbled
to dust. Even the exterior of power has not been kept
up ; he has no guards, no palace, no money. The Governors of Indiana and Illinois have a salary of 1000 dollars
a year, without a house or any accessories. There is not
a trader in Cincinnati, who does not pay his head-clerk
better ; the clerks at Washington have 700 dollars a year.

This fall of power is to be explained by other considerations than those drawn from the principle of self-government. The ancient power was Cæsar, was military in its character. American society has denied Cæsar. In Europe, it has been necessary that Cæsar should be strong for the security of national independence; for in Europe we are always on the eve of war. The United States, on the contrary, are organised on the principle, that war between the States is an impossibility, and that a foreign war is scarcely probable. The Americans, therefore, can dispense with Cæsar, but we are obliged to cleave to him. Yet it is not to be inferred that they can and will long dispense with authority, or that they are even now free from its control. There is, in America, religious authority, which never closes its eyes; there is the authority of opinion, which is severe to rigour; there is the authority of the legislatures, which sometimes savours of the omnipotence of parliament; there is the dictatorial authority of mobs.

Still more; by the side of the power of Cæsar, in political affairs, another regular authority is beginning to show itself, which embraces within its domain the modern institutions and new establishments of public utility, such as the public routes, banks, and elementary schools, that, in the United States, have acquired an unparalleled magnitude. Thus there are Canal Commissioners, Bank Commissioners, School Commissioners. Their power is great and real. The Canal Commissioners establish administrative regulations, which they change at will, without previous notice. They fix and change the rate of tolls; they are surrounded by a large body of agents, entirely dependent upon them and removeable at pleasure; they are charged with the management of large sums of money; the sums that passed through the hands of the Pennsylvania Commissioners amounted to nearly

23,000,000 dollars. They are certainly subjected to a
less minute and rigourous control, than is extended to the
most trifling affairs of our Board of Public Works or our
Engineer Department. If they had had our financial
regulations, our system of responsibility, our court of
accounts, they would, certainly, have spent ten years more
in executing the works entrusted to them, and they would
have executed them no better and no cheaper. The Bank
Commissioners in the State of New York, by the provisions of the Safety Fund Act, are clothed, by right, if not
in fact, with a sort of dictatorship ; they have, in certain
cases, power of life and death over the banks.

It is in the new States, especially, that one should see
the Commissioners exercise their powers. Last summer
the Ohio Canal Commissioners, perceiving or thinking that
they perceived, a conspiracy among the persons engaged
in the transportation of goods on the New York canals to
raise the rates of freight, immediately adopted a resolution
to this effect ; whereas certain persons have shown a disposition to make exorbitant charges, the rates of toll on
all articles that may have paid on the New York canal,
above a certain rate of freight, shall be double. This
was establishing a *maximum*, not only on their own territory, but on that of a neighbouring State. A director-
general of our public routes, who should take such a liberty,
would be forthwith denounced as violating the principles
of commercial freedom. In the United States, every
body agrees that the Ohio Commissioners were right ; that
the profits of the transportation companies would be somewhat less, but the public would be the gainer, and the
former accordingly submitted.

In the United States, then, the general weal is the
supreme law ; and it immediately raises its head and vin-
dicates its rights, when it feels the encroachments of private interest. The system of government in this country

is, therefore, not so much a system of absolute liberty and free will, as a system of equality, or rather it takes the character of a strong rule by the majority. In looking at some of the provisions in the charters of incorporated companies, one is tempted to ask how associations could be formed on such conditions, and how they have been able to procure capital. In Massachusetts, the share-holders are individually responsible for the debts of the company. In Pennsylvania, it is expressly provided, that, if at any time the privileges granted to the corporation shall prove to be contrary to the public good, the legislature may revoke them. This is the germ of despotism; but in the United States, Cæsar is disarmed; the old feudal line has neither fangs nor claws. Industry is prompt to take alarm at the exercise of despotism by Cæsar; but it is only in extreme cases, that it will feel any distrust of a society which lives and flourishes by labour, and all whose ends and aims, public and private, are self-aggrandisement by means of productive labour.

To understand fully the meaning of the word liberty, as it is used in this country, it is necessary to go to the sources of the American population; that is to say, to the origin of the distinction between the Yankee and the Virginian race. They have arrived at their notions of liberty by different avenues, the one by the gate of religion, and the other by that of politics, and have, therefore, understood it very differently.

When the Yankee came to settle himself in the New World, it was not for the purpose of founding an empire, but to establish a church. He fled from a land, which had shaken off the yoke of the papal Babylon, only to fall under that of the Babylon of episcopacy. He left behind him Satan, his pomp, and his works; he shook from the soles of his feet the dust of the inhospitable land of the Stuarts and the Anglican bishops; he sought a refuge

in which he might practise his own mode of worship and
obey what he believed to be the law of God.   The Pilgrims, landed on Plymouth rock, established a liberty
according to their own notion ; it was a liberty for
their own use exclusively, within whose embrace they felt
perfectly at ease themselves, without caring if others were
stifled by it.   It might have been expected, that, proscribed themselves, they would at least have admitted
religious toleration ; but they did not grant it the narrowest
corner, and even now it is far from having elbow room
among them.   Originally, the right of citizenship was
extended only to Puritans like themselves ; the state and
the church were confounded ; it was not until 1832 that
they were definitely and completely separated in Massachusetts.   The Jew and the Quaker were forbidden to
touch the soil under the severest penalties, and in case of
return, under pain of death.   At present, if the law tole-
rates the Roman Catholic, public opinion does not, as the
burning of the Ursuline convent in 1834, and the scandalous scenes exhibited at the trials of the incendiaries, testify.
Still less mercy is shown to unbelief ; witness the trial of
Abner Kneeland for blasphemy, on account of his panthe-
istic writings.*

   The Yankee type exhibits little variety ; all Yankees
seem to be cast in the same mould ; it was, therefore, very
easy for them to organise a system of liberty for themselves, that is, to construct a frame, within which they
should have the necessary freedom of motion.   On their
arrival they accordingly formed the plan of one, not merely
tracing its general outlines and form, but dividing it into
numerous compartments controlling all the details of life,

---

* It is unnecessary to say that the author has here fallen into a gross
error.   Even in the affair of the convent at Charlestown, it was the supposed
abuse of a particular institution, not the Roman Catholic religion itself, that
kindled the flame.—TRANSL.

with as much minuteness as the Mosaic law did that of the Hebrews. Thus organised, it became impossible for any man not cut to the same pattern, to establish himself among them. Although most of those laws which thus reduced life to rules,* have been abrogated, especially since the Revolution, still their spirit survives. The habits which gave them birth, and to which, by a natural reaction, they gave strength, still exist, and to this day it is observable, that no foreigner settles in New England.

As for us, who resemble each other in nothing, except in differing from every body else, for us, to whom variety is as necessary as the air, to whom a life of rules would be a subject of horrour, the Yankee system would be torture. Their liberty is not the liberty to outrage all that is sacred on earth, to set religion at defiance, to laugh morals to scorn, to undermine the foundations of social order, to mock at all

---

* I doubt if the power of the community over the individual has been pushed to such an extent anywhere else as in New England ; in Connecticut there were laws forbidding a person to continue tippling more than half an hour at a tavern, or to drink more than half a pint of wine, and it was ordered that taverns and victualling-houses should be closed at half past nine o'clock. No young man not married could keep house without the consent of the town ; and no housekeeper could receive a young man to sojourn in his family without the same permission. Laws were made against swearing, lying, uttering false news or reports, or using tobacco without a certificate from a physician that it was necessary to health. Other regulations prohibited smoking in public places, and this very year the city government of Boston has forbidden smoking in the Mall, which, however, I do not consider a measure of excessive rigour. It is unnecessary to say that the laws of the New England colonies were extremely severe in religious matters ; every individual was required to join some Congregational society, and no one was eligible to any public trust, unless he had so done. Dissenters were taxed for the support of the established church. Jews and Quakers were banished, and forbidden to return under pain of death. The *Blue Laws* of Connecticut contained some curious provisions in respect to marriage, and at Taunton, in Massachusetts, in 1836, two justices forbade the bans of matrimony, on the ground that the parties could not provide for themselves after the marriage, and that they had not sufficient discernment to enter into a contract of such moment.

traditions and all received opinions ; it is neither the liberty of being a monarchist in a republican country, nor that of sacrificing the honour of the poor man's wife or daughter to one's base passions ; it is not even the liberty to enjoy one's wealth by a public display, for public opinion has its sumptuary laws, to which all must conform under pain of moral outlawry ; nor even that of living in private different from the rest of the world. The liberty of the Yankee is essentially limited and special like the nature of the race. We should consider it as framed after the model of the liberty of Figaro ; but the Yankee is satisfied with it, because it leaves him all the latitude he desires, and because of all the lessons of the Bible, that of the forbidden fruit, which we have not been able to fix in our brain, has made the deepest impression on his.

As the Yankee does not suffer under these restraints, as he is, or what amounts to the same thing, thinks himself, free, a preventive authority is unnecessary for him. This is the reason why there is no appearance of authority in New England, and that an armed force, a police, are even more unknown there than in the rest of the Union. The absence of a visible authority imposes on us, and we think that the American in general, and the Yankee in particular, is more free than we are. I am persuaded, however, that if we measure liberty by the number of actions that are permitted or tolerated in public and private life, the advantage is on our side, not only in comparison with New England, but also with the white population of the South.

The Virginian is more disposed to understand liberty in our manner. His disposition has a greater resemblance to ours ; his faculties are much less special, more general than those of the Yankee ; his mind is more ardent, his tastes more varied. But it is the Yankee that now rules the Union ; it is his liberty which has given its principal features to the model of American liberty. Yet to extend its empire, it has been obliged to borrow some of the characteristic traits of Virginian liberty ; or, I might say, of French liberty, for the high-priest of American democracy was a Virginian, who had imbibed in Paris the doctrines of the philosophy of the 18th century. American liberty, as it now is, may be considered the result of a mixture, in unequal proportions, of the theories of Jefferson with the New England usages. From these dissimilar tendencies has resulted a series of contradictory measures, which have become strangely complicated with each other, and which might puzzle and deceive a careless observer. It is in consequence of these opposite influences in the bosom of American society, that such conflicting judgments have been passed upon it ; it is because the Yankee type is at present the stronger, whilst the Virginian was superior in the period of the revolution, that the ideas which the sight of America now suggests, are so different from those which she inspired at the epoch of Independence.

LETTER XXVII.

SOCIAL IMPROVEMENT.

CHARLESTON, SEPTEMBER 1, 1835.

THE United States are certainly the land of promise for the labouring class. What a contrast between our Europe and America ! After landing in New York, I thought every day was Sunday, for the whole population that throngs Broadway seemed to be arrayed in their Sunday's

best.   None of those countenances ghastly with the privations or the foul air of Paris ; nothing like our wretched
scavengers, our ragmen, and corresponding classes of the
other sex.   Every man was warmly clad in an outer gar-
ment ; every woman had her cloak and bonnet of the
latest Paris fashion.   Rags, filth, and suffering degrade the
woman even more than the man ; and one of the most
striking features in the physiognomy of the United States,
is, undeniably, the change which has been introduced,
in the train of the general prosperity, into the physical
condition of women.*   The earnings of the man being
sufficient for the support of the family, the woman has no
other duties than the care of the household, a circumstance
still more advantageous for her children than for herself.
It is now a universal rule among the Anglo-Americans,
that the woman is exempt from all heavy work, and she
is never seen, for instance, taking part in the labours of
the field, nor in carrying burdens.†   Thus freed from
employments unsuited to her delicate constitution, the
sex has also escaped that hideous ugliness and repulsive
coarseness of complexion which toil and privation every
where else bring upon them.   Every woman here has the
features as well as the dress of a lady ; every woman here
is called a lady, and strives to appear so.   You would
search in vain among the Anglo-Americans, from the
mouth of the St. Lawrence to that of the Mississippi, for
one of those wretched objects, who are feminine only with
the physiologist, in whom our cities abound, or for one of
those haggish beldams that fill our markets and three

---

* The legal condition of all classes of females in the United States is
the same as that of the women of the middle classes in England.   The
same is the case with their moral condition, except that they have even more
liberty before marriage, and are more dependent after.

† In England a woman is never seen, as with us, bearing a hamper of
dung on her back, or labouring at the forge.

fourths of our fields. You will find specimens of the former class only among the Indians and negroes, and of the latter, only among the Canadian French and Pennsylvania Germans ; for their women labour at least as much as the men. It is the glory of the English race, that they have ever and every where, as much as possible, interpreted the superiority of the man to the woman, as reserving to the former the charge of the ruder and harder forms of toil. A country in which woman is treated according to this principle presents the aspect of a new and better world.

Figure to yourself an Irish peasant, who at home could scarcely earn enough to live on potatoes, who would look upon himself as a rich man if he owned an acre of ground, but who, on stepping ashore at New York, finds himself able to earn a dollar a day by the mere strength of his arm. He feeds and lodges himself for two dollars a week, and at the end of a fortnight he may have saved enough to buy ten acres of the most fertile land in the world. The distance from New York to the West, is great, it is true ; but the fare on the great canal is trifling, and he can easily pay his way by the work of his hands. It is also true, that the poorest Irishman would not think of buying so little as ten acres ; the least that one buys in the West is eighty. What of that ? The savings of a few months will enable him to compass them ; besides, *Uncle Sam* favours emigrants, and if, in theory, he does not sell his land on credit, he is, in fact, very indulgent to the pioneer who comes to subdue the savage wilderness, and he allows him to occupy the soil temporarily without charge. Thus the Irish, who would go to fisticuffs with any body for denying in their presence that the isle of Erin was a terrestrial paradise, and who, under the inspiration of whiskey, sing the glories of that *first pearl of the sea*, quit it by fifty thousands for the United States. On their arrival, they cannot believe their own eyes ; they feel of themselves to find out whether they are not under some spell. They do not dare to describe to their friends in Europe the streams of milk and honey that flow through this promised land.*

Even in this section of the country, where the workman in the towns and the labourer in the country, instead of being as in the North the sovereigns of the country, are slaves, there is more plenty, more physical comfort among the labouring class than is found amongst us. The coloured population, therefore, increases in numbers faster than our rural population. Not that our peasant gives birth to fewer children than the blacks of Virginia and Carolina; but death, led by the hand of want, is active in keeping down the excessive multiplication of arms that would soon become formidable competitors of the fathers, and in closing forever mouths that would cry for bread which their parents could not supply. The attention of the benevolent in Europe has long been directed towards the reduction of the public expenditures, and a more equal distribution of the burden of taxation, as a means of improving the condition of the poor; but all these plans, supposing them to succeed according to the views of the projectors, would merely amount to taking a few coppers less from the pockets of the poorer class. Whilst a system of measures concerted in such a manner as to diffuse among them a love of order and habits of regularity and industry, to enlarge the field of labour, and to render its terms more favourable to them, would have the effect to fill those pockets. The relief of one class of the community by merely shifting its burden to the back of another, has a

* An Irishman, who had recently arrived, showed his master a letter which he had just written to his family: "But, Patrick," said his master, "why do you say that you have meat three times a week, when you have it three times a day?" "Why is it?" replied Pat; "it is because they wouldn't believe me, if I told them so."

revolutionary character which ill agrees with the notions of a generation that is weary of revolutions, or with the nature of a government established for the very purpose of staying the revolutionary flood ; on the contrary, all that develops the resources of industry is in harmony with the present leaning of all minds.   Labour is an admirable instrument of concord, for all interests gain by the prosperity of industry.   This is the pure and true source of all wealth, public and private.   Labour alone creates ; and it is it alone that can relieve the wants of the needy, without impoverishing him who has enough, or even reducing the luxury of the opulent ; that can give wealth to some, competency to others, and to all *the fowl in the pot*, which, since the revolt of Luther, has been the great social problem in the material order of things.

The admirable prosperity of the United States is the fruit of labour, much more than of any reform in taxation. The soil has not the luxuriant fertility of the tropical regions ; roasted larks fly into nobody's mouth ; but the American is a model of industry.   This country is not a second edition of the Greek and Roman republics ; it is a gigantic commercial house, which owns its wheat-fields in the Northwest, its cotton, rice and tobacco plantations in the South, which maintains its sugar works, its establishments for salting provisions, and some good beginnings of manufactures, which has its harbours in the Northeast thronged with fine ships, well built and better manned, by means of which it undertakes to carry for the world, and to speculate on the wants of all nations.   Every American has a passion for work, and the means of gratifying it.   If he wishes to cultivate the ground, he finds waste land enough for his farm in the Northwest or the Southwest.   If he chooses to be a mechanic, that he may finally become a manufacturer, he has no difficulty in getting credit ; he finds unemployed waterfalls all along the rivers, of which he takes possession, and on which he sets up his wheels. If he has a taste for commerce, he puts himself into the hands of a merchant, who after some years of apprenticeship and trial, sends him to take charge of his business in the interior, or to the Antilles, or South America, or Liverpool, or Havre, or Canton. He may labour without apprehension, and produce without stint; having no rent to pay, his flour, his salt provisions, fear no competition in the markets of South America and the sugar islands. As for cotton, the United States alone almost supply the world, and he cannot plant enough. The career open to the Americans, as active, bold, and intelligent merchants, is unlimited, and is entered with admirable spirit and success; they beat their rivals, even the English, on every field. If the American devotes himself to some branch of domestic industry, here he finds ample room for activity, for the home consumption is indefinite; every body here enjoys himself, or at least spends. Every one produces much, because all consume much; each consumes freely, because he gains freely, has no fears for the morrow neither for himself nor his children, or at least takes no thought for it.

The most efficient measures of the public administration for the amelioration of the condition of the people in France, would be such as would tend to increase the industrial qualities of the mass, and to furnish them with the means of putting these qualities in action; such are, a system of industrial education; the establishment of institutions of credit, which should place within the reach of all, the instruments of industry, or, in other words, capital, which is now inaccessible not only to the operative and the labourer, but to a great proportion of the *bourgeoisie;* the execution of a complete system of routes of communication, from village roads to railroads, for manufactures and commerce are impracticable where facilities of transportation do not exist; the modification of many laws and customs, judicial and administrative, that now embarrass industry, without being of the least advantage in any point of view.

I dare hardly speak of popular education, where I now am. The people in the Southern States, are slaves. The maxim here is that they need no instruction; to instil into them a sentiment of fear is the only moral nature suitable to their condition. They have, therefore, no other education than that of their own hands, and that, of course, must be limited, because their intellectual and moral nature is in fetters. In the Northern States, the labouring classes are whites, and there the law makes a liberal provision for popular instruction. Almost every where in the North, all the children go to the primary schools. Elementary education is there of a more practical character than with us; it is our primary instruction, with the omission of the ideal, and the addition of some instruction in commercial and economical affairs; but there is no practical industrial education here except by apprenticeship. There are no mechanical or agricultural seminaries. It is not thought necessary here to shut up the young in such institutions to inspire them with a taste for commerce, agriculture, or the mechanical arts; they suck it in with their mother's milk; they breathe the air of industry under the paternal roof, in the places of public resort, in the public meetings, every where, at all times, and in every act of life. When an American wishes to learn a trade, he goes into the work-shop, the counting-house, the manufactory, as an apprentice. By seeing others act, he learns how to act himself; he becomes an artisan, a manufacturer, a merchant; all the faculties of his firm and watchful mind, all the energies of his ambitious spirit are centred in his workshop or warehouse. He directs all his powers to making himself master of his business, to learn the lessons of others' experience, and he succeeds of course, as every one does who obeys the voice of his destiny. I do not pretend that the Americans are right in not having recourse to a theoretical preparation for a particular branch of business, for which we have instituted such costly establishments. I only record the fact, with the observation that they get on very well without it. Our national character has little disposition for business ; we work from necessity and not from choice. Our ideas have little of a commercial or mechanical turn. To make a Frenchman a skilful husbandman, an able merchant, a dexterous mechanic, a long and painful training is necessary ; he must change his natural bent, and metamorphose all his thoughts and habits ; in a word, with us a special professional education must precede apprenticeship. The American learns by example merely ; we must learn by general principles ; we stand more in need of them, and we have a greater aptitude for mastering them, than they.

*   *   *   *   *   *

Before passing to the institutions best suited to develop industry, I would observe that a political system which should be particularly calculated to create and sustain them, cannot be taxed with materialism. Industry influences the moral nature of man ; the material prosperity of a people has an important bearing on the public liberties. Men cannot practically enjoy the rights secured to them by law, when they are manacled and fettered by poverty ; the English and their children in America call competency, *independence*. The Anglo-Americans have reached wealth through their political liberty ; other nations, and we, I think, are of the number, must arrive at political franchises by the progress of national wealth. I now come to the consideration of a credit system.

Suppose, on one side, the land-holder who has granaries bursting with corn, his stable filled with cattle, his storehouse crowded with barrels of whiskey and salt meat ; then, the merchant with his warehouses full of cloth, and the grocer, well supplied with tea, coffee, and sugar ; and on the other, the labourer, the mason, the carpenter, the smith, all skilled in their trade and wanting work to supply them with daily food. A canal or a railroad is projected ; the country has capital enough to construct it, since it contains the arms to execute the works, and the necessaries for subsisting the labourers. The construction of the work is indispensable in order to enable the workman to turn his muscles to account, and gain his daily bread, and to give the merchant a market for his goods. Now in this case, amongst us, there is no other medium of communication between the labourer and the holder of articles of consumption, than the engineer, a man of science but not of capital, and the citizens of the towns which are interested in the scheme ; these last have a competence and no more, and they have no means of raising, on their lands or their houses, the ready money which must serve as a medium of exchange between the wares of the merchant, the produce of the cultivator, and the labour of the operative. Amongst us, therefore, the most useful projects remain on paper. In this country, by the side of the engineer and the citizen, you have one or more banks, in which all, labourers, landholders, and traders, put confidence, often, indeed, much more than is deserved. The bank guaranties to the cultivator and the trader payment for their produce and merchandise, and to the labourer, his wages ; for this end, it offers the share-holder of the projected enterprise, in exchange for his personal engagement renewable at a certain date, and often on the pledge of the very canal or railroad shares, a paper-money, which the labourer receives in payment of his wages, and with which he procures the necessary supplies from the pro-

ducer or the trader. Thus every judicious and practicable project is at once carried out into execution.

In order to arrive at the same result amongst us, it
would be necessary, in the first place, that we should
possess somewhat more of that genius for business which
is the characteristic of the American, and, in the next,
that the banks should be able to accept with confidence
the engagements of the share-holder of the work ; the latter
requisite, could not be obtained as in the United States,
because amongst us, except in the manufacturing towns,
the *bourgeois* in general does not engage in business ; he
is a proprietor living on his income and not increasing it.
The American *bourgeois*, on the contrary, is actively engaged in business, and is constantly employed in increasing his means ; and besides, the banks have more hold
on his real property, than they could have in France.

Finally, it would be necessary that the public, proprietors and labourers, traders as well as landholders, should
have full confidence in the bills issued by the bank, which
is impossible in a country where all paper-money suggests
the idea of *assignats*.   Even if the people had not that
disastrous experiment before their eyes, it would be difficult to teach them to look upon a scrap of paper, although
redeemable at sight with coin, as equivalent to the metals.
A metallic currency, has, in our notions, a superiority to
any other representative of value, which to an American
or an Englishman is quite incomprehensible ; to our peasants, it is the object of a mysterious feeling, a real worship ;
and, in this respect we are all of us more or less peasants.
The Americans, on the other hand, have a firm faith in
paper ; and it is not a blind faith, for if we have had our
assignats, they have had their continental money, and
they need not go far back in their history to find a record
of the failure of the banks in a body.   Their confidence
is founded in reason, their courage is a matter of reflexion.

Last winter, for example, it was known to the public that certain banks in New York had on hand only five dollars in specie for one hundred paper-dollars in circulation, and even less. In France this would have been the signal of a general panic, and the bill-holders would have thrown themselves in crowds upon the bank to exchange their paper for coin. The bank, thus stormed, would have stopped payment; fifty or seventy bills in a hundred, would have become mere rags in the hands of the holders, and what would be more fatal, the banks, which lean upon each other, and hold each other's notes to a large amount, would have failed one after another, as those of the Federal District did last April. Each bank failure would have been followed by numerous individual failures, which would have involved other banks in their fall, and the country would have been ruined. The Americans in this fearful crisis, did not quail ; they stood firm, like veterans under the fire of a battery or encountering a cloud of Arabs at the foot of the pyramids with bayonets crossed and serried files. None of the New York banks stopped payment, and scarcely six or seven small banks failed through the country.

Let us not deceive ourselves; it will be a long time before we shall be in a condition, in France, to enjoy such a system of credit as exists in the United States or England; in this respect we are yet in a state of barbarism, from which we cannot pass to a more perfect condition of things, except by a complete revolution in our commercial habits and ideas, and even to a certain degree of our national manners.

I do not pretend to decide beforehand what the precise organisation of a system of credit for France should be ; but I think it may be safely affirmed, that the system which prevails here would not do for us. In appropriating to ourselves the improvements of the English and of their successors in America, we must modify them in conformity with the genius of the nation, or they will wither on our soil.   As the East is the cradle of religion, so England in our day is the mould in which the political and commercial institutions that seem destined to rule the world have been cast; but as the religious conceptions of the East have had to undergo a radical change in order to gain a footing in the West, so the political and commercial creations of our neighbours, must undergo a transformation before they can become fixed amongst us.   Coming into the world under circumstances of a peculiar nature, amidst a people of an original and peculiar character, born under the unhealthy shadow of conquest and civil war, they are not suited to be transferred bodily to another soil. They are already undergoing modifications in America, although they are here amongst the scions of the English stock.   Among the people of the south of Europe and among us, when they have taken their final shape, it is probable that they will no more resemble their British type, than a Benedictin or a Sister of Charity resembles an Indian fakir or dervish.   It would be presumptuous to attempt to pronounce at present what precise form the institutions of credit will assume;   yet it is reasonable to presume, that to be in harmony with our character and disposition, they must lean upon the government, combine their operation with its action, become, in a word, public establishments, and they must be ready to extend a large share of their benefits to the agricultural interest.

The public credit, which, in France, must be the bulwark of private credit, still feels and will continue to feel the effect of our former bankruptcy.   It should be our aim to make the breaches of the public faith under the monarchy and under the republic forgotten, and to strengthen the foundations and enlarge the sphere of the national credit, which will thus become a suitable basis for the banks, for in France we shall not trust in the bankers, nor will the banks have confidence in themselves, any further than they are propped up by the government, and become in fact public establishments. Many sound heads consider it indispensable that the system of credit, should be, in many respects, amalgamated with the financial system of the State. This is no rash speculation, or untried novelty. In the Southern and Western States, which, like France, are chiefly agricultural, the principal banks are dependent on the State governments, they are employed in collecting the taxes, and transferring funds on account of the State treasury. This is the case, in a greater or less degree, in the Carolinas, Georgia and Alabama, and still more so in Indiana and Illinois.

The greatest change, which institutions of credit will have to undergo in their introduction amongst us, will be the adaptation of them to the wants of agriculture. We are more an agricultural than a manufacturing people ; three fourths or four fifths of our population live by agriculture. The English are especially devoted to manufactures and commerce ; their banks are most easily accessible to the merchant, next to the manufacturer, and but little or not at all, to the agriculturist. The feudal traits, which landed property still retains among them, contribute to this result. In this country, the banks have been organised on the English model. They have become excessively numerous in the Northern States,* which are

---

* In 1811, out of 88 local banks, there were 55, or two thirds, in New England and New York, although those States contained but little more than one third of the population. In 1834, the States north of the Potomac had 414 banks, with a capital of 106 millions ; the Southern and Western States had only 88 with a capital of 60 millions, about one half of which were in a few commercial towns. The population of the former was then 6,500,000, of the latter 7,500,000 ; the ratio of the banks, therefore, was as 4 to 3, while that of the population was as 6 to 7. Massachusetts and Connecticut alone, in which the character of the mother-country is most strongly pre-

inhabited by a people eminently possessing the manufacturing and commercial spirit. Those which have been
established in the agricultural States of the South and
West, have fallen through at different crises, of which
the most disastrous was that of 1819. In 1828, the local
banks had ceased to exist in Kentucky and Missouri; each
of the States of Tennessee, Indiana, Illinois, Mississippi,
and Alabama, had but one, or had not yet established any.
At present they are created in the South and West with
something of a public character, the state either becoming
the principal share-holder or guarantying the loan for raising
a capital. Several of them have a decided tendency to
connect themselves with the agricultural interest. Louisiana has adopted the most comprehensive and important
measures in this respect.*

It is evident that the extension of credit in France
would be the means of a greater saving to the people,
than any reform in the budget. The average rate of
interest on all transactions of all kinds is at least 15 or 20,
perhaps, 25 per cent. Suppose that this could be reduced

---

served, had 174 banks or one third of the whole number of local banks,
with a capital of 40 millions, or one-fourth of the whole banking capital
of the country, although their population was only one thirteenth of the
whole population. The extension of the culture of cotton, and of the trade
which it creates, has since, however, tended to turn the balance in favour of
the south, and several large banks have been established in the southern
capitals with branches in the interior.

* Several bank charters in Louisiana contain a provision obliging the bank
to lend a large proportion of the capital to the planters. The Citizen's
Bank is bound to advance one half its capital to landholders, beside which
they have the advantage of being share-holders without having paid up anything. The bank borrowed its effective capital of European capitalists; its
nominal capital is double that sum. It gives in return mortgages on the
estates of the share-holders to that amount, with the guarantee of the mortgage
by the State. Each share-holder is entitled to credit to the amount of half
his stock at the rate of six per cent. The other half of the capital is devoted
to the commercial operations of the bank. The share-holders then, have their
share in the profits. It will be seen that this system depends on the legislation in regard to mortgages.

only two per cent., a result which does not seem very difficult to be obtained, it is plain, that as positive a saving would be made to the country as could be made by a diminution of the expenses of government, and that the former would he applicable to as many millions as the latter would be to thousands.   It is not possible to give an exact estimate of the amount of the annual transactions in France, it must be enormous, for every time an article of property changes hands, there is a transaction affected by the rate of interest ; now the total annual produce of French industry is estimated at nearly 2,000 millions dollars ; and we must suppose the amount of transactions to be ten or twelve times greater.   The annual amount of commercial transactions alone is about 4,000 millions.   Admitting the average credit to be four months, and the mass of transactions to amount to 16,000 millions, a saving of two per cent. a year would be equal to 100 millions.   Add to this that the creation of institutions of credit would make a saving once for all of 300 or 400 millions, by the substitution of paper for a portion of the metallic currency. (See *Letter V.*)

It would be superfluous to dwell upon the salutary influence of a judicious system of public works on the prosperity of all classes, and more especially of the lower classes.   On this point every one is already convinced ; it would be an enterprise worthy of a great people to undertake such a system, which should include canals, local roads, and railroads on the great routes ; which should drain our bogs and supply water to the districts that need irrigation ; which should convert Rouen and Havre, Lille and Calais, Orleans, Reims, and Troyes into suburbs of Paris ; should consummate the union of Belgium with France ; should make Strasburg one of the greatest *entrepôts* in the world ; should restore life to Bordeaux, which is now pining away, by giving it a more easy access to the central and southern departments ; should revive Nantes,

which is dead, by connecting it with the flourishing interior provinces, and particularly with Paris, the heart of
France ; should bring Lyons into contact with the Rhine
and the Danube ; should develop our mineral wealth,
which now lies useless in the bowels of the earth, for
want of means of transportation ; should not, as is too
often the case, overlook our peaceful and laborious country
population, but should deliver every farm and village from
the six months' blockade, to which they are now condemned by the mud of every winter. This would be
a grand and noble enterprise.

There is a common bond of union between the various
branches of social improvement ; a good system of public
works would exercise a powerful influence on the extension of credit, and, reciprocally, a liberal system of public
and private credit, would communicate activity to public
enterprises.   I go further ; it is impossible that our public
works should be carried forward with vigour, without the
aid of credit.   To pretend to execute them wholly by
means of taxes, would be madness.   Without public and
private credit, the Americans would never have had any
public works.   They have entered upon the construction
of their great canals and their innumerable railroads only
through the instrumentality of the banks and their loans.
In 1828, the three cities of the Federal District, Washington, Georgetown, and Alexandria, having together a population of 32,000 souls, with little trade, no manufactures,
or agricultural resources, for the country around is sterile,
subscribed 1,500,000 dollars towards the construction of
the great canal from the Chesapeake to the Ohio, raising
the funds by a loan in Holland.   Our large towns Bordeaux, Marseilles, Rouen, Lyons, will have canals and
railroads, whenever they shall see fit to do with moderation
what Washington, Georgetown, and Alexandria have
attempted on too great a scale.

The improvement of the means of transportation often causes such a fall in the price of articles, that the construction of a canal or road relieves the inhabitants to an extent much exceeding the amount of the most oppressive tax. In France, where wine is abundant, and where it is a light drink which does not brutify a man, it is important to bring it within the reach of the poorer classes, and to accustom them to the daily use of it. There are still several districts in central and southern France, in which wine is transported on the back of mules, for a distance of 40 miles. Transportation, the same distance, by a canal, would only be one sixth of the price of mule carriage, or would make a saving of five cents a gallon, which is more than the excise on the common wines; so that the construction of a canal, considered in this light, would be a greater relief to certain consumers, than the suppression of the excise.

In regard to legislation, we have reason to congratulate ourselves on having a uniform system of laws, instead of a jumble of rules and customs derived from all ages and various sources. The spirit of Napoleon pervaded the creation of this noble work; but Napoleon was wholly pre-occupied with Roman ideas; he wished to found an empire of adamant on the Roman model; his counsellors were possessed with the notion that the Roman law was pure, absolute, immutable justice. They have, therefore, given us a code of laws, protecting various interests rather according to the degree of importance which they possessed eighteen hundred years ago, than that which they have acquired in modern times. In the time of the Romans, landed property was almost the only property; agriculture was the only branch of industry held in respect; manufactures were merely a department of domestic labour, and were carried on by the slaves in the house; commerce was abandoned to foreigners and freedmen. At that time, no one dreamed of the possibility of those huge factories

on the English plan, or of that powerful machinery which
is the soul of our industry ; or those immense docks and
and store-houses, which enable a man, in his closet, to
arrange and direct the most extensive operations, without
touching an article of merchandise, or even inspecting
samples, merely by setting his signature to a warrant or a
receipt. The system of accounts was then unknown ; the
idea of banks did not occur to the most far-sighted intellect. Governments took little thought for the means of
making exchanges sure, easy, and speedy ; the great roads
opened by the prætors and emperors, were military roads.
Little care was given to economy of time ; for time has a
value only in an industrious community.*   On the contrary, there was every reason for endeavouring to keep
property in the great families.   Landed property, with reference to which all the laws were framed, is inconsistent
with the idea of constant change.   The object of legislation was stability and permanency ; the forms which it
established, were favourable to delay.

Following this example, Napoleon and his counsellors
have given us a code of laws, in which every thing is
sacrificed to landed property.   The law treats the manufacturer and the merchant with suspicion ; it looks upon
them as the sons of the slave and the freedman, or at
least, as persons of no consideration, commoners whom it
is permitted to treat without ceremony.   On the other
hand, the presumption is always in favour of the proprietor ; he is protected not because he is a cultivator and producer, but simply and abstractly because he is a proprietor,

---

* The Neapolitans are said to have made the following objection to a
company, which proposed to run a steam-boat between their city and Sicily :
" Your boat takes us over in one day, and yet you demand the same fare, as
a sail vessel which is three days.   That is absurd ; how can you expect that
we will pay as much for being found one day as for three ? "   This is the
reasoning of a people, who have no idea of setting an economical value on
time.

the owner of the soil, the successor of the Roman patrician and the feudal lord. Thus our laws overlook the importance of manufacturing industry, and the great destiny which awaits it; they shackle and check ti by the complicated formalities to which they subject it, and the vexatious details with which they embarrass its movements.

Let me not, however, be too severe on our code; I do not know any other, which, all things considered, is more advantageous to industry. Even the American legislation has retained the defects of the English laws; it partakes in their vagueness and uncertainty; it is under the almost exclusive dominion of precedents which it still borrows from English decisions as if North America were still an English colony. In most of the States, the undefined and conflicting pretensions of the common law and equity jurisdiction still remain in force. In some of the old States, as Virginia, the legislation yet bears many of the features of the feudal system. American law, however, has the great advantage of a simpler and less expensive process than ours or the English, and especially of a great economy of time by a reduction of the delays attending the English and French practice. As for the use of the jury in civil cases, it is of doubtful expediency. I often hear it said, that it would be better to leave them to three judicious and irremoveable judges, than to twelve citizens, who often carry their individual prejudices, or party passions, or class jealousies into the jury-box. With a jury, the influence of a skilful advocate often weighs much, the merits of the cause too little. Finally, in this country, the commercial tribunals have no compulsory jurisdiction; the ordinary courts take cognizance of all causes, unless there is a previous agreement between the parties to submit all differences that may arise between them to arbiters or a committee of the chamber of commerce, which is merely a voluntary association, and is not to be found in all parts of the country.

LETTER XXVIII.

SOCIAL REFORM.

AUGUSTA, (GEORGIA,) SEPTEMBER 3, 1835.

IT is impossible to foresee the time when the blacks in this country shall be set free; there is here a great gulf between the black and the white. The difficulty here is not exactly of a pecuniary kind; for, to apply to the two million and a half of American negroes the process which the English have applied to their colonies, only 300 millions would be required, a sum which is not beyond the means of North America. By rendering the process of emancipation more gradual, so as to render it more slow and safe than in the English Islands, a much less sum would be sufficient; but another obstacle occurs, against which money can do nothing. The English nature is exclusive; English society is divided into an endless number of little coteries, each jealous of its superior, and despising its inferior. The Englishman is in his own country, what his country is in reference to the rest of the world, an islander.

This spirit of exclusiveness which prevails in society at home, appears again in the relations of the English with other people. The Englishman cannot fraternise with the Red Skins or the blacks; between him and them there is no sympathy, no mutual confidence. The Anglo-Americans have retained and even exaggerated this trait of their fathers; and to the men of the North as well as to those of the South, to the Yankee as well as to the Virginian, the negro is a Philistine, a son of Ham. In the States without slaves, as well as in those in which slavery is admitted, the elevation of the black seems impossible.

An American of the North or of the South, whether he be rich or poor, ignorant or learned, avoids a contact with the negro, as if he were infected with the plague. Free or slave, well or meanly clad, the black or the man of colour is always a Pariah; he is denied a lodging at the inns; at the theatre or in the steamboats he has a distinct place allotted him far from the whites; he is excluded from commerce, for he cannot set his foot on 'Change nor in the banking rooms. Everywhere and always, he is eminently unclean. Thus treated as vile, he almost always becomes so.

In Europe, blacks or coloured persons have sometimes filled high stations; there is not an instance of the kind in the United States. The republic of Hayti has its accredited representatives at the court of France; it has none in Washington. An anecdote was told me at New York of the disappointment of a young Haytian, who was a near relation of one of Boyer's ministers, and who had received a good education in France; having arrived in New York, he could not get admittance into any hotel, his money was refused at the door of the theatre, he was ordered out of the cabin of a steamboat, and was obliged to quit the country without being able to speak to any body. At Philadelphia, I heard of a man of colour who had acquired wealth, a rare thing among that class, who used sometimes to invite whites to dine with him, and who did not sit at table, but waited upon his guests himself. At the dessert, however, upon their pressing him to be seated with them, he would yield to their urgency. At the end of 1833, in one of the New Engg-land States, and I think it was in Massachusetts,* a man

* In Massachusetts and most of New England the blacks are legally citizens, and, as such, have the right of voting; they do not, however, at present exercise this right, either because they are prevented from doing so, or because their names are designedly omitted on the list of tax-payers,

of colour being on board a steamer with his wife, wished
to get her admitted into the ladies' cabin ; the captain
refused her admission.   A suit was, therefore, brought
against the captain, by the man, who was desirous of
having it decided by the courts, whether free people of
colour, conducting themselves with propriety, could enjoy
the same privileges with whites in a State, in which they
were recognised as citizens by the laws.   He gained his
cause on the first hearing, but was cast on appeal.

The different nations of the great christian family, after
having for ages received the doctrines taught by the successors of St. Peter, have selected out of the christian
scheme, some one principle most congenial to their nature,
and made it the basis of their character.   The French, a
most christian people, have chosen the principle of universal charity.   In our eyes, there are no longer Gentiles ;
our prepossessions in favour of foreigners increase as the
square of the distance that separates their country from
ours.   The Spanish, a chivalric people, have adopted with
enthusiasm the adoration of the Virgin, which is of a
more modern origin.   The Protestants have taken up the
principle of individual conscience, and this is nearly all that
they have accepted from Christianity ; they have renounced
the successive additions of the church to the faith of the
Apostles, and they have even rejected a part of what
Christ himself had engrafted on the Jewish theology.

---

which in some States forms the list of voters.   [Blacks vote and always have
voted in Massachusetts.—TRANSL.]   The constitution of Connecticut,
formed in 1818, excludes them from this franchise.   In New York, real
estate of the value of 250 dollars, and the payment of taxes is made
the electoral qualification of blacks.   [The new constitution of Pennsylvania,
formed in 1838, restricts the right of suffrage to the whites, although it was
extended to blacks by the old constitution.—TRANSL.]   The Western
States, in which slavery does not exist, do not admit blacks to vote, and in
the slave-holding States, it may readily be imagined that they do not enjoy
that privilege.

Among Protestants, the Yankees have carried this retro-grade tendency to the greatest extreme ; they have, except in some few points, relapsed into Judaism, and returned to to the Mosaic law. They appeal in preference to the maxims and doctrines of the Old Testament ; they borrow their names from it, and amongst the peculiarities that strike a Frenchmen in New England, one of the strongest is the great prevalence of Hebrew names, such as Phineas, Ebenezer, Judah, Hiram, Obadiah, Ezra, &c., on the signs and in advertisements.

As the religion of the people exercises a controlling in-fluence over the general tone of its feeling and character, the Yankees, having thus fallen back into Judaism, possess, like the Jews, that exclusive spirit which was already in-herent in their insular origin. The fact is, that their religious notions square exactly with this depression of the blacks. The blacks seem to them inferior beings ; they revolt against the thought of any assimilation with them, even in the slightest degree ; a mixture of the two races, or, as they call it, *amalgamation,* is in their eyes an abom-ination, a sacrilege, which would deserve to be punished, as the sin of the Hebrews with the daughters of Moab was punished. The emancipation of the negro comprises two things ; the one, formal, that is manumission by the mas-ter, which it would not be difficult to effect, if a sufficient indemnity were offered to the planters and the country could pay it ; and the other, moral, that is, a real acknowl-edgment of the rights of the black, by admitting him to the personal privileges of the white man, which would meet with insurmountable obstacles at the North as well as the South, and would, perhaps, be even more repugnant to the former than to the latter.

The principal difficulty of emancipation, so far as re-gards the slave himself, is also of a moral character. To render him fit for the enjoyment of liberty, it is necessary

that he should be initiated in the duties and dignity of
man, that he should labour in order to pay his tax to society, and maintain his family with decency, that he should
learn to obey other motives than the fear of the lash.
He must learn the sentiment of self-respect ; he must wish
and know how to be a father, son, husband.   He only can
have a perfect right to liberty, who is in a condition to
enjoy it with profit to himself and to society.   Slavery,
odious as it is, is one form of social order, and should be
preserved where no better form can be substituted for it,
as it must disappear where the inferior is ripe for a better
state of things.

    In regard to the lower orders in Europe, the difficulty is
of the same kind with that which stands in the way of the
emancipation of the American slaves ; it is only different
in degree, and it is already half overcome.   In order that the
hireling should be raised from his present abject state, the
higher classes must be ready to treat him as a being of the
same nature with themselves, and he himself must have
acquired higher sentiments than such as belong to his
present condition.   He must not only be inspired with the
desire of being happier, but also with the ambition of being
better.   To establish new relations between the different
classes, both parties must labour with that firm will, which
recasts ideas and habits.   The question of the improvement of the condition of the lower classes is essentially a
moral question.   A moral remodelling of society is the
necessary preliminary.   Now, whoever pronounces the
world moral in the wider sense of the term, means religion.
Philanthropy and philosophy have no hold on the moral
nature of man, unless they borrow it from religion.   Religion only can move the hearts of all classes deep enough,
and enlighten the minds of all strongly enough, to cause
the rich and the poor to conceive new ideas of their mutual relations, and to realize them in practice.

History teaches us, that civilisation, in its successive phases, has gradually improved the condition of the lower classes ; it proves also that each of the great changes that have taken place in the condition of the multitude, has been consummated or prepared by religion, and accompanied by a change in religion itself. It was religion that struck off the fetters of the slave, that gradually freed the serf from the glebe. The free principles of the French revolution were only the precepts of the Christian religion practised by persons who were no longer Christians, and the revolutionary actors themselves gave to Christ the title of *sans-culotte*, in their eyes a title of honour.

To render the efforts of the higher classes in favour of the people vigourous and sustained, they must, then, be directed by religion. To raise the lower orders effectually from their abasement, religion must fix them steadily on that high moral level, to which they have occasionally soared by sublime, but fitful and soon drooping flights. Now, the higher classes have not faith. If among the highest, the irreligious philosophy of the 18th century has of late lost adherents, it restores and increases its numbers from among the lower ranks. Incredulity has lowered its aim a peg ; its train has lost in quality, but gained in quantity. Irreligion is at work among the populace of the cities, disposes them to revolt, and would make them unfit for the regular enjoyment of liberty. When we have roads, when schools have taught the whole population to read, which will be soon, you will see irreligion infecting the country people, if you do not provide against its approaches beforehand.

Christianity, or at least Catholicism, seems to be on the eve of suffering a general desertion amongst us. And yet how far are we from having drawn from the Christian principles, which some among us affect to consider as exhausted, all the elements of popular liberty and happiness which they contain ! We are a most Christian people in this sense, that we believe in the unity of the whole human family, and we prove it by our good will to all nations; but it seems as if we expend abroad all the heat that Christianity has developed in our souls. We, the apostles of the brotherhood of nations, we have not yet breathed into our relations to each other the principle of the fraternity of men. We of the middle class, the sons of freedmen, think that labourers, the sons of slaves, are of a different nature from ourselves. We have still a remnant of the old pagan leaven at the bottom of our hearts. We do not, indeed, with Aristotle, teach the doctrine of two distinct natures, the free nature and the slave nature, but we act in practice as if we were brought up in that faith. We are not yet become the fathers and elder brothers of the peasant and the operative; but in our relations to them, we are still their *masters*, and hard masters too.

And unfortunately, whilst society, driven about by the waves, at the mercy of chance and without a compass, is exposed to disasters, which the control of religion alone can prevent, religion makes no effort to resume the helm and recover her authority. In the midst of nations which are rushing onward at every risk, Catholicism stands still, silently shrouded in her mantle, with her arms folded, and her eyes bent on heaven. The Church bore all the shocks of the revolutionary storm with a heroic resignation; she meekly submitted to be scourged with rods, like the Just One; like him she has been fixed to the cross, and has opened her mouth only to pray for her executioners. But the sufferings of the Just have saved sinners and changed the face of the world; nothing betokens that the recent sufferings of the Catholic church will have any saving power. From the tomb where it was laid for dead, we see it bring back no scheme for the restoration of suffering, longing humanity.

The Roman Church is yet what it was four hundred

years ago ; but within that period the world has become quite another thing ; it has made great progress, and freed itself from the meshes of the past, with the firm purpose not to be again involved in them. If civilisation, then, is about to assume a new form, as every thing forebodes, religion, which is at once the beginning and end of society, the key-stone and the corner-stone, religion, must also recast herself. Would it be the first time that Christianity has modified her forms and rules, to adapt herself to the instincts and the tendencies of the nations she has sought to bless ?

In this country, religion has wrought the elevation of the lower classes. Puritanism has been the starting point of the democratic movement. The Puritans came to America, not in quest of gold, nor to conquer provinces, but to found a church on the principle of primitive equality. They were as I have before said, new Jews ; they wished to govern by the laws of Moses. In the beginning the state was completely swallowed up by the church ; they divided themselves into religious congregations, in which all the heads of families were equal, conformably to the Mosaic law, over which the elders and the saints presided, and in which all earthly distinctions were abolished or contemned. One of the first objects of their care, under the influence of their religious views, was to establish schools, in which all the children should be educated together and in the same manner. Although unequal in respect to property, all adopted the same habits of life. The physical exertions, to which all were obliged to devote themselves in common, in order to defend themselves from famine and the savages, strengthened their habits and feelings of equality. Now, New England, which is inhabited exclusively by the sons of the Puritans, and in which their traditions and their faith are still kept unchanged, has ever been, and is yet, the focus of American democracy.

Thus American democracy has been enabled to organise and establish itself. All our efforts, on the contrary, to found a democracy in France in 1793, would have been vain, even had we not been unfitted for democratic habits, because we wished to build on irreligion, on the hatred of religion. Manners and feelings must prepare and inspire the means of social improvement ; the laws must express and prescribe them. Politics and religion, then, must join hands in this difficult task. Politics, as well as religion, must be transformed for the furtherance of civilisation, and the safety of the world.

I admire the results, which the political system of the United States has produced in America. But it seems to me impossible, that the institutions by which the condition of the people has been so much bettered here, can be naturalised amongst us. There must be harmony between the political and religious schemes that are suited to any one people. Protestantism is republican ; puritanism is absolute self-government in religion, and begets it in politics. The United Provinces were Protestant ; the United States are Protestant. Catholicism is essentially monarchical ; in countries, which are Catholic, at least by recollections, habits, and education, if not by faith, a regular democracy is impracticable. The anarchy of the former Spanish colonies fully proves to what bitter regrets Catholic nations expose themselves, when they attempt to apply to themselves the political institutions of Protestant countries.

Under the influence of Protestantism and republicanism, the social progress has been effected by the medium of the spirit of individuality ; for protestantism, republicanism, and individuality are all one. Individuals stand apart from one another, or if they are associated together, they have formed only limited associations, which have no common bond of union. The republic of the United States is indefinitely subdivided into independent republics of various classes. The States are republics in the general confederation ; the towns are republics within the States ; a farm is a republic in a county. Banking, canal, and railroad companies, are so many distinct republics. The family is an inviolable republic in the state ; each individual is a republic by himself in the family. The only effective militia consists of volunteer companies, which have no connexion with each other. The religious organisation of the country resembles its civil and political organisation. The different sects are independent of each other, and most of them tend to split up into completely detached fragments.

Our national genius, on the contrary, requires that in France we should act chiefly under the influence of association and unity, which are characteristic traits of Catholicism and monarchy. France is a specimen of the completest political and administrative unity that there is in the world. Our individual existence must be bound up with others ; we love independence, but we do not feel that we live unless we make a part of a whole. Solitude overpowers us ; the personality of the Englishman or the American can sustain itself alone ; ours must be linked with that of others. For a people eminently social, like the French, how is it possible that the spirit of association should not be the best ? But it must retain the distinction of ranks ; for with us, a republican association would degenerate into anarchy.

If, then, I should attempt to define the conditions most favourable to the improvement of society in France, I should say that they require it to be undertaken under the influences of religion ; that its accomplishment should be confided to the constituted authorities, central and local, and particularly to royalty ; that it should be effected by means of institutions bearing the double impress of unity and hierchical association, and reposing immediately on the general association, which is the state, or supported by powerful intermediary associations, which should be themselves attached to the state.   The nearer we approach these conditions, the more complete will be our success, the sooner shall we have the happiness of seeing our beloved France, prosperous within, recover the high station which she ought to occupy in the world.

LETTER XXIX.

THE EMPIRE STATE.

ALBANY, SEPTEMBER 11, 1835.

It has been already shown (*Letter X.*), that there are in the United States two strongly marked types, the Yankee and the Virginian, the mutual action and reaction of which have hitherto been the life of the Union.   A third is rising in the West, which seems destined to become the bond and umpire of the two others, if it is able to preserve its own unity ; which will not, however, be easy, for the West comprises slave-holding and non-slave-holding States. For the present, this high office is filled by the Middle States, or rather by New York, which is the most important State not only of this group, but of the whole Union. To be a mediator between two types, it is necessary to unite in one person the principal qualities of both ; the State of New York, then, should combine the large views of the South with the spirit of detail that marks the North. To be, even imperfectly, the personification of the principle of unity in the great American confederation, it is indispensable that the claimant of that honour should possess in a high degree the spirit of unity. To achieve the work of centralisation or consolidation in America, even partially, demands a high degree of the genius of centralisation. For some time there has appeared in the administration of the State of New York, a character of grandeur, unity, and centralisation, that has procured it the title of the *Empire-State*. Although it is the nearest neighbour of the New England States, and actually borders upon three of them, although a large number of its inhabitants are of New England origin, it has succeeded in freeing itself from the spirit of extreme division that is characteristic of the Yankees, or rather in counterbalancing it by a proportional development of the spirit of unity.

The Opposition, which is in the minority in the legislature in the State, and does not, therefore, feel in good humour, endeavours to create among the people a dislike to this control of the central power. " You are led," it says, " by the Albany Regency ; a half-dozen of the friends of Mr Mr Van Buren, taking their cue from Governor Marcy, make you their puppets." The Opposition exaggerates ; but it is certain, that the organisation of the State, and the forms of administration, which have been established of late years under the influence of Mr Van Buren, and which form a precedent for the future, bear the impress of a centralism, at which the friends of unlimited individual independence have a right to take alarm, but which wise men must applaud ; for it is by means of it that the State of New York is become superiour to the others, and it is by it alone that it can maintain its superiority. This combination of expansive force, which prevails every where else in the American confederacy, with a sufficient cohesive power, has given to the constitution of New York an elasticity, which, for communities as well as for individuals, is the condition of a long and prosperous existence.

The organisation of the public schools and of public instruction in general is centralised. Most of the States have a school-fund, the income of which in New England is distributed among the towns, who dispose of it according to their own good pleasure, without the State having the right to exercise any real control over it, or imposing any conditions in regard to it. New York proceeds more imperially ; it obliges the different towns to raise a sum equal to that to which they are entitled from the State, under penalty of not receiving their share of the State fund. This method is preferable to that followed in Connecticut, which distributes annually among the towns about the same sum as New York, but exacts no account of the manner in which it has been employed, and cannot even be sure that it has been actually devoted to the purpose of instruction.

In 1834, the public schools in New York were attended by 541,400 pupils ; now the number of children between five and sixteen years of age in the districts from which returns were received, comprising very nearly the whole State, was only 543,085. The whole expenditure for schools was 1,310,000 dollars, of which 750,000 dollars was for pay of teachers. The amount expended in France for the same object is only three times as great as that expended by New York, which has one sixteenth of the population of France. The number of children in our schools is 2,450,000, or one thirteenth of the population, which is only one third of the proportion in New York.

All the common schools in New York are under the supervision and control of a board of commissioners, mostly composed of several of the chief officers of the government, and of which the Secretary of State is the most active

member. The commissioners make provision for the instruction of teachers, require an account of the condition of the school, and select the text books. Virginia,
Ohio, and some other States have adopted a similar system
in this respect ; but New York has this peculiarity, that it
has also a board, styled the board of Regents of the University, who are appointed by the legislature, and have the
control of the higher schools called academies. There are
seven colleges in the State, one of which is styled the University of New York, and corresponds, very remotely it is
true, to the English and German Universities.

The control of the government over the academies is at
present very limited ; it is little more than an annual visit
by one or more of the Regents of the University, but it can
easily be extended, whenever the State shall think proper,
by means of the system of pecuniary aid ; in 1834, the
sum distributed among these seminaries was 12,500 dollars.
The number of pupils in the Academies was a little more
than 5,000, or two and a half pupils out of each thousand
souls. In France, there were 80,000 pupils in the colleges, which is the same ratio to the whole population.
It would appear from this comparison, that in the United
States, where the advantages of elementary instruction are
universally realised, the desire for a higher degree of instruction is less general than with us, for the number of
families that can afford to pay is proportionably much
greater in the United States than in France. Thus in
regard to a higher education, we recover, in some measure,
the superiority, which the Americans, at least in New
York, have over us in respect to elementary education.

The same spirit of unity and centralisation has dictated
a general regulation of a singular character in respect to
the banks, which may prove to be of great value in practice, and to which there is nothing similar, either in the
other States, or in any other country. The Safety-Fund-

Act establishes a bank fund appropriated to making good any losses incurred by the failure of any of the banks. Each bank is required to pay annually to the State treasurer, a sum equal to one half of one per cent. on its capital, until it shall have so paid in the sum of three per cent. on the capital stock. Whenever the bank fund is reduced by paying the debts of an insolvent bank, it must be restored to the proper amount by the same process. The banks, together with the fund, are under the supervision of three Commissioners, one of whom is appointed by the Governor, and the two others by the banks. The Commissioners visit each bank at least once in four months, examine into its operations, and satisfy themselves that it has conformed itself to the provisions of its charter. They are beside required to make a particular examination of any bank on the demand of three other banks, and in case of detecting any violation of the charter, to apply to the court of chancery for an injunction against it.

This law contains several sections designed to aid the Commissioners in the execution of their duties, and to prevent their being imposed on by the banks ; it gives them the right to inspect the books, and to examine the officers of the bank under oath. The salary of the Commissioners is 2,000 dollars, which is paid out of the bank fund. Any bank director or officer who shall make false returns to the legislature, or false entries in the books, or exhibit false papers with intent to deceive the Commissioners, is subject to imprisonment for not less than three nor more than ten years. Every bank subject to this act may receive legal interest on loan and discounts ; but on notes which shall be mature in sixtythree days from the time of discount, it shall receive only six per cent. per annum. It is further provided that the issues or circulation of any bank shall not exceed twice its capital stock, and that its loans and discounts shall never exceed twice and a half that amount; but this provision has not hitherto been rigidly observed.

The number of banks in the State is eightyseven, of which only seventyseven are subject to the provisions of the Safety-Fund-Act, the others having been established before the date of the act. But as all will be obliged to renew their charters within ten years, with the exception of the Manhattan bank alone, which has a perpetual charter, they will all, with one exception, be brought under the act. The aggregate of the bank capital in the State is 31,280,000 dollars; the bank fund amounts to above 538,000 dollars. The annual amount of the loans and discounts of the banks is estimated at about 300 millions, exclusive of the operations of the three branches of the United States Bank; that of the banks of the city of New York alone, is about 180 million, or twice as much as that of the Bank of France.

Nothing, however, has contributed so much to give New York its *imperial* reputation, as the energy it has displayed in canalling its territory. All the resources of the State were devoted to this object; all the energies of its citizens were bent for eight years on the accomplishment of this great work. In spite of the worst predictions and earnest remonstrances of some of the most respected men in the Union, the confidence of this young [State never faltered for a moment. Complete success attended its efforts; the great canal, begun in 1817, was finished in 1825. The State has since executed a great number of canals, at an expense of above twelve millions, the greater part of which has been raised by loan. Several others are still in progress.

The Erie canal, the most important of these works, is simple in construction, not very deep nor very wide. But if it is not peculiarly interesting as an object of art, it is an object of admiration considered as a great commercial artery. From our canals, which are navigated by heavy and clumsy boats slowly and painfully dragged forward by a man, you can get no idea of this great channel, with its fleet of light, elegant, covered barks gliding along at a rapid rate, and drawn by a powerful team. Every minute boats are passing each other, and the boatman's horn warns the lock-master to be in readiness. Each moment the landscape varies ; now you pass a river by an aqueduct, now you traverse large new towns, fine as capitals, with all their houses having pillared porticos and looking externally like little palaces ; it is an admirable spectacle of life and variety. The amount of property annually transported on the Erie Canal is 430,000 tons, on the Champlain canal, 307,000 tons, at very moderate rates of toll. The annual amount of tolls is 1,500,000 dollars ; that on the French canals and rivers is only 900,000 dollars.

In 1817, when it began the great canal, the State of New York contained 1,250,000 inhabitants, scattered over a surface about one fourth as large as France. Whilst in Europe, grave publicists were discussing the question, whether a State should undertake the execution of public works, and the most powerful governments were listening scrupulously to the debate, in order to determine whether they had the right to enrich their subjects by productive enterprises, — the same governments who never doubted their right to waste millions of men and treasure in devastating Europe, — the modest authorities of this miniature empire solved the question, without dreaming that it could embarrass great potentates in other quarters. The State of New York undertook the execution of public works, and has found its advantage in them ; after having executed them, it has managed them itself on its own account, and found even greater advantages in this. The income from the canals, with the aid of some slight additions, has been

sufficient to sink nearly half the debt contracted in their construction. Thus the brilliant success of the Erie canal, became the signal for the greatest undertakings of a similar
character by the other States. Pennsylvania, Ohio, Maryland, Virginia, and Indiana have followed the example of
New York, and have undertaken to open routes of communication of every kind, through their territories, at their
own expense, even at the risk of incurring the reproaches of
the timid economists of Europe.

New York has carried her interference in public works
still further; in all the charters for railroad companies, the
State reserves to itself the right of acquiring the property
of the railroad, after the expiration of ten years, and on
certain conditions named in the act of incorporation, which
are truly liberal on the part of the State; they stipulate
the re-payment of the first cost and the sums expended in
repairs, and the supply of any deficiency in the dividends
below ten per cent.*

Thus the State of New York, in its imperial humour,
has laid hands on public instruction, banks, and the
means of communication, with the purpose of centralising
them; the design is already effected in respect to public
works; it is not yet fully accomplished in regard to the
schools and the banks; but its fulfilment approaches gradually and surely. As I have already said, the spirit of
centralisation has penetrated more deeply into the administration of the State, than into the acts of the legislature;
a guarantee, that the laws of unity will not remain paper
rules.

The lessons of New York have turned to the profit of

---

* Several States have reserved to themselves a similar right, but generally
on less liberal conditions. Massachusetts, however, has adopted the same,
extending the term of possession by the company to twenty years. New Jersey has stipulated that it shall have the right of acquiring the property of
several works, at a price not exceeding their first cost.

its neighbours; like it, they also begin the work of centralisation, in embracing schools, banks, and public works within the action of the State. They see, by its example, that the spirit of individual enterprise does not suffer, when the government subjects to its control and its authority these three great springs of national prosperity, and even when it sets them in action on its own account; for nowhere is the spirit of enterprise more vigourous and clearsighted than in New York. In spite of the Safety-Fund-Act, there are nowhere more numerous applications for the incorporation of banking companies. Notwithstanding the school laws, nowhere do institutions of education increase more rapidly. Nowhere are there more railroads in progress. The State contains 80 miles of canal and 100 of railroads, constructed by companies; from 150 to 200 miles of railroad are now in process of construction, and a company has been organised for constructing a railroad from the Hudson to Lake Erie through the southern counties, a distance of 350 miles.

It would be too much to suppose that a country like France, where so much value is set on the principles of unity and centralisation, would be less courageous than these little republics, born under the influence of the individual principle, and that we should any longer delay to take an *imperial* course in regard to institutions of credit, public works, and industrial education. The object to be accomplished is not merely to increase the wealth of the country. But there are other and more elevated motives to induce modern governments to take part in such institutions, and thus to extend their control over the interests and operations of industry.

The progress of civilisation, considered with reference to the individual, consists in this; that each becomes more and more suited to bear the weight of his individuality. Social order, being thus supplied with stronger individual

guarantees, seems to require less and less of legal and public ones; but in this matter, there is an important distinction to be kept in view. Civilisation gradually strips man
of the grosser habits and the brutal propensities of savage
life. There are many prohibitions and commands in the
Deuteronomy, which in our day would be perfectly superfluous. Mankind hardly has further need to be taught :
Thou shalt not kill. The lictor and the headsman are
losing their social importance ; the constable, the sheriff,
and the gaoler are, it is to be hoped, on the eve of taking
their places every where. Public order has begun, and
will continue more and more, to dispense with the use of
the sword ; and thus individual reason substitutes its voluntary sanction for the imperative sanction of political
power and the force of arms.

The human understanding is expanded and enlightened
by cultivation ; the heart is elevated and purified ; yet the
elementary passions are the same. They are combined
under different forms, and are turned to different objects ;
but if they are moderated, it is only in outward appearances ; if they are polished, it is only on the surface ; within
all is as rough and fierce as ever.* In politics, particularly, jealousy and ambition exist in the same degree
amongst us as they did amongst the Greeks and Romans ;
they no longer wield the dagger or administer the poison,
they do not even employ an assassin or a Locusta ; but
they are neither less unjust, nor less insatiable, nor less
bitter than in ancient times ; they do not stab the body,
but they wound the honour ; slander takes the place of the
stiletto, and serves them as well as the juices of venomous
plants ; civilisation furnishes them a thousand new means

---

* Mde. de Stael exclaims; " Strange destiny of mankind, condemned
ever to retrace the same circle by the passions, whilst it is ever advancing
in the career of thought !"

of assuaging their thirst.　I do not believe that Sylla and Marius, Cæsar and Pompey, hated each other more cordially than General Jackson, President of the United States, and Mr Biddle, president of the United States' Bank.　If one were to search out the types of Cain and Abel among modern statesmen, the list would be of frightful length.

To that force of dissolution, which increases instead of diminishing, in proportion to the increasing number of individuals admitted to a share of political influence, it is necessary to oppose cohesive elements of equal activity and intensity.　It is for this reason that in the future, as well as in the past, the existence of society involves that of religion. Even did not religion touch the tenderest cords and stir the liveliest sensibilities of the human heart ; if it did not offer to the imagination a vast field in which to wander in safety ; even if it were not indispensable to peace of conscience and to domestic tranquillity, it would be impossible to get along without it, for it has also a political necessity.　It has been rightly said, that if there were no God, it would be necessary to feign one.

A single institution, however, would not suffice to regulate and govern the passions at all times and in all places, unless it were to follow men in all their movements, control them in all their acts, bind them hands and feet, or, in a word, unless it were despotic, after the image of the old theocracies.　It is not, then, to be hoped, that, in our free countries, religion alone can counterbalance human passions and confine them within the limits, in which they subserve the progress of society ; or at least, if it can do this in one of the social hemispheres, the family, it will always be insufficient in the other, the state. For this reason, the Middle Ages established a salutary principle, when they separated the temporal power from the spiritual authority, and gave strength and independence to each.　From that time, all efforts to confound these two powers, or, which amounts to the same thing, to dispense with one of them, have been completely unsuccessful; they have generally resulted in establishing a tyranny.*

A temporal authority, armed with ample prerogatives, is, then, indispensable at the present day, even in behalf of liberty itself. On the other hand it is impossible to deny that the tendency of civilisation is to strip the throne of its ancient attributes, either in whole or in part. On this head, our age has taken a decided stand. The resistance of kings to the efforts of those who have assailed the throne, has served to exasperate the latter to such a pitch, that a party, — that of the republicans, — has been formed, the sole object of which is the complete and radical abolition of monarchy, and the singular doctrine of the inutility and even the danger of all power has found numerous and warm adherents.

The people are right to desire the kings to lay down or to curtail their old prerogatives; the governments, that are the heirs of conquest, ought to abdicate whatever there is of violence and brutality in their authority. It would be premature to assert that universal peace is about to dawn

---

* I have already said, that when the Puritans landed in New England they wished above all things to found a religious society. They organised themselves by the laws of Moses. Political society did not exist in fact, although there was a nominal governor to represent the temporal authority, or was swallowed up in the church; the town was merged in the congregation. Thus in a short time, their government came to resemble that of the Jesuits in Paraguay, with only this difference, that each one here had his share in the tyranny. The Blue Laws of Connecticut are a monument of this state of things, in which the common acts of life were subjected to the most vexatious restrictions. The New Englanders were soon obliged to renounce their Mosaic system of government, and without perfectly separating politics from religion, they gave to each of the two powers an independent existence. They did not establish the political power firmly beyond the town; but the municipal constitution was solid and firm, sometimes even to excess, for the very reason that it started from the religious organisation.

on the earth ; it is not so to affirm that war is henceforth to be a secondary and accidental matter in the history of nations. Industry, that is to say, the art of creating wealth, multiplying the means of happiness, and adorning the globe, the residence of the human family, will henceforth take precedence of the art of slaying and wasting. The sword is ceasing to be the highest emblem of power. But kings are right, in their turn, to prevent their power being reduced to an empty shadow. Independently of all individual ambition, from the lofty height on which they are placed, they see that the preservation of the order of society demands the presence of a power worthy of the name. And what proves the justness of their view is the fact, that men of all parties who have taken part in the government during our revolutionary crisis, have all agreed in this point whatever may have been their former opinions ; it is the only point on which they have been unanimous.

The truth is, that while we are taking from governments, we must also be giving to them. War is no longer the principal object of the activity of nations ; the employment of brute force becomes less and less necessary to the preservation of society ; let us then gradually reduce, with a firm hand, those prerogatives of power which give it an exclusively warlike character, and which leave our lives and liberties at the discretion of its armed creatures ! Since industry is occupying a wider and wider space in the existence of the individual and the nation, let us cause it to enter more and more completely into the sphere of government, by including in the attributes of government its three springs, banks, means of communication, and schools ; on condition, be it understood, that government shall use the new powers with which it shall be thus invested, for the general good.

The banks, means of communication, and schools are instruments of governments, which it would be unwise to leave wholly out of the influence of the public authority, but which there could be no harm in partially incorporating with it, in such a manner as not to stifle the spirit of individual enterprise. The public authority would then exercise its functions conformably with the tendencies of the national character, and would preside over the most important events of the national life ; it would then really deserve the name of government ; it would possess a new means of coercion and restraint, which is the only one compatible with the progress of the spirit of liberty. Instead of having a hold on the body and blood of the subject, it would have a hold on his industry and his purse. A new degree of inviolability would thus be secured to the individual, without the social order losing its needful guarantees. By this means in fine the political advent of industry would be accomplished. Instead of being a cause of agitation and change, once sure of its rank and secure in its seat, industry would act an important conservative part in society.

Every thing is now ripe for this political transfiguration. Forty years ago, the people looked for their own elevation in the overthrow of the old order of things. Hatred has now ceased to be their chief counsellor ; the thirst for destruction is cooled ; they think less of shaking off the yoke of tyrants, more of freeing themselves from the burdens of ignorance and poverty. The road to liberty which would now be preferred in Europe, passes through competency, education, and industry. Those who were once the temporal and spiritual heads of the people would soon regain their lost rank, if calming the fears with which the curses uttered against the last of kings and the last of priests had filled them, they knew how to put themselves at the head of such a march ; for the people could follow them with joy. By what fatality is it, that they still doubt and hesitate ?

I know not if I deceive myself, but it seems to me, that, in this matter, the example must come from France. Not that she has greater sums in her treasury; not that she counts more soldiers under her flag, more ships in her ports, more cannon in her fortresses, but that she has the most sagacious intellect, and the noblest heart; that the world is accustomed to receive the watchword from her. London, with its thousands of ships, might be burnt to the ground, and the rest of the world would be no otherwise affected by the event, than as by a lamentable disaster which has befallen a foreigner; the recoil of a mere riot in Paris is felt to the ends of the world. The revolution of July gave birth to Parliamentary Reform; the Reform bill would never have brought forth July. It is because France is the heart of the world; the affairs of France interest all; the cause which she espouses is not that of a selfish ambition, but that of civilisation. When France speaks, she is listened to, because she speaks not her own feelings merely, but those of the human race. When she acts, her example is followed, because she does what all desire to do.

France was the first on the European continent to enthrone liberty; it is for her to re-seat the principle of authority, for the fulness of its time is come. She protected the people when protection was necessary; it is now for her to protect kings; not by the edge of the sword, although she must not break her own, which has done so much for civilisation (for that would be sacrilege), but by the wisdom and the moral superiority of her new principles of government, by the creative power of the new attributes with which she invests authority.

LETTER XXX.

SYMPTOMS OF REVOLUTION.

BALTIMORE, SEPTEMBER 25, 1835.

Two years ago Mr Clay began a speech in the Senate, with these words, which have become celebrated on this side of the Atlantic : " We are in the midst of a revolution." It was at the time, when by an act of authority before unheard of in American history, General Jackson had just settled the bank question, which his friends in Congress and even his own ministers had refused to decide. These words have often been repeated by others. More recently, since the scenes of murder, outrage, and destruction which have been exhibited through the United States, both in the slave-holding States, and in those in which slavery does not exist, in the country as well as in the towns, at Boston, the republican city *par excellence*, as as well as at Baltimore, for which the bloody excesses of which it was the theatre in 1812, have gained the title of the *Mob Town*, good citizens have repeated with grief ; " We are in the midst of a revolution."

It must be granted to the honour of the English race, that it is, more deeply than any other, imbued with a feeling of reverence for the law. Until lately, the Americans have shown themselves in this respect, as well as in others, to be double-distilled Englishmen. There are nations, who conceive of law under a living form, that is, only so far as it is personified in a man. They know how to obey a leader, but they cannot learn to respect a dead letter. With them the glory and prosperity of a State depend little on the character of the laws, but much on that of the men who are their organs. In their view, the empire rises and falls by turns, according as the sovereign, whatever may be his title, is a superior man or an ordinary personage. Such appears to be, in general, the character of the Asiatics. The Englishman is formed in a different mould ; he willingly bows to the authority of a text ; but he stoops to man with reluctance. He does not need that obedience to law should be inculcated by the voice of man, he obeys it without an effort and by instinct. In a word the Englishman has in himself the principle of self-government. This fact accounts for the success of his political system in the United States, where the native character of the English race is fairly developed.

Unfortunately the reverence for the laws seems to be wearing out with the Americans. This people, eminently practical in every thing else, have allowed themselves to be pushed into the excess of theory in politics, and have here taken up the *quand même* logic ; they have shrunk from none of the consequences of popular sovereignty, at least while those consequences were flattering to their pride ; as if there were a single principle in the world, not excepting Christian charity itself, which could be carried to its extreme logical consequences without resulting in absolute absurdity. They have, therefore, been driven in the United States to deny that there is any principle true in and by itself, and to assert that the will of the people is, always and necessarily, justice ; the infallibility of the people in every thing and at all times, has, in fact, become the received doctrine, and thus a door has been opened to the tyranny of a turbulent minority, which always calls itself the people.*

The appearance of this miscalled popular justice, admin-

---

* It has been observed, that the disorders are always committed by a handful of men followed by a train of a mischievous boys. It is rare that more than one hundred persons take part in the acts of violence, and often not half that number is engaged in them.

istered by the hands of a few desperate or furious men, who call themselves the successors of the Boston *Tea Party* of 1773, is a great calamity in the bosom of a country, where there is no other guarantee of the public peace than a reverence of the laws, and where the legislator, taking for granted the prevalence of order, has made no provisions against disorder. This popular justice has the greater condemnation of being for the most part grossly unjust. Most of the men who have been atrociously hanged, or flogged, or tortured in twenty other ways in the South,* as abolitionists, that is as guilty of instigating the slaves to rise against their masters, were, according to all appearances, merely guilty of having expressed their abhorrence of slavery with too little caution. It is even doubtful whether the pretended plots, for being engaged in which whites and blacks have been summarily executed, had a real existence. At least no proof of their reality has yet been brought forward, which would be admitted by a court of justice. During the outrages last month at Baltimore, which were continued for four days, this self-styled justice was most stupidly unjust. The mob gave out that it wished to punish those knaves who had shamefully abused the credulity of the poor in the affair of the Bank of Maryland. It is a matter of public notoriety, that the bankruptcy of the bank was fraudulent ; that just before it stopped payment, it had offered a high rate of interest on deposits of any amount, in order to attract to its counter the savings of the labouring classes ; but it was also a matter of notoriety, that the criminal acts of the bank were wholly the work of one Evan Poultney, who alone was,

---

* A Virginia newspaper relates that an abolitionist, having fallen into the hands of a Commitee of Vigilance, was stript naked, and stretched at his length on his face, when a cat was several times dragged across his bare back by the ruffians. A New York Journal repeats the statement with no other comment than some witticism.

in fact, the bank. Instead of going to take vengeance for the ruin of the artisan, the widow, and the orphan, on the author of it, the mob went to call to account the bankruptcy commissioners, appointed by the court. It was not till the third day that it bethought itself to make a visit to Poultney, who, without being at all disconcerted, began to cry out that he was a sinner, that he had been guilty of wronging his neighbour. He beat his breast in sign of repentance, and in a puritanical slang accused himself more loudly than the rioters had done. Blinded, like Orgon, by so much sanctity, they excused themselves to Tartufe like him, carefully swept the hall and the marble door-steps which they had soiled, and hastened to sack the house of the mayor, because a small detachment of militia, spontaneously assembled, had fired upon them in self-defence, after having stood patient for some time under a shower of stones.

These disorders are alarming from their general prevalence, and from their frequent repetitions, and they are the more so, the less their importance is realised. They meet with few voices to condemn them, but they find many to excuse them. One of the defects of democracy is that it is forgetful of the past, and careless of the future. A riot, which in France would put a stop to business, prevents no one here from going to the Exchange, speculating, turning over the dollars, and making money. On meeting in the morning, each one asks and tells the news; here a negro has been hanged, there a white man has been flogged; at Philadelphia, ten houses have been demolished; at Buffalo, at Utica, some people of colour have been scourged. Then they go on to the price of cotton and coffee, the arrivals of flour, lumber, and tobacco, and become absorbed in calculations the rest of the day. I am surprised to see how dead the word equality falls, when a good citizen pronounces it; the reign of law seems to be at an end; we have fallen under that of expediency. Farewell to justice, fare-well to the great principles of 1776 and 1789! All hail to the interest of the moment, interpreted by nobody knows who, for the success of some petty intrigue of politics or business!

Five men, five white men, have been hanged at Vicks-burg in Mississippi, without even the form of a trial ; they were gamblers, you are told, the scourge of the country. The *most respectable* citizens of Vicksburg assisted in their execution. But the law which guaranties to all your fellow-citizens the trial by a jury of peers ; but that old Saxon justice of which you boast! What is become of them ? No tribunal would have been able to rid us of the rogues ; morality and religion condemn them, and their decree, for want of others, we have executed ; it was necessary. *Expediency !* In Virginia, travellers from the Northern States, on the slightest pretences, for some tavern gossip, or some conversation in the coach, have been drag-ged before the self-styled *Committees of Vigilance,* beaten, tarred, and feathered. Others, whose crime consisted in inadvertently having in their pocket, some papers which the slave-holder has been pleased to pronounce abolition writings, have been seized by these fanatics, and hanged as emissaries of insurrection. What is become of that article of the constitution, which secures to the citizens of each State the protection of the laws in every other State ? If we were to insist on these points, we should endanger our union with the South. *Expediency !* Merchants of New York! The planters of one of the parishes of Louisiana have set a price on the head of one of your number, because, as they say, he is an abolitionist, an amalgamator. Will not your national sensibility, so lively in regard to France, be touched by this act of audacity ? Our commerce with the South constitutes half the prosperity of New York. *Ex-pediency !* Men of New England ! Citizens of the cradle

of American liberty ! Sons of the pilgrims, self-exiled first
to Holland, and then to the sandy shores of Massachusetts,
rather than bow their opinions to the will of the Stuarts!
You, so proud of your liberties, how can you abandon the
dearest of all, the liberty of the press, to the hands of a
postmaster ?   Always the same reply : *Expediency !*

It would seem as if political principles no longer existed
in the United States but at the pleasure of the passions, and the laws had no force when they jarred with interest.   When a State feels itself injured by a tariff, it
declares the law null and void, arms its militia, buys powder and throws down the glove to Congress.   When
another State, as Ohio, is dissatisfied with the boundary
line assigned to it, it declares war against Michigan, its
neighbour, in order to extend its frontiers by force.   When
the fanatics of Massachusetts, in their savage intolerance,
feel offended by the presence of a Catholic convent, in
which the sisters devote themselves to the work of edu-
cating young girls without distinction of sect, they plunder it and set it on fire, and the sacred edifice is burnt, in
sight of a city with 70,000 inhabitants, without a drop of
water being thrown upon the flames, and without its being
possible to find a jury that would convict the authors of
the cowardly outrage.   When a Governor of Georgia*
comes into collision with an upright magistrate, who inter-
poses his authority between the rapacity of the whites and
the poor Indian whom they are impatient to rob, he de-
nounces the just judge to the legislature, and urges the
passing of a law that will make him a State criminal.
And, I repeat it, the worst and most fatal symptom of the
times is, that the perpetration of these outrages, however
frequent they become, excites no sensation.   The destruction of the churches and school-houses of the blacks in

* Gev. Lumpkin,

New York was looked upon as a show, and the merchants of the city as they passed, paused to take a moment's relaxation from the sight; the fall of the buildings was greeted with loud cheers. In Baltimore, a numerous crowd applauded the work of demolition without inquiring whose house was pulled down, and the women, in the excitement of the moment, waved their handkerchiefs in the air.

Another symptom still more alarming! Civil courage, the virtue of the Hampdens, the glory of the English race, which shone with so pure a lustre in the United States whilst the authors of their independence survived, seems to be for a time extinct; I say for a time, for there is a stock of energy in the American character, which cannot fail some time or another to revive and put forth its strength anew. The press, which with a few honourable exceptions, does not possess and does not merit, in the United States, the consideration which it enjoys in France; the press, which is here so outrageously violent and brutal in its treatment of members of Congress belonging to the opposite party, is, on the other hand, more cautious and reserved in regard to the multitude. The American press is free in so far as it gives no bonds and pays no stamp duty, but it is dependent on a capricious, despotic, and not very enlightened public opinion, which requires it to flatter the passion of the hour, and does not look to it for lessons of morality. The public opinion of the democracy is a master who is easily offended, and who quickly shows his displeasure. The American journalist is well aware that for the slightest display of boldness he will be deserted; and since the late events, this is not his only fear, for he knows that if his enemies should choose to brand him as an abolitionist, for example, it would be easy to raise a mob of vagabonds, who would pillage and pull down his house, tar and feather his person, and drive

him from home without any interference by the public
authorities.* He is therefore exceedingly circumspect.
In a word, the *reign of terrour* is begun in the United
States. Men of courage and devotion to the cause of law
have no rallying point in the press; and even when the
public authority would be disposed to support them, it
proves insufficient, either through fear, or concern for party
interests, or want of physical force. To the small number
of good citizens in whom the state of the country excites
the liveliest alarm, there appears to be no resource left, but
that of organising themselves in patriotic societies, forming
themselves into military companies, of creating, in fine, a
national guard, under the form which the laws and national customs would sanction. They feel that this step is
necessary, but they hesitate, because they fear to kindle a
civil war. The Baltimoreans, however, seem determined
to make the trial.† It has also been proposed to make the

---

* An editor of a newspaper was lately driven from Boston by a mob, on
account of his abolition principles, and not long since another was subjected
to the same ostracism in New Orleans for having offended a militia company
by his remarks.

† The question of an armed police has for some time attracted the attention of enlightened individuals in the United States; the constable's staff
and the *posse comitatus* of the sheriff are no longer sufficient to maintain
order and keep the peace. Independently of political difficulties, however,
economical considerations stand in the way of the project. Virginia, for
example, has nearly two-fifths of the superficial area of France. An armed
police of one thousand men, which would be inconsiderable for that
extent of country, would cost her about 800,000 dollars a year, a sum, say
the calculators, which would more than pay the interest of a loan that would
enable us to construct a canal or a railroad from Richmond to the Ohio. So
the canal is made, and the armed police put off for another day. Meanwhile if some travellers from the North are hanged or flogged as abolitionists
by the slaveholders, in a moment of excitement, the affair is regretted at
first, but it is thought to be more important to have a canal or railroad which
shall make Richmond the rival of New York, than to save two or three
fanatics from the lash or the halter. This system is deplorable. But I
know not that we have a right to denounce it, for we must confess, that
something analogous prevails amongst us. We demand money without

towns responsible by law for the damages committed within their limits. Such a law, if it did not have the effect wholly to prevent the disorders, for the taxes here are mostly paid by the rich, would at least have the merit of repairing the losses suffered by means of them.

The present generation in the United States, brought up in devotion to business, living in an atmosphere of interest, if it is superiour to the last generation in commercial intelligence and industrial enterprise, is inferiour to it in civil courage and love of the public good. Deplorable fact ! When Baltimore was not long since given up to the genius of destruction four whole days, when the protection of the city had been vainly transferred from the mayor to the sheriff, and from the sheriff to the commanding officer of the militia, when the prisons had been forced, and the spirit of order began at last to revive, not a man was found in this city of 100,000 souls to put himself at the head of the movement. When the most respectable citizens, and those most deeply interested in the restoration of the public tranquillity held a meeting in the Exchange, the mountain in labour brought forth only a long series of whereases on the advantage of public order, and a string of wordy resolutions which resolved nothing. Nothing, shameful to relate, but the presence of a veteran relic of the Revolution with the weight of eightyfour years on his head, who had retired from Congress to end his long career in repose, but who felt his blood boil in his veins and mantle in his cheeks at the spectacle before him,—nothing but his presence gave courage to this assembly of men in the vigour of life, who were letting their city fall a prey to a handful of drunkards and depraved boys. The indignant

---

hesitation for war, for organising and keeping up a large military force, for filling our arsenals with cannon ; but how difficult is it to procure any for useful enterprises, roads, canals, railroads, schools, penitentiaries, to which the United States devote almost all their resources ?

old man, started up and interrupted the reading of the resolutions ; " Damn your resolutions !" cried he ; " give me a sword and thirty men, and I will restore order ?" " What ! General Smith," said one of these irresolute makers of resolutions, " would you fire upon your fellow citizens ?" " Those who break the laws, drive their neighbour from his house, plunder his property and reduce his wife and children to beggary," answered Gen. Smith, " such fellows are not my fellow-citizens." These words, which expressed the thoughts of all, but which no one dared utter, were received with a thunder of applause. The aged senator was named commander of the military force by acclamation, and a few days after was chosen mayor. Since that time Baltimore has been quiet. But when we reflect that order has been restored in a large and flourishing city, only because there happened to be present a veteran whom death had spared, and who had energy enough, with one foot in the grave, to come forward and teach his fellow citizens, by example, the lessons of the golden age of American liberty, are we not forced to exclaim with Mr Clay ; " We are in the midst of a revolution."

Mr Clay is no false prophet ; for the events that have succeeded each other since he uttered these words, announce that a crisis is at hand. The American system no longer works well. In the North, the removal of all restrictions on the right of suffrage, without the creation of any counterpoise, has destroyed the equilibrium. In the South, the old foundation borrowed from the ante-Christian ages, on which it has been attempted to raise the super-structure of a new social order in the nineteenth century, shakes and threatens to bury the thoughtless builders under the ruins of their half-finished work. In the West, a population sprung from the soil under the influence of circumstances unparallelled in the history of the world, already affects a superiority, or rather lays claim to dominion, over the North and South. Everywhere, the relations established by the old federal compact, become unsuited to the new state of things. The dissolution of the Union, the mere thought of which would have caused a shudder of horrour, ten years ago, which was numbered among those acts of infamy that are not to be named, — the dissolution of the Union has been demanded, and no thunder fell upon the head of the perpetrator of the sacrilege. At present it is a common topic of conversation. The dissolution of the Union, if it should take place, would be the most complete of all revolutions.

What will be the character of this revolution, which is felt to be approaching ? To what institutions will it give birth ? Who must perish in the day of account ? Who will rise on the storm ? Who will resist the action of ages ? I have not the gift of prophecy, and I shall not try to pierce the mystery of the destinies of the New World. But I have a firm faith, that a people with the energy and intelligence which the Americans possess ; a people which has like it the genius of industry, which combines perseverance with the resources of ingenuity, which is essentially regular in its habits and orderly in its disposition, which is deeply imbued with religious habits, even when a lively faith is wanting, such a people cannot be born of yesterday to vanish on the morrow. The American people, in spite of its original defects, in spite of the numerous voids which a hasty growth and a superficial education have left in its ideas, feelings, and customs, is still a great and powerful people. For such nations, the most violent storms are wholesome trials which strengthen, solemn warnings which teach, elevate, and purify them.

LETTER XXXI.

THE MIDDLE CLASSES.

BALTIMORE, OCT. 8, 1835.

AMERICAN society is composed of quite different elements, from those of which European society in general, and French society in particular, consists. On analysing the latter, we find, in the first place, the shadow of an aristocracy, comprising the wrecks of the great families of the old order that have been saved from the revolutionary storm, and the descendants of the Imperial nobility, who seem to be already separated from their fathers by the distance of ages.

Next below this is a numerous body of the Middle Classes (*bourgeoisie*), consisting of two distinct sets; the one, the active class, is engaged in commerce, manufactures, agriculture, and the liberal professions; the other, generally designated amongst us as the *bourgeoisie oisive*, consists of men without active employment, landholders who derive an income of 500 or 1500 dollars from their estates, by rents or sharing the produce with the cultivator, without attempting to increase it, and the small body of holders of public stock.

These two divisions of the Middle Class differ essentially from each other, the one labouring, the other only consuming and enjoying what they have. The one increases its means, and consequently is able to keep itself above the waves, and maintain, if not to raise, its level; the other, as M. Lafitte has said, successively transported by time into one stage of society after another, in each of which large additions are made to the general wealth, finds itself growing relatively poorer, and must decrease in numbers. They differ no less in their origin; the one belongs essentially to the commons; the other has some pretensions to nobility, it is the offspring, or at least the heir and successor of the country-gentry. During the period of the Restoration, they differed also in their political views; the members of the one class for the most part took the left side, those of the other preferred the right side. At present, the former accepts the new dynasty without reluctance; the latter, more difficult to be satisfied in regard to the preservation of order, and ready to take alarm at every violation of old established privileges, still preserves a secret preference for the legitimate line. In respect to religious sentiments, the latter is sceptical, and prone to believe that the Voltairean philosophy and the theories broached by the Opposition during the fifteen years, are the *nec plus ultra* of the human understanding; the former, shaken in its faith, still keeps alive the sacred fire of religious feeling, rejects the disorganising doctrines of the 18th century, and holds in scorn the lucubrations of the liberal publicists of the Restoration. The one piques itself on its adherence to the positive, the material; the other concerns itself about the great conservative principles of society, but refuses to recognise the new interests, which must be allowed to share in the privileges of those of the past.

These two sections of the Middle Class are not wholly and sharply separated from each other; but they run into and across each other. A large proportion partakes somewhat of both characters, and joins one side or the other, according to times and circumstances. Yet, although often confounded in the same individual, the two interests are, nevertheless, substantially distinct from each other. The base of the pyramid is occupied by the peasants and operatives, divided into two sections; the one of which has become possessed of property, the other has not yet reached that point but aspires after it with eagerness. On one side, we have the mechanics and small proprietors ; on the other, the labourers. It is universally acknowledged that the Middle Class, at present, rules in France. The aristocracy is driven from power or keeps itself aloof. The mechanics and small proprietors hardly yet begin to raise their heads. The labourers are nothing.

In the Northern States of the American Union, society is much less complex in its composition, than in France. Exclusive of the coloured caste, there are here only two classes ; the middle class and the democracy. Of the two conflicting interests, one only has a public existence here ; it is labour. The Middle Class consists of the manufacturers, merchants, lawyers, physicians. A small number of cultivators, and persons devoted to letters or the fine arts, is to be added to these.

The democracy is composed of the farmers and mechanics. In general, the cultivator is the owner of the soil ; in the West, this rule is without exceptions. Great landholders do not exist, at least as a class, in the North and the Northwest. There is strictly speaking no class of mere labourers ; for although there are day-labourers, and both in the cities and country many workmen without capital, yet these are in fact apprentices, for the most part foreigners, who become in turn proprietors and master-workmen, and not unfrequently rich manufacturers, wealthy speculators.

Between these two classes there is, however, no line of demarcation, for the attempts of some coteries to establish certain fashionable distinctions do not deserve notice, or at least are only of a negative value, as timid and often absurd protestations against the abuse of equality. The two classes have the same domestic habits, and lead the same life, and differ considerably only in respect of the sect to which they are attached, and the pews they occupy. The relations which exist at present between the wealthy *bourgeoisie* and the wrecks of the aristocracy in France, give an accurate notion of the relative condition of the two classes of American Society.

Political influence is, at present, entirely in the hands the American democracy, as with us it is monopolised by the Middle Classes. The latter have no chance of getting possession of power in the United States, except temporarily, or by means of accidental divisions in the democratic ranks, when they may rally to their standard a portion of the farmers and mechanics, as happened in 1834, after General Jackson's attack on the Bank. So in France, it will be impossible for the aristocracy to raise, not its own banner (for it has none), but that of the legitimate line, unless the folly of the government should excite new troubles, and inspire the Middle Class, who now support it heartily, with fears for the public security.

In the Southern States, the existence of slavery produces quite a different state of society, from that of the North ; half of the population there consists of mere labourers in the strictest sense, that is of slaves. Slavery necessarily requires great estates, which in fact, form aristocracy. Great estates still continue to be held in the South, notwithstanding the custom of equal partition has very much narrowed them.

Between these two extremes in the South, an intermediate class has sprung up, consisting, like our Middle Class, of the workingmen and the men of leisure, the new interest and the old interest. Commerce, manufactures, and the liberal professions, on one side ; on the other, the land-holders, corresponding to our moderate country land-holders, living on their estates by the sweat of their slaves, having no taste for work, not prepared for it by education, and even taking little oversight of the daily business of the plantation ; men who would be incapable of applying themselves to any occupation if slavery were abolished, just as our proprietors would be unable to get a living, if they were to be deprived of their estates.

It is plain that the equal partition of estates must have tended to increase the number of this class of men of leisure ; it is numerous in the old Southern States, Virginia, the Carolinas, and Georgia, and also in Louisiana ; the check which these States at first experienced in their career, whilst the North was advancing without let, and the contemporaneous increase of this class, are two correlative facts, which account for each other. But we do not find this class in the new States of the South. The new generation there, as in the North, devoured with the the passion of making money, has become as industrious as the Yankees. The cultivation of cotton offers it a wide field of activity ; in Alabama and Mississippi, the cotton lands are sold at a very low price. The internal slave-trade furnishes hands in abundance, which are easily procured on credit when one has friends, but no patrimony. The sons of the old Southern States, instead of vegetating on a fragment of the paternal estate, with a handful of negroes, sell off their property at home, extend their means by aid of a loan, which they are sure of being able to repay promptly, and go to the Southwest, to establish a a cotton-plantation, a sort of agricultural manufactory, in which they are obliged to exercise more or less of the activity, and to feel more or less of the hopes and fears of a manufacturer.

Thus the class which works little or not at all, is disappearing in the United States. In the Western States, which are the true New World, it no longer exists at all, in the North or in the South ; you meet with no one there who is not engaged in agriculture, commerce, manufactures, the liberal professions, or the clerical office. The

United States, then, differ from us in having no aristocracy, no idle Middle Class, no class of mere labourers, at the least in the North. But a distinction should be made in regard to the absence of these three classes; for while it may be admitted that the two last are absolutely becoming extinct, it would be more correct to say that the first has not yet begun to exist.

Civilisation, in its passage from one continent to the other, has, then, got rid of two classes. This twofold disappearance is, however, only a single phenomenon, or, at most, two phases of a single fact, the industrial progress of mankind. It seems to me to be inevitable, that, in this matter, the Old World should follow the example of the New; it moves towards the same end under the influence of peculiar causes, and it is irresistibly driven onward by what is commonly called the force of events, that is, by the decree of providence.

There is a rule superior to all social conventions, codes of legislation, or systems of jurisprudence · it is, that when a class has ceased to take part in the workings of society, its doom is pronounced; it cannot preserve its privileges, unless the march of civilisation comes to a stand, and it is kept stationary, as it was in Rome from Augustus to Constantine; but when the column again sets forward, those who will not serve as soldiers, and are unfit to be officers, those who can do duty neither in the ranks nor in command, who can act neither in the tent nor the field, all these are abandoned as stragglers, and their names are struck from the roll. The law is inflexible and unsparing; no human power can rescue those whom it condemns from their doom; they only can save themselves, by taking part in the general movement.

This explains the annihilation of the aristocracy of the nobility in France. Between it and royalty, as between royalty and the English aristocracy, there was a long

struggle, but the results were as different as the characters
of the nations.   In France, monarchical unity triumphed ;
Louis XI. struck down the aristocracy ; Richelieu muzzled
it ; Louis XIV. obliged it to wear the collar.   Thus reduced in a political point of view, it was left in possession
of the field of taste and art, which it devoted to the promotion of irreligion and corruption of manners.   When,
therefore, it was weighed in 1789, it was found wanting ;
the decree of destiny had gone forth, and the revolution
executed it with a cannibal ferocity.   The unhappy aristocracy remembered its lofty nature only at the point of
death ; it mounted the scaffold with dignity.

For the same reason, the idle portion of the Middle Class
tends towards its fall, for it accomplishes no purpose,
which cannot be effected without it.   It does not enrich
society by its labour, although it lays claim to be reckoned
in the number of producers, under the pretext that it holds
the soil and exercises a sort of superintendence over its
cultivation.   The truth is, that it is wholly ignorant of
agriculture ; it has received by tradition a certain routine,
but the peasantry is as fully possessed of the tradition, and
needs no teachers on that matter.   The proprietor is sometimes, indeed, paid in kind by the peasant, and then sells
the grain himself ; but the peasant could easily attend to that
business, and would manage it quite as well as his landlord.   Neither does this class serve as the representative of
knowledge ; for in this respect, its acquisitions are limited
to a little polite literature, an agreeable accomplishment
surely, but not answering to the wants and spirit of the
age.

Where a nobility exists and maintains its prerogatives,
as in England, it performs a twofold office.   In the first
place, it devotes itself to the most difficult of all arts, that
of governing men, and in this it excels ; whether because
it cultivates it by the traditions of experience, or because

it vigilantly recruits its ranks by enlisting in them such men as have already proved their superiour knowledge of the different interests of society. This reason cannot be urged by our idle Middle Class as an argument for its preservation ; for it is notoriously ignorant of the science of government.

The second office of a nobility, not less essential than the first in our polished age, is to serve as a pattern and example in the art of living, to teach the art of consuming, without which that of producing procures only partial and illusive gratification, and to encourage the fine arts. On this head nothing can be said in favour of the class alluded to. It excels neither in grace, nor elegance, nor address. The importance which it has acquired by the destruction of the aristocracy, has been fatal to the old French politeness, to that exquisite courtesy on which our fathers prided themselves. Within the last fifty years, whilst the English have been improving in this respect, much more successfully than their stiff and unpliant humour seemed to promise, we have forgotten much and unlearned much, under the controlling influence of our Middle Class.

As for the art of consuming with grace and living well, and that care of the person, the only fraction of which that they can be sensible to, the English call comfort, our Middle Class has lessons to learn, but none to give. It is not, however, the fault of nature ; for no people has received finer and acuter senses than ours. Surely, our nerves are more sensitive, our ear and our palate more delicate than those of the English. Our superiority on these points, is attested by the fact, that, from one end of the world to the other, we are in possession of most of the trades which relate to the person ; the office of cook, head-dresser, dancing-master, valet, or tailor, is everywhere monopolised by the French. But to surround oneself with the English comfort, and that more refined comfort which we can

conceive of, one must be rich. Now our Middle Class is
poor, and politically considered this is one of its greatest
faults ; it grows poorer daily, either by the operation of
the law which commands the equal partition of estates, or
of that idleness which condemns it to a stationary income,
whilst public wealth and luxury are increasing all around
it. It cannot, therefore, encourage the fine arts, for the
patronage of the arts is costly ; besides taste is growing rare
in France since the fall of the aristocracy.

Nor can it be affirmed that the unemployed Middle Class
in France represents the element of order, and that if it
were to disappear, France itself would perish in frightful
convulsions. For the labouring class is already ripe for a
better state of society, and requires only the advantages of
instruction, and of more favourable terms and more numerous opportunities for industry, to be in a condition to
exercise all the rights of a citizen as usefully as the greater portion of the Middle Class. And even if the latter represents in whole or in part the element of order, it is only
by the aid and the instrumentality of four hundred thousand
bayonets, exclusive of those of the Middle Class itself, and
thus it retains its predominance only by opposing the multitude to the multitude ; a critical and dangerous position,
which cannot long be held, for the very bayonets are beginning to become intelligent.

The *bourgeoisie oisive* has, then, only one course to take ;
that is, to pass into the ranks of the working men, to fit
themselves to become the leaders of the people in its labours. When this is done, our fields, which belong especially to their domain, will change their aspect as if by
enchantment, and our peasants, who, it cannot be too
often repeated, at present form the poorest and most numerous class in France, will be raised to a better condition,
of which they are worthy. The idle Middle Class must
now become with the government, to which the first step

in all great projects of improvement belong, responsible for the progress of twenty-five millions of agricultural labourers.

In this change it has every thing to gain itself. By this means it will maintain and confirm its own social rank, for it will thus recover the confidence of the multitude, and will turn its superiority to a good account by exercising a beneficent patronage towards its inferiours. It will exchange a straitened condition for competency or even wealth, and the tedium of a life of inaction for the satisfaction of having done well, the consciousness of having faithfully performed a great duty. This honourable desertion of the standard of idleness for that of industry is now going forward daily. Let us rejoice at it: let us pray that it may speedily become universal. Let us especially urge government to accelerate it, by encouraging the development of industry, by all the means and aids that can improve the condition and resources of agriculture, and inspire the young generation with a desire to devote themselves to this first of arts.

LETTER XXXII.

ARISTOCRACY.

PHILADELPHIA, OCT. 13, 1835.

No great society can be durable, except in so far as authority is established in it. We may easily imagine a case, however, in which the authority may be temporarily thrown into the shade; when a great nation is in search of political and social forms suited to its wants, when it

is obliged to pass from trial to trial, to feel its way, and turn
itself successively to different points ; when, beside, its separation from the rest of the world guaranties its independence, and frees it from the necessity of organising itself
under the apprehension of assaults from abroad, it is then
permitted, it is even necessary, that it should provide for
the greatest possible freedom of motion, and that it should
cast off all unnecessary and unprofitable restraints.   But
then a society without a fixed order and political ties, is
an anomaly, a passing phenomenon.   The social bonds of
opinion and religion, the only ones which exist here, cannot supply the want of political ties, unless they are
straightened to such a degree as to become despotic.
Besides, when large towns like New York, Philadelphia,
and Baltimore, have once grown up, and there is a numerous floating population, which opinion and religion cannot
watch closely, manners and belief have need of the firm
support of the laws.

The serious character and frequent occurrence of disorders in the American Union, at the present time, prove
that the period has come, when it will be necessary for
authority to be organised.   There are interests in the
South, for example, which are filled with alarm, and
which for want of legal protection, protect themselves,
right or wrong, in a brutal manner, and feel the necessity
of a power upon which they can rely for safety.   In the
Middle Class of the cities of the North, there is a popula-
tian, enervated or rather refined by wealth, which is no
longer ready to exercise that portion of self-government
that consists in the suppression of violence by force, and
in the democracy, there is a restless and turbulent element
which force alone can hold in check.   These two classes,
which are peculiar to the North, and whose numbers daily
increase, will soon be unable to live with each other, without the intervention of power.

Authority has two bases, upon which, to stand firm, it must be supported, like man upon two feet; these are unity or centralisation, and the distinction of ranks. The corresponding bases of liberty are equality, and independence. The spirit of unity or centralisation is already beginning to appear in several of the United States. (See *Letter XXIX.*).

It is not strictly correct to say that the Americans have renounced the principle of authority; for they have from the beginning adopted the principle of the sovereignty of the people. It is true that they understood it, at first, negatively; that is as a simple denial of authority in the European sense, or of military power founded on conquest; but when the doctrine of equality had once secured to the democracy the superiority over the Middle Class, the democracy gradually took upon itself the exercise of that sovereignty, for its own interest, well or ill understood, at the dictation of its passions good or bad; here, then, was power in the fullest extent of the word, here was a dictatorate : not indeed permanent and steady, but showing itself by starts and at intervals. For the most of the time it may be said to have slumbered, and left the field free to the spirit of individuality; it has roused itself occasionally only to strike a decisive blow, and to sink back again into its slumbers; but however irregular may have been its action, still here has been power, and power legal in its character and bold in its operations, and gradually extending their sphere.

The New England States, which are the incarnation of the spirit of division and individualism, have advanced little in this direction. The old Southern States, although they have more of the spirit of centralisation, have also shown themselves timid in this matter. The Middle States, and particularly New York, have made the greatest progress; those of the West, and particularly of the Northwest, seem disposed to imitate them.

This centripetal power has operated in two ways; negatively, in setting limits, and sometimes narrow ones, to the independence of personal action, whether exercised singly by individuals or collectively by companies. It has, for example, reduced the privileges of incorporated companies in general, and the railroad and banking companies in particular, or rather it has assumed to itself to be omnipotent in regard to them; at this moment, the democracy in the North is raising the hue and cry after all companies. It has imposed various restrictions upon commerce, such for instance, as the inspection laws relative to exported produce. Positively, it has interfered with the private transactions of individuals, and suspended or annulled them; thus in the West, *ex post facto* laws have been passed in favour of debtors; or the courts which refused to yield, have been abolished in a body, as in Kentucky; or monopolies have been created and sold for the profit of the State, as in New Jersey. Within a few years other measures of a more fundamental and comprehensive nature have been adopted, and the centralisation of the schools, the means of communication, and the banks, the three institutions of the most vital importance in a society devoted to industry, has already been commenced. Thus the germ of a vigourous central authority, which will embrace all the ruling interests of the country, is already beginning to sprout. In this respect the North and the South, the East and the West, with the exception of New England, which is held back by its spirit of subdivision,* seem to be unanimous.

---

* It has already been mentioned that Massachusetts has lately adopted the new policy in regard to public works. [And it might be added in respect to the school-system.—Transl.]

If any danger is to be feared in the Northern States, during the coming period, it is not the absence, but the excess of power that is to be apprehended. Whilst the democracy in these States retains its jealousy of the military, it appears to be regardless of the accumulation of power in the hands of the legislators. It refuses to appeal to arms, even for the suppression of the most brutal violence ; but it is willing to use or abuse the omnipotence of the popular representation, and it would not hesitate, in case it should be provoked by circumstances, to exercise it in the most tyrannical manner. A representative government loses the character of a compromise between the different social interests, and degenerates into an instrument of despotism in the hands of the multitude. In America, it had its origin in the concessions of the Middle Class to the democracy. At present the positions are reversed ; the Middle Class now stands in need of concessions and does not seem likely to get them.

Instead of the physical tortures of the Inquisition, this despotism, if it gains strength and stability, would practice the most cruel moral tortures, it would have its Procustes' bed for intellect and wealth ; its level for genius. Under pretence of equality it would establish the most fatal uniformity. As it would be successively exercised by the changing favourites of the multitude, it would be eminently fickle and capricious ; ever calling in question and unsettling all that was established,* it would end by palsying

---

* In 1834, the Ohio legislature incorporated a Life and Trust Company, with very great powers; the company was organised in 1835, and in 1836, a proposition was made in the legislature 'the effect of which would have been indirectly to abolish it. Happily the legislature saw the necessity of keeping up the credit of the State by a faithful adherence to its engagements, and the proposition was rejected. Mr Dallas, of Philadelphia, who has been a Senator of the United States, has quite recently urged the adoption of *ex post facto* measures, with the object of annulling the charter of the United States Bank.

the spirit of enterprise, which has created the prosperity of the country.

In the Southern States, the white democracy has a pedestal in slavery. In order to realise its own elevation, it is not obliged to be continually engaged in lowering the superiour classes; it exercises its authority on what is beneath, and thinks less of attacking what is over it. In the South, society is divided into masters and slaves; the distinction of higher and lower class is there of secondary importance, particularly at the present time, when the alarming state of their relations with the blacks, obliges all whites to act in concert. In the South, moreover, slavery will soon oblige the local governments to maintain an armed police, which, while it keeps down the slaves, will also serve to prevent the repetition of excesses, by which this section of the union has recently been sullied, and the imitation of those outrages on private property and public order, of which the North has, of late, so frequently been the theatre.

Centralisation is one half of authority; distinction of ranks, the other half, cannot be easily supplied in the United States, particularly in the North, where, however, it is necessary that some institution should give stability and strength to authority. There are two sorts of aristocracy; aristocracy of birth, and aristocracy of talents. I do not now speak of the aristocracy of money, for this has no chance of establishing itself, and can acquire influence only by being merged in one of the two others.

All great societies which have existed up to this time, have established with more or less solidity, one or the other of these aristocracies, or, to speak more correctly, both. An aristocracy of talents existed even in the bosom of the Egyptian and Hindoo castes; but Christianity first distinctly established an order of classification founded on intellect, not only in each nation, but throughout the

Catholic Church ; the Roman Catholic clergy was organised on this principle. It could not be otherwise ; the unity of God and of the human race was an article of faith ; for the christian there was only one God, the father of all men, before whom all distinctions of birth were as nothing.

But by the side of this aristocracy of intellect, all nations which have reached a lofty political elevation, and founded durable empires, have had an aristocracy of birth, a civil and military nobility. Among some not very numerous peoples of antiquity, the nobility was composed of all free citizens, who were inferiour in numbers to the slaves. Such were the republics of Greece, whose political superiority, however, was of short duration. Such were the Arabs, among whom there were rayas, christians, and Jews, below the faithful. The nations which have had most weight in the balance of European civilisation, have been differently constituted ; above the free citizens, they had a hereditary privileged class. Such was Rome ; such is England ; in the same way the empire of Islam was not solidly or firmly fixed, until a handful of Turks was placed over the Arabs, as a privileged class.

It is worthy of notice, that the last of the great societies which have passed over the face of the earth, christian society, or that in which the aristocracy of intellect was first fully developed, is also that in which aristocracy of birth has been most strongly marked. The sons of Japhet, who gave the impulse and acted as leaders to this movement of civilisation, brought with them from the North, a strong spirit of family, with which their political systems have been deeply impregnated ; thus arose the most strictly hereditary nobility which has ever been seen. Till that time the hereditary system had been applied to caste ; the Germans extended hereditary distinctions and functions to family, with the additional restriction of primogeniture. What before had been an exception in favour of royal families, they applied to all noble families. This organisation, more or less modified, still prevails in most of the European States. But yesterday, it seemed as vigourous as ever in England. It is true that it has there conformed itself to the spirit of the age, that it has become pliant and elastic, opened its ranks to the aristocracy of intellect, and consecrated its wealth and employed its privileges, not in gratifying its own caprices, nor in satiating its passions, but in spreading all around it, the network of a vast and beneficent patronage.

At the present day, there is a violent reaction against hereditary distinctions and aristocracy of birth. On all points of the territory occupied by the Western civilisation, the aristocracy of feudal origin is battered down, here by the democracy, there by the Middle Class, and elsewhere by royalty. In the general league against it, the emperor of Russia gives his hand to the American democracy and the French *bourgeoisie,* and the British democracy in the person of O'Connell, is allied with the king of Prussia and the emperor of Austria.

Whatever opinion we may entertain of the present value of aristocracy of birth, we are obliged to acknowledge, that, in the past, it has rendered great services to the human race. But for the establishment of the feudal system, the barbarian hordes would have continued to drive over the face of Europe, tribe dashing against tribe, nation hurled against nation. The principal distinction between the Germans or Normans, and the followers of Attila or Genghis Khan, is that the former had the instinct of organisation, as is manifested by their conception of the feudal system, and the latter were destitute of it. England is chiefly indebted to her aristocracy for her brilliant success.* I do not regret the past, for our share of glory is still great, although France has been conquered by her rival in the field and in the cabinet, and in every part of the world, in Europe, America, and Asia. Yet I may be permitted to say, that if the French aristocracy had triumphed in its struggle with Richelieu,† the destinies of the world might have been completely changed ; and France, perhaps, would then have played the part which has fallen to the lot of England.

The right of primogeniture, extended beyond the limits of the aristocracy, ought not to be looked upon as a senseless imitation of the customs of the nobility by vain common- ers. Although it may be difficult to defend this custom, on the ground of equity, yet it has been one of the causes of the greatness of England. It is clear that it is favoura- ble to the accumulation of capital in few hands ; now capital is like man, powerful when united in masses, fee- ble when divided. England is indebted to the law of primogeniture for an ever swarming army of younger sons, eager to exercise their enterprise in the colonies, and con-

---

* The English aristocracy is accessible to every man of superior qualities. The king can and often does make a peer of a commoner, and the order of knights, which is the lowest degree of nobility, is essentially an aristocracy of talents and personal services, not being hereditary. But if the aristocra- cy of intellect has thus got a footing in the aristocracy of birth, the latter has also encroached upon the former; for with the constitution of the An- glican church, and in the absence of monasteries and the numerous gratui- tous institutions of the olden time, it is more difficult for a swine-herd, like Sixtus V., to rise in the establishment at the present day, than it would have been for him to reach the summit of the Catholic hierarchy in the Middle Ages.

† The French aristocracy which fought the fight with Richelieu was Protestant, and was more enlightened than the English aristocracy of the same day. French protestantism was the flower of Europe in every respect, even in industry. It is well known that the English and German manu- factures made great progress immediately after the revocation of the edict of Nantes, w drove four hundred thousand of our fellow countrymen from France.

tented with their lot, whether because they readily obtain assistance from the head of the family, or because they are full of energy, and know that by industry they will obtain wealth, or because they do not think that the world can be arranged on a different system. Meanwhile, the elder sons have formed an opulent metropolis, which has given ample aid to its distant possessions in all emergencies, and has gradually gained the supremacy in Europe.

But it would be madness to think of repairing the broken walls of feudalism, or to wish to copy, in France or the United States, the English aristocracy, even with its mode of recruiting its ranks by those distinguished for merit and services ; these orders of things have had their day. Yet all nations which aim to become or to remain powerful, must have an aristocracy ; that is to say, a body, which, whether hereditary or not, may preserve and perpetuate traditions, give system and stability to policy, and devote itself to the most difficult of all arts, which every one at the present day thinks he knows without having learned it, that of governing. A people without an aristocracy may shine in letters and art ; but its political glory must be as transitory as a meteor.

I know not if I allow myself to be deceived by my admiration for the past, although I do not conceal from myself how much of tyranny has been exercised over the great mass of mankind. But I cannot bring myself to believe, that the hereditary principle, or, in more general terms, the sentiment of family, should be entirely excluded from the aristocratical part of the new social order, which, although yet wrapped in uncertainty and mystery, is now struggling into existence on both sides of the Atlantic. The sentiment of family is not becoming extinct. Like all other social institutions, the constitution of the family has undergone various changes, since the beginning of the historical period. In the earlier times, every thing was swallowed up in the father, and the individuality — the rights, privileges, and duties — of the wife and children was the successive growth of ages ; but through all these changes, the family sentiment has gained, rather than lost. If this progressive movement is not violently checked, the new institutions with which our civilisation is now big, must give a place in the political system to the family sentiment, and it is not easy to conceive how this can be done, without a certain infusion of the hereditary principle.

It may be objected, that, in the United States, the family sentiment is much weaker, than it is in Europe. But we must not confound what is merely accidental and temporary, with the permanent acquisitions of civilisation. The temporary weakness of the family sentiment was one of the necessary results of the general dispersion of individuals, by which the colonisation of America has been accomplished; the effect must cease with the cessation of the temporary cause which produced it, that is, with the interruption of emigration to the West. As soon as they have got their growth, the Yankees, whose spirit now predominates in the Union, quit the paternal roof never to see it again, as naturally and with as little emotion, as young birds desert forever their native nest as soon as they are fledged ; but the predominance of the Yankees, at least, as they now are, does not seem to me destined to be perpetual ; I do not see in them the ultimate and permanent type of the American.

Even amongst the Yankees themselves the family sentiment has maintained a strong hold, by means of the bible, the sanctity and strictness of the marriage tie, the ample powers left to the father in disposing of his property.

Within the three last centuries, the moveable elements have shot up with a wonderful vigour in western civilisation. Manufactures and the press, the organ of philosophy and profane learning, have destroyed the balance between the opposing forces of innovation and conservation, whose equilibrium is necessary to constitute order. These two new powers, whose tendency is to reform every thing, have gained the advantage over the old powers of society, and trampled down the twofold aristocracy of birth and talents, the clergy and the nobility. Must we, then, conclude that these two aristocracies, or even either of them, are stone dead ; or must we not rather admit that order, that is to say, the equipoise of the innovating and the conservative powers, cannot subsist, unless authority is reconstructed in its ancient strength, without, however, retaining the brutal traits of its former character ? Is not this a reason that the hierarchy should be established at least as firmly as in past times ? Although it need not borrow from the past the unyielding, unelastic, and absolute features of the old aristocracies. And is there any principle of stability and solidity, comparable to that of hereditary transmission ? One may be permitted, or rather is obliged, to doubt it.

Systems of great stability have, doubtless, been organised without hereditary succession. The Catholic hierarchy offers the most complete example of this fact ; it has now stood eighteen hundred years. But in order to produce this result, it was necessary to root out the sentiment of family from the bosoms of its members, by binding them to celibacy ; and to substitute for the natural principle of stability, that of hereditary succession, a merely artificial principle, that of rigourous discipline, and passive obedience,—or in other words, stability has here been obtained at the sacrifice of liberty.

The two powers of commerce and the press are eminently fluctuating and unquiet, only because they are not yet regularly organised. They are susceptible of being modified, and of being restrained in their innovating tendencies, so as to render the restoration of the conservative force in all its vigour less necessary. The industrial interest would certainly be less averse to the privileges of the lay aristocracy, if it were permitted to participate in them, or if it had its own peculiar prerogatives. Learning, of which the press is the sword, would have showed less antipathy towards the spiritual hierarchy, had not the latter repulsed and rejected it. It is not impossible that we may be destined to witness a sort of industrial nobility; it is even possible that we may come, by degrees, in the course of time, to entertain the question of a more or less complete monopoly of learning and the press under some form or another. Instead of throwing down the aristocracy, we might give it additional strength and stability, by connecting it with learning and industry, which would then serve as its buttresses, instead of becoming the instruments of its ruin. In such a system as this, the aristocracy would be less compact and less exclusive ; it would soar less loftily over the rest of mankind ; but it would cover more ground, it would gain in breadth and length what it lost in height, and it would leave nothing beyond the reach of its influence. Equality would probably gain by this arrangement ; but human independence would lose by it.

It would be idle to attempt to guess at the future forms which the hierarchy may assume, to foresee the different interests of which society will hereafter be composed, or to name beforehand the institutions in which they will embody themselves. A multitude of combinations, which no one can divine, are possible. Many will take place, either successively in the same country, or simultaneously in different countries. But two things appear to me to be certain : one of these is, that new social phenomena of great magnitude are on the eve of being exhibited, either in America or in Europe ; and the other, that the sentiment of family cannot be ultimately and absolutely erased from the political catalogue.

For Europeans, the immediate and complete abolition of a hereditary aristocracy seems to me beset with the greatest difficulties. The nations of Western Europe have received their laws and usages from the Germans and Romans, that is, from two stocks strongly impregnated with the sentiment of family; there is not an inch of their soil, a stone of their monuments, a line of their national songs, which does not awaken this sentiment by recalling this two-fold origin; it seems, then, impossible that they should be ready to adopt at once a political system, in which it was allowed no place nor consideration. We may, however, be sure that the principle of hereditary succession must henceforth be limited within certain bounds. The idea of perpetuity, whether of punishment or of reward, is foreign from our age, and will not, certainly, be more acceptable to future ages. We live longer in the space of time than our fathers; the same number of years, therefore, represents a much greater duration than formerly. If the aristocratic investiture were to endure only for a few generations, aristocracy would not cease to be the most coveted of privileges and the most stable of institutions; while the jealousy of the non-privileged classes would be less keen in regard to its prerogatives, if the nobility bore upon its front the inscription; " Dust thou art, and unto dust shalt thou return."

This, however, would not be enough; the aristocracy of birth requires a spur. To exercise the most important functions, it is not enough that one has taken the trouble to be born. There is something monstrous in the privilege of the English peerage, of being legislators by hereditary right. In the Middle Ages it was necessary to have gained the spurs, before one could gird on the sword and raise the banner of a knight. In Rome, birth made

Patricians, but not Senators. Similar restrictions would be useful in all countries ; with a people like the French and the Southern Europeans, they would be indispensable.

It is not easy to say whence a hereditary aristocracy in France is to be derived, if we must really have one. A nucleus of old families or of military men would be wanting, around which the new elements might group themselves. Now, the old French nobility allowed itself to be degraded to the state of menials under Lowis XIV., and sunk into the grossest debauchery under Louis XV. ; the trials of exile did nothing for those who escaped the revolutionary axe ; when they re-appeared amongst us, they had forgotten nothing, and learned nothing. The infusion of the military aristocracy of the empire has not regenerated it. Is the retirement to which the old nobility has condemned itself since the revolution of 1830, a retreat, in which by meditation and repentence it is to renew its youth, or is it not rather a tomb, in which it has buried itself forever ? Will the old soil be heaved by earthquakes into new inequalities of surface ? Have we among our peasants some unknown scions of the slayers of Cæsar, or of the children of Brennus, who will be revealed to the world by some mighty convulsions ? Or will some Tartar horde from the North, the great hive of nations, put an end to our domestic quarrels, fix themselves in our palaces, seize our most fertile fields, wed our noblest, richest, and loveliest heiresses, and, sword in hand, proclaim to us ; " The reign of lawyers is over, ours is begun."

If the United States have also to constitute an aristocracy, and give political existence to the sentiment of family, their future would be yet more cloudy and uncertain than our own. The hereditary element of aristocracy has always come from conquest, or, at least, has supported itself, by alliance or compromise, by the sword of the

conqueror.   How can there be a conquest in the United
States ?   It is possible that they may conquer Mexico, but
they cannot be conquered by it.   It cannot be supposed that
some red Alexander or Charlemagne from the distant
steppes of the West, heading the fierce tribes of the Paw-
nee braves, and dragging in his victorious train swarms of
revolted negroes, can ever become the founder of a military dynasty and aristocracy.   If the Union should ever
be dissolved, and the hardy sons of the West, pouring
down from the Alleghanies, should ever conquer the people of the North, enervated by luxury and enfeebled by
anarchy, and those of the South, weakened by servile
wars, still no germ of a hereditary aristocracy would exist
in such a conquest ; for the victors and vanquished would
all be of the same family.

The Southern States, however, are already organised
on the principle of hereditary aristocracy.   It is true that
the privileged class is so numerous, that, unless a privilege
is established within a privilege, they do not form an
aristocracy properly so called ; but the fear of a rising of
the blacks keeps the whites closely united and forces them
to submit to a vigourous organisation of authority at
every sacrifice.   The relative situation of the whites and
blacks admits of no hesitation.

It is evident that the establishment of a hierarchy possessing any stability, would be the most difficult in the
States without slaves, and that the elevation of the sentiment of family to political dominion, would there encounter the most vigourous resistance.   In the maritime States
north of the Potomac, the difficulty would seem to be
insurmountable.   These States contain large towns, with
an extensive commerce carried on by great houses, great
factories in the English style, powerful trading, financial,
and manufacturing companies, that is to say, the germs of
an extreme inequality ; yet their laws consecrate a system

of absolute equality, and the sovereign democracy shows itself resolved to maintain it at all costs. Between these two counteracting forces, a struggle is going on, and cases might be imagined in which the contest may assume a terrible character. If any cause were to interrupt the prosperity of these States ; if, by means of a separation, which, however, is daily becoming less and less probable, the markets of the South were to be shut against their merchants and manufacturers ; if the sons of the farmers and their hired workmen could no longer have access to the lands and growing cities of the West ; if, to crown their misery, a foreign war should blockade their harbours, they would be exposed to the most frightful convulsions. The Northern States, then, must remain indissolubly wedded to the Union of the States, and firmly devoted to the policy of peace with the European monarchies.

If, then, it were proved that there was an irresistible necessity for a distinction of ranks in every society, and that the principle of inheritance or sentiment of family must be one of the constituent principles of a privileged class, which is requisite to form the apex of the social pyramid, it must be acknowledged that the prospect of the North is more dark and alarming than that of the South. By the exercise of unyielding vigilance over the slaves, the South may continue to maintain the outward forms of a regular social system. It would, indeed, be a retrograde system, for it would be morally a copy of the ancient order of society, which had its day before the advent of the Christ, patched up with the improved material order of modern times ; it would be despotism, but an orderly, organised despotism, which after all would be a less terrible scourge than the anarchy which threatens the North.

Nevertheless, whatever may be the destiny of aristocracy and the political fate of the family sentiment, I am loath to believe, that all that energy and intelligence which I have witnessed in the Northern States of the Anglo-American Union, can be swallowed up and lost. No deductions of logic can force me to conclude, that a society, superiour to any that has yet flourished in our ancient continent, will not, one day, and that soon, exist in the fine regions on the east and the west of the Alleghanies, around the wide basin of the great lakes, and along the far-stretching banks of these mighty rivers. It cannot be that a superiour race has transported its children to these shores to devour each other. If, on the one side, American civilisation seems to be exposed to formidable dangers, it presents itself in other points of view, with strongly marked features of permanency and stability. If great perils encompass its cradle, is it not the cradle of an infant Hercules ?

LETTER XXXIII.

D E M O C R A C Y .

NEW YORK, OCTOBER 22, 1835.

OUR old European societies have a heavy burden to bear ; it is that of the Past. Each age is the guarantee of the acts of those that have gone before it, and imposes a similar obligation on those which follow it. We are paying interest on our fathers' errors ; we pay it in the first place under the form of the public debt ; we pay it also in the charges for the support of our fine army, for among the causes which oblige all Europe to keep the flower of its population under arms, we must reckon the animosities of our fathers. We pay it, and at a higher rate, in all those habits of distrust and suspicion, which have been bequeathed to us from times of anarchy and despotism. The accumulated weight of a long Past must, indeed, be an insupportable burden, since the Roman empire, first in Rome, and afterwards in Constantinople, whither it was removed to escape the load, crumbled and sunk beneath it. All nations, which have been the glory of the world, have been ground to a lifeless dust, like the ashes of the tombs, by the pressure of a Past, which hemmed them in on every side. Will the Europe of our age undergo the fate of its predecessors? There is reason to hope that it will be more fortunate ; for, having their example before its eyes, it must be wiser than they, and it is at the same time more pliant in its temper, and more elastic in its forms.

One of my friends, some time ago visiting the great iron-works of Crawshay & Co., in Wales, was struck with the fact, that the numerous railroads connected with the works, were constructed on an old and very imperfect system. On inquiring the reason, and observing that the saving in traction, would pay the expense of a re-construction with the improved rail, "Nothing is more just," he was told ; " but we retain our old flat rails, and we shall do so for a long time, because it would take two or three years to make a change ; and in the mean while, it being impossible to keep the wagons running on both rails at the same time, we should have to stop operations, and to leave fifty thousand workmen without work and without bread. The difficulty is merely in the transition, but at present it seems to be insurmountable." So it is in regard to society. It is easy to see that one system has decided advantages over another, and that if society could be transported from one to the other by a blow of the wand, much would be gained ; but between the two there is a great gulf. How can it be passed ? How is it possible to assure vested right, to which nothing seems to be guarantied on the opposite side ? How overcome the opposition of the privileged class, who resist the change ? How check the impatience of the multitude, eager to enter into the enjoyment of the benefits which it expects to find on the other shore ?

In regard to social reforms, the question is wonderfully simplified, by merely transplanting it, that is, by going into new countries to resolve it. The old country is then abandoned to old interests and old ideas, and the emigrant lands disengaged and unembarrassed, ready to undertake every thing, and disposed to try every thing. He has left behind him in the mother-country a thousand associations and relations, which surround existence, and give it, if you please, its ornaments and its charm, but which also tend to check its activity, and make society slow to answer the demands for reform. The first of all innovations is the change of soil, and this necessarily involves others. Vested rights do not emigrate ; they are bound to the old soil ; they know no other, and no other knows them. Privileges, which are respected because they are consecrated by time, do not venture upon a new soil, or if they hazard the trial, they cannot become acclimated there. A colony is like a besieged city ; each one must serve with his person ; each one passes only for what he is worth personally. In a society which has no Past, the Past counts for nothing.

It is to be remarked, therefore, that projects of social reform, conceived in the bosom of established societies, in which opportunity is afforded for the calm exercise of thought, have generally been obliged to be transported to other shores, and to take root in barbarous lands, in order to be carried into execution, and to be embodied under the form of a new society. Civilisation has advanced from the East toward the West, increasing in vigour at every remove, although the founders of new colonies have generally quitted a more civilised country for a barbarous one.   Thus Italy and Greece, daughters of Asia and Egypt, have gone beyond their mothers ; thus western Europe has eclipsed the glories of Greece and Rome. Soon after having given birth to the new nations, the old ones have perished violently, or have fallen into an obscurity worse than death, merely from a want of will or energy to apply the principles which gave vigour to their offspring, — principles of a new social order, founded on the wider extension of liberty and the greater diffusion of privileges, — to their own wants.

Providence had done much to prepare the European races, when transported across the ocean, for becoming the founders of great and powerful nations.   The English-Americans, who were the last comers, and did not arrive until after the Spaniards had established their dominion over equinoxial and southern America, left the Old World only after it had been aroused and agitated by the intellectual revolution of which Luther was the Mirabeau, and of which in England, Henry VIII. was the Robespierre and the Napoleon.   This great event had already sown those seeds in the human breast, which were to swell and expand through succeeding ages.   England was already big with those habits of industry and order, which were destined to make her the first nation of the Old World in the sphere of industry and in political greatness.   Her children, therefore, carried with them the germ of those principles and institutions, which were to secure to them the same supremacy in the New.   They embarked, at least this was the case with those of New England, the pilgrims, the fathers of the Yankees, after having undergone the ordeal of fire and water, after having been seven times tried between the sledge and the anvil, between persecution and exile.   They arrived wearied out with political quarrels, and bent on devoting their energies to pacific and useful purposes.

They seated themselves under a climate which differed little from that of their native skies. Thus they escaped the danger of becoming enervated by the influences of a warm and balmy atmosphere, like that in which the fiery spirits of the Castilian race were tamed ; they landed on an almost uninhabited shore, and had only a few poor tribes of Red Skins for enemies and neighbours, whilst the Spaniards had to contend with the numerous armies of the brave Aztecs in Mexico, and their successors, the Creoles, have had to keep in check on the one side the Camanches and the *Indios Bravos* of the north, and on the other the Araucanians of the southern Cordilleras. If the English had encountered a numerous population like that which resisted Cortez, they would have had to conquer it, and doubtless they would have succeeded in so doing ; but after the victory, they would have been obliged to keep it in subjection, and the yoke of the English race is harder than that of the Spaniards. Their social organisation would then have been founded on the servitude of the inferiour castes, red and mixed ; the new society would have been tainted with a deep-seated disease, which would have reduced it to a much lower state than European society, and have sunk it to the level of ancient communities, which were founded on personal slavery. It is not, indeed, completely free from this taint at present ; since negroes have been brought into the country, and twelve States out of twentyfour are defiled with the pollution of slavery. The portion of the country which has been left for the pure white race, is, however, ample enough to receive a large community composed of the same materials with the European nations, and affording great facilities for combining them in a better order.

If they had found powerful enemies to combat, if war

had been constantly hanging over their heads, they would have been obliged to submit themselves to a military aristocracy, spite of the instinct of self-government and independence which runs in British veins, and of which they had a double share. In that case, the Anglo-American society would have been only a copy, and an inferiour copy of the English; as the Canadians, for example, were merely an imitation of the French, under the old order of things. The English colonists sometimes had to repel the attacks of the French, who had possession of the west and of the basin of the St Lawrence; but after the capture of Quebec, they found themselves completely delivered from the most momentous public charge, that of defending their territory and their independence. They were, therefore, able to dispense with a military establishment, to turn all their thoughts and energies to their domestic concerns, and to devote themselves exclusively to the work of colonisation. They ceased to stand in need of the English guardianship, and they freed themselves from it, that they might expand themselves and take their own course without let or hindrance. Finally, yielding to their natural impulse, they tried their great democratic experiment, which is already shedding such a brilliant light upon the prospect of improvement in the condition of the lower classes in all countries. From these circumstances and influences, has resulted a new political and physiological phenomenon, a hitherto unknown variety of the human race, inferiour to the English and French types in many respects, particularly in taste and philosophy, but superiour to the rest of the human family by its extraordinary combination of sagacity, energy of will and hardy enterprise, by its admirable aptitude for business, by its untiring devotion to work, and above all by its recognition and protection of the rights of the labouring classes, hitherto treated as the offscourings of society.

It seems, then, that the Americans are called to continue
the series of that succession of progressive movements
which have characterised our civilisation ever since it
quitted its cradle in the East.   This people will become
the founders of a new family, although perhaps the features which now predominate in it will hereafter cease to
be the prominent traits ; whilst the Spanish-Americans
seem to be an impotent race, which will leave no posterity
behind it, unless by means of one of those inundations
which are called conquests, a current of richer blood from
the North or the East, shall fill its exhausted veins.

An eminent philosopher, who is an honour to the French
name,* defines the progress of the human race in its slow
and majestic pilgrimage round our globe, by the term
initiation.   Following out this thought, we may pronounce North America, at least the non-slave-holding
States, to be already in advance of us ; for, in many
respects, what amongst us is accessible only to a small
number of the elect, has become common property in the
United States, and is familiar to the vulgar.   The conquests of the human mind, to which the Reformation gave
the signal and the impulse, and the great discoveries of
science and art, which, in Europe are yet concealed from
the general eye by the bandage of ignorance and the mists
of theory, are, in America, exposed to the vulgar gaze and
placed within the reach of all.   There the multitude
touches and handles them at will.   Examine the population
of our rural districts, sound the brains of our peasants, and
you will find that the spring of all their actions is a confused medley of the Bible parables with the legends of a
gross superstition.   Try the same operation on an American farmer, and you will find that the great scriptural traditions are harmoniously combined, in his mind, with the

---

* M. Ballanche.

principles of modern science as taught by Bacon and Descartes, with the doctrine of moral and religious independence proclaimed by Luther, and with the still more recent notions of political freedom. He is one of the *initiated*.

Amongst us the powerful instruments and machinery of science and art, the steam-engine, the balloon, the voltaic pile, the lightning-rod, inspire the multitude with a religious dread. In France, out of a hundred peasants in the recesses of our provinces, you will not find one, who, after having witnessed their effects, would dare to lay his hand upon them ; they would fear to be struck dead, like the sacrilegious wretch who touched the ark of the Lord. But to the American, on the contrary, these are all familiar objects ; he knows them all by name, at least, and he feels that they are his. To the French peasant they are mysterious and terrible beings, like his fetisch to the negro, his manitou to the Indian ; but to the cultivator of the western wilds, they are, what they are to a member of the Institute, tools, instruments of labour or science ; again, therefore he is one of the *initiated*.

There is no *profanum vulgus* in the United States, at least amongst the whites ; and this is true not only in regard to steam-engines and electrical phenomena, but the American multitude is also much more completely *initiated* than the European mass, in all that concerns the domestic relations and the household. The marriage tie is held more sacred amongst the lowest classes of American society, than among the Middle Class of Europe. Although the marriage ceremony has fewer forms than amongst us, and the connexion is more easily dissolved,* cases of adultery are extremely rare. The unfaithful

---

* As in some of the States there is no law of divorce, the legislatures grant it in virtue of their legislative omnipotence. Out of less than 150 acts passed by the New Jersey legislature in 1836, thirteen were acts authorising divorces.

wife would be a lost woman ; the man, who should seduce
a woman, or should be known to have an illicit connexion,
would be excommunicated by the popular clamour.   In
the United States, even the man of the labouring class is
more completely *initiated* in the obligations of the stronger
sex toward the weaker, than most of the men of the
Middle Class in France.   Not only does the American
mechanic and farmer spare his wife, as much as possible,
all the hard work and employments unsuitable to the sex,
but he exhibits towards her and every other woman, a
degree of attention and respect, which is unknown to
many persons amongst us, who pride themselves on
their education and refinement.   In public places and
in the public conveyances, in the United States, no
man, whatever may be his talents and his services, is
treated with any particular attention ; no precedence or
privilege is allowed him ; for all men are equal.   But a
woman, whatever may be the condition and fortune of her
husband, is sure of commanding universal respect and
attention.*

In political affairs, the American multitude has reached
a much higher degree of initiation than the European
mass, for it does not need to be governed ; every man
here has in himself the principle of self-government in
a much higher degree, and is more fit to take a part in

---

* In the mail-coaches, the best seats are always yielded to women, without regard to the order in which the names are booked.   The husband also
does the marketing and often brings home the provisions himself.   Nothing
is more common than to see men carrying home a goose or a turkey by the
legs, or a basket of fruit.   I have before observed that the conjugal and
social submission of the woman is more complete in the United States than
in France.   In France, a woman engages in business, and with the consent
of her husband is acknowledged as a responsible agent ; but there is nothing
of this sort in England and the United States.   Our children in Canada
have even gone beyond us in this respect, and have admitted females to the
electoral franchise.

public affairs. It is also more fully *initiated* in another order of things, which are closely connected with politics and morals, that is, in all that relates to labour. The American mechanic is a better workman,* he loves his work more, than the European. He is *initiated* not merely in the hardships, but also in the rewards, of industry ; he dresses like a member of Congress ; his wife and daughters are dressed like the wife and daughters of a rich New York merchant, and like them, follow the Paris fashions. His house is warm, neat, and comfortable ; his table is almost as plentifully provided as that of the wealthiest of his fellow citizens. In this country, the articles of *the first necessity* for the whites, embrace several objects, which, amongst us, are articles of luxury, not merely among the lower, but among some of the middle classes.

The American multitude is more deeply *initiated* in what belongs to the dignity of man, or, at least, to their own dignity, than the corresponding classes in Europe. The American operative is full of self-respect, and he shows it not only by an extreme sensibility, by pretensions which to the European *bourgeoisie* would appear extraordinary,† and by his reluctance to make use of the term *master,* for which he substitutes that of *employer,* but also by good faith and scrupulous exactness in his engagements ;

---

* The English workman is very skilful. Although in certain branches we excel the English, it appears to me incontestable, that at present the English workman is the first in Europe. In some respects, he is also superiour to the American ; he will, for example, finish a particular piece of work in a better style, but when out of his special sphere, and separated from the tools of the English workshops, which are of a superiour kind, he will be at loss. The American workman has a more general aptitude ; his sphere is larger, and he can extend it indefinitely at will. He accomplishes at least, as much as the English workman, and when he devotes himself for a long time to the same task, which is not usual with him, he does it better.

† Thus a shoemaker or tailor will not go to a customer's house to take a measure, but requires all, women and men, to come in person to his shop.

he is above those vices of slavery, such as theft and lying, which are so prevalent amongst hirelings with us, particularly amongst those of the towns and their manufactories.* The French operative is more respectful and submissive in his manners, but hard-pressed by poverty, and surrounded by temptations, he rarely neglects a chance of cheating his *bourgeois*, when he can do it with impunity. The operative of Lyons practises the *piquage d'onces;* those of Rheims secrete the gold lace.† There are, doubtless, frauds committed in America ; more than one smart fellow has his conscience oppressed with numerous peccadilloes. How many strolling Yankee pedlers have sold charcoal for indigo, and soapstone for soap to the rural housewives ! But in the United States these petty frauds are rare exceptions. The character of the American workman is in a high degree honourable, and excites the envy of the European when he compares the prospect here presented to him with the aspect of things in his own country.‡

---

* In the relations between the master and the operative, the most deplorable usages prevail in our large manufacturing towns. Many of the masters are reduced to practise the most disgraceful artifices on their workmen, in order to sustain themselves against the violence of competition ; thus, in some workshops and factories, the hands of the clock are put forward in the morning and backward in the evening. The operatives commit reprisals in every possible manner.

† The *piquage d'onces*, or secretion of silk by the workmen, is one of the cankers of Lyons. The value of the silk thus stolen is estimated at nearly one million of dollars a year ; the thefts committed in the Rheims factories are stated to exceed 600,000 dollars. The operatives exchange the gold-lace at the dram-shops for about one fourth of its actual value.

‡ The domestics in the United States are almost everywhere much inferiour to the operatives, personal service being here looked upon as degrading. In many of the States the domestics will not bear to be called servants, and take that of *help ;* this is the case in New England. The domestic is there a hired agent whose task is light, and who in many houses takes his meals with the family. On these conditions, native servants may be had in New England who are attentive and intelligent ; they stand upon their

What has been said above applies still more strongly to the farmer ; not being obliged, like the operative, daily to contest the rate of his wages with an employer, surrounded by his equals, and a stranger to the seductions of the city, the American farmer possesses the good qualities of the operative at least in an equal degree, and has his faults in a much less degree. He is less unjust and less jealous towards the richer or more cultivated classes.

If then we examine the condition of the American multitude, we find it, taken as a whole, to be much superiour to that of the mass in Europe. It is true that it appears to be almost completely destitute of certain faculties, which are possessed by the European populace. There are, for instance, at times, a hundredfold more gleams of taste and poetical genius in the brain of the most beggarly *lazzarone* of Naples, than in that of the republican mechanic or farmer of the New World. The houseless young vagabonds of Paris have transient flashes of chivalric feeling and greatness of soul, which the American operative never equals. This is because the national character of the Italians is impregnated with a love of art, and that generous sentiments are one of the distinguished traits of the French character, and the very lowest classes of each nation have some portion of the national spirit. But it does not belong to the multitude to be poets and artists, in Italy, or models of chivalry, in France. Their perfection, above all and in every country, consists in knowing and fulfil-

---

rights, and expect to be treated with respect by their employers, but they perform their duties with an honourable fidelity. In most of the non-slave-holding States, the servants are chiefly free blacks, who are generally lazy and depraved, or newly arrived emigrants from Ireland, who are ignorant and without skill, prone to be most provokingly familiar, and in the intoxication of their new condition, so different from the squalid misery they have left behind them, more disposed to take airs upon themselves, than the natives of the country.

ling their duties to God, to their country, to their families, to themselves, in assiduous and honest industry, in being good citizens, good husbands, and good fathers, in providing for the welfare and guarding the virtue of those dependent upon them. In order to make a fair comparison between the multitude in Europe and the multitude in America, we should consider them in reference to these qualities ; for these belong to all varieties of the human race and all forms of civilization, and upon their development and stability in the greatest number, depends the strength of empires. To render the parallel between the two hemispheres perfect, it would be necessary to set against the mechanic and the farmer in the United States, the members of a corresponding class among a people of Teutonic origin, language, and religion, that is, the English operative and farmer. European civilisation, setting aside the Sclavonians, who have recently appeared with brilliant success upon the stage, divides itself into two branches, that of the North, and that of the South, one Teutonic, the other Latin, distinguished by different qualities and tendencies. American society, being a scion of one of these branches, can be more readily compared with it, than with any of the offsets of the other. It is easy, therefore, to determine the superiority of the American mechanic and farmer to those of England, but it is difficult to decide how much inferiour or superiour any class of American society is to the corresponding Spanish, Italian, or French class ; it is only necessary, however, to open one's eyes to be convinced, that the multitude among these three people are far from having reached, in the direction in which nature points their career, the same degree of progress that the Americans have done in theirs.

The American democracy certainly has its faults, and I do not think that I can be accused of having extenuated them. I have not concealed its rude demands upon the higher classes, nor its haughty airs of superiority to other nations. I will even admit, that, in many respects, it is rather as a class, and in the lump that it recommends itself to favour ; for the individuals that compose it, are destitute of those hearty and affectionate qualities, by which our French peasantry would be distinguished, if it were once delivered from the wretchedness which now brutifies it ; but it is in the mass and as a whole, that I now judge the American multitude.

The American democracy is imperious and overbearing towards foreign people ; but is not a keen sensibility, a good quality rather than a defect in a young nation as in a young man, provided that it is backed by an energetic devotion to a great work ? Pride is ridiculous in an enervated and inert people, but in an enterprising, active, vigourous nation, it is consciousness of power, and confidence in its high destiny. The foreign policy of the American democracy is profoundly egoistic, for national ambition is the characteristic of a growing nation. Cosmopolitanism is generally a symptom of decline, as religious tolerance is a sign that faith is on the decay. The pretensions of the United States are unbounded : they aspire to the sovereignty over South America ; they covet one by one the provinces of Mexico ; but in spite of the rules of morality, it is might which makes right in the relations between people and people. If the United States should wrest the Mexican provinces from the Spanish race, partly by craft and partly by force, they would be responsible to God and to man for the consequences of the robbery ; but they would not be alone guilty. If the country which they had seized, flourished in their hands, posterity would pardon the act ; but, on the other hand, it would condemn the Mexicans, if, with such neighbours at their doors, they should continue as at present, to stagnate in stupid security and in a miserable lethargy, and the powers of Europe, if they neglected to warn them and to rouse them from their torpor.

The Romans were intolerably arrogant towards other people ; they spoke to the all-powerful sovereigns of the monarchical East, and to the heirs of Alexander the Great, that brutal and imperious language, which General Jackson has flung into the face of a monarchy of fourteen centuries. They treated all who stood in the way of the gratification of their insatiable thirst for conquest, as slaves who had re-volted against the divine will. That Punic faith, with the charge of which they branded the memory of their rivals, was often the only faith which they practised. Posterity, however, has proclaimed them the greatest people of history, because they were successful ; that is, because they formed a durable empire out of conquered nations by the wisdom of their laws. The Anglo-Americans have much resemblance to the Romans whether for good or for evil. I do not say that they are destined to become the masters of the world ; I merely mean to affirm that by the side of faults which shock and offend foreign nations, they have great powers and precious qualities which should rather attract our attention. It is by these that posterity will judge them ; by these they have become formidable to other people. Let us aim to get the vantage-ground of them, not by denouncing their defects to the world, but by endeavouring to make ourselves masters of their good qualities and their valuable faculties, and by cultivating and developing our own. These are the surest means of maintaining our rank in the world in spite of them and in spite of all.

At the same time that the American democracy conducts itself more and more haughtily abroad, it is jealous of all who fall under the suspicion of seeking to encroach upon its sovereignty at home. In this, it only imitates the most boasted of aristocracies. The system which it has pursued

towards the higher classes, is dictated by the instinct of
self-preservation, just as that of the European aristocracy
and Middle Class toward the classes respectively below
them, has been instinctive with them. The democracy is
determined to lose none of its conquests, which have been
gained, not by plundering its neighbours, not by pillaging
provinces, not by robbing travellers, but by the sweat of
its brow, by its own resolute industry. Who, then,
amongst us will cast the first stone at it? I can readily
conceive, that, at first sight, we of the Middle Class in
Europe, should be offended by its pretensions, and that we
should feel our sympathy excited by the spectacle of our
American fellows conquered and bound. But let us, nevertheless, confess, that this democracy has managed the
affairs of the New World in such a manner as to justify the
supremacy it has won. and to excuse its jealousy towards
every thing that might have a tendency to spoil it of its
conquest. This is the first time since the origin of society,
that the people have fairly enjoyed the fruits of their
labours, and have shown themselves worthy of the prerogatives of manhood. Glorious result! Even though it
has been obtained by the temporary humiliation of the
classes with which our education and habits lead us to
sympathise, it is the duty of every good man to rejoice at
it, and to thank God for it!

Wo to tyranny by whomsoever exercised! Far be it
from me to apologise for the brutal and savage, and sometimes bloody excesses, which have lately been so often
repeated in most of the large towns in the United States!
Should they be continued, the American democracy will
be degraded and will lose forever the high position it now
occupies. But criminal as these acts are, it would be
unjust to impute them to the American people, and to condemn to ignominy the whole body of these incomparable
labourers. Popular excesses in all countries are the work

of an imperceptible minority, which the existing system
in the United States is sufficient to restrain. That system needs, then, some amendment, which shall suit it to
preserve the good qualities of the nation in their purity,
and which, indeed, seems already on the point of being
introduced, for theories of absolute liberty are evidently
losing favour in the United States.

It would be a mistake to infer from what has been said,
that the American civilisation is superiour to our own.
The multitude in the United States is superiour to the
multitude in Europe ; but the higher classes in the New
World are inferiour to those of the Old, although the merits of the latter are rather virtual than real, and belong
rather to the past or the future than to the present ; for
the higher classes in Europe, both aristocracy and *bourgeoisie,* turn their good qualities to little account, whether
on behalf of themselves or the people. The higher
classes in the United States, with some exceptions and
taken as a whole, have the air and attitude of the vanquished ; they bear the mark of defeat on their front.
As they have been always and in almost all circumstances much mingled with the crowd, both parties
have naturally borrowed many habits and feelings from
each other. This exchange has been advantageous
to the multitude ; but less so the higher classes. The
golden buckler of the Trojan has been exchanged for the
leather shield of the gallant Diomed. Each of the two is,
therefore, superiour in one of the two great elements of
society, and inferiour in the other. This is the system of
compensation.

If, then, from the superiority of the labouring classes in
the United States, it were necessary to draw a conclusion
as to the relative rank of European and American civilisation in the future, the following would be the only necessary inference : in order that American society should have

the advantage of ours, it would be requisite that it should comprise a class, which, intrinsically and in its exterior, should be as much elevated above the people, properly so called, as our higher classes are above the great mass of our population ; or, in other words, it depends upon ourselves to give to our social order the advantage over that of the United States, by raising our lower class both of the towns and the country from the ignorance and brutal degradation in which they are plunged, and developing their powers and qualities in conformity with our national disposition and the character of the race to which we belong.

N O T E S .

NOTE 1 — page 26.

Use of Iron.

ONE must go to England to appreciate the value of iron, the scarcity of wood having obliged the English to apply it to a great number of purposes to which no one on the continent would dream of its being applicable. At every step and under all forms, you meet with cast-iron, bar-iron, sheet-iron, and steel ; machines, piles, columns of all dimensions from two inches to four feet in diameter, water-pipes and gas-pipes, posts, grates, bridges, roofs, floors, whole quays and roads, of iron. But for it, those light and airy structures, so slender in appearance, yet supporting such enormous weights, the huge six story warehouses of St Catharine's docks for instance, would be heavy and gloomy dungeons. The gas which comes from a distance of seven or eight miles, is made and brought in by the aid of iron. Those bridges, springing as it were across the water, those graceful and elegant footways across the canals, as well as the fluted columns of Regent's Street, are of iron, cast or wrought. The quantity of pig-iron annually produced in Great Britain and Ireland, is about 800,000 tons ; in France it amounted in 1834 to 269,000 tons, beside 177,000 tons of bar iron. The ordinary price of both kinds with us is about double the price in England.

Until the present day, stone has been almost the only material employed in durable works of architecture ; but stone having much less cohesive force than iron, is only suited to the Egyptian, Greek, and Roman styles of architecture. The light and airy architecture of the Middle Ages, requires a material possessing great strength in a small compass, such as the metals ; and some attempts have already been made in France and Germany to apply cast-iron to the construction of Gothic structures. Stone has already done all that it is capable of doing, and we can have nothing new in architecture, except by means of new materials. In my opinion, iron is to be the instrument of this regeneration of the architectural art. The price of pig-iron is now so low, that the cost of a building of this material, would not exceed that of one constructed of hewn stone.

——

Note 2 — page 26.

Quantity of Coal mined in France, England, and Belgium.

Mr McCulloch, in his Dictionary of Commerce estimates the quantity of coal annually mined in England to amount to 16,000,000 tons.* The extensive inquiries of M. Le Play, who has carefully examined all the English coal-fields, have led him to estimate it much higher; it does not, probably, fall short of 30,000,000 tons, of which 5,000,000 are consumed in the iron manufacture. Mr McCulloch estimates the amount of capital employed in the coal-trade at 10,000,000 pounds, and the number of persons engaged in it at from 160,000 to 180,000. Other estimates carry this last number to 206,000, of whom 121,000 work in the mines.

In France 2,500,000 tons of coal were raised in 1834, and about 18,000 persons were employed in the mines. France also imports coal from Belgium and England. Next to England, Belgium furnishes the largest quantity of coal; the three great coal-fields of Mons, Charleroi, and Liege with some smaller basins, yielding about 3,200,000 tons annually.

---

* In a later work (*Statistics of the British Empire,* 1839), Mr McCulloch estimates it at 26,188,000 tons. — Transl.

NOTE 3 — page 33.

Value of Exports of Domestic Produce and Manufactures from England, France, and United States, from 1820 to 1835.

Years.	France.	England.	United States.
1820	francs. 543,100,000	fr. 910,600,000	fr. 275,400,000
1821	450,700,000	917,500,000	232,700,000
1822	427,600,000	925,000,000	265,800,000
1823	427,100,000	890,000,000	251,300,000
1824	505,800,000	960,000,000	269,900,000
1825	543,800,000	972,500,000	356,800,000
1826	461,000,000	787,500,000	282,700,000
1827	506,800,000	930,000,000	314,000,000
1828	511,200,000	920,000,000	270,000,000
1829	504,200,000	895,000,000	296,800,000
1830	452,900,000	955,000,000	316,900,000
1831	455,500,000	930,000,000	326,600,000
1832	507,400,000	921,000,000	336,500,000
1833	559,400,000	992,500,000	374,700,000
1834	509,300,000	1,041,000,000	432,100,000
1835	577,400,000	1,184,200,000	539,700,000

England exports hardly any but manufactured articles. The United States export chiefly raw produce. Raw Cotton forms half of the value of their exports, as manufactured cotton forms about half of those of Great Britain. Agriculture furnishes three fourths or four fifths of the exports of domestic articles from the United States, and manufactures, only one tenth. Above two thirds of the exports of France are manufactures, and nearly one third, agricultural produce.

NOTE 4 — page 36.

Shipping.

Statement of the tonnage belonging to the principal ports of France, England and the United States in 1835.

Ports.	Tonnage.	Ports.	Tonnage.
London	566,152	Whitehaven	65,878
New York	376,697	Hull	63,524
Boston	226,041	Bordeaux	69,690
Newcastle	208,100	Marseilles	68,314
Liverpool	207,833	Havre	68,070
Sunderland	132,070	Portland (U. S.)	57,666
Philadelphia	86,445	Baltimore	54,416
New Orleans	79,467	Nantes	51,528
New Bedford	76,533	Bristol	42,913

To render the comparison exact, it would be necessary to deduct one fourth from the French tonnage, in order to allow for the different modes of measurement. The French method is mathematically more correct, but it lays our vessels under the disadvantage of being obliged to pay heavier tonnage dues ; but a law of 1836 has authorised the government to make a change in this respect.

Out of 1,824,000 tons of shipping entered and cleared at the French ports in ‖1835, only 31 per cent. was French shipping ; out of 5,025,000 tons entered and cleared at the British ports, 75 per cent. was of English vessels. In the United States, from 1817 to 1830, foreign shipping formed less than 15 per cent. of the vessels in the foreign trade ; in 1831, it was 26 per cent., and in 1832, 30 per cent., leaving 70 per cent. for the American shipping.

French navigation is in a deplorable state of feebleness, and the evil increases daily. In 1832, the total amount of French shipping was 670,000 tons, of British 2,225,000, of American 1,440,000. In France and England the amount varies little from year to year, but in the United States it increases rapidly, and in 1837 it was 1,896,685.

NOTE 5 — page 38 — *omitted.*

NOTE 6 — page 38.

All the banks in the United States, like the Bank of France in Paris, are at once banks of discount and loan, and banks of deposit and circulation. Almost the whole currency of this country consists of paper-money, the metals being chiefly in the the vaults of the banks, which cannot dispense with them, because their bills are payable on demand in gold and silver.

The old Bank of the United States, founded in 1791, had a capital of ten million dollars, the Federal government holding one fifth of the stock. The present Bank was incorporated in

1816, with the right of establishing any number of branches. The Bank of England also has branches in Manchester, Birmingham, Liverpool, Leeds, Gloucester, Bristol, Hull, Newcastle, Norwich, Swansea, and Exeter. The Bank of France has but two branches, one at St. Etienne and the other at Rheims, both established since 1836.

The capital of the Bank of the United States is 35,000,000, in 350,000 shares of 100 dollars each. That of the Bank of England is 11,000,000 pounds, divided into shares of one hundred pounds; and that of the Bank of France is 90,000,000 francs, in shares of 1000 francs, of which 22,100 are held by the Bank itself. The United States' Bank stock was at a premium of 25 to 30 per cent. before General Jackson began his war upon it, that of the Bank of France is at an advance of 129 per cent., and that of the Bank of England at 116 per cent. advance.

The operations of the Bank of the United States consist in discounting commercial paper with two names, in making advances upon public stock and other securities, and in trading in the precious metals. The Bank of France discounts commercial paper with three names, or with two names and a deposit of Bank stock as collateral security. It is at present authorised to advance four-fifths on public stock on the sole guarantee of the depositor. It also makes advances on deposits of bullion and foreign coins, charging a commission of one eighth for forty five days, or one per cent. a year. The commercial attributes of the Bank of England are still more limited than those of the Bank of France. It makes no advances on public securities, except while the transfer books are closed, which occurs for a certain period in London.

The Bank of the United States discounts at the rate of six per cent.; the Bank of France at four per cent.; and the Bank of England at different rates, but rarely at less than four per cent., which is high in London. In 1836, the rate was advanced to four and a half and five per cent. The Bank of the United States effects foreign and domestic exchanges; the Bank of England only domestic exchange, which it does without charge for those who have an account open with it; and the Bank of France operates neither.

The circulation of the Bank of the United States has varied within late years from ten to twenty millions ; in October 1835, it was twentyfive millions, consisting chiefly of five and ten dollar notes. Of late years the circulation of the Bank of England has amounted to about 100 million dollars. Since 1830, the Bank of France has usually had a circulation of forty millions, so that the two last institutions play a more important part as banks of circulation, than the first. In the United States, the five or six hundred local banks, whose aggregate circulation is five or six times greater than that of the United States' Bank, perform this service. This coëxistence of more than five hundred distinct currencies is the great defect in the financial system of this country. The joint-stock banks, which have been of late much multiplied in England, tend to introduce the same confusion into that country.

The Bank of the United States has generally in its vaults about ten millions in specie, but during the struggle with General Jackson, it had, at times, a sum equal to its bills in circulation, or from sixteen to eighteen millions. The Bank of England endeavours to keep on hand from forty to fifty millions, but it sometime sinks as low as thirty. The Bank of France always has at least twenty and sometimes more than forty millions ; in 1832, it had fiftythree millions, or more than its whole paper circulation.

The Bank of the United States does not discount notes of above four months' date, although this restriction is voluntary ; the great mass of its discounts is on paper of two months date. The Banks of France and England cannot discount bills of more than 90 days date.

The bills of the United States Bank circulate throughout the Union ; the revenue officers are obliged to receive them on the same footing as specie. The Bank, in return, is obliged to redeem them in specie on demand, under penalty of paying interest on the sum demanded at the rate of 12 per cent. per annum, and of forfeiting its charter. It is not, however, bound to redeem the bills of the branches, except at their respective counters, although it does so in fact. The bills of the Bank of England are a legal tender in England, and with the exception of those of the branches, are redeemable in gold and silver only in London. The bills of the Bank of France are current only in Paris, and are not there a legal tender.

The Bank of the United States and the Bank of France only issue bills payable to bearer ; the Bank of England has a certain amount of Bank post-bills, or bills payable to order at seven days sight, being equivalent to about one tenth or one twelfth of its whole circulation.

The Bank of the United States receives deposits, on which it pays no interest. The Scotch banks pay interest on deposits at the rate of 2 to 2½ per cent. The Banks of England and France do not pay interest on deposits, but the latter gets bills on Paris cashed for its depositors without charge.

The number of accounts current opened by the Bank of the United States is indefinite ; in that country and Scotland almost all persons have an account with the banks, and are thus freed from the necessity of keeping any considerable sums on hand. They hardly keep enough in the house to defray the expenses of the household for a few days, and payments are made by checks on a bank. The banks are, therefore, the cashiers of the whole community. This concentration of the whole disposable fund of the country in the banks, gives them the means of extending their operations greatly, and renders the capital, which would otherwise be scattered about and lie idle, active and productive.

The dividends of the Bank of the United States have been regularly at the rate of seven per cent. ; those of the Bank of France vary from eight to ten on the original capital ; those of the Bank of England are at present eight per cent. on the nominal capital, which is the original capital successively modified by acts of parliament. Independently of the ordinary dividends, which were originally seven per cent., afterwards rose to ten, and are now eight, the Bank of England has made several extraordinary dividends, and it increased the nominal capital on which the dividends are paid, twentyfive per cent. in 1816. Mr McCulloch makes the total sum of the extraordinary dividends and of the reserved profits carried to the extension of the capital, from 1799 to 1832, eightytwo millions, which with the reimbursements required by the new charter, amounts to one hundred and five millions. The Bank of France has divided beyond its ordinary dividends, the sum of four and a half millions.

The Bank of the United States, previous to 1834, was charged with the keeping of the public moneys, which were remitted to it by the collectors and receivers and of which it was the legal depository, with the transfer of funds for the service of the Treasury, and with the payments on the public debt and of pensions. It is forbidden to lend more than 500,000 dollars to the Federal government, and more than 50,000 to any State. In this respect it differs from the Banks of France and England, which make, and especially once made, enormous advances to the state. This is the principal object of the Bank of England, the whole çapital of which is lent to the government at the rate of three per cent. Besides this the Bank of England receives the Exchequer Bills, and the Bank of France the Treasury Certificates *(bons du Tresor)*, which bear a low rate of interest. These banks have made inconceivable loans to the state in time of war ; in 1814, the advances of the Bank of England amounted to 165 millions, inclusive of the public deposits, which sometimes amounted to 60 millions. The Bank of France, however, has at present little connexion with the government, and has, therefore, greatly extended its commercial operations. In 1836, it had on hand notes to the value of 27 million dollars, without reckoning four millions advanced on deposits of public funds ; from 1830 to 1835 the amount had not exceeded seventeen millions.

The local or State banks in the United States are organized on principles analogous to those of the National Bank. They are incorporated companies, receiving their corporate privileges from the States, and, therefore, confined to the limits of the State. Sometimes their bills are not current out of the town or county in which they are situated. They are institutions of credit and circulation almost exclusively for the use of merchants. Not having the resource of exchanges, and rarely having any deposits, they aim to enlarge their profits, by extending their circulation through excessive discounts and loans, which often floods the country with an excess of paper money. Their capitals seldom exceed one million dollars, and are often much less ; but several have lately been established in the South with capitals of from three to ten millions.

In England the private bankers have the right of emitting bills payable to bearer, except, if there are less than six partners in the house, within the distance of sixty miles of London ; in point of fact there are none issued within that space. The bills issued by private bankers amount to about 8,500,000 pounds. In Paris, the Bank of France has the exclusive privilege of issuing bills payable to bearer.

The joint stock banks in England are not chartered companies, nor are they under any control. All the partners are personally responsible. These country banks are very numerous, and they offer, perhaps, less security than the American State banks. In all times of crisis, in 1792-93, 1814-15-16, 1825-26, many of them have become bankrupts or suspended payment ; in 1816, 240 were obliged to take one of these alternatives. In 1809 their issues amounted to 24 million pounds ; in 1821-23, they had fallen eight millions, and in 1825, had again risen to fourteen millions. Since the suppression of notes of less than five pounds, they have been much reduced. At present (1836), these institutions are becoming multiplied to such a degree as to inspire serious alarm in prudent men.

Note 7 — page 49.

Failures in the United States.

It would be excessively unjust to the Americans not to acknowledge that they are improving daily in respect to failures. In a new country it is natural that a failure should be little thought of, because every thing is necessarily an experiment, and all speculation is a game of hazard. The public is very indulgent on this point, because it considers a failure what it really is, nineteen times out of twenty, a misfortune and not a fraud. The bankrupt is looked upon as a wounded soldier, who is to be treated with sympathy, and not with contempt. Congress has the power of passing a bankrupt law, but it has not yet exercised this power, and the different States have made temporary provisions for the case, which treat the insolvent debtor with great indulgence, discharging him from any further obligation towards his creditors on his giving up all his property for their benefit. It is felt that too much severity in regard to failures would have the tendency to check the spirit of enterprise, which is the life of the country. None of those rigourous provisions which disgrace French legislation and endanger the interests of creditors, exist here ; and if the lenity of the laws is sometimes abused, the inconvenience is much less than that caused by the harshness of ours.

In the large maritime towns, however, it is felt, that if bankruptcy is not a disgrace, it is at least a private and public calamity, which is to be averted by every exertion. The history of the great fire in New York in 1835 affords ample proof of this. The amount of the loss exceeded fifteen millions, and the insurance companies found themselves unable to meet their engagements. On the receipt of the news in Europe, there was not a merchant who did not tremble for his American debts ; for in Europe, in general, and in France, in particular, such an event would have deprived the sufferers of all credit, of all means of repairing their losses. In France the singular custom prevails of offering you credit, if you do not need it ; but if you stand in want of it, you will get none. In the United States, on the contrary, immediately after this disaster, the President of the United States Bank hastens to place two millions at the disposal of the New York merchants, and the banks in general give out that they shall discount the paper of the sufferers in preference.

Although the sphere of the public authorities in the United States is very narrow, the corporation of New York and the State government, rivalled each other in offers of assistance ; the former offered an advance of six millions, not to individuals, as was done in France in 1830, but to the insurance companies, whose ruin would have led to a general bankruptcy ; it thus strengthened the hands of commerce, by relieving its citadel. Even Congress, which is not allowed to take a step out of its little district, and is scarcely permitted to notice what is going on beyond the Capitol, was moved, and extended the term of payment of custom dues.   The result of this admirable coöperation of individuals, companies, and public authorities was to prevent any considerable failures.

The Americans have a courage in presence of commercial disasters, like that of the soldier on the field of battle.   In a critcal juncture, they face bankruptcy, as old grenadiers march upon a battery under a fire of grape-shot.   If it is true that commerce is to supplant war in the future, it must be confessed that the Americans are more advanced on the march than we are ;   for they have applied all their energies and qualities to commerce, whilst we still devote ours to war.   They have discovered a new sort of courage which produces and enriches ; we shine only by that courage which perishes or destroys.

The merit of this new spirit does not belong exclusively to the Americans ; they had the germ in their blood, and have received the gift from the mother country.   At the period of the late calamity, the English were no more subject to a panic terrour than their New York descendants.—It is within my knowledge, that American merchants established in Paris and having houses in the United States, having applied to London bankers for a continuation of credit, were immediately assured, that not only the former amount of credit should be continued, but that they should be allowed an unlimited credit in order to enable them to repair their losses.   Some French bankers, on the contrary, similarly situated, hastened to cut off the credit they had previously given.

In a country organized for commerce, and having the proper institutions of credit, the money and merchandise of the merchant, are not his only capital ;   the most valuable part of his capital consists of his experience, his correspondents and connexions, the weight of his name.   This constitutes a moral capital, which conflagrations cannot destroy, nor accidents of any kind injure.   In New York, by the aid of this moral capital, on which a high value is set in commercial countries, a merchant who has not property to the amount of more than 50,000 dollars, operates as if he had five or six times as much.   In Paris, the same man, with the same fortune, would operate with only about twice as much. Thus the wealth of the United States increases in a much faster ratio than in France.

Note 8 — page 54.

The American newspapers are very numerous, but in consequence of their great number their circulation iscomparatively small. There are few daily papers, whose circulation exceeds 2,000, and not one, which exceeds 4,000 ; that of most of the newspapers is not more than 400 or 500. The American newspapers have little resemblance to the French and English. They are chiefly mere advertising sheets ; they do not direct public opinion, they follow it. This local character does not allow of their having much influence out of their particular district. In New York, only the city newspapers are read ; in New Orleans, those of New Orleans are the only ones generally seen ; whilst in France those of Paris, and in England those of London are read every where. The Globe and the National Intelligencer of Washington are, however, pretty generally circulated. Newspapers in the United States are not powers, they are mere instruments of publicity within the reach of all. They are consulted for the news, nor for opinions. The profession of a writer does not stand so high in England as in France, and is less honourable in the United States, than in England. With the exception of a very few newspapers, at the head of which are the New York American edited by Charles King, and the Philadelphia National Gazette, edited by Robert Walsh, the American press occupies a low rank in the social scale.

Notwithstanding their large size, the American newspapers are low-priced ; the cause is plain enough ; the profits are derived chiefly from advertisements, and the expenses of editing are inconsiderable, as there is generally but one editor. There is no stamp duty ; but the postage on them is higher than in France.* The circulation of some of the French newspapers

---

* The postage of newspapers in France is two fifths of a cent within the department where it is published, and four fifths on any distance beyond it.

exceeds 10,000 ; and some cheap publications have lately had a circulation of 90,000 or 100,000.

Note 9 — page 53.

In 1832, the transfer of funds between different points of the Union, or between the Union and foreign countries, effected by the Bank of the United States, amounted to 255 millions, of which 241,718,710 was for domestic, and 13,456,737 for foreign transactions. The Bank received only 217,249 dollars for commissions on this vast sum.

Note 10 — page 64.

Specie and Paper Money.

The quantity of gold and silver coined in France with the new die, amounted, up to 1836, to about 750 million dollars, of which three fourths were in silver. It is not probable that more than one fourth of that sum has been melted and exported ; there would then remain about 550 millions. A part of this immense sum is out of circulation, and is buried in the coffers of individuals or in the pockets of the poor, who do not dare trust their savings to any person or institution.

In the United States, in 1834, the 405 local banks from which official or semi-official statements had been received, had 65 million dollars paper in circulation, and 14,250,000 dollars in specie in their vaults. There were beside, 101 banks, estimated to have in circulation 12,650,000 dollars of paper, and 2,825,000 dollars in specie on hand. The Bank of the United States had at that time a circulation of 10,300,000 dollars, and specie to the amount of 13,865,000 dollars. The whole currency of the United States, exclusive of the small amount of specie in the hands of individuals, amounted, therefore, to 88 millions in paper and specie. At this time, the banks had withdrawn a large amount of their bills from circulation, their issues before the war on the Bank having exceeded 100 millions. Since 1834, the amount of specie in the United States has been considerably increased, several of the States having prohibited the emission of bills of less than five dollars, a measure, which would tend to promote the use of the metals.

The following statement, showing the quantity of paper money in circulation in the United Kingdom at the end of 1833, is chiefly from McCulloch's Dictionary of Commerce.

Of Bank of England - -	£19,500,000
Of Branches of do. - - -	3,300,000
Of Private Bankers - - -	8,500,000
Of English Country Banks - -	1,500,000*
Of Scotch Banks - - - -	2,000,000
Of Irish Banks - - - -	7,500,000
Total	42,300,000

At the same time the amount of the precious metals in circulation and in the banks, was estimated at 45,800,000 pounds, of which seven millions were in silver.

———

NOTE 11† — page 96. *Cherokees and other Indians.* Omitted.

———

NOTE 12† — page 98. *Public Lands.* Omitted.

———

NOTE 13† — page 119. *Temperance Societies.* Omitted.

———

NOTE 14 — page 132.

Cotton Manufacture.

At the end of 1836, the Lowell cotton factories comprised

---

* In August 1836, this had been increased to 3,600,000 pounds.

† These notes, with several others, have been omitted, as they contain merely statements familiar to most readers in this country.

129,828 spindles and 4,197 looms, and employed 6,793 operatives of whom 5,416 were women. The quantity of cloth made was 849,300 yards a week, or at the rate of 44 million yards a year ; raw cotton consumed 38,000 bales, or 15 million pounds yearly.

In 1831, the American manufacture employed 62,157 operatives, of whom 38,927 were women and 4,691 children. There were beside 4,760 hand-weavers, 40,709 persons employed in accessory labours, making the whole number of persons engaged directly and indirectly 117,626. The factories contained 1,246,503 spindles, and 33,506 looms, and produced 230,461,990 yards of stuffs, besides 1,200,000 pounds of yarn, which were woven in families during the winter. The consumption of raw cotton was 77 million pounds. The value of the products was 26 million dollars, eleven millions of which were paid in wages. (*Pitkin's Statistics*, 526.)

There were in England, in 1834, according to Baines, (*History of Cotton Manufacture,*) 100,000 power-looms, and 250,000 hand-looms. The difference between the number of the hand-looms in England and the United States deserves to be noticed. The hand-weavers in ¦Great Britain form one of the most wretched classes of the population. The English factories employed 729,000 persons, or with the dyers, bleachers, measurers, folders, packers, &c., and all hands employed in building and repairing the mills, 1,500,000. In 1833 the English factories consumed 332 million pounds of cotton. The value of their annual products is estimated at from 30 to 34 million pounds sterling; the wages of the 724,000 operatives amount to 13 millions.

In 1834, the French manufacture employed 600,000 persons, and the annual value of its products was about 110 million dollars ; quantity of cotton consumed 100 million pounds. If these statements are correct, it follows, that our operatives produce less than the English or Americans.

NOTE 15 — page 186.

Production and Consumption of Cotton.

In 1834, one of our most able manufacturers, M. Kœkhlin, made the following estimate of the production and consumption of cotton throughout the world.

Production.

In the United States - - -	437,500,000 lbs.
In India - - - - -	75,000,000
In Brasil - - - - -	30,000,000
In Bourbon, Cayenne, &c. - -	7,500,000
In Egypt and the Levant - -	25,000,000
Total	575,000,000

Consumption.

In England - - - -	375,000,000 lbs.
In France - - - -	100,000,000
In the United States - -	45,000,000
In China - - - - -	37,500,000
In Switzerland, Belgium, &c. - -	42,500,000
Total,	600,000,000

Several other countries not enumerated above yield cotton. China produces some which she consumes, or exports under the form of nankeens ; Mexico produces nearly enough for her own consumption ; Mr Koekhlin has meant to speak only of what belongs to the general commerce. He has somewhat overstated the consumption of England, and underrates that of the United States.

NOTE 16 — page 154 — *omitted.*

NOTE 17 — page 161.

Trial of the Incendiaries for burning the Ursuline Convent.

The intolerant spirit of a part of the Protestant population was

offended by the sight of the Ursuline Convent on Mount St. Ben-
dict, within the limits of Charlestown, a town adjoining Boston.
The sisters devoted themselves to the instruction of young girls,
and many Protestant families had confided daughters to their
care. Every thing proves that they were by no means devoured by a spirit of proselytism. In the beginning of August, 1835,
a report got about in Charlestown, that one of the sisters, a young
woman, was detained in the convent by force. The Selectmen
of the town had a meeting, five of them went to the convent,
which they examined from cellar to garret, had an interview
with the sister who was represented as a victim of the Catholic
discipline, and became satisfied that she was there of her own
free will. This conviction was made known to the public. But
on the night of August 12th, the convent was surrounded and attacked by a handful of ruffians, at the head of whom was one
John Buzzell, a brickmaker, noted for his brutal character.
The sisters were driven from the convent with violence ; every
thing was plundered ; the tombs of the dead were forced open.
The building was then fired ; it was burnt in sight of the Selectmen ; the Boston firemen hastened to the spot, but were repulsed by the populace by main force.

Several men, taken in the act, were arrested, and among
others Buzzell ; they were tried in Boston in 1835.* The wit-
nesses were afraid to bear testimony, a mysterious influence had
changed their language ; the public prosecutor, who had previously demanded in vain a postponement of the trial, until the
causes which instigated the violence had been traced, pleaded
the cause of order with a generous indignation. All the prisoners were acquitted, except one poor youth of the name of Marcy
who was sentenced to fifteen or twenty years imprisonment ;
but public opinion soon after obliged the Executive to grant him
a pardon. Buzzell and Kelly, one of his accomplices, became
heroes ; they were carried about in triumph, and a subscription
was made for their benefit. The sisters petitioned the Massachu-

---

* The author is mistaken ; they were tried in the county in which the offence
was committed. Boston is in a different county. TRANSL.

setts legislature for indemnity ; the most intelligent citizens of Boston interested themselves in their favour, but the House of Representatives rejected the petition by a large majority. On the anniversary of the outrage, the populace of Charlestown celebrated it as a day of rejoicing, and got up a shooting match, the target being a representation of the lady superior of the convent. The Selectmen succeeded in suppressing the figure, but not the procession.   Finally, to crown these deeds of impudence and savage violence, two of the incendiaries, in 1836, presented a petition to the legislature to be indemnified for the damages they had suffered by the trial.   The committee to whom the petition was referred, reported a grant of 500 dollars to each of these wretches ; but to the honor of Massachusetts, their report was rejected on the second reading.

Note 18 — page 172.   *Omitted.*

Note 19 — page 180.   *Omitted.*

Note 20 — page 193.

Taxation.

It has repeatedly been made a question of late, whether the United States were more or less heavily taxed than France. The subject may be considered under several points of view. The systems of Taxation in the two countries are very different.   The taxes in the United States are less numerous then they are in France, and are differently distributed.   The country population, that is the great majority, pay much less in the United States than in France ; but in the large towns the inhabitants pay nearly as much as with us, except in Paris.   The disproportion between the two countries becomes much greater, if instead of estimating the amount in money, we give it in day's labour, which is the most rational manner.   The day-wages of a labourer being about threefold as much in the United States as they are with us, and other things being in the same proportion, it follows, that, in the former, a tax of three dollars to three dollars and a half, which is about the general average, is not more burdensome to the mass of the people, than a tax of one third that sum would be in France. The average tax in France, or six dollars a head, is equivalent to twentysix days' work in our country; while the average in the United States is only equivalent to four days' work in that country.

It is true, that, amongst us, all the public expenditures are comprised in the budget; all our taxes amount to 190 million dollars. But in the United States, there are various expenses supported by individuals and companies, which do not appear in the sum of the public taxes. Toll is paid on a very large number of roads : public worship is maintained at the expense of the worshippers; hence heavy charges on the rich.

It is important to remark, that the public revenue in the United States is almost wholly employed in a productive manner, in useful undertakings, in public works, schools, and various kinds of improvements. There is no Federal debt, that of most of the States and towns is inconsiderable, there are no retiring pensions, and the army is small ; whilst more than half of our budget, or 118 million dollars, is devoted to the charges on the public debt, pensions, and the sea and land forces, we cannot expect to restore the balance in our favour, because we cannot dismiss our soldiers, nor declare a national bankruptcy ; but we might diminish our present inferiority (paradoxical as it may seem), by adding some millions to our budget for useful and productive works.

The military service itself is a public burden and a very heavy one ; but it is difficult to rate the amount of this in money. In France it takes one man out of eighty inhabitants from labour, but in the United States only one out of 2,300. This tax might be lightened, by employing the army in public works. .

We may also notice the two following differences, which appear to me essential ones, between American and French taxes : —

1. The American taxes, whether it be from the mode of their assessment, or from the difference of conditions of the two countries, never press heavily upon the taxables, nor give them any uneasiness; they never embarrass transactions nor interrupt business. On the contrary, amongst us the tax is often an oppressive burden ; our registry dues, and excise on property changing hands, often occasion serious embarrassments and even insurmountable obstacles in the way of enterprise.

2. In the United States the treasury fears to incur the public odium ; amongst us the most respectable citizens are subjected to the most vexatious treatment ; our officers of the customs have adopted practices unworthy of a civilised people ; our wives and daughters must submit to be searched in the most shameless manner by vile hags, and these brutal proceedings have not the poor excuse of being useful to the customs. Their avowed object is to prevent the smuggling of articles, with which, in spite of three lines of custom-house officers, the country is inundated, and which it is well known are brought in by dogs* on a large scale, and not in the pockets of private persons. The branches of industry, which they are designed to protect, are altogether of secondary importance, and cannot be weighed in the balance against public decency.

Note 21 — page 11.

Construction and Cost of Steamboats in the West.

The western steamboats are on the high pressure principle, with a force of six or eight atmospheres. The boilers are on deck, in the bow of the boat; the cylinder is horizontal ; there are two wheels, one on each side. Formerly, a single stern wheel was generally used. Only one engine is used to a boat. The pistons are not of metal, an arrangement which necessarily involves a great loss of power, but which renders repairs more

* On the northern frontier there are from 500,000 to 600,000 dogs which enter annually ; not more than 6,000 or 7,000 are seized.

easy, an important consideration with inexperienced engineers. The engines are of very simple construction and cost little ; those for the largest boats cost from 10,000 to 14,000 dollars ; the engines of the French government packets in the Mediterranean cost nearly 60,000 dollars. The cylinders of the most powerful engines in the western boats are of 30 inches diameter, and seven feet stroke. These boats consume enormous quantities of wood ; the larger ones burning from one and a half to one and three quarters cords an hour ; the rate of speed rarely exceeds ten miles an hour even down stream.

In the east a good steamer from 175 to 200 feet in length with copper boilers, which are necessary to resist the action of salt water, costs from 70,000 to 80,000 dollars, including the furniture. The carpenter's work of the hull costs about thirty dollars a ton, exclusive of the iron. The engine, when there is but one, costs from 12,000 to 15,000 dollars, exclusive of the boilers. The North America cost 100,000 dollars ; a good boat, well taken care of, lasts about twelve or fifteen years in the east. The eastern boats are very fast and safe, and of late years, great improvements have been made in their construction, principally by Mr Stevens of New York. They move at the rate of fifteen miles an hour in still water, and generally carry nothing but passengers. Their usual length is from 180 to 200 feet, with a breadth of twentyfour or twentysix, without including the paddle-boxes ; their usual draught of water about four or five feet in the rivers, and from six and a half to nine feet in the bays and seas. Their engines are on the low or mean pressure principle ; the cylinder is vertical, and they often have two engines ; the stroke of the piston has been carried to ten or eleven feet ; the diameter of the cylinders, in some of the boats, is five feet four inches. They consume from twentyfive to thirty cords of wood an hour.

The number of steamboats in the United States, at the end of 1834, was 386 of an aggregate of 95,648 tons, of which 237, with a tonnage of 64,347 tons, were on the western waters. [In 1839 the number of boats was about 800, with an aggregate tonnage of 157,473 tons ; of these about 300 were on the western rivers and 70 on the lakes. — TRANSL.] There were in France, in 1834, 82 steamboats, with a total tonnage of not more than 15,000 tons, beside 37 belonging to the government. The whole number of steamers in England is about 480.

NOTE 22 — page 268.

Summary Statements of the Public Works in the United States.

The six tables which follow present a recapitulation of the statements given in Letter XXI., with the cost per league in francs. [Many of the statements in the Letter are slightly varied from the original, in conformity with official reports, and the cost and distances have there been reduced to English measures and Federal money. In these tables the author's statements are given without change because sufficient materials for a total re-casting of them are not accessible to the translator. In reducing federal money to francs, M. Chevalier assumes the dollar to be equal to 5.33 francs; the league is of 4,000 metres, and consequently equivalent to two and a half English statute miles. — TRANSL.]

I. LINES BETWEEN THE EAST AND WEST.

Length. Leagues. Total Cost. Francs.

Names.	Canals.	Railroads.	Canals.	Railroads.	Cost per League.
1st Line, *Erie Canal,*	146½		} 65,000,000		262,600
Branches,	101				
Lateral Railroads,					
Albany and Schenectady,		6½		4,000,000	615,400
Schenectady and Utica,		31½		8,000,000	254,000
Rochester and Buffalo,		29		3,000,000	103,000
2d Line, *Pennsylvania*					
Canal,	111		} 95,000,000		392,300
Branches,	131¼				
Columbia Railroad,		33		19,200,000	581,800
Portage ,,		14¼		8,550,000	600,000
Bald Eagle Canal,	10		1,000,000		100,000
Union ,,	33		13,870,000		420,300
3d Line *Baltimore and Ohio*					
Railroad,		34		16,000,000	470,600
4th Line, *Chesapeake and*					
Ohio Canal,	74¾		33,000,000		442,800
Georgetown and Alexan-					
dria Canal,	3		2,600,000		866,700

5th Line, *Virginia Canal*,	100		25,000,000		250,000
Railroad section,		60		15,000,000	250,000
Old James River Canal,	12		5,300,000		441,600
6th Line, *Richelieu Canal*,	4¾		1,870,000		393,700
Laprairie Railroad.		6½		800,000	123,100

727¼ 214¾	242,640,000 74,550,000		

II. LINES CONNECTING THE VALLEYS OF THE MISSISSIPPI AND ST. LAWRENCE.

Length. Leagues Total Cost. Francs.

Names.	Canals.	Railroads.	Canals.	Railroads.	Cost per League.
Ohio Canal,	122		22,720,000		186,200
Miami (1st section,)	26½		5,227,000		197,200
" (2d section,)	50¼		11,000,000		219,000
Wabash and Erie Canal,	84		16,800,000		200,000
Michigan "	37½		37,500,000		1,000,000
Pittsburgh and Erie "	41½		5,000,000		120,500
Beaver and Sandy "	36¼		7,250,000		200,000
Mahoning "	36		7,200,000		200,000
Mad River Railroad,		61½		10,500,000	170,700
Welland Canal.	11¼		11,040,000		982,300
Canals on the St. Lawrence,	13		20,000,000		1,538,000
Louisville and Portland Canal,	¾		4,053,000		5,400,000
Totals	459	61½	147,790,000	10,500,000	

III. LINES ALONG THE ATLANTIC.

Length. Leagues. Total Cost. Francs.

Names.	Canals.	Railroads.	Canals.	Railroads.	Cost per League.
Raritan and Delaware Canal,	17		12,000,000		705,900
Delaware and Chesapeake Canal,	5½		14,000,000		2,545,500
Dismal Swamp Canal,	9		} 3,733,000		324,600
Branch,	2½				
2d Line, *By the Cities.*					
Boston and Providence Railroad,		17		8,000,000	470,600
Providence and Stonington Railroad,		21		8,000,000	381,000
Amboy and Camden Railroad,		24¼		12,250,000	505,200
Newcastle and Frenchtown Railroad,		6½		2,130.000	327,700
Baltimore and Washington Railroad,		12		8,000,000	750,000
Winchester Railroad,		13		2,600,000	200,000
Federicksburg and Richmond Railroad,		23¾		3,900,000	164,200
Petersburg and Roanoke Railroad,		24		3,470,000	144,600

Belfield Branch Railroad,		6	840,000	140,000
Portsmouth and Roanoke Railroad,		31	4,000,000	129,000
Charleston and Hamburg Railroad,		54¾	6,400,000	116,900
Georgia Railroad.		46	8,250,000	179,300
Totals	34	279¼	29,733,000	67,840,000

IV. Lines radiating from the Large Towns.

Length. Leagues. Total Cost. Francs.

Names.	Canals.	Railroads	Canals.	Railroads	Cost per League.
Boston and Lowell Railroad,		10¼		8,000,000	780,000
Boston and Worcester Railroad,		17¾		6,670,000	375,800
Middlesex Canal	12		2,800,000		233,000
New York and Paterson Railroad,		6¼		1,100,000	176,000
Harlaem Railroad,		2		2,000,000	1,000,000
Jersey City and New Brunswick Railroad,		11¼		1,800,000	160,000
Brooklyn and Jamaica Railroad,		5		1,600,000	320,000
Philadelphia and Norristown Railroad,		6¼		2,500,000	400,000
Westchester Railroad,		3½		540,000	154,300
Philadelphia and Trenton Railroad,		10½		2,133,000	203,100
Baltimore and Susquehannah Railroad,		24		7,100,000	295,800
Santee Canal,	9		3,470,000		385,600
New Orleans Canals,	4		12,000,000		3,000,000
New Orleans and Carrolton Railroad,		3½		2,000,000	571,400
New Orleans and Lake Pontchartrain Railroad,		2		2,300,000	1,150,000
Schenectady and Saratoga Railroad,		8½		1,600,000	188,200
Troy and Saratoga Railroad,		9¾		1,800,000	184,600
Totals	25	120½	18,270,000	41,143,000	

V. Lines connected with the Coal Mines.

Length. Leagues. Total Cost. Francs.

Names.	Canals.	Railroads.	Canals.	Railroads.	Cost per League.
Chesterfield Railroad,		5¼		1,050,000	200,000
Schuylkill Canal,	43		16,000,000		372,100
Lehigh "	17½		8,300,000		474,300
Delaware " (see Letters)					
Morris "	48½		11,000,000		226,800
Carbondale and Honesdale Railroad,		6½		1,600,000	246,200

Hudson and Delaware Canal,	43	12,600,000		293,300
Pottsville and Sunbury Railroad,	17¾		6,000,000	338,000
Philadelphia and Reading Railroad,	22¾		8,000,000	351,600
Various works,	66		6,000,000	90,900
Totals				
	152	118¼ 47,900,000	22,650,000	

VI. DIFFERENT LINES.

Length. Leagues. Total Cost. Francs.

Names.	Canals.	Railroads.	Canals.	Railroads.	Cost per League.
Cumberland Canal (Me.) Farmington and Blackstone Canals, Mass. &c.	67		10,400,000		155,000
Conestoga Navigation,	7¼	⎱	1,000,000		95,700
Codorus ,,	4¼	⎰			
Muscle-Shoals Canal,	14		7,000,000		500,000
Savannah and Ogechee Canal,	6½		850,000		130,800
Improvement of the Hudson,	11¾		5,000,000		425,500
Quincy Railroad,		1¼		180,000	144,000
Ithaca and Owego Railroad,		11¾		2,700,000	230,800
Lexington and Louisville Railroad,		36		6,000,000	166,700
Tuscumbia and Decatur Railroad,		18		3,000,000	200,000
Rochester Canal,		1¼		160,000	128,000
Buffalo and Blackrock Canal,		1¼		50,000	40,000
Totals					
	110¾	69½ 24,250,000	12,690,000		

VII. SUMMARY OF THE ABOVE TABLES.

	Length. Leagues.		*Cost. Francs.*	
Tables	Canals.	Railroads.	Canals.	Railroads.
I.	727¼	214¾	242,640,000	74,550,000
II.	459	61½	147,790,000	10,500,000
III.	34	279¼	29,733,000	67,840,000
IV.	25	120½	18,270,000	41,143,000
V.	152	118¼	47,900,000	22,650,000
Total.	1,397¼	794¼	486,333,000	216,683,000
Deduct	144	105	72,500,000	21,750,000
	1,253¼	689¼	413,833,000	194,933,000
VI.	110¾	69½	24,250,000	12,690,000
Totals.	1364	758¾	438,083,000	207,623,000
	2,122¾		645,706,000.	

If to these are added some unimportant works, about which I have not been able to obtain exact statements, the total length of the railroads and canals may be estimated at about **2,150** leagues, and the cost at **660** million francs. If we take into account a number of important works, which have been undertaken in the last part of **1835** and the beginning of **1836**, it will be necessary to add **900** leagues and **300** million francs to the above totals, making an aggregate of **3,050** leagues (**7,625** miles) and **960** million francs (**180** million dollars). I do not include the Nashville and New Orleans and the Charleston and Cincinnati railroads, which, however, will probably be executed before long, and with their branches will make an addition of more than **500** leagues. The Americans have already surpassed in the extent of their works, and the rapidity of execution, the most active and wealthy European nations. Almost all the works above enumerated have been executed in fifteen years.

The following table gives a summary view of similar works in Europe :

Countries.	Canals.	Railroads.
England	1,100 leagues.	313 leagues.
France	998	50
Belgium	115	74
Other States	400	50
Totals	2,613	487

General Total of Europe   3,100
"   United States   ·3,050

NOTE 23 — page 281.

Geological Surveys.

The legislatures of several States have lately shown a laudable zeal for geological examinations of the soil. Maryland has a State geologist (Mr Duchatel) who is engaged in preparing a a geological map of the State, particularly with reference to economical purposes. Dr Duchatel has already made some important discoveries in agricultural geology, especially in respect to the use of marl. Tennessee has also its geologist, Dr Troost. Massachusetts has a geological map prepared by Professor Hitchcock. Congress has caused some examinations to be made on the upper Mississippi. Dr Jackson has been several years employed in making geological surveys in Maine, and is at present occupied in Rhode Island ; he has also been appointed by New Hampshire to explore the geology of her mountains and valleys. New York, Pennsylvania, New Jersey, Virginia, Ohio, Indiana, Connecticut, Kentucky, Michigan and Georgia, have also engaged in the same enterprise, and partial examinations have been made in North Carolina. New York has in addition to a corps of four geologists, Messrs Vanuxem, Mather, Emmons and Conrad, a chemist (Dr Beck,) a botanist (Mr Torrey,) and a zoologist, (Dr DeKay.) It is principally to the efforts of the late Secretary of the State, General Dix, that New York is indebted for this great undertaking. Massachusetts has also organised a board of naturalists, to report upon the different branches of botany and zoology. In many of the States, a topographical survey more or less minute, has been connected with the geological explorations. Massachusetts has been trigonometrically surveyed.